People say I am ruthless. I am not ruthless. And if I find the man who is calling me ruthless, I shall destroy him.

– Robert Francis Kennedy

Jack Kennedy could have been a movie star himself. He had the charisma, the charm, that come-hither quality that can never be duplicated. Is it any wonder he got elected president?

– Marilyn Monroe to Lawrence Quirk (November or December 1960)

It's not what you are. It's what people think you are.

– Joseph P. Kennedy, Sr.

Marilyn Monroe:
A Case for Murder

Jay Margolis

iUniverse, Inc.
Bloomington

Marilyn Monroe: A Case for Murder

World Copyright © 2011 Jay Margolis
World Copyright © 2011 George Barris for the front cover photograph
World Copyright © October 1993 Michelle Justice. Reprinted with permission
from fan newspaper *Runnin' Wild: All About Marilyn,* Number 12

All rights reserved. No part of this book may be used or reproduced by any means, graphic, electronic, or mechanical, including photocopying, recording, taping or by any information storage retrieval system without the written permission of the publisher except in the case of brief quotations embodied in critical articles and reviews.

iUniverse books may be ordered through booksellers or by contacting:

iUniverse
1663 Liberty Drive
Bloomington, IN 47403
www.iuniverse.com
1-800-Authors (1-800-288-4677)

Because of the dynamic nature of the Internet, any Web addresses or links contained in this book may have changed since publication and may no longer be valid. The views expressed in this work are solely those of the author and do not necessarily reflect the views of the publisher, and the publisher hereby disclaims any responsibility for them.

ISBN: 978-1-4620-1755-3 (sc)
ISBN: 978-1-4620-1756-0 (hc)
ISBN: 978-1-4620-1757-7 (ebk)

Library of Congress Control Number: 2011907146

Printed in the United States of America

iUniverse rev. date: 12/12/2011

Contents

Acknowledgements v
Foreword vii

THE OFFICIAL VERDICT: PROBABLE SUICIDE 1

The Greenson and Engelberg Agreement 3

Marilyn's Other Friends Get Suspicious 7

Was Accidental Suicide Even a Medical Possibility? 10

Greenson Calls the Police to Say Marilyn
Monroe Committed Suicide 18

The Miner Memorandum 23

An Afternoon Visit from Bobby Kennedy and Peter Lawford 27

One Last Walk at Santa Monica Beach? 31

How Did Marilyn Monroe Really Die? 33

Bobby Kennedy Brought Along His Own
Doctor to Sedate Marilyn 36

C. David Heymann's Interview with Peter Lawford 41

Falling in Love with the President 45

Frank Sinatra Gets the Kennedy Boot 46

FBI Notes Killer All But Named in
Photoplay Magazine (August 1963) 51

Marilyn Monroe's Last Morning Alive 53

The Concentration of Drugs in Marilyn's Blood and Liver 56

One Last Fling with Bobby Kennedy? 59

Marilyn Monroe Threatens a Press Conference 59

Bobby Kennedy's Friendships with Top Police Officials 61

Did Marilyn's Free-Association Tapes for Greenson Exist? 64

Did Miner Accurately Translate Marilyn's Free-Association Tapes? 70

Were Marilyn and Peter's Homes Bugged
and Their Phones Tapped? 72

Did JFK Have More Than a One-Night Stand
with Marilyn Monroe? 75

Did Marilyn Sleep with the President
at the Carlyle on May 20, 1962? 81

Marilyn Monroe Plays the Secretary! 83

Jack Kennedy and Judy Campbell 84

Did Marilyn Monroe and Bobby Kennedy Share a Bed? 88

Greenson Tells the Suicide Team
Marilyn Had Affairs with Both Kennedys 91

Was Marilyn Monroe Bobby's Only Sexual Affair? 93

Was Marilyn Monroe Pregnant with Bobby Kennedy's Child? 98

What Really Happened to Marilyn at the Cal-Neva? 101

Pills, Pills, and More Pills 104

Keya Morgan and the Million-Dollar Marilyn Monroe Sex Tape 105

What Reason Would Greenson Have for Killing His Patient? 108

Was Greenson Obsessed with Marilyn Monroe? 117

Did Greenson Have a Sexual Affair with His Patient? 122

Did Marilyn Monroe Keep a Little Red Diary? 129

Sam Giancana and the "Double Cross" 132

Who Gave Marilyn the Enema of
Nembutal and Chloral Hydrate?... 138

A Surprise Visit from Bobby Kennedy.. 139

Schaefer Ambulance Attendant
James Edwin Hall Told the Truth 143

Who the Hell is Ken Hunter?... 157

The Santa Monica Hospital "Story" 161

Beverly Hills Police Officer Lynn Franklin Connects the Dots........... 164

Strange Remarks Attributed to Strange Men...................................... 166

Greenson's Guilt After Marilyn's Death? 168

Does Greenson's Official "Story" Check Out?.................................... 169

At About 10:30 – 10:40 P.M. Natalie Trundy
Learns Marilyn's in Trouble 176

Officer Lynn Franklin Pulls Over a Very Drunk Peter Lawford.......... 181

Bobby Kennedy and the Plane Back to San Francisco........................ 185

What Happened to Marilyn's Diary
Before Bobby Kennedy Got It?... 186

Did Chief Parker Cover Up Bobby Kennedy's
Tracks in Los Angeles? 188

Bobby Kennedy Publicly Praises the FBI Director 193

THE KENNEDY VERSION: 195

Was Peter's Call to Ebbins a Cry for Help or a Really Good Alibi?..... 195

The Account of Peter Lawford's Friend Director Bill Asher 200

Dolores Naar Claims Peter Said Greenson Gave Marilyn Sedatives.... 201

CONCLUSION: **204**

THE OTHER "MURDERERS" OF MARILYN MONROE: **207**

Her "Secret Husband" Robert Slatzer (1927 – 2005) 207

Her "Best Friend" Jeanne Carmen (1930 – 2007) 211

Her "Flirtation" with Colin Clark (1932 – 2002) 215

Blonde, My Week with Marilyn, or Tarantino? 220

EPILOGUE: **223**

Her Idol Was Lincoln and
Carl Sandburg (1878 – 1967) Was His Biographer 223

TIMELINE: **227**

Autopsy Report: 241

Bibliography: 257

Documentaries: 271

Major Newspaper Articles: 272

Major Magazine Articles: 275

Donald Spoto's Interviews: 276

Jay Margolis' Interviews: 277

Miscellaneous Interviews: 278

Endnotes 281

Index 429

Acknowledgements

This is a scholarly work with extensive source notes. In the past, no one biographer has successfully explained how Marilyn Monroe died. I put together a large amount of never-used information from previous works on the subject, including past interviews. One in particular is a revealing interview by private investigator Cathy Griffin with the psychiatrist's wife Hildi Greenson.

As for the eighteen interviews I cited from Donald Spoto, most of the individuals interviewed are now deceased. In that regard, I found his collection quite helpful. Additionally, I interviewed twenty-two individuals. Many were carefully chosen from among Marilyn's friends and others who knew her during the last year of her life and whose testimony is key to the story. In this manner, I have reached a definitive conclusion as to what really happened to Marilyn Monroe. It wasn't an accident. And it wasn't suicide. Then-Deputy District Attorney John Miner came to the conclusion that someone killed her. He's right. Marilyn Monroe was murdered.

Miner, who oversaw her autopsy with Dr. Thomas Noguchi, told *Playboy* in an interview for their December 2005 issue, "How can the woman rest in peace when there's a lie about how she met her death? My response is that Monroe was denied the basic right to which every American, dead or alive, is entitled – due process of law." I share Miner's rationale and that is the reason why I wrote this book. I have many people to thank for it.

I thank my parents and my friends. I thank Dr. Elias Amador for his brilliant expertise on a complicated medical case. I would also like to thank my interview subjects and the biographers whom I cite in this work, especially C. David Heymann at Simon & Schuster, Anthony Summers, and Donald H. Wolfe.

I owe thanks to Greg Schreiner, President of *Marilyn Remembered*, who provided me with much support. I thank Michelle Justice, co-author of the scholarly fan newspaper *Runnin' Wild: All About Marilyn*. Her newspapers have fascinating interviews with George Barris, Whitey Snyder, and many more of Marilyn's friends.

I would also like to thank Mrs. Gloria Romanoff for her kindness and patience with my tough questions. I thank actresses Terry Moore and the late Jane Russell. I thank Mike Selsman, a guy with a true love for history. I want to say a special thank you to actress Jayne Mansfield's press secretary Raymond Strait for his generosity and time in speaking with me. This book would have been incomplete without my interviews with him.

Most of all, I thank an excellent photographer George Barris who took the most natural pictures of Marilyn Monroe. On August 3, one day before she died, he was one of the last to speak to her over the phone. Mr. Barris is a wonderful man. He loved Marilyn very much. I hope my research on his friend's death will bring closure. I dedicate the book to the memory of Marilyn Monroe. In that respect, I have written it as truthfully as I know it.

J.M.

Foreword

JANE RUSSELL TO JAY MARGOLIS (11/29/2010): "That's the first time I got to know her was when we made *Gentlemen*. Her makeup man told mine that she was all ready. She had come in at least an hour before I did. She just felt nervous about going out alone. I'd go by her dressing room and say, 'Come on, baby, we got about ten minutes to go.' And she'd look up at me and say, 'Oh, alright.' And we'd trot on together. Those other idiots would just sit there and sulk because she was late on other pictures but nobody went by to get her! The press were trying to have us hate each other. But it wasn't that way at all. She was like a little sister to me. She was very sweet and got very upset about a lot of things that I wouldn't have gotten upset about at all. But this was Marilyn. I think she felt alone and she didn't know who her dad was. Her mother was in a sanitarium… On *Gentlemen*, the guy playing 'Daddy' had a friend of his come up and say, 'Well, you just kissed Marilyn Monroe. Now what was it like?' He said, 'It was uh, it was uh, it was like being – swallowed alive!' Marilyn heard that and she ran to her dressing room crying. If that had happened to me, I'd say, 'Honey, you'd be so lucky.' "

JOAN GREENSON (Manuscript by the psychiatrist's daughter, p. 46): "Marilyn couldn't even have her own phone number on the phone. She found out that often people who came into the house would write it down and sell it, or call her. So as a joke, she put on her phone dial the phone number of the local police department, so anyone thinking they had pulled a fast one was in for a big surprise."

GEORGE BARRIS TO JAY MARGOLIS (01/07/2011): "When I was in the country, I was with my brother-in-law. We went to a local grocery to get some milk and bagels. I sat in the car and he went in to buy it and he came running out. And he looked at me, 'It just came over the radio.' I said, 'What are you talking about?' 'Marilyn is dead.' 'You shouldn't make jokes like that. It's not nice.' 'No, it's true. Honestly.' I couldn't believe it. I was just in a shock. I dropped him off then I drove all the way back to New York where I lived at Sutton Place. It was about a 100 miles. Luckily I didn't get a ticket or in an accident I was driving so fast. When I got back, the doorman told me that there was a bunch of press and photographers and reporters looking for me. 'If they come back, tell them I'm not here.' I went upstairs. I put on the television and radio. All that came over was 'Marilyn is dead. Marilyn is dead.' It was too much. I shut everything off. I couldn't take it."

RAYMOND STRAIT (11/28/2011): "Jay Margolis' *Marilyn Monroe: A Case for Murder* is without a doubt the most thoroughly researched (and most on point) as any I have ever read – and I've read them all. Much in his book I can vouch for because of my twenty-year relationship with Fred Otash, Hollywood's top private detective."

GLORIA ROMANOFF TO JAY MARGOLIS (01/28/2011): "They're coming very close on whatever verdict they give Dr. Murray in the Michael Jackson situation. I think the two cases coming simultaneously will create a huge excitement. Are you quite prepared for what you may be dealing with once your book is published?"

MARILYN MONROE
Norma Jeane Mortenson
June 1, 1926 – August 4, 1962

THE OFFICIAL VERDICT: PROBABLE SUICIDE

How Marilyn Monroe died is considered one of the greatest mysteries of the 20th century. While it's certainly true Marilyn almost overdosed on a number of previous occasions, most suicide attempts were accidental in that she would miscalculate how many pills she had taken. After her death, Coroner Theodore Curphey hired a team of three psychologists from an organization first established in 1958 called the Suicide Prevention Team. This would be the Team's most high-profile case to date. Curphey told them Marilyn Monroe committed suicide. Their job was to establish her motive in taking the drugs then write a report. The Team assumed the worst. According to them, her past suicide attempts were intentional.

Close friends like her makeup man of sixteen years Allan "Whitey" Snyder and her wardrobe supervisor Marjorie Plecher, later Mrs. Allan Snyder, believe Marilyn would not have wanted to take her own life, at least not intentionally. On the evening of August 2, a couple days before she died, Marilyn invited Marjorie and Whitey over for caviar and her favorite champagne Dom Pérignon. They reported she was in great spirits.

Oscar-nominated actress Terry Moore, for her role in 1952's *Come Back, Little Sheba*, knew Marilyn since March 1948 when Moore was nineteen. She told me, "The first time I met Marilyn I was working with Natasha Lytess at Columbia. We were trying to do a scene on Elizabeth the Great. And Max Arnow, who was head of talent, brought Marilyn Monroe in and he said, 'This is the new girl we've put under contract. You'll now have someone to do scenes with.' I was so happy because she could play Mary, Queen of Scots. I was the only one underage in the drama class with Natasha. So they put her under contract, and we did scenes every day and we'd go to Freddy Karger and do our singing lessons together. Then we both left Columbia at the same time and went to Twentieth Century-Fox." Moore always believed Marilyn's death to be accidental.

Gloria Romanoff is the widow of the late Michael Romanoff, who owned the famous Beverly Hills restaurant to the stars called Romanoff's. Mrs. Romanoff was a close friend of Marilyn Monroe. She said she inherited the friendship from her husband when Marilyn started going to dinners at the home of Joe Schenck, one of the most influential producers in Hollywood history. It was February of 1948 and Marilyn was just twenty-one.

Jay Margolis

As for August 4, 1962, Mrs. Romanoff told me her friend had absolutely no intention of taking her life deliberately. I asked her, "Marilyn was in an up frame of mind. She didn't sound like she wanted to kill herself, is that correct?" "Oh no. She was in one of her better moments and had been for the whole week preceding this and was looking forward to the next day. Marilyn was not a person given to hate. She had the most benevolent attitude towards everybody and was terribly shy. She didn't have a large social life. Marilyn wasn't even a girl who would contemplate anything like suicide." In fact, Mrs. Romanoff told me she planned to see her that Sunday evening August 5.

Dean Martin of Frank Sinatra's Rat Pack was Marilyn's co-star on her last incomplete film *Something's Got to Give*. On August 6, Martin said to reporter Vernon Scott, "I'm sure it was an accident. She was at my home a few days ago and she was happy. She was in excellent spirits and we were making plans to resume the picture. She was a warm, wonderful person who never hurt anyone but herself."

His second wife Jeanne told me, "Marilyn was the sweetest woman. She was gentle, endearing and quite charming." On her death, Mrs. Martin said, "She just OD'd, not surprisingly. Why anybody would wonder with all the medications she was taking why she would *not* kill herself. There was nothing mysterious about Marilyn's death. She could have OD'd hundreds of times." Milt Ebbins, Vice President of Peter Lawford's production company Chrislaw and one of his best friends said, "She didn't commit suicide. She OD'd."

Another one of Peter's best friends is Joseph T. Naar, a former television producer. He said to me, "The truth is, I do think she died of an overdose. But your most important interview will be Pat Newcomb. I don't think she'll grant you an interview, by the way. She's a real pain in the ass. She's the closest thing to anyone I know who's still alive who knows what happened." Four months later, I called Marilyn's last publicist Pat Newcomb, 80, and had the following conversation with her:

MARGOLIS: Hi. I'd like to talk to Ms. Pat Newcomb, please.

NEWCOMB: Who's calling, please?

MARGOLIS: Jay Margolis.

NEWCOMB: This is she.

MARGOLIS: Hey, how are you doing? I'd like to ask you a few questions, if you don't mind.

NEWCOMB: Who are you?

MARGOLIS: I'm a biographer and I want to talk about Marilyn's accidental suicide.

NEWCOMB: I don't.[1]

Then she hung up.

The Greenson and Engelberg Agreement

Virtually unknown to the public, Betty Robin was a personal assistant to Marilyn Monroe in New York and California during the last eight months of her life. In the 1980s, Robin spoke out for the first time with the sole purpose of exonerating her former employer from the stigma of suicide. Marilyn's attorney Milton "Mickey" Rudin hired Robin who used to work for David O. Selznick and his brother Myron, best known for producing one of the greatest motion pictures of all time *Gone with the Wind* (1939). Daily, Robin reminded Marilyn of her professional commitments. She would fix dinner.

Robin said Marilyn was quite a reserved individual who saw a selective number of friends. She remembered how Marilyn often visited poet Carl Sandburg. She shared some of the happiest moments of her life spending time with him. He was a good singer and played the guitar and would sometimes carry on rambunctiously until 3 o'clock in the morning. Since Marilyn could never sleep, this suited her perfectly fine.

While she knew Marilyn to be an unhappy person, Robin is clear that her employer did not intentionally commit suicide. She said the doctors may have been responsible for her death because of all the pills they were prescribing for her. The medications should have been professionally monitored. Marilyn Monroe's psychiatrist Ralph "Romi" Greenson, M.D. and her physician Hyman "Hy" Engelberg, M.D., long-standing friends, failed to let each other know what they were prescribing for Marilyn days before she died. Anthony Summers wrote, "Dr. Greenson would later say he had brought in Dr. Engelberg to try to wean Marilyn away from sleeping pills. The two doctors agreed to keep in touch concerning the drugs they prescribed for her, but the system may have broken down."

Greenson said he didn't know anything about Engelberg's Nembutal prescription, while Engelberg would afterwards claim he knew nothing about

Greenson's chloral hydrate prescription. If what both these doctors claimed is true then they negligently placed Marilyn Monroe in a highly perilous situation. Chloral hydrate decreases the metabolic rate of Nembutal, making the Nembutal less likely to be absorbed in the liver as quickly and more likely to be lethal. These doctors know the effect of chloral hydrate on Nembutal. Yet their claims of ignorance took first place to anything else.

In fact, Engelberg emphatically stated that only in Tijuana could Marilyn have obtained chloral hydrate because he believed no American doctor would write the prescription. But Greenson *did* write it and Engelberg claimed ignorance of it. As noted by Detective Sergeant Robert E. Byron and his team, there was a prescription bottle recovered from Marilyn's bedroom dated July 25 for fifty 500-milligram chloral hydrates, and it was refilled on July 31. The toxicologist Raymond Abernathy also noted the same dates for the original and the refilled chloral hydrate prescriptions, which is detailed in the coroner's report.

In total, fifteen pill bottles were found on her bedside table, according to Westwood Memorial Mortuary employees Guy Hockett and his son Don yet Abernathy only inventoried eight (an unidentified bottle was later added to the original seven). The statements Greenson made to biographer Maurice Zolotow, *Something's Got to Give* photographer William Read Woodfield, and even Marilyn's housekeeper Mrs. Eunice Murray confirm that Greenson prescribed chloral hydrate for his star patient. Mrs. Murray wrote in her book, "Under Dr. Greenson's guidance, she was taking only chloral hydrate pills for sleep." After interviewing Greenson, Zolotow wrote in his September 14, 1973 article, "Her psychiatrist, Dr. Ralph Greenson, was attempting to cut down her dependence on Nembutal by switching her to chloral hydrate as a sleep-inducer."

When Woodfield telephoned Greenson and asked him why he prescribed such heavy doses of chloral hydrate for Marilyn, Greenson snidely replied, "Well, I've made a number of mistakes in my time." Engelberg stated it wasn't unusual to prescribe Nembutal for Marilyn. In fact, Engelberg told the District Attorney's Office in 1982 that Nembutal was the only sleeping medication he ever prescribed for her. In the same interview, Engelberg relayed, "I don't know of anything Dr. Greenson gave her. Maybe he did. I cannot answer for him… As far as I know, I was the only one writing prescriptions but I couldn't swear to that."

Greenson's wife Hildi told private investigator Cathy Griffin, "The idea was that she was never to be said no to when she wanted a prescription because the only thing that would happen was she would go somewhere else… so whenever she asked for a drug, she would get it." Greenson's daughter Joan explained, "Father had a policy that if Marilyn wanted to have sleep medication, that all she had to do was call her doctor and he would prescribe it to her. Then the physician was to call later and tell him that she had a new sleeping medication and what the name of it was and how much was in it. If Father felt that it was an excessive amount or too dangerous, he would usually pour some out when he was at Marilyn's house."

Greenson wrote in a 1964 paper, "The administering of a drug is a responsibility since it may cause physical side effects, it may be emotionally upsetting to the patient, misused by the patient, and it may lead to addiction and death." If it's true that Greenson never told Engelberg about the chloral hydrate and Engelberg thought it normal to prescribe only Nembutal then there was no plan to "wean" Marilyn from barbiturates as Greenson relayed to the Suicide Prevention Team.

Greenson wrote in a letter to his friend and colleague Dr. Marianne Kris on August 20, 1962, "I later found out that on Friday night she had told the internist [Engelberg] that I had said it was all right for her to take some nembutal, and he had given it to her without checking with me, because he had been upset himself for his own personal reasons. (He had just left his wife after some 27 years of marriage)." Biographer Donald Spoto made a chilling point on how Greenson knew Marilyn well enough to know on which medication she was "somewhat drugged."

The accounts of biographer Fred Lawrence Guiles and Engelberg himself directly contradict Greenson's story about Marilyn "tricking" Engelberg into giving her some Nembutal on August 3. According to Guiles, Marilyn asked for the Nembutal prescription because she considered chloral hydrate a mild sedative which didn't always do its job. She wanted something that actually worked because apparently she had developed a tolerance to the other drug. In 1982, Engelberg told the District Attorney's Office it was standard-operating procedure to write Nembutal for Marilyn, so to him it was not an unusual request.

Hildi Greenson discussed what she claimed her husband did in the weeks before Marilyn's death, "In trying to help Marilyn get off the barbiturates she was on, he was giving her a different kind of medication [chloral hydrate] that is not quite as addictive and he was able to turn the tide, as it were. She was getting less and less dependent on the drugs." Mrs. Murray discussed in her own book the ineffectiveness of chloral hydrate as it related to her employer. Marilyn had said to her, "You know they used to give these to the soldiers in the war for sleeping. They're really very mild." Mrs. Murray told *Hard Copy* who subsequently released their reenactment of Marilyn's last night on April 20, 1992, "She was taking something she said was very mild. She called it chloral hydrate. And she would take it with a glass of milk or something of the sort." Why would chloral hydrate be found in Marilyn's system the night she died when she specifically requested from her physician the stronger drug? I made this point to Gloria Romanoff and she replied, "It doesn't make sense. It didn't happen."

Greenson attempted to resolve this discrepancy in his letter to Dr. Kris. He claimed the following on his alleged final 7:30 – 7:40 P.M. phone call with Marilyn, "At the end of the conversation she asked me whether I had taken away her nembutal bottle. I was surprised that she asked me that because I did not know she was taking nembutal. She had stopped taking all barbiturates for three weeks… I said to Marilyn I had not taken her nembutal, and I didn't know she was taking nembutal, and she quickly dropped the subject. I thought perhaps she was just confused." Greenson dismissed the remark, thinking nothing of it when several other doctors would have.

Greenson's daughter Joan later claimed, "Ironically, one of these doctors, Dr. Hyman Engelberg, gave her a prescription for Nembutal the Friday before she died, but he didn't inform my father because he separated from his wife that day. He was moving out of the house that day." Joan explained what her father did when he got to Marilyn's, "That Saturday he had checked her medication. No new pills were there. He had not received a call that she had gotten new medication. It was a small oversight." Hildi Greenson relayed a similar account, "It happened on a bad day. A divorce either became final or he was moving out of his house. The internist forgot to call. My husband didn't know that she had the Nembutals or Seconals, or whatever they were."

In the police report #62-509 463, Engelberg stated that by the time Marilyn refilled his original prescription for 25 pills, there should have been a total of 50 Nembutals. Engelberg is right. In Anthony Summers' updated version of *Goddess* (2000), there is a photograph of a prescription for Marilyn (following page 432) in which Engelberg's name and the date July 25, 1962 are visible. This is the original 100-milligram Nembutal prescription for 25 pills.

That same prescription was then refilled on August 3, one day before Marilyn died. The 1982 District Attorney's Report read: "The refilled prescription recovered at the scene dated August 3, 1962, was attributed to a refill Dr. Engelberg had given Miss Monroe on that date." Not only did Engelberg "forget" to tell Greenson about the August 3 refill but he also "forgot" to tell him about the original prescription on July 25. Pat Newcomb told Spoto, "She asked for some Nembutals. Engelberg was having problems with his wife… Greenson didn't know she was in this state of wanting these pills. The fact that Engelberg forgot to tell Greenson was malpractice. It was 50 pills and she already had chloral hydrate."

If Greenson and Engelberg are not lying about being ignorant of each other's prescriptions, we would have to assume Marilyn took only 3 Nembutals before her final day, the evening of which she supposedly took the rest of the 47 Nembutals that killed her. Marilyn would have had to hoard Engelberg's pills from the original prescription (July 25) *and* the refill on August 3. Given her regular use of these drugs, could she really wait almost a week and a half before she finally decided to take most of these pills on August 4?

The two doctors knew this didn't make any kind of sense so Greenson and Engelberg concocted a cockamamie story about how she went behind both their backs to get *another* Nembutal prescription and *another* refill. The doctors weren't very creative. The 1982 District Attorney's Report read in part: "The Suicide Team found that Dr. Siegel had prescribed an unknown quantity to Miss Monroe on July 25, 1962, and also noted that she had received a refill of pills on August 3, 1962, and attributed that prescription to Dr. Siegel." The dates of Siegel's alleged prescriptions are the same dates for both of Engelberg's prescriptions. To put it simply, Greenson and Engelberg said she went doctor shopping in order to make it appear as if Marilyn had access to 50 Nembutal pills the day she died.

The late Dr. Robert Litman was a member of the Suicide Prevention Team investigating Marilyn Monroe's death. He told Spoto, "I am stuck with the information that she went out and got pills from Siegel and Engelberg." Dr. Lee Siegel, who worked for Twentieth Century-Fox, vehemently denied that he saw Marilyn for weeks before her death once the studio had fired her on June 8. Siegel's alleged Nembutal prescription and refill is not mentioned in any of the police reports. In fact, the 1982 District Attorney's Report conceded: "The prescriptions attributed to Dr. Siegel were not recovered by the Coroner's representatives," so there is no proof that they ever existed. [2]

Marilyn's Other Friends Get Suspicious

George Barris, who freelanced for *Cosmopolitan*, was the last professional to photograph Marilyn Monroe before she died. Initially, for her services rendered on her last incomplete film *Something's Got to Give*, she was to be paid a mere $100,000. After she was fired, Marilyn was rehired one week later with a new deal and two-and-a-half times more money. In a 1980s documentary, the narrator had this to say about Marilyn's future, which was looking good, "She obtained a new contract with Fox. She was also planning new projects with George Barris."

As for August 3, 1962, Barris said, "When I was in New York after I left Los Angeles and Marilyn Monroe, I was putting together the story for

Cosmopolitan, which was to be about 12 pages and a cover. She called and asked 'How is everything going?' 'Fine.' 'George, you must come back. I have some very important things we have to talk about. It's very important.' 'Marilyn, it's Friday. I'll try to come out by Monday if it's alright.' 'Please, promise me.' I said, 'I promise.' "

Years later, Barris reflected, "She never seemed happier… I was very happy for her. I asked about her plans for the weekend, and she said she'd probably just relax, go out to dinner, and then maybe go over to the Lawfords' for their regular Saturday night party. Then she said, 'Love you – see you Monday.' I said I loved her, too."

Barris asked me, "Why would she take her life?… We did photographs at Santa Monica beach near Peter Lawford's. Marilyn bought a new house in Brentwood but it wasn't furnished. She had gone to Mexico to furnish it Mexican style. She was waiting for the furniture to arrive. Marilyn said to me, 'How can we photograph there if it doesn't look right? What can we do?' 'If you want to go back where you lived with your first husband in Catalina, I'll try.' 'No, I don't want to go back.' 'My friend's home in the Hollywood Hills would be perfect. When I brought it up, he said all he wants is a picture of you and him as a souvenir. You don't have to do it if you don't want to.' 'No, it's okay.' I took a picture of him with Marilyn. All the other photos are at his home."

In 1995, using the pictures taken at Santa Monica Beach and North Hollywood, George Barris would create a very touching and tender book about Marilyn Monroe, her own words guiding the narrative. It was a project they had planned to do sometime in the future just days after they became friends in September 1954. At the time, Marilyn was making *The Seven Year Itch* in New York and Barris was photographing her. He wrote, "What I particularly liked about Marilyn was that she didn't act like a movie star. She was down to earth. Although she was then twenty-eight, she looked and acted like a teenager. Sure, she was beautiful and sexy, but there was an almost childlike innocence about her. I was most impressed that Marilyn was always polite and friendly to everyone on the set. She was no phony or snob."

After working briefly with Elizabeth Taylor in Rome, Italy for a *Cosmo* Story on *Cleopatra*, Barris approached Marilyn on the set of *Something's Got to Give* on Friday, the day of her birthday, June 1. "When I arrived, she said, 'What are you doing here?! I heard you were in Rome with Elizabeth Taylor! So, you found a new girl, huh?' 'No, we were just doing the story. She's impossible to work with.' 'Can you imagine they're paying her a million dollars for that picture?' They later brought out the cake and we all sang 'Happy Birthday' with me at her side. I was supposed to meet her at the studio Monday to start on our story. She wasn't there when I got there. She called in. She was a very frail person. They sent their own studio doctor [Dr. Lee Siegel] to investigate if she was really sick. He confirmed she was *really* sick. The studio was desperate. They had all these technicians, cameramen, and actors and actresses on salary. They're paying them and they were going broke. They had paid Elizabeth Taylor on *Cleopatra* a million dollars. The studio was in bad shape financially." Marilyn was temporarily fired on June 8. She and Barris began their projects during the weeks from June 9 to July 18. He remembered, "I don't think anyone was ever more determined, and I never encountered a model who worked as hard as she did."

In his book George Barris wrote, "I will never believe that she took her own life. It will always be my conviction that she was murdered." He told me, "I'll never forget her because she was kind, and she was honest, and she was loveable, and she was a girl who became what she was because she was determined and she had been through her whole life making everyone happy. She was always a caring person. She was a timid person but also a very lonely person. Unfortunately, her marriages were not very successful. Only if Marilyn had a child, I think that would have saved her life."

One of Terry Moore's best friends was wonderfully versatile actress Jane Russell from Howard Hughes' *The Outlaw* and Howard Hawks' *Gentlemen Prefer Blondes*. In an interview on November 29, 2010, she confirmed for me a story about an unpleasant one-time run-in with Robert Kennedy. I asked her, "I saw an article. It was dated 2007. It said that you didn't believe Marilyn took her own life. Is that true or is that inaccurately quoted?... Did you later meet Bobby Kennedy?"

Russell said, "I met him one time after his brother had been killed. I was working with this organization. We called it WAIF to get kids adopted. You couldn't get them from the United States but you could from other countries. The kids would come in with the parents that had all been picked, and he happened to be there one of these times. He met other people, and he was very friendly and nice. Then he was introduced to me, and the face just went *huh!* It was not friendly at all. I thought, well boy, something's funny there. So I guess he thought I knew all about whatever went on." I told Russell, "That face you saw was a guilty face." "I just think there was something very strange. When the Lord gets here, we'll know exactly what happened... There were things that she looked forward to. The studio had said okay. There were so many things that were happening that she wanted to happen. I think she was going to remarry Joe DiMaggio."

Author Wendy Leigh released an intriguing article in the United Kingdom on March 3, 2007. After interviewing Jane Russell, Leigh discovered the actress believed her friend had been murdered. Russell relayed to Leigh, "I don't think she killed herself. Someone did it for her. There were dirty tricks somewhere." Leigh wrote, "I suggest that Jack and Bobby Kennedy – both Marilyn's lovers – may have been involved, and Jane nods darkly." Russell told her, "Soon after Marilyn died, I met Bobby Kennedy and he looked at me as if to say: 'I am your enemy.' "

Actress Debbie Reynolds (1952's *Singin' in the Rain*) relayed to Britain's *Daily Express* newspaper how she told Marilyn to watch herself in dating the Kennedy brothers, "We knew each other because we attended the same church [Church of the Nazarene]. Marilyn was very religious, which may surprise some people... I saw her two days before she died and warned her to be careful. She was such a sweet and innocent girl but she was used by men. I believe she was murdered because too many people were afraid the truth would come out." Years earlier, Reynolds remembered, "Her life was very sad. And the ending was very sad indeed. And those of us who knew Marilyn, always were kind of dreaming for that great white knight to arrive and really love her and not take advantage of her." [3]

Was Accidental Suicide Even a Medical Possibility?

Reportedly, Marilyn Monroe swallowed 47 Nembutals and 17 chloral hydrates. I brought to Gloria Romanoff's attention the number of pills Marilyn supposedly took and she said, "You don't find it ludicrous of someone suggesting she swallowed *sixty-four* pills?" In the 1980 "In Search Of" *The Death of Marilyn Monroe* documentary, Dr. Sidney B. Weinberg, the former coroner of Suffolk County, New York, said, "People who have died as a result of excessive ingestion by mouth of barbiturates, in their agonal stages, as they're dying, they throw up. They have regurgitation and this regurgitated material comes out onto the pillow cases or whatever they're resting on." Weinberg then posited, "Now if the death was caused by injection, and she did it herself then where's the syringe? It was not present at the scene. And if she didn't do it then someone else had to do it."

On the same documentary, the first policeman officially at the Monroe residence Sergeant Jack Clemmons deduced, "So I do not hesitate at all to call this what it simply is. It is a murder. And I do not hesitate at all to further go and say that a conspiracy existed between the police department, between the Coroner's Office and between the L.A. County District Attorney's Office to conceal this murder and to pass it off as a suicide." In 1982, Dr. Weinberg told *Globe*, "From everything I see, these drugs were injected into Miss Monroe's body. It would have been impossible for her to have taken the barbiturates orally and not have some residue turn up in the stomach. The evidence points to all the classic features of a homicide, much more so than suicide – and certainly not an accidental death."

Deputy Coroner's Aide Lionel Grandison concluded, "I believe there was a cover-up of Marilyn Monroe's death. It's not really clear to me whether she was murdered or if in fact it was suicide. But I know based upon my particular involvement in it that there was a cover-up of some of the information to the public… No one in the office saw this report from the Suicide Team. At the time when Dr. Curphey told me to sign the death certificate, that was one of the specific questions I asked him, 'What about the report from the Suicide Team?' He said we were covered by the fact that we stated 'probable suicide' and that he had both an oral and a written report from the Suicide Team that would come into the report at a later date."

Dated August 17, 1962, the following is the official statement released during a press conference regarding Marilyn Monroe's death written by Theodore J. Curphey, M.D., Chief Medical Examiner-Coroner for Los Angeles County:

> Now that the final toxicological report and that of the psychiatric consultants have been received and considered, it is my conclusion that the death of Marilyn Monroe was caused by a self-administered overdose of sedative drugs and that the mode of death is probable suicide.
>
> The final toxicological report reveals that the barbiturate, previously reported as a lethal dose, has been positively identified as nembutal by the toxicologist.
>
> In the course of completing his routine examination, the toxicologist, Mr. Raymond Abernathy, discovered in addition to the nembutal present a large dose of chloral hydrate.
>
> Following is the summary report by the Psychiatric Investigative Team which has assisted me in collecting information in this case. This team was headed by Robert Litman, M.D., Norman Farberow, Ph.D., and Norman Tabachnick, M.D.:
>
> Marilyn Monroe died on the night of August 4th or the early morning of August 5, 1962. Examination by the toxicology laboratory indicates that death was due to a self-administered

overdose of sedative drugs. We have been asked, as consultants, to examine the life situation of the deceased and to give an opinion regarding the intent of Miss Monroe when she ingested the sedative drugs which caused her death. From the data obtained, the following points are the most important and relevant:

"Miss Monroe had suffered from psychiatric disturbance for a long time. She experienced severe fears and frequent depressions. Mood changes were abrupt and unpredictable. Among symptoms of disorganization, sleep disturbance was prominent, for which she had been taking sedative drugs for many years. She was thus familiar with and experienced in the use of sedative drugs and well aware of their dangers.

"Recently, one of the main objectives of her psychiatric treatment had been the reduction of her intake of drugs. This has been partially successful during the last two months. She was reported to be following doctor's orders in her use of the drugs; and the amount of drugs found in her home at the time of her death was not unusual.

"In our investigation, we have learned that Miss Monroe had often expressed wishes to give up, to withdraw, and even to die. On more than one occasion in the past, when disappointed and depressed, she had made a suicide attempt using sedative drugs. On these occasions, she had called for help and had been rescued.

"From the information collected about the events of the evening of August 4th, it is our opinion that the same pattern was repeated except for the rescue. It has been our practice with similar information collected in other cases in the past to recommend a certification for such deaths as probable suicide.

"Additional clues for suicide provided by the physical evidence are: (1) the high level of barbiturates and chloral hydrate in the blood which, with other evidence from the autopsy, indicates the probable ingestion of a large amount of the drugs within a short period of time; (2) the completely empty bottle of nembutal, the prescription for which was filled the day before the ingestion of the drugs; (3) the locked door which was unusual.

"On the basis of all the information obtained it is our opinion that the case is a probable suicide."

Below is the question and answer session that followed the statement above:

Q: Was Marilyn Monroe a dope addict?

A: No, not in the normal sense that we use the term addict. But she was psychologically dependent upon drugs. Miss Monroe took drugs daily and, in the last two months of her life, was taking low to moderate doses.

Q: Were you able to ascertain the exact time of death?

A: Rigor mortis was far advanced and she was dead a minimum of three hours, probably more. The autopsy also revealed that she had an empty stomach, but there is no way of knowing when she took her last meal.

Q: Did she take the lethal dose in one gulp or was there an interval of time involved?

A: We estimate that she took one gulp within – let's say – a period of seconds.

Q: Will you tell us who supplied the basis for your findings?

A: We will not expose the names of the people who gave their accounts and reports to us in confidence.

The report concluded, "Beside her bed was an empty bottle which had contained 50 nembutal capsules. The presumption is that Marilyn took 47 of them at one time" in addition to a large amount of chloral hydrate.

Marilyn made her last phone call at 10:00 P.M. to best friend Ralph Roberts and reached his answering service. She died shortly before midnight. Had she swallowed 64 pills within that less than two-hour time frame, 47 Nembutals and 17 chloral hydrates, it would be more than a little bit curious why her stomach, according to the official autopsy report, had been almost completely empty.

The autopsy report also noted no refractile crystals from either drug in her stomach, something suspect to any competent medical professional. Elias W. Amador, M.D. told me, "I am surprised that there are no capsules in the stomach. I am very surprised." Unaware of Marilyn's 10:00 P.M. call, Dr. Litman explained this discrepancy in 1980, "At the autopsy, her stomach was empty. What that means is that a considerable period of time, several hours had elapsed between the time she ingested the fatal pills and the time she died."

The Suicide Prevention Team investigating Marilyn's "suicide" was comprised of Robert Elkon Litman, M.D., Norman Donald Tabachnick, M.D., and Norman Louis Farberow, Ph.D. Since Marilyn's psychoanalyst Dr. Ralph Greenson was at the death scene when the police were called, they each consulted with Greenson over what happened to Marilyn. Spoto interviewed Dr. Litman, who had been a former student of Greenson's. Litman told Spoto that the Team "didn't consider the murder hypothesis" yet "Greenson wasn't at all sure if she committed suicide. Greenson felt very much undecided in his own mind… All I heard from Greenson was that she was involved with men at the very highest level of government. The name Kennedy was not mentioned specifically… A sexual goddess of the country with no date for Saturday night, feeling rejected and abandoned." Oddly, Litman next said to Spoto that, in 1962, at the time of the Marilyn Monroe investigation, "I didn't see any record of no drugs in the stomach."

In addition, Litman said Curphey told the Team it was suicide and that their function was to determine Marilyn's state of mind: did she or did she not intend to kill herself? Curphey instructed them not to determine *how* she died but only to determine whether she accidentally or intentionally killed herself according to her past history of suicide attempts. Anthony Summers noted, "The head of the Team, Dr. Norman Farberow, said neither Kennedy brother was questioned. He added, 'I'm sure discretion entered into it.' " Farberow attempted to interview Marilyn's last publicist and long-time Kennedy confidant Pat Newcomb, but "she stone-walled me, was uncommunicative."

Dr. Farberow told me Marilyn's housekeeper Mrs. Murray was also interviewed and that she believed Marilyn accidentally committed suicide, "She said she didn't realize how many pills she had taken." Regarding Marilyn, Farberow relayed, "The general pattern that we had found common among women of her age was that she was unhappy and it [suicide] was not a very difficult possibility" yet he conceded, "I have no idea now, at this time, what her intention was in taking so many."

Next, the Suicide Prevention Team queried a different set of individuals whose attitudes would act as the basis for their conclusions. The Team was of the opinion that her suicide was *intentional* when they "learned that Miss Monroe had often expressed wishes to give up, to withdraw, and even to die." On August 16, 1962, a Canadian newspaper article in the *Winnipeg Free Press* stated, "In Miss Monroe's case, there were four reported earlier attempts at suicide. The Team contacted Miss Monroe's psychiatrist in New York [Dr. Marianne Kris] and the doctors at the Payne Whitney Clinic, where she was hospitalized three years ago [actually February 5 – 10, 1961], after a reported breakdown."

On February 5, Dr. Kris had placed Marilyn Monroe in a locked cell at the Payne Whitney Psychiatric Division after an alleged suicide attempt. Gloria Romanoff told me, "When she was hospitalized in New York, I think the whole behavior of the staff was not to be explained and she reached out to Joe [DiMaggio] to help her and he stormed in there and took her out over his shoulder. She was the first one to say he saved her life. She suffered such indignities in that hospital and she was quite helpless." Pat Newcomb reflected to Spoto, "That was the worst experience. One person she could trust to get her out was Joe. One phone call and she said to me, 'It's so awful. I mean all these people don't want to treat you like a person.' It was so degrading. It really affected her badly." [4]

British actor Peter Lawford, once a member of Frank Sinatra's Rat Pack, was the most important suspect regarding the death of Marilyn Monroe. The day of her funeral on August 8, Peter told a reporter that he may have been the last one to speak to the actress while on the phone with her. He would later report the time at around 7:30 P.M. on August 4. Marilyn's ex-husband Joe DiMaggio "held Bobby Kennedy responsible for her death" according to good friend Harry Hall. With such animosity towards the two brothers, DiMaggio told the funeral director, "Be sure that none of those damned Kennedys come to the funeral." Morris Engelberg (no relation to Marilyn's physician Dr. Engelberg) was one of Joe DiMaggio's best friends and the executor of his estate. He said, "No woman in the world will ever be loved the way he loved her. He loved her in life and in death."

According to Engelberg, Marilyn and Joe had considered adopting a child days before she died because she couldn't have any. He said taking this step "was huge for Joe but he knew that Marilyn wanted more than anything to be a mother." Biographer Richard Ben Cramer suggested the child would be Mexican. As for Marilyn and Joe's plans to get remarried, Engelberg relayed, "He said, 'You know, Morris, instead of kissing her at the altar, I kissed her in her casket…' But when I would say, 'Joe, if that was my wife, I would have gone after them,' he'd say, 'They're the Kennedys. They're too big. They're bigger than life. And why would I want to embarrass her?' Did he hate the Kennedys? Beyond anything you can imagine."

Another close friend of DiMaggio's, Dr. Rock Positano, a New York foot specialist, remembered, "It was pretty heavy to be with him when he got into one of those moods. He wouldn't get mean but he would get stone silent." DiMaggio often played Ella Fitzgerald's "Embraceable You" in the car. "He used to tell me, 'Doc, that was our song.' And he'd play it over and over again. You could see he would be somewhere else."

Morris Engelberg relayed what Joe DiMaggio said to his son, "The Kennedys killed her." Engelberg wrote in his book:

> DiMaggio told me that he had given his son a manila envelope containing a statement concerning Monroe's death, to be opened after he died. "Something the world should know about is in there," DiMaggio told his son. When Junior came to Florida after his father's funeral, I asked him about that envelope. He had given me an opening by volunteering that he had talked with Marilyn the night she died – he said "murdered." He claimed he hadn't opened the envelope because he already knew the message his father had left behind… When I asked him if he agreed with his father that the Kennedys were responsible for her death, he said it was probably true. "She didn't die of natural causes, and she wasn't going to kill herself, not when she was about to remarry my father."

Pat Kennedy Lawford was Marilyn's closest girlfriend. Pat was Jack and Bobby Kennedy's sister. Gloria Romanoff told me Marilyn was very shy and often had a hard time meeting others. She said, "Not many people really got to know her. It's a puzzle to me how you can become such a large figure in that business and really not be known by most people. It's really quite astonishing. She didn't have a framework. She didn't have family members and did not have that many close friends.

"Marilyn just felt inadequate in so many ways. It was really heart breaking. Of those people who filled her life were people who worked for her one way or another" and Pat Kennedy Lawford "was a good friend of Marilyn's to the degree that she could be. Pat spent enormous periods of time with her own family on the East Coast. She wasn't available to Marilyn all the time but she was as friendly as can be and cared about Marilyn. Marilyn knew it and was very appreciative. Pat also thought all her family members would get a hoot out of meeting Marilyn. She'd say, 'I've got some family coming in. I'd like you to join us.' Marilyn was just amazed. Amazed."

Pat and her husband Peter Lawford were quite upset when DiMaggio barred them from the service. Peter remarked, "It seems to be a concerted effort to keep some of Marilyn's old friends from attending." DiMaggio privately growled, "If it wasn't for her so-called friends, Marilyn would still be alive today." After they were denied entrance to Marilyn's funeral, Peter and his wife got on a plane to Hyannis Port, Massachusetts, the Kennedy compound.

Pat Newcomb joined them soon and they all subsequently went on a Maine cruise as a surviving picture on the Manitou proved dated August 12, 1962, four days after Marilyn's funeral. Pat Newcomb, Jack Kennedy, and Peter Lawford are smiling in the photograph. According to biographer C. David Heymann, three days after she was murdered, Bobby Kennedy had "left San Francisco on a camping trip to Oregon with his children. Ironically, they were joined there by his early travel companion, Supreme Court Justice William O. Douglas."

The official police report #62-509 463 by Detective Sergeant Robert Byron on August 8, 1962 read in part: "An attempt was made to contact Mr. Lawford, but officers were informed by his secretary that Mr. Lawford had taken an airplane at 1:00 P... It is unknown at this time the exact destination, however his secretary stated that she did expect to hear from him and that she would request that he contact this Department at his earliest convenience." Peter would continue to ignore the police department's interview requests for thirteen years. This is strange behavior when the issue at hand is an alleged suicide.

Coroner Curphey gave Dr. Litman and the Suicide Prevention Team the conclusion to the case *before* they began their official investigation. Declaring it a suicide, Curphey told them to work backwards. Litman said to Spoto that the Team eventually decided it was a case of "probable suicide" based on the "physical evidence" and the "past history of having made overdoses."

Deputy District Attorney John Willis Miner disagreed. In 1962, serving under District Attorney William McKesson, he was also the liaison to the coroner. In his capacity, he oversaw Marilyn's autopsy performed by Dr. Thomas Noguchi. Miner related, "It takes time to swallow 30 or 40 capsules. As soon as the first ones hit her stomach they would start dissolving and start being absorbed, probably before she swallowed all 30 or 40 of them. She would have been unconscious. And if she had swallowed them, she would have been dead before they all dissolved. There would be residue in her tummy."

Then something unheard of happened next. Miner remembered, "I was called on a Sunday, and the techs wouldn't even have gotten to the specimens until the following day, but all the specimens disappeared – I'd say by the following day. I've never seen that happen before or since. This was deliberate. Somebody took those specimens and flushed them down the toilet… So there were no microscopics, no laboratory work on anything other than the blood and liver.

"Noguchi really couldn't come up with a diagnosis at this point. Somebody wanted the diagnosis of suicide to stick and didn't want any interference by analysis of the scientific evidence." Noguchi told Anthony Summers, "For some reason I felt uncomfortable and shortly after the case was formally closed I called Toxicology and requested the check… Abernathy told me the organ specimens had been destroyed." Noguchi said years later of Coroner Curphey, "He certified the manner of death to be 'probable suicide.' When you weigh all the factors, it tends to indicate a more likely suicide. But the office could not find necessary factors to state it as suicide."

Oddly, Greenson told Litman he wasn't sure if Marilyn Monroe had committed suicide. On August 8, the day of Marilyn's funeral, Greenson would tell John Miner a different story in the late afternoon. Coroner Curphey had sent Miner to interview Greenson in his Beverly Hills office on 436 Roxbury Drive. Greenson told Miner, who happened to be a colleague of his from the Psychoanalytic Institute, that he was certain his star patient *did not* commit suicide.

Miner was adamant about this point for years, "What we really have is a coroner chief medical examiner who had a preconceived notion of what happened and labeled it accordingly and was *completely wrong*. Curphey chose to adopt it and in a way it was the easiest political solution." Miner ruled out suicide by oral ingestion as not medically possible. He said, "With that massive amount of intake, there would have been undissolved capsules. She would have died before all of those capsules had been absorbed. So the notion of oral intake of the barbiturates simply does not scientifically stand up. It just didn't happen that way." [5]

Greenson Calls the Police to Say Marilyn Monroe Committed Suicide

Contrary to the official report, Greenson phoned in the "suicide" for the most famous woman in the world. Sergeant Clemmons consistently throughout the years told documentarians and biographers that Greenson called it in. As for the August 5 phone call at 4:25 A.M. from 12305 Fifth

Helena Drive, biographers Brown and Barham noted, "At first the man on the phone was so agitated that Clemmons couldn't understand him. He was talking very fast and seemed to have a European accent." Greenson had a soft Brooklyn/Viennese accent.

The caller said, "Marilyn Monroe is dead. She just committed suicide." Miner reacted rather strongly to this information, "That's right. Clemmons says Greenson said he was calling with respect to Monroe, that she had committed suicide. I don't think that ever happened. It's contrary to the kind of man Greenson was. I think Clemmons said that to cover himself for not having followed department regulations."

In an article released on August 5, 1973, Greenson stated that he told Engelberg and the housekeeper, "O.K., I'll call the police." Speaking to Sergeant Clemmons, Greenson claimed he said, "I want to report the death of a person, a sudden and unexplained death." Clemmons came right over. When he arrived he found three people: a sarcastic Greenson, a frightened housekeeper Mrs. Murray and Marilyn's sullen physician Dr. Engelberg. Greenson pointed to the empty bottle of Nembutal, implying that it spoke for itself. The psychiatrist did not cry over the death of his patient. Clemmons told Brown and Barham, "I strongly disliked Greenson's attitude. He was cocky, almost challenging me to accuse him of something." [6]

Biographer Keith Badman called into question Clemmons' murder suspicions. Badman said that soon after Clemmons confronted Murray, Greenson, and Engelberg, he called up Marilyn's first husband, LAPD detective Jim Dougherty, to say Marilyn was dead, not revealing what he would later say was "an out-and-out case of murder." Clemmons himself stated, "I didn't call Jim from the house. I went back to the station and called." As for the apparent discrepancy of information to Dougherty, private investigator Milo Speriglio noted in his book, "Clemmons did not tell him what he really suspected; that Marilyn was not a suicide but a murder victim." Since Clemmons was a good friend of Dougherty, he said, "It looks like an OD" out of respect. Dougherty replied with sorrow, "I was expecting it."

Badman claimed Dougherty was not at his house when he received Clemmons' call but rather "sitting in his squad car in North Hollywood, just 10 miles from the actress's home (and not lying in bed with his wife, as some previous Monroe biographers have claimed)." Regarding Clemmons' call, Dougherty reported in his second Marilyn Monroe book, "And yet when Jack finished speaking... I could not breathe, or see or hear. Suicide they told me later. But no. She would never have done that. Not her. I turned and looked down at my wife Pat... 'Say a prayer,' I said, my voice breaking. 'Norma Jeane is dead.'" [7]

In addition to Sergeant Clemmons, Greenson later told his family that

Marilyn had committed suicide but repeated over and over that it must have been an accident. On June 23, 2010, Christopher Turner released a United Kingdom article including an interview with the Greenson children. Danny and Joan spoke publicly for the first time in years. "He always felt that it was an accident that she killed herself," Joan said. "That she was getting better and that she no longer had a tolerance for barbiturates and sleeping medication and stuff like that because she had been slowly weaned off it."

Danny, who believes Marilyn committed suicide intentionally, reflected, "My father was hurt by the fact that she killed herself, and he would tell himself that it was accidental. People who take a lot of pills – and she took a lot of pills – can get so stoned from all the pills they're taking that they lose track and they think they haven't taken enough and they take more and then it kills them. That was his rationalization." Their mother believed the same. Hildi Greenson told Cathy Griffin, "I think it was accidental suicide, like probably the others had been, too, where it was simply a matter of having overdosed herself, and help just didn't come early enough. Before it used to come earlier."

Chris Turner wrote that Marilyn "was the only one of his patients to die in his care." This is not true. In fact, while treating actress Inger Stevens, she died from an overdose of sleeping pills on April 30, 1970, almost eight years after his star patient. I discussed Greenson's version of what happened with Gloria Romanoff: Marilyn took some pills, forgot, took some more then died. She said, "That's a very pat solution to the problem. That's pretty much the story of her life in her late years. To say that is all too easy." [8]

In the documentary *Marilyn Monroe: The Final Days*, Engelberg diagnosed his patient a manic-depressive. Referring to her last night, he relayed:

> Peter Lawford got a call from Marilyn and she was mumbling. Apparently she was going under from the pills she took and perhaps was calling him as a cry for help. He didn't run over. He was the one who then called Mickey Rudin [Marilyn's lawyer and Greenson's brother-in-law] to tell Mickey Rudin that he'd had this call and Marilyn sounded funny and would Mickey check. And that's when Mickey called the housekeeper… Dr. Greenson got there first. She was dead when he got there. I went into the bedroom and made sure she was dead. There was some rigor mortis, yes but it wasn't extreme then. I suspected that she'd been dead at least a few hours.

I believe she was in a manic phase and that something happened to suddenly depress her and she grabbed pills. She had plenty of pills at her bedside. I think she was suddenly depressed and in that sense, it was intentional. *Then* I think she thought better of it when she felt herself going under because she called Peter Lawford. So, while it was intentional at the time I do believe that she *changed her mind*... I had several phone calls from ordinary women. The general feeling was that if they had only known Marilyn was in trouble, they would have done everything they could to help her. And so I realized that Marilyn didn't just have appeal for men. Women were aware of the lost little girl inside of her and they reacted to that.

In a 1983 interview with biographer C. David Heymann, published in full in 1998, Peter Lawford agreed with Engelberg's diagnosis for Marilyn: she was bi-polar. Peter said, "Marilyn had a death wish of sorts but didn't actually want to die, at least not in her more sane moments. In my opinion, she had manic-depressive tendencies and should have been on a different type of medication."

In 1982, Engelberg told the District Attorney's Office, "I saw her Friday evening. It was to give her an injection of liver and vitamins... usually in the buttocks, sometimes possibly in the upper arms where you usually give intramuscular injections... Probably in the buttocks because that's the usual place I would put it." Greenson explained to Dr. Marianne Kris, "I had an internist who would prescribe medication for her and to give her vitamin injections and liver injections, so that I had nothing to do with the actual handling of medication."

Richard Meryman of *Life* magazine conducted Marilyn's last interview and oddly enough he noticed an abrupt, sharp, stimulant-like change in Marilyn's attitude after Engelberg's visit on July 5, 1962. She seemed up and manic within a matter of minutes, he reported, which is consistent with a methamphetamine shot. Marilyn came back to Meryman and said, "No, kidding. They're making me take liver shots. Here, I'll prove it to you." She then talked endlessly until midnight when apparently still in a manic-like phase, she suddenly suggested they grill a steak. When Marilyn returned from the kitchen, she disappointedly informed Meryman no food was left in the refrigerator. [9]

On October 13, 1973, biographer Maurice Zolotow publicly released portions of an interview he conducted with Greenson discussing Marilyn's last day on August 4. The Greenson family sealed the full Greenson – Zolotow interview from the public in Special Collections at UCLA until January 1,

2039, along with most of Greenson's other writings alluding to Marilyn Monroe. Greenson told Zolotow:

> I came over and remained about two hours. She was quite upset. She was also somewhat disoriented. It was clear she had taken some sleeping pills during the day… At this time, I didn't know she had been given a Nembutal prescription she had filled the day before…
>
> At about 7:30 P.M., I received a happy phone call from her and again told her where she could reach me if necessary. That is the last I heard until I received a call from Mrs. Murray at about 3 A.M. I will always believe it was an accidental suicide, because her hand was on the receiver, her finger still in the dial. I'm convinced she was trying to phone me. If only she had reached me…
>
> I can assure you that contrary to Norman Mailer's speculations, Marilyn did not have any emotional involvement with Robert Kennedy or any other man at this time. Furthermore, Engelberg and I made no attempts to resuscitate her, as it was evident from the skin discoloration that she had been dead for many hours.
>
> I did not attempt to pump her stomach. Dr. Engelberg did not pump her stomach. Marilyn was at home all evening and saw nobody except Miss Newcomb, Mrs. Murray and myself. Her room was locked and bolted – doors and windows. How could a murderer have entered: There were no signs of violence. In my opinion, Marilyn Monroe died of an accidental overdose of barbiturates. She was a good human being. She was a lost and very lonely woman who had never gotten over being a waif. She needed to belong or have a family. It is a tragedy that her artistic achievement as an actress, and all the wealth and fame it brought her, did not give her peace. She had a good future ahead of her. She was making progress. If only she had completed that call to me.

Referring to the issue dated July 16, 1973, author Norman Mailer noted in his Marilyn Monroe book, "Dr. Thomas Noguchi stated for *Time* magazine that 'no stomach pump was used on Marilyn.'"

On October 23, 1973, an article was released entitled, "Psychiatrist Breaks Silence In Defense of Marilyn Monroe." Greenson attempted yet again to dispel murder rumors and any sexual affairs with men in government. The article read, "Breaking years of silence, Dr. Ralph Greenson, of Los Angeles, Marilyn Monroe's psychiatrist at the time of her death, has denied that the actress may have been murdered. He also denied that she had been having an affair with the late President John F. Kennedy or his brother."

Greenson himself said, "I've decided that all I can do I've tried to do, and somewhere it is written that this woman is not a bad woman and was not involved with all the political figures. Somewhere, if you will read long enough, you will find it." Days after Marilyn died, to the Suicide Prevention Team, Greenson would say the opposite: Marilyn was in a "close relationship with extremely important men in government." It was "sexual" and the men were "at the highest level." [10]

Soon after Marilyn's death, Mrs. Murray relayed a similar accidental suicide story to Mr. and Mrs. Landau, the movie star's next-door neighbors to the west. Abe C. Landau said to author Robert Slatzer, "Mrs. Murray told us that Marilyn had taken an overdose of sleeping pills. She said Marilyn would take pills. Then she would wake up, forget that she had taken some, and take some more. And that's what Mrs. Murray said happened." On July 16, 1973, *Time* magazine wrote, "It was not a case, says Noguchi, of 'automatism' – that gray area in which a person used to taking pills becomes groggy, takes a few too many, and slips over the edge of death." [11] Under scrutiny, Greenson's story that night falls apart.

The Miner Memorandum

As a former colleague of his, John Miner highly respected Greenson and has defended the doctor for years against charges that he killed Marilyn Monroe either accidentally or intentionally. Yet Miner believed Marilyn *was* murdered nonetheless with the cooperation of Mrs. Murray and a Nembutal enema. As for the purplish discoloration of Marilyn's colon, Miner told Brown and Barham, "I have witnessed more than two thousand autopsies – scores and scores of which involved barbiturate poisoning and I have never seen that phenomenon – before or since." He said the actress was possibly slipped chloral hydrate in a soft drink to knock her out and then the enema was given to her. This scenario can't be true because if Marilyn had been unconscious, she wouldn't be able to make her final call at 10:00 P.M. to the answering service of her best friend and masseur Ralph Roberts before passing out. [12]

Keeping in mind that John Miner highly revered Greenson, the following is Miner's memorandum to Dr. Theodore Curphey where Greenson changed his mind on the suicide verdict and said Marilyn *did not* commit suicide. Oddly, Greenson told Miner, "If at the end of our interview, you reach any kind of conclusion, I have no objection to you stating that conclusion to Dr. Curphey." Was Greenson implying a conclusion other than suicide? Miner recollected the contents of his memorandum:

> To: Theodore J. Curphey, M.D.
> Chief Medical Examiner, Coroner of Los Angeles County,
> Hall of Justice,
> Los Angeles, CA
>
> After I attended her autopsy, you asked me to interview Marilyn Monroe's psychiatrist, Ralph Greenson, M.D. on the suicide issue.
>
> Dr. Greenson granted the interview on condition that I would not ever reveal what was said or heard during the interview, but I could make known whatever conclusion I reached on the suicide question.
>
> Dr. Greenson said, "Marilyn Monroe did not commit suicide. However, my opinion is subject to bias, because a patient's suicide is a catastrophe for her psychiatrist, so I will let her own voice on a tape she recorded for me at her home help you. It is a stream of consciousness of her thoughts which she was unable to say in her office sessions."
>
> Ted, what she said on her tapes rules out any possibility that Marilyn Monroe either deliberately or accidentally killed herself. She did not commit suicide. [Miner's emphasis]
>
> Dated 8/8/62 John W. Miner
> Deputy District Attorney,
> Head, Medical Legal Section,
> Liaison Officer to the Coroner

John Miner later discovered that his memorandum to Curphey and to Chief Deputy District Attorney Manley J. Bowler had mysteriously disappeared. Miner relayed on *The Marilyn Files* documentary, "There's a certain stigma attached to suicide and if Miss Monroe *did not* commit suicide then she is entitled to have that stigma *removed* from her life story." When interviewed by Brown and Barham, John Miner said, "Of course the Suicide Prevention Team reached a different conclusion from mine, namely that Miss Monroe's death was a 'probable suicide.' But I don't think they had the same facts at their disposal."[13] Indeed they did not.

Noguchi didn't have all the facts either but he would find out too late. Still distracted by the findings of the Suicide Prevention Team, Noguchi stated in a February 1976 article for *Oui* magazine, "Our physical examination was coupled with what we call a psychological autopsy. In the case of Miss Monroe, there had been previous suicide attempts. In fact, her whole lifestyle, as we reconstructed it, pointed toward suicide rather than an accident."

Initially suspicious of the findings at Marilyn's autopsy, Noguchi wrote in his book *Coroner to the Stars* that back in 1962 he had asked a member of the Suicide Prevention Team, Dr. Robert Litman, who participated in the psychological autopsy, "Any chance of murder?" and Litman said, "The door to the bedroom was locked from the inside. They had to break a window to enter the room. And Mrs. Murray was in her room all evening only a little way down the hall from Monroe's." Noguchi remained skeptical yet in the end with no further evidence at his disposal, he agreed with Dr. Curphey's official conclusion: "probable suicide."

In the early 1980s, Noguchi had more details, including Miner's memorandum, which emphatically went against the suicide theory. Noguchi would write in his book that as for the ingestion of 64 pills, "In Monroe's case… an accidental overdose of that magnitude was extremely unlikely. From my forensic experience with suicide victims, I believe that the sheer number of pills Monroe ingested was too many to swallow 'accidentally.' Thus, if Miner's evaluation in 1962 was correct, the only conceivable cause of Monroe's death was murder." Noguchi curiously noted, "I found absolutely no visual evidence of pills in the stomach or the small intestine. No residue. No refractile crystals. And yet the evidence of the pill bottles showed that Monroe had swallowed forty to fifty Nembutals and a large number of chloral hydrate pills."

Raymond Strait was Jayne Mansfield's press secretary for 10 years (1957 – 1967). He told me, "Noguchi never believed it was suicide but they shut him up real quick. I knew Tom Noguchi. He said he never believed for a minute that she committed suicide. He wanted to blow the whole thing on Marilyn Monroe but they [his superiors] weren't having it." Dr. Sidney Weinberg told *Oui* magazine for its October 1975 issue, "The findings in the autopsy report are certainly not characteristic of an oral ingestion of large amounts of barbiturates." I asked Dr. Amador, "Is taking 64 pills too many to take accidentally?" "I agree with that statement. You would expect to find tablets in the stomach or residue. Tablets are not immediately dissolved. Those take a while to dissolve."

Dr. J. DeWitt Fox stated for *The Marilyn Files* documentary that there should have been pills in the stomach if indeed she swallowed all these drugs as Coroner Curphey had publicly claimed. Fox said, "The crux of the entire case is the percentage of pentobarbital in her bloodstream and also the chloral hydrate which was found in autopsy toxicology studies and that is a very high lethal level. The other very questionable factor is there was very little in the way of fluid in her stomach. Only 20 cc of fluid was noted. And she was supposed to have taken 47 capsules of Nembutal in a very few seconds and had she done so, she would've probably choked on them.

"And they would've been present in her stomach. At the autopsy, there was not a single capsule found." When Fox was told that there was no drinking glass in Marilyn's bedroom, he stated, "One could never take that many Nembutals without water. The tablets themselves would choke the patient and would be so dry and sticky in his mouth he couldn't tolerate it. And without water being present, I don't see how she could've gotten them down." Therefore, death by oral ingestion of Nembutal was impossible.

In the early 1990s, Noguchi told Brown and Barham not to discount the possibility that Marilyn could've been given a drug-laced enema or suppository. Noguchi concluded in his book, "The remaining questions will go unanswered, and no one will ever be able to say definitely what went on that evening which… transformed Marilyn Monroe from a beautiful and talented actress… to a dying movie star – and an undying legend." [14]

An Afternoon Visit from Bobby Kennedy and Peter Lawford

It's worth noting the way the media functioned in 1962 is not the way it operates today. Then, the press gave politicians more privacy in regards to their personal lives and tabloid media was virtually non-existent. Yet there were gossip columnists like Walter Winchell, Florabel Muir, Louella Parsons, Dorothy Kilgallen, Sheilah Graham, and Hedda Hopper. Today with the advent of consumer-friendly miniature audio and visual recording devices, a politician's secret love affair can easily be exposed in every tabloid newspaper across the country or even broadcast over the Internet via YouTube. Anyone who doubts the sexual proclivities of politicians in high office need only remember that in 1962, when Puritan values dominated the country's mores, such antics were never disclosed. This is why the public still doubts and debates whether Bobby Kennedy ever slept with Marilyn Monroe.

A year before his death in 1984, Peter Lawford stated in his last full-length interview that he and Robert Kennedy visited Marilyn at her home in the early afternoon on August 4, 1962. According to the John Bates family, Kennedy never left their Gilroy ranch south of San Francisco after he arrived on August 3 with his wife and four of their children. Bates said Robert Kennedy couldn't have been in Los Angeles on August 4 "unless he had a twin." He argued, "Even Peter Pan would have had a hard time doing that. It's mind-boggling." Pat Newcomb would later say to Slatzer for his 1974 book, "Bobby did not talk to Marilyn that night. I know that for a fact. I know that from him." However, she conceded, "Peter did call her that night."

This is true but as we will learn later, Marilyn was perfectly fine and *not* dying at the time of Peter's call around 7:30 P.M., as many previous Marilyn Monroe biographers have contended. Private eye to the stars Fred Otash bugged the homes of Marilyn Monroe and Peter Lawford on behalf of Jimmy Hoffa with the sole intent of getting Bobby Kennedy off his back. Hoffa knew Bobby and Marilyn were sleeping together, and Hoffa wanted wiretaps proving it so he could later blackmail Kennedy.

According to Otash and what he overheard on the phone taps, Marilyn declined Peter's dinner invitation and said, "No, I'm tired. There is nothing more for me to respond to. Just do me a favor. Tell the President I tried to get him. Tell him goodbye for me. I think my purpose has been served." Marilyn had failed in her attempts to reach Jack Kennedy. She wanted him to tell his brother Bobby to stop using her.

During Peter's first interview with police on October 16, 1975, he would claim that when he phoned her at 7:30 P.M., Marilyn was dying at the time of this call and that she had said to him instead, "Say goodbye to Jack [Kennedy], say goodbye to Pat [Kennedy Lawford] and say goodbye to yourself because you're a nice guy." Milt Ebbins told Spoto a similar version.

Ebbins claimed that at 7:15 P.M. *Marilyn* had called and said, "Peter, you're a wonderful man, you're a terrific guy. Pat is terrific and Jack is great. I just want you to know that everything you've done is beautiful. I really can't thank you enough for what you've done. Say goodbye to Jack…" Gloria Romanoff told me she didn't fall for the "Say goodbye to Jack…" speech. Mrs. Romanoff said with certainty that Peter made it up: "That has been printed and reprinted. It's fantasy."

Mrs. Murray related to Slatzer, "After Dr. Greenson left, I had all sorts of chores to take care of around the kitchen and other things, personal things. Then the telephone rang [at 7:00 P.M.], and I answered it. It was Joe DiMaggio, Jr., and he was given the privilege of getting through immediately. I called Marilyn, and she left her bedroom and went into the telephone room, the third bedroom, and sat on the floor and talked with him. He evidently gave her some good news, and she was delighted about it.

"She was laughing and speaking in her loudest voice, 'Oh, that's wonderful' and that sort of thing, you know. As a matter of fact, I thought she was calling to me, so I went closer and discovered she was still on the telephone. Then as a result of this good news, she made a telephone call to Dr. Greenson to tell him what she had just learned. She was in a great mood. It was hard to get the feeling that just a short time after that she might have been depressed. This I can't believe." Joe DiMaggio, Sr. later said his son and Marilyn "spoke for about fifteen minutes and Marilyn seemed quite normal and in good spirits." [15]

In 1983, Peter Lawford discussed his friend Marilyn Monroe at length with biographer C. David Heymann for his Jackie Kennedy biography. Peter said that at approximately 2 o'clock on the afternoon of August 4, 1962, he and Bobby Kennedy arrived at Marilyn's home. Peter told Heymann she had set aside some Mexican food, which suggested she was expecting Bobby's visit. Heymann wrote that the buffet included "guacamole, stuffed mushrooms, spicy meatballs… plus a chilled magnum of her favorite beverage, champagne. Lawford poured himself a glass and went out to the swimming pool so Marilyn and Bobby could talk." An existing receipt proved she had in fact purchased this food from Briggs Delicatessen the day before in the amount of $49.07. On Bobby and Marilyn, Peter relayed to Heymann:

They argued back and forth for maybe ten minutes, Marilyn becoming more and more hysterical. At the height of her anger she allowed how first thing Monday morning she was going to call a press conference and tell the world about the treatment she had suffered at the hands of the Kennedy brothers. At this point Bobby became livid. In no uncertain terms he told her she would have to leave both Jack and him alone – no more telephone calls, no letters, nothing. They didn't want to hear from her anymore. Marilyn presently lost it, screaming obscenities and flailing wildly away at Bobby with her fists. In her fury she picked up a small kitchen knife and lunged at him. I was with them at this time, so I tried to grab Marilyn's arm. We finally knocked her down and managed to wrestle the knife away. Bobby thought we ought to call Dr. Greenson and tell him to come over. The psychiatrist arrived at Marilyn's home within the hour.

To Spoto, Pat Newcomb confirmed Peter's account, "I was at her house that afternoon until 3 and that's when Greenson came and told me to leave. He wanted to deal with her... She was very upset... Greenson told Mrs. Murray to take her out for a walk on the beach in the car... And that's the last I saw of her." When interviewed by Maurice Zolotow in October 1973, Greenson would tell him that when he arrived at Marilyn's in the early afternoon, "It was clear she had taken some sleeping pills during the day." Attempting to mask why she was *really* upset, Mrs. Murray and Greenson claimed that Marilyn was mad at Pat Newcomb, who had slept over on August 3, because Pat actually had a good night's sleep and Marilyn didn't.

Mrs. Murray told Rose Shade, "Pat had stayed overnight, and apparently had taken sleeping pills, perhaps some of Marilyn's Nembutal. Pat was still asleep, and would sleep serenely until noon – the way Marilyn longed to sleep. Marilyn was not pleased. To sleep twelve hours in her house was like feasting in front of a starving person."

Greenson relayed to Zolotow, "Marilyn was talking in a confused way. It was hard to know exactly what was bothering her. I finally gathered that she resented the fact that Pat Newcomb had taken some pills the night before and slept 12 hours and Marilyn had also taken pills and slept only six hours. At this time, I didn't know she had been given a Nembutal prescription she had filled the day before. Anyway, I listened to her jumble of confused talk, I said that instead of Pat staying overnight, Pat should go home and Mrs. Murray remain the night. I didn't want Marilyn to be alone. Pat went home. Mrs. Murray stayed over."

Weeks after Marilyn died, Greenson wrote in a letter to Dr. Marianne Kris that it was *Marilyn* who wanted Pat to leave, "I finally asked the girlfriend to leave because this was Marilyn's request, and I asked the housekeeper to stay overnight, which she did not ordinarily do on Saturday nights." The housekeeper related to Slatzer, "Dr. Greenson asked me if I had planned on staying that night. He asked this in a rather offhand way, without any special reason for my staying at her home, for Marilyn felt secure. She often told me that staying alone was no problem with her. She enjoyed being in the house, and it didn't matter if anyone was with her."

Greenson, Mrs. Murray, and Pat Newcomb didn't want to admit that Marilyn was really upset over her row with Bobby Kennedy. Years later, Mrs. Murray would concede to Anthony Summers that the argument was indeed over Bobby's earlier visit. In the *Say Goodbye to the President* documentary Mrs. Murray and Summers shared the following exchange regarding Marilyn's last day on August 4:

> MRS. MURRAY: Well, over a period of time, I was not at all surprised that the Kennedys were a very important part of Marilyn's life. I was not included in this information but I was a witness to what was happening.
>
> SUMMERS: And you believe that he was here?
>
> MRS. MURRAY: At Marilyn's house?
>
> SUMMERS: Yes.
>
> MRS. MURRAY: Oh, sure.
>
> SUMMERS: That afternoon?
>
> MRS. MURRAY: Yes.
>
> SUMMERS: And you think *that* is the reason she was so upset?
>
> MRS. MURRAY: Yes and it became so sticky that the protectors of Robert Kennedy had to step in and protect him.

Summers asked Mrs. Murray why she lied to police and she said, "I told whatever I thought was good to tell."

In 1956, Marilyn Monroe met her last publicist Pat Newcomb after a few days on the set of *Bus Stop*. Irritated and annoyed, she believed Pat showed an interest in a man Marilyn liked. Pat said to Anthony Summers, "We had this terrible falling out almost immediately. I didn't know why for years, but it turned out to be over some guy that Marilyn thought I liked, someone I didn't have any interest in at all. I didn't know how to cope with it, and Arthur Jacobs told me I'd better get out of there at once." Pat told Spoto something similar, "I think she thought I was interested in a guy that she was interested in."

Marilyn and Pat didn't work again together until 1961. As for Marilyn's last afternoon, Pat relayed to Spoto, "Marilyn seemed angry that I had been able to sleep and she hadn't – but something else was behind it all." That "something else behind it all" may have been an argument between Pat and Marilyn over Bobby Kennedy before his visit with Peter Lawford, which led to an even bigger argument with Bobby. Jeanne Martin told Anthony Summers, "Pat got far too involved: she was deeply in love with Bobby Kennedy. She's only just got over that." George Barris, an old friend of Pat Newcomb, told me, "That's the way she was. They both were interested in the same men." [16]

One Last Walk at Santa Monica Beach?

More than two weeks after Marilyn died, Greenson informed a colleague that he encouraged his patient to walk along the beach, "Marilyn wanted to go for a walk on the pier in Santa Monica, and I said she was too groggy for that but if she drank a lot of fluid I would allow the housekeeper to drive her to the beach." Contradicting himself more than a decade later, Greenson would claim he discouraged such an action. He told Zolotow that Marilyn "said she thought she would go to the beach and walk. She lived about 10 minutes drive from the Santa Monica beach. I said, 'Don't do that as people might recognize you, but why don't you go for a drive up the coast highway with Mrs. Murray?' I told her to be sure and drink a large Coke before she went out."

Milt Ebbins said, "We were gonna have Mexican food at Peter Lawford's... Peter calls me. He said Marilyn had a little anxiety and her doctor told her to walk along the beach. She walked at the beach. She stopped at Peter's house. She told him, 'Peter, I don't think I'm gonna be able to make it.' He said,

Jay Margolis

'Come on! Go home. Take a shower. Stay here.' She said, 'I gotta go.' So she went home. She walked on the beach because Dr. Greenson told her. Then she called Peter and told him she couldn't make it."

Peter's good friend director Bill Asher was playing volleyball near the Lawford mansion when he claimed Marilyn arrived sometime after 3 o'clock on Saturday, August 4. Bill Asher told Spoto, "All that bullshit about Bobby being at Peter's that afternoon. I remember Milt being there. No, Milt wasn't there. Maybe Joe Naar. No. Marilyn was there. Took a little walk on the beach… She wasn't too steady in the sand." Because Asher mentioned the alleged presence of Bobby and Peter that last day, Spoto correctly jumps in with, "Saturday afternoon." Asher said, "Either Saturday or Sunday." "No. Saturday. Saturday afternoon." "Or Sunday." Marilyn died Saturday so Sunday's out.

It's difficult to believe after Marilyn's big fight with Bobby that she would want to go to Peter's house knowing that Bobby was there. She was angry with him. Thus, the "walk on the beach" sounds like a manufactured alibi to protect Bobby Kennedy: in hiding Marilyn's anger that afternoon, the rationale was Marilyn couldn't possibly be upset that day if she had gone to Peter's.

James Spada was interviewed by fan newspaper *Runnin' Wild: All About Marilyn* for the October 1993 issue, Number 12. He was the only other biographer to speak with Bill Asher regarding Marilyn Monroe. After reading Spoto's book, Spada reported to the newspaper, "I interviewed Bill Asher for two hours, and we discussed in detail the death of Marilyn Monroe. At no time did he mention anything about a party Saturday afternoon."

In short, Bill Asher didn't tell Spada about a Saturday afternoon walk on the beach while Asher *did* mention it to Spoto. Despite the testimonies of Newcomb, Ebbins, and the questionable Greenson and Asher, there is still not enough evidence to support the notion that Marilyn went for a walk near Peter's house that last Saturday. According to the housekeeper's book, Marilyn had said to her, "I don't think we'll take that drive after all, Mrs. Murray." [17]

How Did Marilyn Monroe Really Die?

In 1983, during his last interview, apparently out of deep guilt (he had always held himself responsible for her death) Peter Lawford conceded to knowledge of a conspiracy to murder Marilyn Monroe. Peter labeled himself a co-conspirator along with his brother-in-law Bobby Kennedy and Marilyn's psychiatrist Dr. Ralph Greenson. Apparently, the secret was kept all these years. The public had been deceived into believing the accidental suicide scenario, successfully played out by Arthur P. Jacobs, who represented Marilyn's publicity, and Margot Patricia "Pat" Newcomb, then employed by Mr. Jacobs.

Natalie Trundy, Jacobs' 21-year-old girlfriend at the time, told Anthony Summers that shortly after 10:30 P.M. Arthur "went to Marilyn's house, and I don't think I saw him for two days. He had to fudge the press." Marilyn's close friend and former publicist Rupert Allan told Brown and Barham, "It was carefully done and beautifully executed… It was decided to play up the 'accidental death' scenario but none of us believed it."

Marilyn's friend reporter George Carpozi, Jr. said in 1992, "Bobby then calls Peter Lawford and says to him, 'Okay, this time she's getting out of hand.' Peter Lawford knows this because Marilyn has been crying on his shoulder all along. Peter calls up Dr. Greenson – this was all organized beforehand – and he says, 'Look, doc, let's get the show on the road,' and right after that afternoon call, Greenson goes to Marilyn's." Peter told Heymann:

> The most surprising revelation of Marilyn's tapes was that in addition to her affairs with the Kennedys, she was also involved with Dr. Greenson, who appeared to be deeply in love with her. I myself knew nothing about any of this until after Marilyn's death, at which time I heard those portions of the tapes she'd made for Greenson in which she alluded to her affair with him. I also got hold of portions of the Mafia-Teamster tapes, and heard what seemed to be sounds of their lovemaking. Greenson's wife presumably knew nothing about the affair… Somehow Bobby learned of Marilyn's liaison with her therapist. He had spoken to Greenson and convinced him that his star patient intended to disclose her romantic dealings

not just with the Kennedys but also with her psychiatrist. This would certainly mark the end of the doctor's career; it would also very likely land him in prison. "Marilyn has got to be silenced," Bobby told Greenson – or words to that effect. Greenson had thus been set up by Bobby to "take care" of Marilyn.

Heymann wrote in his book, "The most surprising revelation of Marilyn's 'free-association' tapes…" In Heymann's hand-written notes, the word free-association is absent. Heymann simply added the word free-association and subsequently put it in quotes to clarify what Peter meant by Marilyn's "tapes." Into a recorder, as part of her psychotherapy, she would speak her random thoughts when she was alone in her home or on the go in her limousine.

Best friend and sometimes lover Frank Sinatra was more than a little suspicious after learning a crucial detail from the autopsy. Sinatra's valet George Jacobs stated, "The bottom line on August 5, 1962, was that Marilyn was dead, and Mr. S was devastated. When the cops said it was an overdose, he had no doubt about it, nor did I. We had both seen her pop pills galore, and mix them with booze, cursing the life that the rest of the world would have done anything to have. She was a walking pharmacy, an overdose waiting to happen. It was only later when the autopsy revealed no residue of pills in her system that we got curious. Mr. S began to suspect Lawford and his brothers-in-law of possible foul play."

Pat Newcomb countered to Spoto, "There's no way they could've done this. I resent it so much… I'd like to see Bobby exonerated from this. He would never do it… He wouldn't hurt her… He was in San Francisco." Former Police Chief Daryl F. Gates conceded in his autobiography, "The truth is, we knew Robert Kennedy was in town on August 4. We always knew when he was here. He was the Attorney General, so we were interested in him, the same way we were interested when other important figures came to Los Angeles." On Marilyn and Bobby, Gates continued, "Frankly, I never bought into the theory that she killed herself because he dumped her – if he did. My feelings were that she was emotional over many things; a relationship gone sour would be just one of many problems she had." I interviewed Michael Selsman, then a 24-year-old press agent working alongside Pat Newcomb in the Arthur P. Jacobs Company. I asked him what he knew about that last day:

> MARGOLIS: Did Arthur Jacobs tell you Bobby Kennedy was at Marilyn's home the day she died either in the afternoon or in the evening?

Marilyn Monroe: A Case for Murder

SELSMAN: Yes.

MARGOLIS: Was it afternoon or evening?

SELSMAN: It was the afternoon.

As for Peter's last interview, Dean Martin's ex-wife Jeanne told me, "If any of that were true, you would not know it. You would not know it at all and somebody would've said something years ago. The mystery of her death, people have let up on that one ages ago." When I told her that many now agree Bobby Kennedy was in Los Angeles on August 4 *before* Marilyn died and *after* she died, Mrs. Martin said, "I don't care where he was. He didn't kill Marilyn. Bobby Kennedy would not kill anybody. He would *kill* somebody? It's impossible. It's such yellow journalism." When I brought to her attention that biographer Heymann had actual interview tapes of Peter's own voice mentioning the conspiracy to murder Marilyn, Mrs. Martin told me, "I knew the Kennedys very well. I knew Peter very well. If anybody took pills, it was Peter." [18] Regarding the Mafia-Teamster tapes he heard, Peter reflected to Heymann:

> You could hear the voices of Marilyn and JFK in addition to Marilyn and RFK. In both cases you could make out the muted sounds of bedsprings and the cries of ecstasy. Marilyn, after all, was a master of her craft.

The scenario of Peter obtaining Mafia-Teamster tapes is not unlikely. In fact, as noted by Anthony Summers, Peter tried to obtain tapes in at least one other instance involving the Mafia in regards to gangster Mickey Cohen's female associate Candy Barr, born Juanita Dale Slusher. This information is supported by a D.A.'s investigation into Peter's activities in 1961.

When I interviewed Joe Naar, he said he was absolutely certain that Peter never said those words to C. David Heymann. Joe told me he was one of his best friends and a friend of the Kennedy family. He said he and Peter went over and over Marilyn's last night, and Joe is convinced Heymann never even interviewed him. Keith Badman reported that Milt Ebbins believed Peter Lawford "was already losing touch with reality and almost always 'out-of-it' on alcohol, cocaine and other mind-bending drugs, a totally unreliable eyewitness to almost everything that had transpired in his volatile past." [19]

Peter Lawford was a close friend of Marilyn Monroe for more than a decade. Never a man to make decisions on his own, as Milt Ebbins attested, I believe Peter was an unwilling participant in her murder. By all accounts, feeling extremely guilty for years after his friend's death, Peter told Heymann everything. He realized what the Kennedy brothers had done to both him and her. Peter died just one year later. Remarkably similar word patterns and a large vocabulary are also found in the 1965 private Kennedy family publication edited by Edward "Ted" Kennedy called *The Fruitful Bough*, where Peter wrote an odd yet overall respectful tribute to Joseph P. Kennedy, Sr. [20]

Bobby Kennedy Brought Along His Own Doctor to Sedate Marilyn

According to Joseph Kennedy biographer Ralph G. Martin, Robert Kennedy testified in a sworn deposition that he arrived at Marilyn's home in the afternoon. Marilyn's unidentified next-door neighbor to the east and the neighbor's friend Elizabeth Pollard were busy playing bridge with a few other ladies that day. Joan Greenson relayed more information about the person next door, "Marilyn found out that the neighbor who you could see from her property was a professor at the university." The professor is either the unidentified neighbor or her husband if she had one.

The card-playing ladies next-door who had seen him enter earlier now witnessed Bobby leave Marilyn's and then shortly thereafter, reenter this time with his doctor, who had apparently come along for the ride. The unidentified doctor subsequently injected Marilyn with an intramuscular pentobarbital (i.e. Nembutal) shot to calm her down, soon after Peter and Bobby had taken the knife away. This may account for either of the bruises later found on Marilyn's "left hip" or the "left side of [the] lower back" according to Noguchi's official autopsy report.

In 1978, former OCID (Organized Crime Intelligence Division) detective Mike Rothmiller actually saw the statement made by Bobby Kennedy on Marilyn Monroe and his secret trip to her home on the afternoon of August 4. Rothmiller read that file and others including not the original but a copy of Marilyn's diary, located in the OCID file rooms. Pertaining to the statement, Rothmiller told Brown and Barham that Bobby Kennedy "said he was involved with Monroe – but he wasn't, implying a friendly relationship. He also said he had met with her several times during the summer."

George Barris related to me an event that happened to him in 1986, "I remember the time Gloria Steinem and I were signing the book we did together in Brentwood in a big book store, and a woman came up to me. She was elderly. She wanted me to autograph a book. She said, 'Mr. Barris, I was a neighbor to Marilyn [unidentified]. I was playing bridge with my friends [including Elizabeth Pollard] and there were people coming and going. That afternoon was Saturday. I saw someone who I believed was Bobby Kennedy and another man go into Marilyn's home and they came out a short while later.' She could see people who came and went. She didn't know who the other man was but she assumed he was a doctor and he had a little black case. Doctors carry it." Barris concluded, "It probably was not Greenson because the psychiatrist came later to her house."

Author Robert Slatzer was the first to document the Saturday afternoon card party and the sighting of Bobby Kennedy when he interviewed Betty Pollard, the daughter of Elizabeth, who relayed her mother's story. Brown and Barham wrote, "The Attorney General and another well-dressed man came to the house sometime late in the afternoon. Women at a card party were able to see the man from an upstairs window. One of them, referring to Kennedy, said, 'Look, girls, there he is *again*.'"

That afternoon, the card-playing friends saw Kennedy bring his own doctor. They did not see Greenson. Importantly, Greenson was not qualified to give intramuscular injections. The ladies witnessed Bobby Kennedy leave Marilyn's then quickly return again with a doctor carrying a black bag. Above, the unidentified neighbor said she saw "Bobby Kennedy and another man go into Marilyn's home and they came out a short while later." In fact, since Greenson arrived nearly an hour later, it simply couldn't have been him. Logistically, what the ladies saw was Bobby retrieve his doctor from the car parked out front.

I went to Marilyn's house and noted that there were two homes adjacent to hers that had an upstairs window: 12304 Fifth Helena Drive and 12306 Sixth Helena Drive. Slatzer wrote that the card party was "in a house next to Marilyn's" where one could see "out of the window toward Marilyn's newly installed Mexican gates." Elizabeth Pollard's friend must have lived on 12304 Fifth Helena Drive, the upstairs window directly facing 12305 Fifth Helena. From that window, a person could easily see cars parked up the drive and anyone entering or leaving Marilyn's home. In fact, from the upstairs window, one could also see somewhat over the gates.

Bobby had instructed his own doctor to give Marilyn the Nembutal shot in order to stun her while Peter and Bobby entered her house and searched for her little red diary. Anthony Summers wrote in *Goddess* that a source heard tapes that recorded Bobby and Peter's afternoon visit to Marilyn's home on August 4:

> The source says both Marilyn's and Kennedy's voices were easily recognizable. Like Otash – and it is worth noting that

the source and Otash do not know each other – the source says there was a heated argument. "Their voices grew louder and louder," he recalls. "They were arguing about something that had been promised by Robert Kennedy. Marilyn was demanding an explanation as to why Kennedy was not going to marry her. As they argued, the voices got shriller… He was screeching, high-pitched like an old lady…" Kennedy's anger, the source claims, was because he had learned that some form of bugging was taking place. "He was asking again and again, 'Where is it? Where the fuck is it?' – apparently referring to a microphone or tape-recorder…" The episode ended, says the source, with the sound of a door slamming…

The tape resumed… with Kennedy's return, this time accompanied by Peter Lawford. The source says he would not have been familiar with Lawford's voice, but relied on Spindel's identification. "There were these three distinct voices," he says, "at first echoey again. RFK was saying words to the effect, 'We have to know. It's important to the family. We can make any arrangements you want, but we must find it,' – apparently he was still looking for the recording device. Then they apparently came close to where the transmitter was. There was a clack, clack, clack on the tape," the source recalls, "which [wiretapper] Bernie [Spindel] says he thought was hangers being pushed along a rail. They were still searching for whatever they were after. And there was a flopping sound – maybe books being turned over… Kennedy was again screeching, and Lawford was saying, 'Calm down, calm down…' Monroe was screaming at them, ordering them out of the house."

Slatzer believed Bobby Kennedy was looking for the red diary, not a listening transmitter. Why would Kennedy expect Marilyn Monroe to know where the bug is in her home? The diary is something that Bobby could make "arrangements" for, and it would be "important to the family." "Books being turned over" sounds like Kennedy was searching for something else besides a wire. In fact, Summers himself conceded that was a possibility in the documentary *Marilyn: The Last Word*, "Robert Kennedy is demanding for her to give him something. He keeps demanding, 'Where is it? Where is it, Marilyn? You've got to tell me where it is! We'll come to some arrangement but the family must have it.' Perhaps he was asking about the diary." [21]

Marilyn's handyman and Eunice Murray's son-in-law Norman Jefferies gave a chilling account of that last afternoon. Mrs. Murray and Jefferies agreed that Marilyn was not dressed when Bobby and Peter arrived. She was still in her white terry-cloth robe. Jefferies told Wolfe, "Mr. Lawford made it very clear that he wanted Eunice and I [sic] out of there, and he told us to go to the market. He gave me some money and said to buy some Cokes. When we came back – maybe it was an hour later – their car was gone, and when we went into the house Marilyn was hysterical and looked awful. Something terrible had happened – she was scared out of her mind… It's something I'll never forget. Marilyn was having this hysterical rage. It was like nothing I've ever seen. She was scared and at the same time she was terribly angry."

Now that Joe DiMaggio had recently asked her to remarry him, Marilyn wanted to bitterly remind Bobby Kennedy about his promise to marry her. Marilyn had already come to terms with the fact that Bobby was not going to divorce his wife. However, she wanted to stick it to him about his original promise to marry her because he still wanted sex, which infuriated her more than anything. Marilyn's feelings were being toyed with, and Bobby didn't care. The only thing he cared about was her red diary. Otherwise, he wouldn't have bothered to show up. One of Otash's employees said, "Marilyn had done a turnabout. Lawford said Marilyn had called the White House, trying to reach the President, saying, 'Get your brother away from me – he's just using me.'"

John Miner heard something similar on one of Marilyn's free-association tapes she had recorded for Greenson, "I want someone else to tell him it's over. I tried to get the President to do it, but I couldn't reach him." That afternoon, she felt very upset, used, and betrayed. Bobby had said to her, "It's over."

Marilyn shot back, "But you promised to divorce Ethel and marry me." Otash then claimed she said, "I feel passed around – like a piece of meat. You've lied to me. Get out of here. I'm tired. Leave me alone." Later when Bobby tried to get Marilyn over to Peter's house, she told him over the phone, "Stop bothering me. Stay away from me." I asked Michael Selsman from the Arthur P. Jacobs Company, "Was it to your understanding that one of the brothers had promised to marry her?" "She was convinced that not Jack but Bobby would leave Ethel and all their kids. And they were heavily Catholic. She was under the impression that Bobby would marry her."

Marilyn's hairstylist Sydney Guilaroff knew her since making *The Asphalt Jungle* in 1950. Marilyn phoned Guilaroff twice that last Saturday. The first call was right after Bobby left. Guilaroff told Wolfe, "She was in tears, and I had difficulty understanding her." In his own book, Guilaroff detailed their exchange as follows:

GUILAROFF: What's the matter, dear?

MARILYN: Robert Kennedy was here, threatening me, yelling at me.

GUILAROFF: Why was Bobby Kennedy at your house?

MARILYN: I'm having an affair with him.

GUILAROFF: Marilyn.

MARILYN: I never told you. I never told anyone. But I had an affair with JFK as well.

GUILAROFF: Both of them?

MARILYN: Both… I warned him [Bobby] that I could go public.

Marilyn relayed to Guilaroff that Bobby had then responded, "If you threaten me, Marilyn, there's more than one way to keep you quiet." Asking if Bobby was still there, Marilyn told Guilaroff, "He left – with Peter Lawford." Guilaroff recommended that Marilyn get some rest and they would discuss this further in a few hours. As Peter's friend producer George "Bullets" Durgom told Fred Otash in 1985, "Bobby was very worried about Monroe getting spaced out and shooting her mouth off."

According to Anthony Summers (who only knew of the second call), Marilyn's last call to Guilaroff was at 9:00 P.M. Guilaroff told Wolfe this final call was between "eight and eight-thirty" and that "she was feeling much better and had met with her psychiatrist, Dr. Greenson." Guilaroff relayed to Wolfe they ended the call with the following exchange:

MARILYN: You know, Sydney, I know a lot of secrets about the Kennedys.

GUILAROFF: What kind of secrets?

MARILYN: Dangerous ones.

After that, Marilyn hung up. [22]

C. David Heymann's Interview with Peter Lawford

In 2005, David Marshall and the DD Group (Death Discussion Group) tried to discredit Peter's interview with Heymann. The Group argued, "The curious thing is how Peter's story changed between the publication of the first book and the second." Heymann explained this discrepancy in his 1998 book on Robert Kennedy. He said he couldn't validate the fact that Marilyn had actually made free-association tapes for Greenson, therefore he printed Peter's interview in part only for his 1989 biography *A Woman Named Jackie.*

While Heymann was conducting research for his *RFK* book, he learned that John Miner said Greenson had Marilyn make such tapes. Subsequently, Heymann printed Peter's full interview regarding the last day of Marilyn Monroe's life. In 2005, Hildi Greenson told John Miner and the *Los Angeles Times* that her husband allowing Marilyn to make free-association tapes was a possibility and it seemed in character. [23]

On September 25, 1998, the *Boston Herald* released an article by Gayle Fee and Laura Raposa entitled, "RFK Bio Author Throws Book at Trio Who Disavow Him." Fee and Raposa wrote, "Patricia Stewart, the widow of ex-Kennedy in-law Peter Lawford, was credited along with her late hubby – with all the juicy dirt about RFK's alleged romance with sex siren Marilyn Monroe. But after the book's publication, Stewart claimed she never spilled the beans to Heymann and that the author never interviewed Lawford, who died in 1984."

Heymann countered, "I spent a good deal of time with Pat and have about 15 to 18 tapes of interviews with her." Fee and Raposa ask, "So, David, do you feel the hand of the Kennedys at work here?" Heymann replied, "The Kennedys don't like the book, I know that. But people are out there protecting them. Like when I wrote the Jackie book, bookstores in her neighborhood wouldn't put it on the shelves."

C. David Heymann indeed stirred controversy nine years earlier with the release of his now well-respected *A Woman Named Jackie*, yet Jackie Kennedy herself made an effort to prevent its publication. On April 17, 1989, a *Star* magazine article was released in Tarrytown, New York over the *PR Newswire*. For the article, Heymann said, "Like everyone else, I've always been fascinated by the woman... My most difficult hurdle was deciding whether to proceed with the book knowing that Jackie didn't want it written. Once I decided to go ahead, I left few stones unturned."

Nancy Tuckerman, Jackie Kennedy's spokeswoman, countered, "We've done what we could do to discourage this book. I told Mr. Heymann Mrs. Onassis doesn't want the book done, but there's nothing we can do to stop him." *Star* wrote, "Tuckerman said that Jackie stopped short of warning family friends not to speak to the author. When asked by *Star* if he was worried about any Kennedy backlash, Heymann insists he wasn't." Heymann said, "I taped every interview, so there could be no mistake."

As for Heymann's even more controversial 1998 *RFK* biography, Bob Sherrill reviewed the book then penned an October 11 article "Busy Nights in Camelot" for the *Washington Post*. Sherrill wrote, "Bobby became 'as sexually insatiable as Jack had been.' Movie stars by the dozen, 15-year-old nymphets, socialites, in-laws – the brothers were catholic in their passion. Lawns, closets, airplanes, sailboats, the White House, the family's suite at the Carlyle Hotel – any old place would do just fine… If we can believe actor and Kennedy brother-in-law Peter Lawford – and we have only his word for this – Robert set up Marilyn Monroe for murder by drugs because she was threatening to publicize her affairs with both brothers. This is a solid biography." Heymann has always insisted that when writing a biography about a public figure, the person's sexual life as well as his political life is necessary in understanding the complete person.

A January 3, 1999 *New York Times* article discussed Heymann's *RFK* biography and the plot to murder Marilyn Monroe. The article was called "Political Affairs: A biography of Robert F. Kennedy focuses on his love life" written by John Judis. On Heymann, Judis wrote, "If that weren't enough, he introduces a new conspiracy involving Marilyn Monroe, with whom he says Robert as well as John Kennedy had a love affair. Robert Kennedy, he writes, 'very likely had conspired in the murder of his former lover, the nation's premier cinema star.' Heymann relies on Peter Lawford's account of a conversation between Robert Kennedy and Monroe's psychiatrist, Dr. Ralph Greenson: ' "Marilyn has got to be silenced," Bobby told Greenson – or words to that effect.' Heymann doesn't say how Lawford was apprised of this private exchange, or remark on the telling qualification, 'or words to that effect.' "

Evan Thomas believed call of a conspiracy is shot down based on whether one can rely on primary witness Peter Lawford, who was heavily into drugs and alcohol during the last two years of his life. Thomas wrote in his Robert Kennedy biography, "A small publishing industry has grown up devoted to proving, or at least insinuating, that RFK not only slept with Marilyn Monroe, he then arranged to have her snuffed out – and covered up the sordid mess… At the request of her psychiatrist, Dr. Ralph Greenson, Monroe had spoken her stream-of-consciousness thoughts into a tape recorder as part of her therapy.

"In the course of the medical examiner's inquest into her death, Miner listened to those tapes. The former prosecutor remained silent about them for thirty-five years, until Dr. Greenson's family permitted him to speak up to exonerate the late psychiatrist from charges that he had a hand in murdering Monroe. The tapes strongly insinuate that both JFK and RFK had physical relationships with Monroe. Before he died, Peter Lawford told author David Heymann that he, too, had listened to the tapes and heard Monroe speak of a sexual relationship with both Kennedys.

"Lawford's testimony can be discounted. Plagued by problems with drugs and alcohol, he went through a hostile separation from Pat Lawford in 1963, rejected and scorned by the Kennedy family, particularly RFK. Miner's account is harder to dismiss. Still, it is entirely possible – even likely – that Monroe was engaging in fantasies when she recounted love affairs with both Kennedy brothers. Sick and drug-ridden, she may have been the least reliable witness of all... Myer Feldman, deputy counsel to President Kennedy and a Washington lawyer, told the author that the Kennedy family asked him to check out the rumors about RFK and Monroe."

Countering what Peter told Heymann, Feldman said to Thomas, "I talked to Lawford and Steve Smith. Bobby had no interest in Marilyn Monroe. Lawford was just getting even." Thomas wrote, "Other friends of Lawford, including the writer Dominick Dunne, give more credit to his [Lawford's] account." In fact, Dunne said Peter Lawford was treated terribly by the family, "The Kennedys were the root of Peter's problems... Further, Peter was ill-used by his famous and glamorous brothers-in-law. Get the girls, Peter. Get the blow, Peter. Tell Sinatra we can't come, Peter, we're staying at Bing Crosby's instead. Having to give that message to Sinatra was the kiss of death for Peter. Sinatra hated him from then on."

Many will doubt Peter's account. On July 13, 2010, C. David Heymann told me in a telephone call that he recorded the interview. Even though we were both aware Peter had been a habitual drug user, Heymann said he still couldn't catch him in a lie. On March 17, 2011, I saw the hand-written notes Heymann took while he was interviewing Peter Lawford and I can attest that in the notes, it read: "Greenson had thus been set up by Bobby to 'take care' of Marilyn."

The controlled substances didn't prevent Peter Lawford from being in his right mind when Heymann interviewed him. Peter remembered the same code name Jack Kennedy used with Jayne Mansfield's press secretary Raymond Strait whenever Jack wanted to get in touch with Jayne. Strait told me Jack Kennedy "calls my house and said, 'Tell her Mr. K called.' That's the name he used with me to reach her and he never ever identified himself. As a matter of fact, I never heard him talk to her. I heard her talk to him on the phone." Peter relayed to Heymann, "Jayne, whose marriage to Mickey Hargitay was floundering during this period, used to call Jack 'Mr. K.' Jack spoke of her sexual prowess."

Secondly, Peter Lawford and biographer Evan Thomas relayed remarkably similar accounts when describing the old man. As for Jack Kennedy's run for president, Peter told Heymann, "Joe Kennedy ran the campaign from an outdoor enclosure next to the swimming pool. He called it 'the bullpen.' There was no roof on the structure. Inside were a telephone and a deck chair. Joe spent his mornings on the telephone barking orders at frightened minions and employees. What seemed odd about the arrangement was that he made his calls in the nude, which was the reason for the enclosure. And this is the same man who castigated me for not wearing anything on my feet while playing golf in Palm Beach with Jack." Evan Thomas' text validates Peter's recollection in this instance in that Joseph Kennedy "never discussed his business activities with his children. They could see him sitting in his 'bullpen,' an enclosure that allowed him to conduct business while he sunbathed in Palm Beach or Hyannis." Normally, people who are too badly affected by drugs and alcohol cannot remember such accurate details but there's always an exception like Peter.

A third strong example to prove Peter had a rather sharp mind is to analyze his writing and speaking style. Similar patterns in style do emerge when one juxtaposes Peter Lawford's written tribute to Joseph Kennedy with the more candid way Peter describes him to Heymann. In the *Fruitful Bough*, Peter wrote, "One of the best pieces of advice he ever gave me, and there were many, was 'Always deal from strength…' I could go on at length with many instances of his judgment, understanding, and wisdom, but they would only sound redundant. All of us through the years have heard the pros and cons concerning Joseph P. Kennedy – good, bad, ambitious, kind, ruthless, understanding, tough. To evaluate such adjectives in depth would more than fill a book. He is sometimes grizzly, sometimes gruff, yet always a most kind and gentle bear."

Peter told Heymann, "Joe Kennedy was the world's greatest hypocrite. His philosophy was quite simple: 'Do as I say, not as I do.' But his great gift, his genius, if you will, was that he could simplify a problem rather than make it more complex, as most of us do. He would see one road instead of many and he would follow the road. Most of us, including myself, are victims of our imagination. Not Joe. He had a concept of destiny." By comparing the two quotes, I found them remarkably similar in language and style and at no time did it ever cross my mind that controlled substances impaired Peter Lawford's memory. His recollection of facts to Heymann is remarkable and accurate to the best of Peter's knowledge.

Peter's last wife Patricia Seaton Lawford (now married to former LAPD detective Daniel K. Stewart) accused Heymann of never interviewing Peter. All of my cross-referenced sources show that Mrs. Stewart is uninformed.

Most importantly, during the time he was interviewed by Heymann in 1983, Mrs. Stewart was not in a relationship with Peter and she wasn't living with him; therefore, she was unaware of any interview requests that came Peter's way, including the one from C. David Heymann.

However, sometime after Heymann's interview, Peter and Pat would get back together in mid-1984 and marry in July of that year. Months later, on Christmas Eve, he would pass away. Peter's interview with Heymann is discussed at great length throughout this text. I attempt to prove the British actor was being truthful. Strong and reliable sources can easily back him up in each instance. Many people will now be asking Mr. Heymann if they can listen to his tape-recorded interview with Peter Lawford. [24]

Falling in Love with the President

Marilyn Monroe drew powerful men into her orbit; however, she could never permanently hold onto any of them. But now she wanted one of the most famous men in the world to divorce his wife and marry her. Jack Kennedy was a Catholic and married Jacqueline Lee Bouvier for political reasons, which in his mind justified his rampant womanizing. Marilyn took marriage seriously or at least she tried to assure herself she did. Often in a barbiturate haze from her routine daily intake of drugs, many of her thought-processes were compromised. As a result, monitoring of her business expenditures waned.

Marilyn had just $2,605 to her name when she died. Her inability to save money was mainly due to impulsive shopping sprees and the seemingly never-ending bills to pay for the plethora of advisers employed by her from doctors to makeup artists to hairdressers and many more of the like. In not systematically organizing her finances, it was as if she was always walking away from responsibility, from reality.

But she never did care about money. Instead, Marilyn often escaped into her fantasy world and in her fantasy world nothing else mattered except she wanted to be wonderful. Greenson had once described her as a "Cinderella girl who did not live happily ever after." Although she and Jack Kennedy knew each other as early as 1951, Marilyn became even more infatuated with him when he was elected president. Peter told Heymann:

> She was crazy about Jack. She devised all sorts of madcap fantasies with herself in the starring role. She would have his children. She would take Jackie's place as First Lady. The fact

that he was President allowed her to attach a lot of symbolic meaning to the affair. It was only a lark for him, but she really fell for the guy, for what he represented. In her depressive and doped-out state, she began to fall in love with him – or she convinced herself she was in love, which is basically the same thing. Besides telephoning Jack at the White House, she used to send him copies of her love poetry, most of it written early in her career.

Richard E. Burke was a former aide to Senator Edward Kennedy. While working with Kennedy in-law Stephen Smith, Burke remembered flipping through typed transcripts of edited and unedited erotic phone conversations between Jack Kennedy and his mistresses including Judy Campbell, Marilyn Monroe, and others. His recollection of these phone calls coincides with Peter's.

Burke wrote in his book, "In fact, I was gaining my own view of the late President, which was not the portrait the family painted. One of my duties was to pack up old files, the Senator's legacy of material from the Camelot days, and ship them to Steve Smith, who was then supposed to forward them to the library. To do this, I had to sift through the contents of the locked file cabinet in the inner office, adjacent to my desk...

"They were all personal conversations. Several of the passages were calls from Marilyn Monroe. One was a long, romantic conversation with the woman then named Judith Campbell. I glanced at only a few of these. Some of the conversations were fairly erotic and steamy. It would have taken hours to read them all, but none of them seemed to involve presidential business." [25]

Frank Sinatra Gets the Kennedy Boot

Ever since they first met through Peter Lawford in 1955, Jack Kennedy greatly admired Frank Sinatra for his ability to attract the prettiest girls in Hollywood. Sinatra's valet George Jacobs explained that Jack loved the women Frank used to procure for him. However, Sinatra's run with the law made it difficult to remain his good friend. A Kennedy aide said, "We were discussing Frank one day and all that he was doing for the campaign, and Jack said to a group of us, 'Look, make no mistake about it. Sinatra's a thug. Let's face it. Let's be aware of it and then let's try to use him to our advantage.' "

Joseph Kennedy orchestrated that advantage and personally told Sinatra he wanted Giancana's help to get Jack elected president. Tina Sinatra relayed what Frank then told Sam Giancana, "I believe in this man and I think he's going to make us a good president. With your help, I think we can work this out." Later, Jack Kennedy said to one of his aides, "Every night, before I go to bed, I pray to God that I don't wake up and read in the newspaper that Frank Sinatra has been arrested again, at least not until after I'm elected." Sinatra was always walking on a tight rope with Jack Kennedy. Apparently Marilyn Monroe finally snapped the rope. Peter next explained to Heymann why Frank Sinatra was banished from the Kennedy circle:

> Then one day she told me she had telephoned Jackie at the White House. For all her romanticism and masochism, Marilyn could also be a mean little bitch. Everybody wrote her up as being the poor, helpless victim, but that wasn't always the case. According to Marilyn, Jackie wasn't shaken by the call. Not outwardly. She agreed to step aside. She would divorce Jack and Marilyn could marry him, but she would have to move into the White House. If Marilyn wasn't prepared to live openly in the White House, she might as well forget about it.
>
> Actually, Jackie was infuriated by the call, and for some reason blamed Frank Sinatra for it. She couldn't easily blame me because I was family, so she took it out on him. She and Sinatra had always been on decent terms. He visited the White House, Hyannis Port, Palm Beach... But this was the end of it for Jackie... The break with Jackie occurred at the same time that Sinatra began to have problems with Bobby Kennedy.
>
> Bobby, who at 35 thought of himself as another Wyatt Earp, had been cracking down on many of Sinatra's buddies. He had launched all-out investigations of Sam Giancana, John Rosselli, Mickey Cohen, Carlos Marcello, Santo Trafficante and, of course, Jimmy Hoffa. Some of these guys looked to Sinatra for help, and Sinatra turned to Bobby. I went with him. In so many words the Attorney General told us to stuff it, and he told his brother, the President, to steer clear of Sinatra. "We're going after the bosses of organized crime in this country, and you're socializing with the guy who's pals with half of them," he said to Jack.

Bobby Kennedy and Frank Sinatra were often at odds since Bobby fought against the same members of the Mafia with whom Sinatra had become associated. The account of George Jacobs matches with Peter's. Jacobs related that Sinatra became angry when it was apparent that Bobby had it in for all of his friends whether Bobby had acquired the support of Senator Joseph McCarthy or Reverend John McClellan.

The sorest point between Kennedy and Sinatra was Bobby's persistence to put away Sam Giancana. Bobby felt it would contradict his public stance if he supported the world famous singer since Sinatra's best friend was a Chicago Mafia boss. After reading C. David Heymann's *Bobby and Jackie: A Love Story*, it's easy to see how Jackie loved Bobby as one of her closest friends and since Bobby clearly hated Sinatra, it's no stretch that Bobby's hatred of Sinatra rubbed off on Jackie but when Joe Kennedy had his stroke on December 19, 1961, all bets were off.

Peter Lawford and George Jacobs both agreed that Bobby and Jackie Kennedy severed their ties with Frank Sinatra at the same time. Jacobs remembered, "Bobby was out to get Mr. S in a big way. He saw Frank as Al Capone, all sex and crime, and he saw himself as Cotton Mather, all fire and brimstone. His liberal, Puritan, Yankee zeal was made more poisonous by his own weakness for an attraction to the carnal pleasures of Hollywood that Mr. S embodied."

In fact, Bobby Kennedy had discreet affairs with high-profile movie actresses including Lee Remick and Kim Novak *before* sleeping with Marilyn Monroe, which will be discussed later. [26] To Heymann, Peter then described in accurate detail how the President and the Attorney General forever broke Frank Sinatra's trust just three months later:

> Jack had planned on spending March 24th to the 26th, 1962, at Sinatra's Palm Springs home. Jackie would be away on her trip to India and Pakistan. It was an ideal time for Jack to relax. In anticipation of the President's visit, Sinatra had added several rooms to his house, two or three cottages for the Secret Service, a heliport to accommodate the President's chopper, even a flagpole. At the last minute, Bobby called me and said I should advise Sinatra that the President couldn't accept his hospitality. I asked him to reconsider, told him how much the visit meant to Sinatra. "Sinatra's connections to organized crime could possibly embarrass the President," Bobby responded.
>
> I telephoned the President. He was sympathetic but adamant. "I can't stay there as long as Bobby's conducting the Giancana

operation. Maybe you can find me another place to stay." So I finally rang up Sinatra and laid it out. I blamed it on security, said that the Secret Service felt his place would be difficult to secure. Sinatra knew bullshit when he heard it. He telephoned Bobby Kennedy and called him every name in the book. He told him what a hypocrite he was, that the Mafia could help Jack get elected but couldn't sit with him in the front of the bus.

Jack, meanwhile, had made arrangements to spend the weekend at Bing Crosby's Palm Springs home. This blew Sinatra's mind. The other singer wasn't even a goddamn Democrat. Sinatra unfairly blamed the whole thing on me. It ended our friendship. I heard later that he grabbed a sledgehammer and tore apart the concrete heliport he'd built for Kennedy.

Milt Ebbins retorted, "Bobby Kennedy not letting Jack stay at Sinatra's house because Sam Giancana was a guest two weeks before doesn't make sense!" George Jacobs again concurred in all the major details with Peter's account. Jacobs said Sinatra made up his Palm Springs home to accommodate the President's visit. He recalled, "Mr. S's total humiliation occurred in early spring 1962... Lawford first tried to blame the Secret Service, saying it was a security issue, then he finally admitted that it was a *Frank* issue and that Bobby was the mastermind behind it... As punishment, Peter was immediately excommunicated by being cut out of the two upcoming Rat Pack movies *Four for Texas* and *Robin and the Seven Hoods*. Lawford, and his career, never recovered." In addition to Heymann, Peter also told Kitty Kelley he blamed it on security.

Above, Peter said, "Jack had planned on spending March 24th to the 26th, 1962, at Sinatra's Palm Springs home. Jackie would be away on her trip to India and Pakistan." Jack then changed the venue to Bing Crosby's because of Sinatra's mob connections. The British actor had a great memory for two reasons: (a) Without mentioning Marilyn at all, Peter accurately recollected how March 24 to 26 were the dates Jack *did* stay at Bing Crosby's and (b) Jackie *was* on a trip during this time to India and Pakistan, respectively. As a matter of fact, she arrived in India first then traveled to Pakistan a little more than a week later. The drugs and alcohol, which later consumed Peter apparently didn't have a drastic effect on his memory.

Marilyn Monroe saw Jack Kennedy in late March 1962 and had a weekend tryst. Florida Senator George Smathers relayed, "JFK told me that they were talking about one thing or another and he happened to say something to her like, 'You're not really First Lady material, anyway, Marilyn.' He said it really stuck in her craw. She didn't like hearing that." Nevertheless, per Badman on March 25, "Marilyn handed the President a gift, a Ronson Adonis chrome cigarette lighter." She "had the initials J.F.K. engraved on it." [27] Although Jack Kennedy treated her in a rather callous manner, Marilyn kept coming back for more.

As for Jackie Kennedy's trips to India and Pakistan, she met with Indira Gandhi in New Delhi, India on March 14, 1962. On March 15, "Jacqueline Kennedy visits... [the] Taj Mahal... [She] exchanges gifts with Indira Gandhi." On March 22, Jackie Kennedy was still in India. The narrator of a documentary who filmed the event on that same date said, "Before leaving the country for Pakistan, Mrs. Kennedy has to ride on an eight-foot elephant. The First Lady is accompanied by her sister Princess Radziwill on the 10 minute ride." After arriving in Pakistan on that same day, Jackie was welcomed by President Mohammad Ayub Khan.

She joined President Ayub Khan on a walk through "the Shalimar Gardens, Lahore, Pakistan... Mrs. Kennedy [wore] the traditional Pakistani hat (called a Jinnah cap) of astrakhan fur that was given to her personally by President Ayub Khan." On March 23, "Ayub Khan, in a gesture of goodwill, gives first lady Jacqueline Kennedy a horse named Sardar. Kennedy [is joined by] Lee Radziwill on a camel ride [in] Karachi [on] March 25." She was still in Pakistan on "March 26... Jacqueline Kennedy [went] on her visit to the Khyber pass. She wears a light suit and sun glasses [and] also a caracul hat. She meets the chieftains of the frontier tribes at the 125-year-old Jumrod Fort. Secret Service agent Clint Hill follows her closely."

Before leaving Pakistan, Jackie Kennedy said of the visit addressing the people, "I must say I am profoundly impressed by the reverence, which you in Pakistan have for your art and for your culture and for the use, which you make of it now. My own countrymen, too, have a pride in their traditions. So, I think, as I stand in these gardens, which were built long before my country was born, that that's one more thing that binds us together and which always will... I had always heard of Pakistan's proverbial hospitality. And it was even more than I had expected. I hope that with my husband, I will be able to return again soon to this vital and beautiful country." Then Jackie Kennedy was "welcomed home to the White House, March 29." [28] While Marilyn Monroe was visiting the President of the United States, Jackie Kennedy was visiting the President of Pakistan. Clearly, if Peter can remember detailed facts and dates that can be cross-referenced with strong sources, he is indeed a reliable witness despite the drugs and alcohol.

Biographers in the past who have relied on Peter's interview, specifically sourced from Heymann's *A Woman Named Jackie*, not the subsequent *RFK* biography, where Peter revealed the conspiracy to murder Marilyn Monroe, include but are not limited to: *Goddess* author Anthony Summers for his J. Edgar Hoover and Frank Sinatra biographies, Brown and Barham for their Marilyn Monroe biography, James Spada for his Peter Lawford biography, Jerry Oppenheimer for his Ethel Kennedy biography, J. Randy Taraborrelli for his Frank Sinatra biography, Curt Gentry for his J. Edgar Hoover biography, and Keith Badman for his Marilyn Monroe biography.

Keith Badman claimed the incident at Bing Crosby's had little or no effect on Jack Kennedy's friendship with Frank Sinatra. Badman wrote that on June 4, 1962, "JFK penned a letter to the singer thanking him for the 'floral rocking chair that you had thoughtfully sent me for my birthday.' " Badman said on August 28, 1962, Sinatra had generously made available to Jack Kennedy a special print of his new film *The Manchurian Candidate*.

But according to George Jacobs, Sinatra's trust of the Kennedys had by now evaporated even if Jack Kennedy thought he was on friendly terms with Sinatra. As for *Manchurian*, Sinatra told Jacobs, "I hope it pisses the shit out of them." Jacobs relayed, "Mr. S took pleasure in sticking it to them, the whole hypocrisy bit, the idea of this rich political dynasty controlling their hero son, using him as a charming puppet." Appearances can be deceiving, Mr. Badman.

Bobby, on the other hand, didn't share Jack's amiability with the singer movie star. Above, Peter said Sinatra "telephoned Bobby Kennedy and called him every name in the book. He told him what a hypocrite he was, that the Mafia could help Jack get elected but couldn't sit with him in the front of the bus." In fact, George Jacobs later said on Sinatra's relationship with Bobby, "After all, one of the few times I ever saw the guy cry was earlier that year when Martin Luther King Jr. was killed. He did *not* shed a tear for Bobby Kennedy, but that's another story." [29] Indeed it was.

FBI Notes Killer All But Named in Photoplay Magazine (August 1963)

Martha Donaldson wrote an intriguing article in the August 1963 edition of *Photoplay*, which promptly made its way into Marilyn Monroe's FBI Files. It's called, "One Year Later: Marilyn Monroe's Killer Still at Large!" The article implicitly pointed the finger at Bobby Kennedy as the killer of Marilyn Monroe. It read in part:

You can see him in a crowd. You can reach out and touch him; because he is a great man... You can see him on television – or even in a movie theater – and you will look up to him and think how lucky his wife is to be married to him and how lucky his children are to have him for a father... You can read about him almost any day in the newspapers and magazines, and you will think, "This is a good person. This is a truly honorable man..." But what you will never read, never see, never know is that this man is a killer. He is the man who killed Marilyn Monroe... When their romance began, nobody – especially Marilyn and the man – could have guessed at the ending. For it began with a kind of love... It was the worst time of her life and the best time of his... He had no intention of ever divorcing his wife. She knew that, too... His career had reached a height he never before dreamed it would, and there were obviously better, much better things in store for him. And what better celebration than to have the world's most desirable sex symbol in love with him?... He is the man they can never arrest. He is the man who is still at-large... Wherever he goes, whatever he touches, whomever he sees; he thinks of Marilyn. His guilt never leaves him, his fear has become his friend. For once, long ago, before all this, he was an honorable man. But he had made a fatal mistake. And now he is lost – not to all the world – but to himself. Some people know who he is. Will they ever reveal it publicly? Does his wife know? Would she tell? And he himself, will his guilt pry his tongue loose? You can see him in a crowd. You can reach out and touch him... And you will never know that he is the man who killed Marilyn Monroe. [30]

Presumably FBI Director J. Edgar Hoover brought the article to Bobby Kennedy's attention had he not already seen it. Known to become enraged at any negative press against his family, Kennedy's reaction to the article must have been priceless.

Marilyn Monroe's Last Morning Alive

Marilyn's morning had a pleasant enough beginning: an hour-long massage. During this time her ex-father-in-law and most caring father figure Isadore Miller (she affectionately called him "Dad") placed a call to Marilyn "at noon, New York time (9 A.M. Los Angeles time)." According to Flora Rheta Schreiber's January 1963 interview with Miller, "The housekeeper said that Marilyn was dressing and would call him back."

Miller said to Schreiber it was out of character for Marilyn not to return his phone calls when she was made aware of them. Miller insisted, "She never got that message. If she had, she would have talked to me. She always interrupted even a business conference to talk to me. So I waited. But Marilyn did not call." Miller wistfully reflected, "She helped a great many people and their names will never be known. She was charitable because there was charity in her heart, not because she wanted thanks."

Ralph Roberts relayed to *New York Herald Tribune* reporter Joe Hyams for a September 25, 1962 article, "I gave her a massage that last day in the morning from 9 to 10:15. She was in wonderful shape and not tense... She loved to have a massage to relax her, and then sometimes she'd fall asleep on my table." Afterwards, Marilyn and Ralph left her bedroom. The table folded under his arm, he then let himself out the front door without saying goodbye, which was standard-operating procedure, as he later told Spoto. Marilyn next went into the kitchen, greeting Mrs. Murray good morning before heading to the refrigerator to pour herself a glass of grapefruit juice. She would consume no food or alcohol for the rest of the day.

Larry Schiller, one of the *Something's Got to Give* photographers who took the world famous shots of Marilyn's nude swimming scene, said he arrived at her home in the early morning "around 9:30 or 10" as reported in *Marilyn: The Last Months*. During this time, however, Marilyn was busy inside getting her back rubbed by Ralph Roberts.

In December 2005, Schiller told Lisa DePaulo, "I stopped by her house on my way to Palm Springs to show her some photos from the shoot and to go over negotiations we were having for a front and back cover for *Playboy*. She was tending her flowers, and nothing was unusual about that day. She seemed completely fine." Then he left.

Schiller would exclusively tell Fred Lawrence Guiles that Marilyn had showed him the guest cottage she fixed up for friends. As for her white French poodle Maf, Marilyn allegedly told him, "Don't mind the doggy smell." This account changed a little more than five years later. Mrs. Murray's co-writer

Rose Shade wrote Schiller's story as if it were true and never confirmed through other sources whether he was actually there that morning.

In fact, Mrs. Murray never claimed to have seen Schiller but since Mrs. Murray was inside Marilyn's home before noon, she didn't deny his account either. The housekeeper told Slatzer, "No. I never met him. Of course, he could have come while I was away." Relying solely on Schiller's recollection, Shade wrote in Mrs. Murray's book, "He came inside the yard and talked with her in the parking area. Marilyn was very gracious, but didn't invite him in the house." The story of Marilyn showing Schiller the guest cottage was not one mentioned to either Mrs. Murray or Lisa DePaulo of *Playboy* magazine. It was a story told once in 1969 and never repeated again.

Guiles explained why Schiller said he was there that day, "In exchange for permitting Schiller to shoot freely, he had agreed that Marilyn would have approval of the pictures… Sometime before noon, Schiller came by to see if Marilyn had signed the *Playboy* magazine contract. Marilyn shouldered up from her wave of melancholy to greet him and to report that she had not.

"Late on Sunday afternoon, Schiller and Woodfield found an unmarked, unstamped envelope shoved under the studio door. They knew by then, of course, that Marilyn had been found dead, and they wondered who had brought them. Had Marilyn driven over with them on Saturday afternoon? Had Pat Newcomb found them so clearly marked for their attention when she visited Marilyn's home briefly on that morning of her death? The photographers were never to know… Either to compensate *Playboy*'s loss for the front and back covers or because she had reconsidered her decision, she wrote across the back of the prints, 'These should go to *Playboy*.'"

Neither possibility seems plausible or even possible. Pat and Marilyn were occupied during this time. Pat Newcomb hated Larry Schiller and would never have done business with the man. Under the influence of drugs that last afternoon, Marilyn was in no condition to drive nor did Mrs. Murray mention that she drove anywhere on her employer's behalf.

Apparently, Larry Schiller stretched out this story even further. After claiming to have Marilyn's "permission" with her alleged written words: "These should go to *Playboy*," Schiller also tried to interject himself into a Sunday meeting at the Arthur Jacobs Office. The meeting was to discuss how best to handle the reporters after Marilyn's death with their seemingly never-ending questions. Press agent Michael Selsman worked at the Jacobs firm:

> MARGOLIS: Besides yourself, who was present at that Sunday meeting the day after her death?

SELSMAN: Arthur and I and that was pretty much it because Pat was incommunicado at that time.

MARGOLIS: Was Rupert Allan present?

SELSMAN: Rupert wasn't even part of the Jacobs Office then. He was much, much later when Arthur merged with John Springer's Office in New York, and Rupert worked for John then. The Jacobs Office was Arthur, Pat, and I. We had a guy who handled TV named Bill Barron, who was not part of our discussions, and Elvira, Arthur's secretary.

MARGOLIS: When did the meeting start?

SELSMAN: It may have been at the office around ten o'clock in the morning.

MARGOLIS: Did Lawrence Schiller drop by at the Sunday meeting?

SELSMAN: No. I didn't like Larry and neither did Arthur. We wouldn't have anything to do with him.

MARGOLIS: He claimed to come by to get release forms so he could get "permission" to use those nude photographs for *Playboy* magazine. Mr. Schiller told this story where Marilyn, Pat Newcomb, or even some mysterious person supposedly put an unmarked envelope under his studio door the day of her death with the "approved pictures."

SELSMAN: I don't believe that ever happened. He's just a total liar. Always has been… Release forms were never a part of what we did for clients. We had neither the permission nor the responsibility to do that. That was handled by the actor, her manager, if she had one, or her lawyer. Not even an agent could do that. As for the mysterious envelope or person that allegedly put that under his door, I would not believe it under torture.

There are two additional holes in Schiller's account regarding the Sunday meeting. First, Schiller told Anthony Summers this meeting was in the *evening*, not the morning. Regarding the Kennedy brothers, Schiller then said to Summers he could hear Pat Newcomb and Arthur Jacobs worrying about "what would be revealed by the telephone records." Before I mentioned Schiller's name, Selsman told me Pat Newcomb was *not* at the Sunday meeting, so the fact that Schiller placed her there is absolutely false. Given these astounding contradictions, Schiller's account is highly questionable. In 1974, more than a decade after her death, Schiller struck an agreement with Hugh Hefner to place an "approved photo" from Marilyn's nude swim on the front cover of *The Pocket Playboy*, Number 4.

According to Mrs. Murray's book, before Pat Newcomb awoke at noon, "Sometime during the earlier part of the day, the bedside table was delivered and Marilyn wrote a check for it. The citrus trees were also delivered that day and were placed in the rear yard." Mrs. Murray relayed to Slatzer, "On the day before [Friday], Marilyn and I went to a small furniture store on Santa Monica Boulevard, and she bought a bed table. That was delivered on Saturday morning." [31] This was the bedside table for the guest cottage. Marilyn already had one for the main bedroom.

The Concentration of Drugs in Marilyn's Blood and Liver

Ralph Roberts told Spoto he learned from Marilyn's secretary May Reis that Marilyn on average took about 6 Nembutals in a day. However, when Dr. Thomas Noguchi performed the autopsy on Marilyn Monroe, he noted two drugs in her body: Nembutal (i.e. pentobarbital) and chloral hydrate. Per the District Attorney's Report, "The results of the blood and liver toxicological examination show that there were 8 mg. percent chloral hydrate [seventeen 500-mg pills] and 4.5 mg. percent of barbiturates in the blood [forty – fifty 100-mg Nembutals] and 13.0 mg. percent pentobarbital in the liver." Suicide Team member Dr. Robert Litman explained, "High content in the liver just means she died slowly, the chance to be absorbed."

According to her regular intake, Dr. Amador presented the possibility that throughout her last day Marilyn took 6 Nembutals or less orally. He estimated that later she received a drug enema containing 17 chloral hydrates and between 15 – 20 Nembutals. Amador relayed, "She could have gotten that by enema very easily."

However, let's account for logistics. From July 25 until August 3, Marilyn took 3 Nembutals or less a day until she ran out of the 25 pills from Engelberg's original prescription. When Marilyn received a refill for 25 additional pills on August 3, if she had orally ingested between 3 – 6 Nembutals on both August 3 and 4, that would leave Marilyn with 13 – 19 Nembutals remaining, the amount most likely used for the enema, in addition to the 17 chloral hydrates.

Using the new figures to account for logistics, the intramuscular injection given to her earlier in the afternoon contained approximately 15 – 24 Nembutals. Dr. Amador told me the injection didn't reach that equivalent right away "because it takes time to distribute. Hours." As we will see later, when Marilyn made her final walk to the guest cottage to investigate a noise, she must have had what equated to less than 15 Nembutals in her body since she was still mobile.

The afternoon injection and the evening enema together contained the equivalent of 28 – 43 Nembutal sleeping pills. Including the 17 chloral hydrates, the pill total would roughly equate to 45 – 60 pills. Adding in oral intake of 3 – 6 Nembutals on August 4, the new grand total is equivalent to 48 – 66. She was estimated to have taken approximately 64 pills.

Marilyn's friend reporter George Carpozi, Jr. relayed that in the afternoon, "The doctor administered what amounted to the fatal overdose of drugs to Marilyn's body, and the intent was actually not to kill Marilyn with that dosage but to merely let it comprise an overdose when she took her nightly going-to-bed drugs... Dr. Sidney Weinberg said she couldn't have died by her own hand because there was no crystal residue in her stomach or in her intestines, which meant that she hadn't even taken her drugs that night."

This means the combination of the Kennedy doctor's afternoon injection along with a little oral intake and later a drug enema, would in a matter of hours travel from the blood to the liver to detoxify the substance. Over this period of time, the liver was allowed to reach that very high Nembutal concentration. It could only reach higher levels while she was still alive. John Miner explained the 13 mg. percent of Nembutal in the liver is a "high concentration" and said, "It indicates that however the drugs were administered, hours and not minutes were involved before she died." In contrast to the 13 mg. percent of Nembutal, the chloral hydrate in the liver was not tested since it would reveal a much smaller amount, incongruent with a suicide.

Spoto contended that had Marilyn taken 40 – 50 Nembutals during the day, the Nembutals would no longer be in her stomach but in her liver for the process of excretion. We have already seen that oral ingestion of this many pills was impossible in Marilyn's case, according to medical professionals Drs. Sidney B. Weinberg, John W. Miner, J. DeWitt Fox, Elias W. Amador, and even Noguchi himself as he finally conceded in his 1983 book. She would have passed out before the pills finished absorbing and there would have been undissolved capsules in her stomach. This is especially true since Marilyn made her last call to the answering service of Ralph Roberts at 10:00 P.M. and died before midnight.

John Miner ruled out death by needle injection. He said, "The amount of drugs found in Marilyn's body was so large that had it been administered by injection, the star would have died almost immediately." Note that a fatal needle injection would not leave Marilyn any time to make one last phone call. The woman on the other end of the line remembered that Marilyn's voice sounded slurred. This suggested a slow death: it will be necessary to keep this information in mind for later to have a complete understanding of how Marilyn Monroe died.

Noguchi wrote in his autopsy report: "The stomach is almost completely empty. The contents is [sic] brownish mucoid fluid… no more than 20 cc." Miner, who was present during the autopsy, related, "There was a small quantity of liquid in the stomach but we did not detect any sign that would indicate it contained any heavy drugs or sedatives… The duodenum was felt all the way down to the ileum, which is at the end of the small intestine and the beginning of the large intestine but there was nothing obstructive."

The pentobarbital injection given by Kennedy's doctor may have been sufficient in itself to account for Marilyn's "somewhat drugged" condition that afternoon as noted by Greenson in his letter to Dr. Kris. According to Anthony Summers' research, Noguchi believed the bruises found on Marilyn's body at the autopsy on her "left hip" and the "left side of [the] lower back" have not been accounted for and are a "sign of violence."

Dr. J. DeWitt Fox said, "She had a bruise on her hip which was possibly from an injection given either the day before by her physician [Dr. Engelberg] or from the intramuscular injection of pentobarbital [on the afternoon of August 4]. So, if she had been given the injection, in the haste of performing the autopsy, it might be easily overlooked."

Drs. John Miner and Robert Litman both agree that the 13 mg. percent of pentobarbital in the liver simply explains that she died slowly. The fact that Marilyn had what equates to 48 – 66 pills in her body at the time of her death is astounding. A lesser amount of drugs surprisingly didn't kill her sooner. At her worst, Marilyn was known to take 20 Nembutals in an entire day as reported by John Huston while directing Marilyn in *The Misfits* (1960). [32]

One Last Fling with Bobby Kennedy?

On September 10, 1973, Maurice Zolotow documented an interesting observation made by Noguchi himself regarding rumored sexual relations involving Marilyn Monroe and Bobby Kennedy that final day. Noguchi told Zolotow, "The examination I made included contents of vaginal passages which were made on a smear and studied under a microscope. There was no indication of sexual intercourse." Noguchi told the same story to *Time* magazine months earlier on July 16, 1973.

I asked Mansfield's press secretary Raymond Strait about these rumors. Strait heard eleven hours of Fred Otash's tapes running the last day of Marilyn's life. He told me, "I know they had a long conversation that afternoon. Mostly it was just fighting back and forth. I don't know anything about any sex. I have no evidence of any kind to substantiate such a statement." [33] Logistically, the sex act never happened on August 4.

Marilyn Monroe Threatens a Press Conference

In her last months, Marilyn Monroe felt powerless against the Kennedys. The brothers had used her for sex and now they were through with the woman but she wasn't through with them. Marilyn idolized the Kennedys, she became close to their sister Pat, and in her mind the last thing she expected was for Bobby and Jack to betray her. Furious, she vowed to wipe the smiles off their faces. She was no joke to be laughed at and forgotten. Unlike the other actresses the Kennedys had treated in kind, Marilyn wasn't willing to just go away. In his interview with Heymann, Peter mentioned Bobby's steadfast efforts to keep Marilyn from going public:

> I certainly think Marilyn would have held a press conference. She was determined to gain back her self-esteem. She was unbalanced at the time – and Bobby was determined to shut her up, regardless of the consequences. It was the craziest thing he ever did – and I was crazy enough to let it happen.

John Gilmore, Donald Spoto, and David Marshall dismissed the possibility of murder in Marilyn's case because according to them, the claim "originated" from sensationalists like Frank Capell, Norman Mailer, and Robert Slatzer, in that order. Marilyn Monroe *was* murdered. Gilmore, Spoto, and Marshall argue that Marilyn would not have called a press conference because they feel author Robert Slatzer made it all up.

I questioned press agent Michael Selsman from the Arthur P. Jacobs Company about this further, "Were you aware that Marilyn was going to give a press conference on Monday morning?" "We had heard rumors but she was out of control. Even though she was still a client of the office, we didn't have any power over her because she had power over us."

Those who knew her understood that a press conference would be considered out of character since Marilyn was not a vindictive person; however, she was furious at what the Kennedy brothers had done to her. When prompted by Brown and Barham, Marilyn's former publicist and close friend Rupert Allan agreed that a press conference was likely. Shortly before Marilyn died, when he returned from Monaco and Princess Grace Kelly, Marilyn had left a message regarding "very important business to discuss."

When Rupert didn't reply, Ralph Roberts communicated Marilyn's message: "Tell him this is very important." Rupert recalled, "Ralph reached me. But I had jet lag after the flight from France and a bad case of bronchitis I had picked up in Monaco. I knew if I spoke one word to Marilyn, she would insist on coming over with chicken soup and aspirin. And I was really too sick for that." Upon learning of the press conference, Rupert reflected, "I don't know how I would have handled that. Of course, I was angry and saddened by the way the Kennedys had treated her, but I think I could have talked her out of making it public knowledge. In my opinion, it would have badly hurt her career."

Judy E. Simms of New Jersey claimed that as an adolescent, she saw Marilyn on television threatening a press conference, in which she would disclose the contents of her "book." This was the late afternoon on August 2, 1962. Mrs. Simms told biographer Keith Badman, "I was just a teenager when I saw it. Marilyn was on the sidewalk flanked by the media… She stated that she had a little book, and said she was going to reveal what was in it. Naturally, my ears perked up when I heard this because I was curious about what could be in that book. I remember thinking, 'This could be trouble.' She seemed very direct and determined. I can still see her with the mikes pushed at her. I don't recall anything else they asked her and it was brief. I have never met anyone that remembers that interview." [34]

Bobby Kennedy's Friendships with Top Police Officials

Peter's account of August 4, 1962 received some validation from FBI Director J. Edgar Hoover. Even though he hated the Kennedy brothers, Hoover assured a neighbor in the late sixties that Marilyn Monroe did not commit suicide. She was murdered, Hoover said to teenager Anthony Calomaris, and he pointed the finger at the Kennedys. While under the influence of drugs, Peter told his third wife Deborah Gould that the Kennedys made sure Marilyn's death was not properly investigated.

Then-Deputy Chief Tom Reddin told Anthony Summers, "The Kennedy connection was a matter of common knowledge at the Police Department I was at. The Kennedy – I should say Kennedys' – relationship with Marilyn Monroe was pretty generally accepted." However, after trying to get information on her death, Reddin relayed, "When I saw the report, it was so fragmentary that I said, 'This can't be the Police Department's complete file.' When they said, 'It's all there is,' I thought, so there is no source... no valid source to help us find out what happened to Marilyn Monroe."

Valerie J. Nelson penned an enlightening article for the *Washington Post* on March 14, 2010 entitled, "Psychiatrist Robert Litman dies; co-founded suicide prevention center." Nelson wrote that in 1958, "The idea for a suicide prevention center came from two Veterans Administration psychologists, Edwin S. Shneidman and Norman L. Farberow, who persuaded Dr. Litman, over drinks in Beverly Hills, to help establish it."

Bobby's best friend since tenth grade, David L. Hackett, assisted him by securing the implementation of a grant, making sure there would be enough funds for the Suicide Prevention Team, which according to Nelson's article, had four years prior "opened in a dilapidated abandoned tuberculosis ward on the grounds of Los Angeles County Hospital."

Such a team had the power to block a possible inquest into the real circumstances of Marilyn Monroe's death. Hiring them would ensure that nobody questioned the suicide verdict. The only thing they could question was whether Marilyn Monroe committed suicide intentionally or accidentally. Nothing more. Dr. Litman of the Suicide Prevention Team conceded to Spoto that they "didn't consider the murder hypothesis."

To help clean things up, Bobby told his good friend Chief William Parker to make sure his other good friend Captain James Hamilton was assigned to the investigation. As confirmed by Tom Reddin, the Marilyn Monroe case was one labeled a "national security" risk under the guise of the association of a national political figure and a world famous movie star.

It only seems logical that the case would be labeled as such had Bobby

Kennedy actually been at Marilyn's home on the day she died, which he most definitely was. Yet Reddin's answer regarding national security is incomplete. Brown and Barham reported, "Through the Freedom of Information Act, Hoover biographer Anthony Summers found memos from Hoover to RFK which referred to copies of surveillance tapes involving Monroe. The substance of the messages remains blacked out 'for reasons of national security.' " As for the connection between Police Chief William Parker and Bobby Kennedy, Reddin said, "Chief Parker was close to the Kennedys."

Former OCID detective Mike Rothmiller told Brown and Barham that the OCID kept Marilyn Monroe's files away from nosy journalists by breaking up the reports. Jeanne Martin said of Rothmiller, "That shows just what a lousy guy he is. I tell you anybody in the police department that goes out and tells anything about someone who died, right away I would think this guy just wants to get some publicity because a decent policeman and a good officer or anyone involved would not be going out and saying anything or did they ever that I read. This is really just yellow journalism. The book has been closed on Marilyn and she's gone." Rothmiller explained that the files would then be placed in storage facilities and even in the garage of detective Thad Brown. Anthony Summers later discovered some of Monroe's telephone records in Brown's estate papers.

Rothmiller was fascinated as he began flipping through files of famous persons. The co-writer of Rothmiller's book Ivan G. Goldman noted that Rothmiller saw "cross files. Marilyn Monroe crossed, of course, with the Kennedys." As for the transferring of confidential and politically sensitive files, Rothmiller told Brown and Barham, "This was common practice. They just rented those anonymous storage lockers and filled them with reports which should never have left police headquarters. This allowed the department to claim that it had no such files." These actions successfully skirted around the Freedom of Information Act.

Rothmiller continued, "We [at the OCID] heard that [Police Chief Daryl] Gates began moving out master files, or what was left of them, six weeks before he left. Almost all of the potentially embarrassing stuff was pulled." Gates countered this accusation by claiming, "We destroy everything after ten years. Pffft, it's gone!"

Tom Reddin disagreed with Gates, "Routinely, such files are held because of their continuing news interest. How else do you explain the large file on the 'Black Dahlia' homicide?… It would have been unheard of for those records to be destroyed – against department policy. Yet I was unable to get a single scrap of that file when I was Chief." Rothmiller explained this apparent discrepancy, "That's because it was hidden from him." [35]

In 1960, Bobby Kennedy mentioned Captain James Hamilton as one

Marilyn Monroe: A Case for Murder

of his "friends" in the Acknowledgments section of his book *The Enemy Within*. Hamilton's son later confirmed to Anthony Summers that Bobby Kennedy and James Hamilton were indeed friends outside their professional titles. Biographer John Buntin provides additional corroboration, "On November 14, 1956, [Bobby] Kennedy... flew out to Los Angeles to meet Chief Parker... Parker took Kennedy's visit seriously. He directed Hamilton... to take the afternoon to meet with the Senate investigators. The men hit it off immediately... Hamilton and Kennedy met as strangers but ended the day as friends. Henceforth, the LAPD intelligence division would be an important source of intelligence to Robert Kennedy. Kennedy's relationship with Chief Parker was different. The two men would never be friends in the way that Hamilton and Kennedy were; their personal styles were too different. But ideologically, the two men were largely in sync. In addition to sharing a faith (Roman Catholicism) and a creed (anti-Communism), the two men shared a worldview: Both saw the underworld as the enemy within... From the start, Parker put the LAPD at the Kennedys' disposal."

In return, said former Mayor Sam Yorty, Bobby convinced Parker he would succeed Hoover as head of the FBI. Biographer Evan Thomas explained that the Rackets Committee was created on January 31, 1957 also known as the Select Committee on Improper Activities in the Labor or Management Field. Bobby Kennedy promised to take down Dave Beck and Jimmy Hoffa. Daryl Gates told Wolfe, "At the invitation of Chief William Parker, Bobby Kennedy set up his offices in the LAPD Intelligence Division. Their desks were next to Captain James Hamilton's. Bobby Kennedy and Hamilton became close friends, and Bobby often relied upon Hamilton for information and guidance during the Select Committee investigations." Wolfe noted that Hamilton's lead detectives James Ahearn and Archie Case were the ones specifically chosen by Hamilton to help Bobby.

Photographer William Woodfield and reporter Joe Hyams saw Captain Hamilton at Marilyn's home and wondered why Hamilton was on the scene had it been just a routine suicide. He wasn't typically assigned to suicide cases. Woodfield and Hyams then figured there was more to the story. Lieutenant Marion Phillips' boss was Captain Hamilton. As for the Marilyn Monroe case, Phillips reported to Anthony Summers, "We knew about the inquiry, but we didn't get in on it at all. It was too damned hot. Captain Hamilton and Chief Parker were conferring on it. It went on and on, and weeks later the file went to the Chief."

Gates detailed in his autobiography, "Jim Hamilton, the captain of Intelligence, had been Parker's man in that position from day one and I had assumed Jim would never leave. But the National Football League was having terrible problems with gambling." Gates then said Chief Parker had remarked to him, "Pete Rozelle thinks the mob's shaving points on football games and he wants to hire a director of security who knows organized crime. Robert Kennedy suggested Jim." [36] What are good friends for?

Did Marilyn's Free-Association Tapes for Greenson Exist?

In 1983, Former Deputy District Attorney John Miner told Anthony Summers about a confidential interview he had with Greenson on August 8, 1962 that made Miner conclusively believe that Marilyn Monroe *did not* commit suicide. In fact, Miner went on record that Marilyn Monroe was a homicide victim and that the "stigma of suicide" should be removed from her name. Miner made a promise to Greenson to never reveal the content of the two tapes he had allowed him to listen to.

He recalled, "Greenson said to me, 'If at the end of our interview, you reach any kind of conclusion, I have no objection to you stating that conclusion to Dr. Curphey [the Coroner], but I will agree to the interview only on the condition you do not reveal any of the contents because I ethically believe that that would be a violation of my duty to Miss Monroe and the psychiatrist-patient privilege relationship.'" [37] The man kept that promise of silence for more than 30 years.

Miner publicly defended Greenson after two incidents attracted widespread attention. In 1992, former Schaefer Ambulance attendant James Hall addressed millions of viewers for *The Marilyn Files* TV Special hosted by Bill Bixby, an actor from the TV show *The Incredible Hulk*, which aired from 1978 – 1982. Hall said as he was reviving the movie star from an alleged overdose, a man identifying himself as "her doctor" came in, told him to remove the resuscitator and then proceeded to inject a hypodermic syringe with a long heart needle already attached to it into her chest. Later, Hall learned the doctor was Greenson and he is now certain Greenson did it to kill her.

Then, in 1993, Spoto's Marilyn Monroe biography held Greenson responsible for accidentally killing his patient. He alleged Greenson told housekeeper Eunice Murray to sedate her hysterical employer with a chloral hydrate enema containing 17 broken-down pills.

Anne W. O'Neill of the *Los Angeles Times* wrote on December 14, 1997, "Miner said he recently received permission from Greenson's widow to bare the secret after published reports speculated – falsely Miner contends – that Greenson and the Kennedys had been involved in Monroe's death."

Marilyn Monroe: A Case for Murder

On August 5, 2005, John Miner released to the *Times* a heavily sanitized transcript of two free-association tapes she made perhaps a week prior to her death for Greenson.

Stephen Robello of *Playboy* wrote that Miner jotted everything down he remembered from the tapes when he arrived home that very night. Welkos of the *Los Angeles Times* wrote, "Miner said he took 'extensive' and 'nearly verbatim' notes, and only broke the promise years after Greenson's death, when some Monroe biographers suggested that the psychiatrist be considered a suspect in her death." Nevertheless, Miner claimed the contents of the tapes prove that Marilyn Monroe *did not* commit suicide. Miner had the uncensored version printed in the December 2005 issue of *Playboy*. [38]

Peter Lawford died in 1984 and Anthony Summers first published his Marilyn Monroe biography in 1985. However, Marilyn's free-association tapes have only been alluded to once before Peter died: in Noguchi's 1983 book where he stated Miner "was allowed to listen to tape recordings of Monroe's own words in her sessions with Dr. Greenson." Noguchi didn't mention the word free-association explicitly but it is suggested.

The only way for Peter to have access to Marilyn's tapes is if he and Bobby confiscated them from Marilyn's home the night that she died. They confiscated the recordings along with Marilyn's tape recorder, spiral notebooks, and any other items that could incriminate the Kennedy name. Peter's third wife Debbie Gould explained that Peter went to Marilyn's home with that specific intent. For the *Say Goodbye to the President* documentary, Gould stated, "He said he went there. He tidied up the place. And did what he could before the reporters found out about the death."

Private eye Fred Otash later conceded that on Peter's behalf, he sent in more help to remove any other items that may have been missed including surveillance bugs. Otash said to Anthony Summers that it was ironic how he was the one who helped put the bugs in on behalf of the Mafia and now he was helping the Kennedys to get rid of them. Milt Ebbins attempted to counter Otash by telling Spoto, "I know Peter Lawford better than anybody. If somebody says to me he called Fred Otash or he went with Bobby, I would be the first to know. He couldn't have waited to tell me."

At the age of 70 on October 5, 1992, Otash died in his suite at the Jonathan Club, a private social club in Los Angeles, California. At the time, he was writing another book entitled *Marilyn, Kennedy and Me*. Mansfield's press secretary Raymond Strait knew Otash for over twenty years. He had ghostwritten Otash's first book *Investigation Hollywood!* and Strait believed Otash died under mysterious circumstances before finishing the second one, "We were working on the book when he died." Strait told me Otash had always given him the okay to go ahead with the project if anything happened. [39]

Spoto asked Pat Newcomb, "Did Marilyn make tape recordings of everyone who visited in her home?" "No, she wasn't that organized." Days before Marilyn died, she gave Peter more than a little worry during her last weekend at the Cal-Neva Lodge in Lake Tahoe. After Bobby failed to meet her there as he had promised, Marilyn told Peter she might make public her recordings of Bobby's telephone conversations with her as a way to get back at him for crassly breaking off the relationship. Marilyn's little red diary was a concurrent threat.

She wanted him to man up and give her an explanation for cutting off their friendship, which was more important to Marilyn than the sexual affair. According to Miner and Otash, she didn't want to be used that way if she wasn't getting anything in return. Peter lamented to Heymann it was true that in Marilyn's mind, she believed both Kennedy brothers at one time or another had promised to marry her. But when she thought they had reneged on their promises, she felt like a sex object. The British actor relayed:

> At the behest of Dr. Greenson, Marilyn was making tapes. Greenson had suggested she tape her daily thoughts while riding to and from appointments in the backseat of her limousine. In a kind of stream-of-consciousness mode, she carried forth on everyone and everything from Joe DiMaggio to Robert Kennedy. The tapes revealed – and I heard several of them – that she had fallen deeply in love with Bobby. She spoke about her desire to be married to him and to have his children. She also spoke about both Kennedys having jilted her, then passing her around like a football.

The relationship Marilyn wanted to continue with Bobby Kennedy was more supportive in nature. The same kind of support Kennedy aide Edwin Guthman said Bobby also often gave over the phone to another insecure actress Judy Garland. This, by itself, presented a real threat to Bobby because Marilyn was needy. She could get childishly upset and angry at the smallest slight. Marilyn and Bobby committed acts of desperation at this time resulting in disastrous results for both involved. When Peter told Bobby about Marilyn's taped phone conversations, Bobby was frantic. That last afternoon, Bobby said to Peter, "Get her to your place. She won't talk to me now, you get her to the beach."

Before Bobby had dropped her, Marilyn actually valued his advice. She asked him important questions and sought his help when she needed it. The statement below by Peter to Heymann indicated Bobby's more than casual relationship with Marilyn:

What she failed to mention, or at least I never heard it, was Bobby's help in trying to settle a dispute with Lew Wasserman and MCA, her final theatrical agency. She wanted MCA to release her from her contract, and Bobby attempted to negotiate an agreement with Wasserman. After she died, MCA sued her estate for more than eighty thousand dollars.

MCA actually asked for $37,228.61 according to a facsimile of the creditor's claim found in the July 1994 issue, Number 15 of the fan newspaper *Runnin' Wild: All About Marilyn*. In Susan Strasberg's book, Marilyn's close friend Ralph Roberts verified Peter's account above. Marilyn told him, "Bobby is trying to break up MCA and he asked me to help him."

In fact, before Marilyn went to sing for the President at Madison Square Garden, she thought Bobby was going to take care of the threats made by the studio to fire her if she went. Marilyn's designer and close friend William Travilla relayed to Brown and Barham, "He led her to believe that the White House was taking care of it. Her impression was that the nasty telegram had been rescinded, so therefore, she ignored it completely." Bobby did make such an effort. When he telephoned Fox, Bobby was put through to Peter Levathes, Executive Vice-President of Production:

> KENNEDY: I'd like you to make an exception for Marilyn Monroe. This is very, very important to the President of the United States.
>
> LEVATHES: I can't. Not this time. The board of directors has already ruled.
>
> KENNEDY: I can't overemphasize the importance of this to Jack Kennedy.

Seeing that he was getting nowhere with him, Bobby then called financier Milton Gould, Levathes' boss, asking his permission instead to let Marilyn go to the Gala:

> KENNEDY: The President wants it and I want it.
>
> GOULD: We can't afford to do it. Marilyn has just returned to the cameras and this appearance could end up costing us millions.

KENNEDY: Think about it and I'll call you back later.

Kennedy phoned again and this time his patience was running out.

GOULD: I don't know what I can do. The board has already decided on this.

KENNEDY: I know what you can do. You can let her go.

GOULD: This actress has missed two weeks because of illness – an illness that isn't over yet. Don't you see that we can't afford to have her appear in public and on *television* as well?

KENNEDY: You know what you are? You're a no-good Jew bastard!

After that, Kennedy hung up. Shortly before Marilyn was fired on June 8, Bobby called his family connection Judge Samuel Rosenman, the board of directors chairman. Rosenman informed Bobby that if he wanted to help Marilyn he would have to talk to Milton Gould. Considering Kennedy and Gould had not ended their last conversation with kind words, he knew this was not a possibility. Having exhausted his resources, Twentieth Century-Fox fired Marilyn Monroe. On June 13, 1962, Marilyn sent off a sarcastic Western Union Telegram to the Kennedys at Hickory Hill (McLean, Virginia):

> DEAR ATTORNEY GENERAL AND MRS ROBERT KENNEDY: I WOULD HAVE BEEN DELIGHTED TO HAVE ACCEPTED YOUR INVITATION HONORING PAT AND PETER LAWFORD. UNFORTUNATELY I AM INVOLVED IN A FREEDOM RIDE PROTESTING THE LOSS OF THE MINORITY RIGHTS BELONGING TO THE FEW REMAINING EARTHBOUND STARS. AFTER ALL, ALL WE DEMANDED WAS OUR RIGHT TO TWINKLE.
> MARILYN MONROE.

Marilyn hinted at how disappointed she was in Bobby for letting the studio fire her after his so-called efforts to secure "permission" to attend the Gala in New York. In her mind, with Bobby's support, it should never have happened. According to Heymann's hand-written notes, Peter Lawford relayed to him:

> Marilyn had tried in vain on a number of occasions to call Jack and then Bobby. When she couldn't get through to them, she called Jackie at the White House and Ethel at Hickory Hill. She apparently admired Jackie but had complete disdain for Ethel, who struck her as a complete phony.

Marilyn became enraged with Bobby and perhaps he told her she was being unreasonable, calling him at his own home. Rupert Allan shed some additional light on the full meaning of the June 13 telegram. Referring to Bobby and Marilyn's February 1, 1962 attendance at the Lawfords' where they had danced the Twist, Rupert relayed to Brown and Barham, "She said they talked of how few really big stars remained. Marilyn was immensely flattered when Bobby told her that she and Elizabeth Taylor were the only stars left."

With the support of Darryl F. Zanuck and her co-star Dean Martin, Marilyn Monroe was rehired a week after she was fired. Martin refused to work with anyone but Marilyn. Greenson's daughter Joan observed, "There was never a line in a paper or trade paper about the fact that they were trying to get her back. You never heard about that... It also confirmed what we all felt that the studio was trying to punish Marilyn. It also was trying to get as much publicity as possible on her firing. They played it up in all the papers, trying to make Marilyn look as bad as possible. Marilyn was really saddened and upset by it all... She had picked up some kind of virus when she had been in Mexico, and off and on seemed to run a temperature, and this really complicated her working on the movie."

As for Zanuck, he eventually bought enough shares to take back control of the studio from shareholders with no knowledge on how to make motion pictures. One of these men was Milton Gould who was subsequently forced to resign. Zanuck had at that point been elected president of Twentieth Century-Fox. However, the act of being fired in itself was a public embarrassment for Marilyn and an emotional slap in the face, which affected her badly. Shooting on the film was scheduled to resume in October after Dean Martin met another film commitment but Marilyn died in the interim.

Alas, David Marshall and his DD Group tried yet again to discredit Peter's interview with Heymann. They claim that Peter couldn't possibly have access to Marilyn's free-association tapes because they were in Greenson's office. Greenson had *some* of Marilyn's tapes in his possession, two of which John Miner listened to. However, Greenson did not possess the tapes still at Marilyn's home, including ones she hadn't given to him yet, which Bobby

Kennedy later kept to blackmail the psychiatrist in case he ever felt like opening his mouth about the plot to kill his patient.

Greenson knew it wouldn't look good if a Marilyn Monroe free-association tape somehow leaked to the newspapers, a tape that referenced Marilyn's affair with him. Peter said he heard several of the movie star's tapes. He and Bobby probably listened to them together. When I interviewed Raymond Strait, he said Peter hired Fred Otash who brought along another man to sweep Marilyn's place for bugs and anything else incriminating *before* midnight *not* the following morning, as had been previously misreported by many a biography.[40]

Did Miner Accurately Translate Marilyn's Free-Association Tapes?

Some biographers speculated that John Miner made up the tapes he claimed to have recollected from memory. Miner said the tapes are not exact yet he believed he did not do damage to Marilyn's intent. After interviewing Gloria Romanoff, I read several selected paragraphs to her from Miner's recollection of Marilyn's tapes. Mrs. Romanoff said, "I think it's so eerie. Really eerie. There are sentiments in there that are very much her sentiments. I don't think she all by herself would have done this. I think she did have some assistance if in truth there is something in hand to see." Miner remembered from the tapes regarding Sinatra, DiMaggio, and Miller:

> What a wonderful friend Frank Sinatra is to me. I love Frank, and he loves me. It is not the marrying kind of love. It is better because marriage can't destroy it. How well I know. Marriage destroyed my relationships with two wonderful men. Joe D loves Marilyn Monroe and always will. I love him and always will. But Joe couldn't stay married to Marilyn Monroe, the famous movie star. Joe has an image in his stubborn Italian head of a traditional Italian wife.
>
> She would have to be faithful, do what he tells her, devote all of herself to him. Doctor, you know that's not me. There is no way I could stop being Marilyn Monroe and become someone else to save our marriage. It didn't take too long before we both realized that and ended our marriage. But we didn't end our love for each other. Anytime I need him, Joe is there. I couldn't

have a better friend… It's different with Arthur. Marrying him was my mistake, not his. He couldn't give me the attention, warmth, and affection I need. It's not in his nature. Arthur never credited me with much intelligence.

When I mentioned John Miner provided the framing for Marilyn's words, Mrs. Romanoff remarked, "The language simply is not hers. She was not that articulate. Some of these sentiments are very much hers. She was a very simple girl. She was not really educated. What education she had was self-education. She was totally sincere in pursuing that to the extent she could."

As for Miner's recollection of what Marilyn said as it pertained to DiMaggio, Sinatra, and Miller, Mrs. Romanoff concluded, "I think her sentiments as regards to Joe DiMaggio are perfectly honest. I think her reflections about Sinatra are perfectly honest. I think her thoughts about Arthur Miller are very honest. DiMaggio was drawn to her certainly because of her celebrity. As sometimes happens, the husband resents the celebrity, the attention and wishes that the wife could be just the wife."

It is this biographer's conclusion that the free-association tapes Peter Lawford and John Miner heard are real. Peter mentioned "a kind of stream-of-consciousness mode" which is what Miner had Marilyn discussing in his recollection of the two tapes he heard, "While reading Molly's blathering, the idea came to me: Get a tape recorder, put a tape in, turn it on and say whatever you are thinking, like I am doing now. It's really easy. I'm lying on my bed, wearing only a brassiere. If I want to go to the fridge or the bathroom, I can push the stop button and begin again when I want to."

Or if her words sounded a little too polished, perhaps she was reading from a notepad while speaking into the recorder. She did this no doubt to further impress Greenson. Either she was talking while reading and/or she pressed the stop button, prepared for minutes to hours then pressed play again. When Marilyn referenced "Molly's blathering" in her tapes, she was describing the character of Molly Bloom in James Joyce's classic book *Ulysses*. Importantly, Marilyn made it clear *she* was the one who came up with the idea of recording herself, *not* Greenson. [41]

Jay Margolis

Were Marilyn and Peter's Homes Bugged and Their Phones Tapped?

Discussing Bobby Kennedy, Teamsters' President Jimmy Hoffa confided in Conservative columnist Victor Lasky, "I used to love to bug the little bastard." In the documentary *Marilyn: The Last Word*, Anthony Summers relayed what he discovered from years of research, "This bugging system in Monroe's house was active from March/April 1962 until the very night of her death." Malibu real-estate agent Arthur James knew Marilyn Monroe from two mutual friends. The first was through Charlie Chaplin, Jr. in the late forties when James first met Marilyn and the second was in 1953 through Edward Robinson, Jr., both former lovers of hers.

In March 1962, James got a call from an associate of Carmine DeSapio who had links to Jimmy Hoffa. James told Anthony Summers, "The request was that I should get Marilyn away from her house for a while, perhaps for a weekend at my place in Laguna Beach. They wanted her place empty so they could install bugging equipment. I knew about Marilyn's relations with Robert Kennedy – she had told me – and that was evidently the reason for wanting to bug her." James said he declined the request.

When television actress Veronica Hamel from *Hill Street Blues* moved into Monroe's house in the 1970s, she tore down part of Marilyn's bedroom and noticed wires sticking out of the roof tiles. She called General Telephone to have them removed and later a GT employee told Hamel, "These aren't phone lines. They're surveillance lines." On behalf of Jimmy Hoffa, Fred Otash bugged the residences and phones of both Peter Lawford and Marilyn Monroe. Peter relayed to Heymann:

> Marilyn's house was being bugged by everyone – Jimmy Hoffa, the FBI, the Mafia, even Twentieth Century-Fox. Jimmy Hoffa wanted to gather information on Monroe and the Kennedys for personal use; the FBI hoped to ascertain what Marilyn knew about Frank Sinatra's connections to the Mafia; the Mafia was curious as to what she knew about the FBI. As for Twentieth Century-Fox, who knows what they wanted?

Biographer Ted Schwarz told Heymann, "Spindel was a crook among crooks in that he would have a client and he'd get paid to install a wiretap, but there would actually be five clients for the same tape. Tapes from Spindel went to J. Edgar Hoover, the CIA, Jimmy Hoffa, and Mafia boss Carlos Marcello, as well as other notorious mob characters."

Marilyn Monroe: A Case for Murder

Even the jealous Joe DiMaggio hired Fred Otash, who worked for wiretapper Bernie Spindel. Biographer Richard Ben Cramer wrote, "Joe would meet with Otash, who'd give him his reports: Marilyn in meetings with the Kennedys at the Lawfords' beach house... Bing Crosby's house with JFK... a weekend with Sinatra's friends at Frankie's new casino resort, the Cal-Neva Lodge, on the border at Lake Tahoe..." DiMaggio was always watching over Marilyn like a protective father. He knew terrible things could happen to her if she wasn't careful. In the end, despite his tremendous efforts even DiMaggio was powerless to alter her tragic fate.

Wolfe revealed in his book actual transcripts from ABC Television's 1985 20/20 program. The segment was later scrapped and never aired. Broadcast journalist Sylvia Chase interviewed Fred Otash:

CHASE: How did you get involved in this?

OTASH: Hoffa was very interested in developing a derogatory profile on Bobby Kennedy – not so much Jack Kennedy, but Bobby Kennedy.

CHASE: And then what followed?

OTASH: Bugs were installed in the Lawford house – in the bedrooms and on the phones. There were four bugs all together installed out there.

CHASE: Why the Lawford house?

OTASH: Well, because the information we had was that it was the Kennedy playhouse – that's where Bobby and Jack played... There were numerous tapes made of Marilyn and Jack in the act of love.

CHASE: But you were really trying to obtain information on Bobby Kennedy.

OTASH: Sure.

CHASE: Did you hear Bobby Kennedy on an eavesdropping tape?

OTASH: Yes.

CHASE: Do they confirm that Bobby Kennedy and Marilyn also had an affair?

OTASH: Of course… sure… Bobby Kennedy and Marilyn were recorded many times.

By late May 1962, Jack Kennedy felt Marilyn Monroe was coming on too strong by liberally calling him several times at the White House. Jack sent Bobby to talk to her. Otash associate John Danoff, who also heard sounds of Jack and Marilyn making love over wiretaps in addition to Bobby and Marilyn, said Jack Kennedy "was tired of her and he gave her to Bobby. In the same time that she was making it with him, Bobby was also playing with her."

In the *Say Goodbye to the President* documentary, Danoff relayed, "Music. People talking. It would fade in and fade out. I then began to recognize the voices. The Bostonian accent and Marilyn Monroe. I heard the President call Marilyn 'Marilyn' and Marilyn call the President 'Prez.' The footsteps left the living room and went into the bedroom where there was another transmitter which picked up all the activity in the bedroom. Cuddly talk and taking off the clothes and the sex act on the bed and you could hear the springs squeaking and so on and so forth."

Fred Otash claimed others beside the Mafia wanted Peter and Marilyn's homes bugged. Otash relayed, "I'm not the only man who was working the Kennedys. I am convinced with moral certainty that there were so many bugs in those houses that there were bugs on top of bugs. A lot of people were involved! J. Edgar Hoover wanted a derogatory profile on the Kennedys. The Republican Party wanted a derogatory profile on the Kennedys… The CIA and the FBI wanted a derogatory profile on the Kennedys… Bobby Kennedy was putting so much heat on everyone."

Ted Schwarz told Heymann, "Fred Otash… had been hired to bug Lawford's house. So he went out there. But before he bugged it, just for the hell of it, he swept it and he detected a bug that was already in place. In other words, before he installed his own wire, he listened with somebody else's. It came courtesy of Howard Hughes, who had long been politically active on behalf of Richard Nixon, who was determined to gather dirt on the Democrats." Lastly, Raymond Strait told me he heard eleven hours of Fred Otash's surveillance tapes that were running the night Marilyn Monroe died, which will be discussed in another section. [42]

Marilyn Monroe: A Case for Murder

Did JFK Have More Than a One-Night Stand with Marilyn Monroe?

Only two Monroe biographers argued that Jack Kennedy had a one-night stand with Marilyn Monroe. The first is Donald Spoto. The second is Keith Badman. Following Spoto's lead, Badman said that Jack and Marilyn's tryst at Bing Crosby's Palm Springs home from March 24 – 26, 1962 was a one-time event. Badman explained, "If you examine the President's and Marilyn's separate itineraries, as I've done, that's the only time they could feasibly have been together alone. Apart from that, their schedules simply didn't match up… But was it an affair? No. A quick fling? Yes." Itineraries are not as solid as rock. If we relied exclusively on Jack Kennedy's itineraries like Badman does then we would incorrectly assume Kennedy never had time to fool around. There is too much evidence to the contrary and Jack Kennedy was anything but discreet.

Peter Lawford told Anthony Summers he knew Marilyn Monroe since 1950 when they first met at William Morris. After interviewing agent Charles Feldman's secretary Grace Dobish and associate Alain Bernheim, Summers suggested that Marilyn may have met Jack at a party hosted by Feldman in 1951. On April 24, 1954, Pat Kennedy and Peter Lawford were married. According to friend Arthur James, shortly before she divorced second husband Joe DiMaggio in late October, a brief affair between Marilyn Monroe and Jack Kennedy went virtually unnoticed. James saw the two at each other's side along the beach near Malibu pier.

He relayed to Anthony Summers, "Although Jack Kennedy was a Senator, he was unknown here, relatively speaking. He and Marilyn could get away with a great deal. They sometimes drank at the Malibu Cottage, which was the raunchiest place you've seen in your life… but in those days it was a hangout for some of the most famous names in Hollywood… I don't think it was ever really important to Jack Kennedy but Marilyn never got over it, least of all when he became president. In the end, though, their headquarters was Peter Lawford's place, back at Santa Monica." James told Summers that Marilyn had informed him that she and Jack would often book rooms in Malibu's Holiday House Motel.

However, the real affair would come years later. Marilyn's long-time friend James Bacon, columnist for the *Los Angeles Times*, then working for the *Associated Press* relayed, "Marilyn told me about her affair with JFK… It began when he was campaigning for president. They had parties out at Peter Lawford's house." Biographer Seymour Hersh interviewed Michael Selsman who told him he knew about the affair with Marilyn and Jack shortly before the inauguration in January 1961.

Selsman said to Hersh, "It was the first thing I was told. We had to protect her, we had to keep her out of print. It'd be disastrous for me. It wasn't hard in those days. It was a different era. Today it would be impossible to keep anything resembling that a secret." George Barris told me, "The Kennedys I think were very much aware of the fact that having relationships with movie stars could be detrimental to their career. Here's the President of the United States and his brother the Attorney General in such high positions in government. It could lead to their downfall for them to be associated with famous actresses who some people claim they had affairs with. The rest of the country doesn't go for this."

Dr. Max Jacobson ("Dr. Feelgood" to several celebrities) first treated Jack Kennedy to a shot combined with amphetamines and steroids during the fall of 1960. The future First Lady sometimes received the shots as well. Jacobson's son Tom told Heymann, "The combination of steroids and amphetamines no doubt increased Kennedy's sexual drive." In addition, Anthony Summers relayed, "People treated with this new drug [cortisone] as it was then for Addison's disease, men and women both alike became exceptionally sexually eager and active. Their libidos were enormously enhanced."

Jack Kennedy's best friend Florida Senator George Smathers, also a handsome lothario in his day, noted what a peculiar role Kennedy's sex life played in his other daily activities. Smathers told Heymann, "My feeling was that Rose, like Eleanor Roosevelt, hated sex, couldn't tolerate it. Joe was chauvinistic, a tremendous skirt-chaser, and Jack had an equally active libido... It was a gift, maybe his greatest gift, the ability to make the most out of every experience."

Smathers said to Kitty Kelley, "There's no question about the fact that Jack had the most active libido of any man I've ever known... I remember one night he was making it with a famous movie star and, by God if Jackie almost didn't catch him right in the act... No one was off-limits to Jack – and not your wife, your mother, your sister. If he wanted a woman, he'd take her... Just in terms of the time he spent with a woman, though, he was a lousy lover. He went in more for quantity than quality.

"One time I caught him messing around in the Cabinet Room in the White House and asked him how in the hell he thought he was going to get away with that kind of thing. He was convinced Jackie would never find out, but the fact of the matter is that she probably knew just about everything that was going on. By God, she knew... And not all of his women were good-looking. He had a couple of dogs working for him in the White House nicknamed Fiddle and Faddle who he was always playing around with."

Smathers told Seymour Hersh that Marilyn Monroe "was a beautiful actress. Probably as pretty a woman as ever lived. And Jack – everybody knew he liked pretty girls." Said the late James Bacon: "Marilyn used to tell me about Jack. She had a big affair with him. It was kind of a slam-bang affair because she'd be ushered in. The Secret Service would take her there to Jack Kennedy. Boom. Boom. She once said to me, 'There's no foreplay.' And I said, 'Marilyn, after all, the guy *is* running the country, you know.' And she says, 'Well, he should show more consideration.'"

Joseph P. Kennedy biographer Ronald Kessler noted in his book *In the President's Secret Service* that the Secret Service themselves validated more than just a one-night stand with Jack and Marilyn. Kessler wrote, "According to Secret Service agents, Kennedy had sex with Marilyn Monroe at New York hotels and in a loft above the Justice Department office of then-Attorney General Robert F. Kennedy, the President's brother. Between the fifth and sixth floors, the loft contains a double bed that is used when the Attorney General needs to stay overnight to handle crises. Its proximity to a private elevator made it easy for Kennedy and Monroe to enter from the Justice Department basement without being noticed. 'He [Jack Kennedy] had liaisons with Marilyn Monroe there,' a Secret Service agent says. 'The Secret Service knew about it.'"

Agent Marty Venker told Heymann that the Secret Service "not only procured for him but partied with him. They were young, handsome, well-educated fellows who enjoyed women and drinking and drugs... And had an agent talked, every other agent would have clammed up or denied the stories, which by the way also included Bobby and Teddy Kennedy... Bobby Kennedy became quite alarmed about all this womanizing. Of course, he engaged in his own extracurricular activities, but he feared that his brother's affairs would bring down the entire administration. He warned JFK to exercise greater prudence... The President's private parties when held at the White House usually took place in and around the swimming pool. Because of his bad back, the pool was heated to more than ninety degrees Fahrenheit... A pitcher of daiquiris would be prepared in anticipation and chilled in a portable refrigerator; little Vienna sausages wrapped in bacon would be kept in a portable heater." Again, Jack Kennedy was anything but discreet.

And neither was Marilyn. She bragged to Sinatra's valet George Jacobs about her clandestine affair with Jack Kennedy and that she had sex with him many, many times. Jacobs reflected, "Marilyn would tell me breathlessly about Jack, though she never mentioned Bobby. Most of the stories involved how sexually obsessed Jack was with her, how many times and where they had made love, from suites at the Plaza in New York to broom closets at the Sands.

"I knew how horny Jack was, so nothing she said surprised me, except her belief in his promises that he would leave Jackie and that she would be his First

Lady for his second term. That guy would say *anything* to score!... Marilyn did concede that the President was not a great lover. His biggest problem, she told me, was premature ejaculation. She tried to take it as a positive, evidence of how she drove the President out of control. 'Jesus, George, he's got a *country* to run. He doesn't have time for that mushy stuff.' " [43]

Keith Badman dismissed the possibility that Marilyn ever attended the Democratic National Convention and stated that she was in New York preoccupied with filming. But as biographer J. Randy Taraborrelli noted, "Marilyn wasn't sure she could make it. She said she had prior commitments with *The Misfits*. However, Pat [Kennedy Lawford] told her that if she missed it she would be 'missing something historical.' So Marilyn agreed to be there. She would be out of town, she said, but she would fly in for the convention and fly right back out that night." Actually, according to Peter Lawford, she would stay more than one night.

Kennedy official Peter Summers, responsible for television coverage, remembered Marilyn Monroe meeting Jack Kennedy during his nomination at the Los Angeles Coliseum on July 15, 1960. Peter Summers relayed, "It was a magical moment like no other I can remember. When he came to the podium, the applause was thunderous but then, as he spoke, you could hear a pin drop. Chills were going up and down your spine. Yes, Marilyn was in the audience, along with many other stars. That night, I think a strong friendship began to develop between her and Jack Kennedy. She was free, but Jack Kennedy wasn't."

Peter Summers verified that a serious affair between Jack Kennedy and Marilyn Monroe most likely began at the Convention and that campaign officials each sat them down as they explained the situation, "Some people on staff said products are sold by star endorsement and that maybe a closeness of this nature will be a benefit to him getting elected. The other side was that you're not going to elect someone president who is perhaps ignoring his wife or cheating on his family. So, yes there was concern. Marilyn was spoken to very frankly about it. The President was spoken to very frankly about it. There was great concern at the time. It could have destroyed him."

Jack Kennedy had come to the Democratic National Convention with the full support of the Los Angeles Police Department. Wolfe explained that the Kennedys were registered at the Biltmore Hotel "down the hall from Chief Bill Parker's private apartment." Those assigned to protect the Kennedys were James Hamilton, Daryl Gates, Frank Hronek, Marvin Iannone, Archie Case, and James Ahearn. Heymann said Marilyn went skinny dipping at the Lawford mansion the night of the Convention. The next day, she attended Jack Kennedy's celebration party at Romanoff's. That evening, she and Jack

Kennedy were together at Puccini's with Kenneth O'Donnell and Peter Lawford. Peter relayed to Heymann:

> Of all his "other" women, Marilyn was perhaps the best for him. They were good together. They both had charisma, and they both possessed a sense of humor. Marilyn proclaimed that night that Jack's sexual performance was "very democratic" and "very penetrating." She also came up with that memorable line, "I think I made his back feel better." Jack liked to pat and squeeze her. He was touching her here and there under the table when this bemused expression suddenly crossed his face. Marilyn said later he had put his hand up her dress and discovered she wore no underwear.

Jack Kennedy and Marilyn Monroe formed a strong bond during the Convention. Kennedy aide Peter Summers said, "They were very close friends. I would say she was a very special guest – the President was really very, very fond of Marilyn. She was delightful, a little bit nervous perhaps, but I think the nervousness was because she was in a new territory with people who were political animals. She wasn't totally at ease. I did feel that she was so impressed by Kennedy's charm and charisma that she was almost starry-eyed... But she was totally able to hold her own conversationally; she was very bright." Entranced by the prospect of Kennedy becoming president, the movie star was smitten with Jack, more so now than years before.

Marilyn didn't want to stop seeing the handsome and smooth-talking Kennedy. As the most famous woman in the world, Marilyn knew she had the power to seduce any man. If she couldn't at first, she became curious and more attracted then she would pursue it further. Peter Summers relayed, "I think that the next couple of times I saw them together, right after the nomination, she seemed so much more comfortable... There were a number of celebration parties going on. Marilyn was at one – at the Beverly Hilton, where there was a private celebration, with dancing. She was there, and I saw Jack, right after telephoning his wife on the East Coast, go out and start dancing with Marilyn. We didn't know how serious this affair would be – platonic or otherwise."

On Friday, November 11, 1960, Earl Wilson wrote the following headline in the *Los Angeles Mirror*, "Marilyn Monroe Will Divorce Arthur Miller." A little more than a week later, humorist and Kennedy confidant Art Buchwald wrote a teaser column in the *Washington Post* on Saturday, November 19, "Let's Be Firm on Monroe Doctrine. Who will be the next ambassador to Monroe? This is one of the many problems President-elect Kennedy will have to work on in January. Obviously you can't leave Monroe adrift. There are too many greedy people eyeing her, and now that Ambassador Miller has left she could flounder around without any direction."

Peter Summers often visited Kennedy at the Lawford beach house. One time, he saw Marilyn Monroe and Jack Kennedy there together. Summers recalled, "I had to go and see Jack. He came out of the shower, putting on his tie, and started talking. And a few minutes later Marilyn came out of the shower, with just a towel around her. She had clearly been in there, in the shower, with him. It was obvious, but neither of them seemed worried about it." Otash's sound man John Danoff claimed that a tryst between Jack Kennedy and Marilyn Monroe occurred in 1961 sometime near Thanksgiving. In 2006, Anthony Summers established for his Frank Sinatra biography that it happened on November 19, 1961 at the Lawford beach house.

British journalist William J. Weatherby met Marilyn during the shooting of *The Misfits* and periodically had drinks with her at a New York bar on Eighth Avenue. On November 4, 1960, filming wrapped. After May 19, 1962, Weatherby saw Marilyn one last time at the same bar in New York. He wrote in his book:

> "Did you know Arthur's married again?" she asked… "Maybe I'll get married again myself," she said with a mysterious smile. She seemed secretly serious, looking at me to see how I reacted. "Have you someone in mind? Is there a leading candidate?" "Sort of." She played with her drink and I thought: she is still beautiful. Her expression was so wistful as she looked down, dreaming. Then she glanced up and laughed. "Only problem is, he's married right now. And he's famous; so we have to meet in secret." Her tone of voice suggested that she found that exciting, romantic. "And he's getting a divorce?" "Arthur had to get a divorce, you know… He's in politics," she said, going as near the point of telling me his name as she could. "In Hollywood?" "Oh, no." She giggled at my ignorance. "In Washington." Okay, so it sounded like one of the Kennedys.

Later in the discussion, Weatherby stayed on the same subject but changed the topic to politics:

WEATHERBY: How do you think President Kennedy is doing?

MARILYN: Wonderfully.

WEATHERBY: He's made some bad appointments in the South.

MARILYN: I'm sure President Kennedy had good reasons.

WEATHERBY: Yeah, he was paying off some political debts.

MARILYN: You don't like President Kennedy?

WEATHERBY: It's not a matter of like or dislike with a president. It's whether he does a good job for all the people. It's too early to tell with Kennedy.

MARILYN: I think he's going to be another Lincoln. [44]

Consequently, any man Marilyn held to ideal standards was eventually destined to betray her in some way and Jack was no exception.

Did Marilyn Sleep with the President at the Carlyle on May 20, 1962?

It is highly unlikely Marilyn Monroe had a tryst with Jack Kennedy after the Birthday Gala. On duty at the time, Secret Service agent Gerald Blaine verified that Marilyn was in fact at the Carlyle yet he is adamant nothing happened between the two on this date. Blaine wrote, "Marilyn was also present in the Carlyle Hotel, as one of many guests, including Bobby Kennedy, Jean Smith, the President's sister, other family members, White House staff personnel, and other entertainers. Miss Monroe left before the other guests." Anthony Summers noted, "The *New York Times*, in its normal coverage, said the President returned to his hotel, the Carlyle, at 2:00 A.M. His recent biographer, Ralph Martin, quotes an unnamed eyewitness as saying that Marilyn joined him there. If she did, she and the President had a fairly brief meeting."

Since Marilyn drove her beloved former father-in-law Isadore Miller home that night, it would be out of character to ditch Miller while she went and had a dalliance with Jack Kennedy albeit how quickly. A surviving photograph taken at Arthur Krim's Manhattan home after the Gala showed Marilyn

Monroe and Isadore Miller sitting not far away from each other while Jack Kennedy is on the other side of the room. She looks bored and unhappy.

Flora Rheta Schreiber interviewed Isadore Miller. Schreiber wrote that Marilyn "insisted upon taking him home. At his elevator they kissed goodby. But, as she was stepping out of the front door, she turned and came back. 'Dad,' she urged, 'come back to the Coast with me tomorrow.' 'Later, Marilyn,' he promised. 'Maybe in November.' Though they talked again many times, this was the last time they saw each other."

By 1962, Marilyn had been friends with 24-year-old Jimmy Haspiel since September 1954 when he was just sixteen. Haspiel firmly denied that Marilyn had time to sleep with the President after the Gala. He wrote in his first book, "I can tell you with *authority*, that I was with Marilyn at her apartment at ten minutes to four in the morning. Categorically, Marilyn was not asleep at the Carlyle Hotel, and I didn't notice the President anywhere nearby us, either!

"The night of entertainment at Madison Square Garden probably got underway at around eight o'clock in the evening... after which there was a party for Kennedy and certain performers from the Garden that Marilyn then attended on the arm of 'my father-in-law, Isadore Miller...' Allowing time for socializing at the party, then getting Isadore back to his home in Brooklyn, Marilyn's return home at nearly 4 A.M. was not unreasonable." Around this time, by Ralph Roberts' account, Marilyn called him over to her apartment for a massage.

Describing the photograph of Marilyn with both Kennedy brothers, Badman said Marilyn Monroe gave Jack Kennedy a nice present, a "gold Rolex President." Engraved were the following words, "Jack, with love as always from Marilyn May 19th, 1962." When Jack put the watch back in the box, he happened upon a folded note from Marilyn, which read:

> Let lovers breathe their sighs / And roses bloom and music sound / Let passion burn on lips and eyes / And pleasures merry world go round / Let golden sunshine flood the sky / And let me love / Or let me die!

While the poem accompanying the President's birthday gift is sexually charged, the evidence is still not sufficient to suggest that Marilyn had a fling with the Commander-in-Chief at the Carlyle Hotel that night.

Secret Service agent Gerald Blaine incorrectly stated Marilyn and the President were only in each other's company two times. The first time they met he claimed was at the Lawford beach house in 1961 and the second time was at the Carlyle. Marty Venker and other Secret Service agents interviewed by Ronald Kessler directly contradict Blaine. Also, Blaine forgot or was not aware of the March 24 – 26, 1962 meeting, a date universally accepted by every Marilyn Monroe biographer as indeed a tryst between the two national icons.

These biographers include but are not limited to Brown and Barham, Anthony Summers, Donald Spoto, J. Randy Taraborrelli, and Keith Badman, all of whom rely on the trusted account of Marilyn's best friend and masseur Ralph Roberts who said he talked to Kennedy himself over the phone and assisted him with his back problems. Ralph Roberts relayed to Brown and Barham what Marilyn had said to him, "Ralph, I've got a friend here I want you to talk with. We have been discussing the way I developed my walk. You know, 'the Marilyn walk.' Anyway, he wants to know the name of the muscles I had to develop in order to achieve this."

In September 1962, Roberts told reporter Joe Hyams, "Back in the days when Marilyn first decided she wanted to be an actress rather than a star, she got a book, 'The Thinking Body,' by Mabel Ellsworth Todd. From it Marilyn got the basic exercise called 'the pelvic girdle' and she developed the walk that made her famous. She always carried a copy of that book with her. And she took lessons in walking and body alignment in New York from Barbara Clark, who's now in her seventies." [45]

Marilyn Monroe Plays the Secretary!

Ralph Roberts told Brown and Barham she would often dress incognito to meet the President, especially at the Carlyle. One ruse was that Marilyn was made up like a secretary with an inexpensive brunette wig, a gray Sears, Roebuck suit, and horn-rimmed glasses accompanied by a notepad aboard Air Force One. Roberts related, "She called me a day later and we joked about it. She said Lawford even made her take dictation just as if she was a real secretary. That particular act burned her up." Eventually, Jack tired of Marilyn and felt that she was nagging him beyond what he could handle.

Jack's friend Florida Senator George Smathers said, "Well, it wasn't a big thing as far as he was concerned... He wanted to stop it because it got to be to a point where it was somewhat embarrassing. She stopped bothering him because he quit talking to her." Smathers told Hersh, "What happened was that she... would like to be close to the President. And then after he had been associated with her some, she began to ask for an opportunity to come to Washington and come to the White House and that sort of thing. That's when Jack asked me to see what I could do to help him in that respect by talking to her." Rupert Allan reflected with sorrow, "If Kennedy had handled Marilyn differently, things might not have turned out so badly. But just ducking her as he did. Not good." [46]

Jack Kennedy and Judy Campbell

"The only Campbell I know is chunky vegetable soup," claimed Kennedy's presidential aide and close friend Dave Powers in 1991. Milt Ebbins relayed to Donald Spoto, "Hell hath no fury like a hooker that becomes an author… You mean to tell me he took her to the White House?" Seymour Hersh wrote, "Exner's FBI file, released in its entirety under the Freedom of Information Act, contains no evidence linking [Judy Campbell] Exner to prostitution, despite years of surveillance." Who was Judy Campbell, the lady eventually forced to testify before the Church Committee in 1975? Walter Winchell wrote in his May 9, 1962 column, "Judy Campbell of Palm Springs and Bevhills is Topic No. 1 in Romantic Political Circles." Press agent Michael Selsman discussed with me Jack Kennedy's affairs:

>SELSMAN: He was doing everyone he could get his hands on, including Judy Campbell. She was my client actually.

>MARGOLIS: Seymour Hersh made a statement that only he and Liz Smith believed Judy Campbell's stories.

>SELSMAN: I believe them, too.

>MARGOLIS: Did you ever hear about Jack and Judy being together during the time that it happened?

>SELSMAN: Jack and Judy? Oh, yes, she was one of the five or six women he would have sex with when he was out here. Angie Dickinson. I mean there were a lot of people.

>MARGOLIS: He had many women, right?

>SELSMAN: Yeah, he did. His right-hand guy-cum-valet Kenny O'Donnell used to smuggle women out of the backdoor of the White House. And Lawford was his pimp out here.

Marilyn Monroe: A Case for Murder

Once married to actor William Campbell whom she wished she never knew, Judy said she first met Jack Kennedy on February 7, 1960 through her friend and occasional lover Frank Sinatra. She claimed she didn't know Jack was Senator of Massachusetts or that he was married. Judy told Hersh, "I knew him as Pat's brother rather than as a senator." Judy Campbell fell in love with Jack Kennedy, which she said wasn't too hard because of his charismatic personality. They made love for the first time one month later on March 7, just before the New Hampshire primary.

Since Judy was a good friend of Sinatra, Jack would hound her for the newest, juiciest celebrity gossip and she would always turn him down. Judy wrote in her book *My Story*, "Oh, but he loved gossip. He adored it. That was something he was always asking me about on the telephone and in person. He would say, 'Who's Frank seeing now?' or 'I heard Frank is seeing so-and-so and isn't she married?' I would say, 'I don't know any gossip.' He would say, 'Come on, let me in on a little of it. You're around those people, you see things going on.' 'If you want gossip, pick up a movie magazine.' He would act shocked. 'I don't want that phony stuff. I want the real inside dope.' " Judy told Hersh, "I now think he may have been interested in some of the women he asked about."

Beginning in 1960, just a few months after they had met, knowing of Judy's friendship with the notorious Mafia boss, Jack trusted Judy enough for her to act as intermediary between him and Sam Giancana. Jack was about to ask Judy for some dangerous favors which soon led to years of incessant FBI surveillance. Jack assured Judy, "You know Sam works for us." Jack gave Judy a satchel of money to give to Sam Giancana, containing as much as $250,000. Jack wanted to win the presidential election and according to Judy, in early August 1960, Jack gave her his second and last satchel of cash telling her, "This is for the campaign." Anthony Summers wrote that Giancana then arranged for "massive vote-stealing in Illinois."

After Jack Kennedy was elected, he approached Judy before the inauguration and asked her to transport documents to Giancana for yet another favor: to kill Castro. Judy told Hersh, "I knew what they [the documents] dealt with. I knew they dealt with the 'elimination' of Castro and that Sam and Johnny [Rosselli] had been hired by the CIA. That's what Jack explained to me in the very beginning... I was aware of 'elimination,' which in my mind just meant removing him from office. Had I realized it was assassination, I'd have been much more frightened."

Intriguingly, Judy said Bobby Kennedy was also fully aware of the role Sam Giancana would play in the plot to kill Castro. Judy told Hersh, "Bobby would come in and bring the information in a manila envelope to Jack. And they would discuss a little bit about it. And Bobby often would put his hand on my shoulder and ask, 'Are you still comfortable doing this? We want you to let us know if you don't want to.' " This was the same Bobby Kennedy who in 1959 had chided Giancana before the Rackets Committee for giggling like a little girl.

Ironically, a year later, Giancana would help Jack get elected president in return for monetary compensation given to him through Judy Campbell. Before the inauguration, the Mafia boss would assist the Kennedys again in a plot to kill Castro, this time to get the FBI off his back. Regarding "the mob donations to the Kennedy campaign," the FBI picked up the following on wiretap in December 1960:

> ROSSELLI: Sinatra's got it in his head that they [the Kennedys] are going to be faithful to him [and, by extension, the mob].
>
> GIANCANA: In other words then, the donation that was made…
>
> ROSSELLI: That's what I was talking about.
>
> GIANCANA: In other words, if I ever get a speeding ticket, none of those fuckers would know me?
>
> ROSSELLI: You told that right, buddy.

Giancana later said to Hoffa's brilliant attorney Edward Bennett Williams, "They can't do this to me. I'm working for the government." Indeed he was but in the end, the Kennedys did him no favors.

The FBI got a real shock in July 1960 around the time of the Democratic National Convention. They eventually learned of the connection between Jack Kennedy, Judy Campbell, and Sam Giancana. Former FBI agent William R. Carter relayed to Hersh his utter disappointment in the people running the country. Carter said, "We considered Kennedy to be no better than Giancana or Rosselli."

On Bobby Kennedy, Jimmy Hoffa relayed in 1973, "A man who would do anything to get himself a headline or a headline for his brother. And used the Teamsters as a stepping-stone to get his brother elected and he become attorney general." FBI agent Carter said other agents noticed the same hypocrisy observed by Giancana and Hoffa. Carter told Hersh regarding Bobby Kennedy's public stance against organized crime, "We attributed it to political ambition. Figured it was the way several people have become famous. Fighting crime means you're a good guy."

On March 22, 1962, over lunch, J. Edgar Hoover finally informed Jack Kennedy he was fully aware of his connection with Judy Campbell, Sam Giancana, and Giancana's lieutenant Johnny Rosselli. According to Judy, Jack was angry at Hoover for throwing it in his face. Judy told Hersh that Jack phoned her mother's house because the FBI probably didn't have that line bugged.

Judy related, "He said he'd just had this meeting with Hoover and Hoover told Jack that he knew, first of all, about Jack's relationship with me. And he also knew that I was carrying documents regarding the Castro assassination plot to Sam Giancana and John Rosselli for Jack. And he knew that they worked for the CIA... That's the reckless side of Jack – that he would allow himself to be in that position. I mean, he never should have been involved with me. They wanted to get rid of Hoover and they couldn't, because of the information that Hoover had on the Kennedys – not just Jack."

Judy told Hersh the last time she slept with Jack Kennedy she became pregnant but it couldn't have been the late summer. Judy said to renowned columnist Liz Smith, "I went to see him one last time – late December 1962. I said I wouldn't see him anymore; it was too painful. But we were intimate that one last time, in the White House. I still loved him with all my heart. I don't know if God was punishing me. But I went to New York and then on to Chicago. I'm in my hotel. I realize I am pregnant. I hadn't been with anyone but Jack – *not ever during the whole time.*" Judy showed hospital receipts to Liz Smith proving that from January 26 – 28, 1963, she entered Chicago's Grant Hospital. With the help of her friend Sam Giancana, she then had an abortion set up by a doctor.

Judy explained to Smith she was emotionally devastated by Jack's next move, "After the abortion, Jack was on the phone to me right away, begging me to come back to Washington. I was so afraid of the FBI, of the CIA, of Sam, of the Mafia, of everyone. Jack kept calling me in California, and I told him I just couldn't go through it anymore... I saw him once after – it's in the records. Funny, it's there, but I have a mental block. I really don't remember it." Judy said to Hersh, "Jack didn't play by our rules; Jack had his own rules. I believe that all of the Kennedys play by their own rules. I don't think they conduct themselves the way we do. I think that's very sad." [47]

According to RFK biographer Evan Thomas, Jack Kennedy loved reading historical fiction. His favorite book was *Pilgrim's Way* by John Buchan. Buchan's *The Thirty-Nine Steps* no doubt influenced Jack's subsequent sexual and political debauchery. Thomas wrote, "Buchan's secret agent, Richard Hannay, was a precursor of James Bond. Together, Jack and Bobby were riveted by Hannay's intrigues in the 'queer subterranean world of the Secret Service.' " By reading such books, Jack often placed himself in the role.

When he really wanted the high-life, Jack actually lived it. How else to explain his reckless behavior during his presidency with so many women including movie stars? Agent Marty Venker agreed, "This was the James Bond era and Kennedy was intrigued by the whole mystique of the Secret Service." Jack thought he could get away with it but he was not at all discreet like his younger brother Bobby. The public may not have known at the time of the Kennedys' infidelities but J. Edgar Hoover would never be far away to remind the brothers he knew their every step. [48]

Did Marilyn Monroe and Bobby Kennedy Share a Bed?

For years, biographers have debated whether Bobby Kennedy was an adulterer. Donald Spoto went so far as to emphatically state that Bobby Kennedy slept with no one else but his own wife. In an interview with Spoto, Peter Lawford's long-time friend Milt Ebbins was asked whether he had any indication of a "relationship with Robert Kennedy." "If there was one, it was very well-hidden." Spoto proudly told Ebbins that because Marilyn's best friends like Ralph Roberts and Susan Strasberg said no affair with Bobby existed then Spoto concluded, it must not have happened. He then used the accounts of Peter's good friends Joe Naar and Bill Asher as additional "proof" of no affair.

Ebbins cautioned Spoto, "I would investigate that if I were you. Oh, yeah, I would investigate that. I have no proof… These guys are known as hit-and-run artists. Jack was hit-and-run with them. We know that from the women. Bing! And up and out. I asked him once about that. I said, 'What the hell is that?' He says, 'You have to take it fast, brother. You don't have much time.' " Ebbins told Spoto in a second interview, "I think that Bobby had an affair with her… It seems to me that Jack passed her to Bobby."

Press agent Michael Selsman agreed. He told me, "The way I understand it is that Jack and Bobby had a routine ever since they were much younger where Jack would have an affair and when he was tired of her, he would pass her on to Bobby." In an ironic reversal, Jack Kennedy's friend George Smathers relayed to Anthony Summers that the President "expressed some concern to me about his brother's relationship with Marilyn." For the *Say Goodbye to the President* documentary, Smathers said that Jack "Kennedy had told Bobby to stop. To break it off."

Marilyn Monroe: A Case for Murder

Even though he believed no affair existed, Peter's friend Joe Naar conceded to Spoto that with the female sex Bobby was "pushy, aggressive. 'I'm Bobby Kennedy, the Attorney General.' That was the attitude... Bobby always had a thing about Marilyn but he had a thing about women. So did Jack... Bob was a little obnoxious. I was dancing with Marilyn and he said, 'Can I cut in?' "

In mid-1962, Bobby approached George Terrien then married to Bobby's sister-in-law Georgeann. Terrien told Oppenheimer, "Bobby was sounding very macho and full of himself. Out of the blue he said, 'George [Skakel] would keel over if he knew who I was screwing.'

"First of all, I was flabbergasted that Bobby used that word because he rarely used that kind of language. Secondly, I thought he was joking because as far as I was concerned, and everyone in the family was concerned, Bobby and Ethel had a good marriage. She idolized him. We all knew Jack was fucking around, but I couldn't conceive of Bobby having a thing with anyone but Ethie. So I said, 'You are the biggest bullshitter in the world. You wouldn't have the balls to play around.'

"And he said, 'Just tell George I've had Marilyn's pussy.' I said, 'What the hell are you talking about? Marilyn who?' And Bobby said, and he was laughing, 'You know, the woman Jack used to jack off over. Marilyn Monroe. After he finished with her, she fell for me. I think she's in love with me.' I told Bobby, 'You're full of shit,' and he laughed and that was the end of the conversation. I thought he was full of shit then, and I think he's full of shit now. I can't imagine Marilyn Monroe getting into bed with that little jerk."

Peter Lawford's neighbor and frequent guest Peter Dye said as for Bobby Kennedy and Marilyn Monroe, "I know she was nuts about him because she told me. She liked that mental part of it. She was fascinated by him. I think she was scared to death of him because he gave this air about himself. I think he was nuts about her. She kind of teased him but then she knew just how far to go and then just kind of back off. And she was kind of cute with him in a way. But she was nuts about him." Peter's ex-wife Deborah Gould relayed, "From what Peter said then Bobby got very infatuated and it led into an affair between Marilyn and Bobby." Peter himself verified a tryst between Bobby and Marilyn in his last interview with Heymann:

> Marilyn realized the affair [between her and Jack] was over but couldn't accept it. She began writing these rather pathetic letters to Jack and continued calling. She threatened to go to the press. He finally sent Bobby Kennedy out to California to cool her off... He tried to explain to her that the President was an extremely busy man, that running the country was an imposing task, that while Jack cared a great deal for her, he

was already married and couldn't very well simply sneak off and see a divorce lawyer. Although it probably wasn't easy for her, she would have to accept this decision and stop calling the President. She took it pretty hard. Bobby felt for her. They met again the following day and passed the afternoon walking along the beach.

It wasn't Bobby's intention, but that evening they became lovers and spent the night in our guest bedroom. Almost immediately the affair got very heavy, and they began seeing a lot of each other. Now Marilyn was calling the Department of Justice instead of the White House… Pretty soon Marilyn announced that she was in love with Bobby and that *he* had promised to marry her. It was as if she could no longer tell the difference between Bobby and Jack…

I told her to get the hell off whatever she was taking and screw her head on straight, or her entire career would go down the tubes. Marilyn couldn't step on the brakes. Bobby was gradually retreating from her the same way Jack had retreated. She went up the wall. "They treat everybody like that," she said. "They use you and then they dispose of you like so much rubbish." [49]

    Others were becoming aware of the close relationship between Bobby and Marilyn. Peter Dye wasn't the only Lawford neighbor who suspected a tryst between the two. Lynn Sherman told Anthony Summers she was absolutely certain that Bobby and Marilyn were intimate, "There were many, many rendezvous there. The official car used to drive up, and you knew Robert Kennedy was in town, and then the help would come in and say, 'Marilyn's arrived.' She'd be wearing maybe a scarf over her head and pants. Sometimes I'd notice Bobby and Marilyn go out through the patio to the beach to walk. From my balcony, it was pretty obvious they were there together on many occasions – there was no doubt in my mind."
    After Marilyn died, Pat had a drink with Lynn Sherman and complained about her philandering husband Peter Lawford. Pat told Sherman, "But we all go through it – look what Ethel's been going through." Actress Terry Moore told me Clark Gable's widow Kay Spreckles, who was in contact with Marilyn in the weeks before her death, heard from Marilyn "that the man she loved the most was Bobby Kennedy." However, Marilyn became disillusioned when

she realized he was just using her and she did not appreciate it at all. It made her very angry.

Peter Lawford's young friend Chuck Pick remembered the first time he met Marilyn Monroe. Twenty-year-old Pick worked as an attendant in front of the Lawfords' one night in mid-1962 and saw more than what he expected. Pick related to James Spada, "Marilyn was there, and so was Bobby. One of the Secret Service guys said to me, 'You have eyes but you can't see, you have ears but you can't hear, and you have a mouth but you can't speak. You're gonna see a lot of things, but you have to keep quiet.' I didn't know what he was talking about, but a little while later I guessed. The party was breaking up, and Marilyn and Bobby were leaving together. I brought around his white 1956 T-bird and Marilyn got into it and I just sat there – I guess I wanted to sit next to Marilyn Monroe for as long as possible. Finally Bobby said, 'Okay, you can get out now' and he got in and they drove away." Per Summers' Hoover biography, Bobby borrowed the white convertible from William G. Simon, Head of the Los Angeles FBI Office. Pick's account is also found in Heymann's *RFK* biography. [50]

Greenson Tells the Suicide Team Marilyn Had Affairs with Both Kennedys

Anthony Summers interviewed the Suicide Prevention Team. Days after Marilyn's death, Greenson told Dr. Robert Litman about her sexual affairs with both Kennedy brothers but never referred to the Kennedys by name. For an October 13, 1973 article with biographer Maurice Zolotow, Greenson contradicted himself, denying that Marilyn was having an affair with either Kennedy brother. Another article released just ten days later voiced a similar opinion. Presumably Greenson changed his tune after Norman Mailer's book hit national headlines that year suggesting Marilyn Monroe may have been murdered. Certainly, this frightened Greenson, who publicly stated that Mailer's last chapter is "all wrong, filled with fallacious statements that give rise to pure fantasy."

However, Greenson's wife Hildi and his daughter Joan agreed that the affairs *did* happen. Joan remembered, "I knew there had been a new man in her life, and I was asking her about her new boyfriend. She had told me she had been seeing someone, but that she didn't feel it was right for her to tell me his name, because he was well-known. So she said from here on, we would just call him 'The General.' With this, we both laughed. We enjoyed the intrigue."

Hildi concurred to Cathy Griffin, "I think she mentioned it in a very veiled way to my daughter. She I think told her that she was seeing somebody called 'The General,' or she called him 'The General…' It wasn't masking very much. Never to me." Heymann noted that General "is a common form of address for the attorney general." Marilyn would often arrive at Greenson's lectures incognito by putting on a dark wig, glasses and a scarf. Hildi relayed, "I imagine she would do similar things to meet somebody as prominent as either the President or Robert."

In the end, Greenson was ambivalent about the affairs. Dr. Litman allowed Anthony Summers to quote from his notes back in the first days of August 1962, referring to earlier that same year: "Around this time, Marilyn started to date some 'very important men.' Greenson had very considerable concern that she was being used in these relationships… However, it seemed so gratifying to her to be associated with such powerful and important men, that he could not declare himself to be against it… He told her to be sure she was doing it for something that she felt was valuable and not just because she felt she had to do it." Unfortunately, during her last months, Marilyn was in sexual affairs with very powerful men that could only have ended in disaster.

Summers wrote, "Dr. Litman says today that Greenson spoke to him of a 'close relationship with extremely important men in government,' that the relationship was 'sexual,' and that the men concerned were 'at the highest level.' Dr. Litman says that while Dr. Greenson did not actually name the Kennedys, he had 'no real doubt' whom he meant by 'important men in government.' Litman also felt that Dr. Greenson had not been 'totally candid' even with him."

Litman told Brown and Barham, "There was evidence of her intimate relationship with Robert Kennedy. But Bobby was no different than any other of the strong men she brought into her life as rescuers. He was another of those father figures who eventually betrayed her… She was always able to attract the highest level of men. She went out after them, and she got them." [51] At the time, Marilyn didn't believe the Kennedy brothers were taking advantage of her. As shown in Peter's last interview, she later made a free-association tape complaining about how they had used her, "passing her around like a football."

Was Marilyn Monroe Bobby's Only Sexual Affair?

Jack Kennedy once confided, "Dad told all the boys to get laid as often as possible." Kennedy biographer and close friend Arthur Schlesinger, Jr. conceded, "Bobby was human. He liked a drink and he liked young women. He indulged that liking when he traveled and he had to travel a great deal." Florida Senator George Smathers said one of those young women was 28-year-old Mary Jo Kopechne who later drowned in Ted Kennedy's car in Chappaquiddick, Massachusetts on July 18, 1969. At the time that Bobby was having an affair with her, she was campaigning for his 1968 presidential run as one of the "Boiler Room Girls."

Smathers told Heymann, "Although she no longer worked for me, Mary Jo and I stayed in touch. I'd become her father confessor, so to speak. She was young, sweet, and impressionable. When she informed me that Bobby had invited her to join him as a secretary on the presidential campaign plane, I warned her against it. I knew Bobby, and I knew that he would take advantage of the situation. And that's precisely what happened. It didn't matter to him whether Ethel was also on the plane. They'd check into hotels at night, and Mary Jo would be given her own room. It didn't take much for Bobby to excuse himself from a strategy meeting for a few minutes and go visit Mary Jo in her room. Nobody was the wiser for it. It reminded me a little of Jack when he campaigned for the presidency in 1960, except that Jackie wasn't around most of the time."

Press secretary Raymond Strait told me that both Jack and Bobby Kennedy had trysts with actress Jayne Mansfield. Bobby's affair with Mansfield occurred almost a year after Marilyn Monroe was murdered. Jack's affair with Jayne continued after Bobby's even when she was noticeably pregnant with Mariska in late 1963, soon before Jack was assassinated. Peter Lawford relayed to Heymann:

> Jayne looked like a dumb blonde but was by no means stupid. There were three meetings that I know of – one in Beverly Hills, one in Malibu, one in Palm Springs… She had the best body in Hollywood, long legs, large firm breasts and a miniscule waistline. The time they met in Palm Springs Jayne was pregnant with Maria, her fourth child, and Jack wasn't aware of it until they got together. She was visibly pregnant. Her condition apparently turned him on, which frankly surprised me.

Strait told me Jayne got mad with Jack one day over the phone at the Beverly Hills Hotel. After she drank a few black Russians at the Polo Lounge, Strait overheard her say the following to him, "Listen to me, buster, you'll only be president two terms at most but I'll be a movie star forever." Then she hung up. They never spoke again.

Bobby Kennedy met discreetly with Jayne Mansfield after her performances at the Casino Royal in Washington, D.C., which began on the Fourth of July 1963. At the time of the tryst, she was 30. Strait relayed to Heymann, "Paul Blane, Jayne's road manager, told me what happened in D.C. On several nights, Robert Kennedy came to see the show. Mickey [Hargitay, her husband] was there with Jayne, even though they weren't getting along at all at that point, so Bobby had to make a delicate arrangement to see her. Paul became the emissary between the two, and after some back and forth he offered the use of a suite of rooms that he had at a hotel around the corner. The Attorney General had sex with Jayne in the bedroom one night while Paul sat in the living room watching a Western on TV. It's noteworthy that JFK had likewise been with Jayne."

Strait wrote in his second book on Mansfield, "Robert Kennedy emerged from the bedroom, hair rumpled, suit disheveled with a frosted pink lipstick smear on his cheek. Jayne remained in the bedroom. Kennedy shook Paul's hand and thanked him. As he quickly exited he added, 'Thanks for everything. Remember, we don't know anything about this, do we?'"

C. David Heymann's 2009 book entitled *Bobby and Jackie: A Love Story* documented the sexual affair between Bobby and Jackie Kennedy, which began in 1964 after the assassination of Jack Kennedy and lasted for four years, until Bobby's assassination. Heymann used strong sources including close contacts to the Kennedys to validate Bobby's tryst with Jackie. Humorist and Kennedy family friend Art Buchwald told Heymann that Jackie "had lovers, many more than people realized, but the only man she loved was Bobby Kennedy." According to Heymann's research, Bobby became a philanderer but was much more discreet about it than his older brother Jack. Anthony Summers came to similar conclusions.

On August 30, 2009, the *Winnipeg Free Press* released an article entitled, "Bobby and Jackie Up In a Tree, K-i-s-s-i-n-g After JFK's Death?" by Winnipeg lawyer Brenlee Carrington. Carrington wrote, "The premise of American writer C. David Heymann's new release is that Bobby and Jackie were the loves of each other's lives. This despite the fact that Bobby was married to Ethel Kennedy, mother of his 11 children, while he was allegedly having numerous liaisons on the side – and despite the allegation that Jackie was also not faithful during her marriage and after her husband's assassination."

Heymann said in the article, "Too often in earlier biographies, Robert

Marilyn Monroe: A Case for Murder

Kennedy was depicted as something of a choirboy, when, in fact, he enjoyed the same proclivity for extramarital affairs as his brothers, Jack (JFK) and Ted (Senator Edward) Kennedy... In the 1960s, the private lives of public figures were simply not covered by the media... As a biographer, it has always been my conviction that sexual or personal behavior is integral to a fuller understanding of a person's life, particularly in the case of public personalities."

Billionaire Aristotle Onassis and Bobby Kennedy never got along with each other. Bobby didn't like how Jackie had considered marrying Onassis, who was twenty-three and a half years older, so soon after Jack Kennedy's death that he suggested she wait until after his run for president to marry him. This was also for political reasons: her marriage to a much-older billionaire would be a distraction. Always loyal to Bobby, Jackie obeyed.

Aide Johnny Meyer said Onassis hated Bobby Kennedy enough to the point where he hired his own investigator to find out if he really did have Marilyn Monroe killed. His investigator could not produce any hard evidence. Onassis bitterly remarked, "The only thing JFK and RFK have in common is Jacqueline Kennedy." Four and a half months after Bobby was assassinated, Jackie finally agreed to marry Onassis on October 20, 1968.

Even though he was known as the moralistic brother, Bobby sometimes strayed in the company of Jack. Peter Jay Sharp, who purchased the Carlyle Hotel in 1967, reflected to Heymann, "Bobby participated in at least some of the notorious swimming pool parties with Jack. I was quite friendly in the early 1960s with a girl [Becky Petersburgh Townley] who used to go down to see Bobby at the White House and also at the Department of Justice, and she reported a kind of orgy in the White House swimming pool with both brothers present.

"I don't know how much of Bobby's activities Ethel knew or cared about. I was always under the impression that all the Kennedy women, in-laws and otherwise, were like Rose – once they had their children they didn't care what their husbands did so long as it didn't happen in front of their noses, though on several occasions it did."

Sharp recalled one day seeing three Kennedy brothers in the same hotel room, each with a different woman, "I didn't own the Carlyle when John Kennedy was president, but I knew him and visited him at the hotel a number of times. Once, I went up to the family's penthouse suite and found a Secret Service guard in front of the door. He ushered me inside and there was Jack in one of the beds with a blonde and Bobby on the living room floor with a brunette. I was actually looking for Teddy, but Robert told me he was in the bathroom with another girl. I didn't want to bother Ted, but as I was leaving I asked Bob to tell him to call me when he was finished. Bobby carried on this conversation without missing a beat with his girl."

Jay Margolis

The brunette was Carol Bjorkman, bearing a slight resemblance to Jackie Kennedy. At the time, she worked for *Women's Wear Daily*. Bobby met Bjorkman in 1961 at a dinner event in Manhattan. Peter Lawford told Heymann, "The day I accompanied him, he seemed extremely impatient. I heard a rumor – and only a rumor – that he asked Carol to marry him. He promised he would divorce Ethel. Carol purportedly turned him down. She had no intention of becoming a home wrecker." [52]

Lee Remick, the actress who replaced Marilyn after she was temporarily fired from *Something's Got to Give*, caught Bobby Kennedy's eye in 1961 while at a Justice Department function. When Bobby came out to Los Angeles again, he asked Peter if he could arrange something with Lee. At the time, Remick was 25. One weekend, they had a tryst at a private residence in Malibu, California. When Bobby went to Florida in early 1962, he even brought Lee along to the Palm Bay Club. Bill Walton, JFK's director of the White House Fine Arts Commission, reflected to Heymann, "As far as I recall, Bobby abandoned his friendship with Lee Remick when she became overly aggressive, calling him at all hours at home and in his office."

Within months of Jack Kennedy's assassination, Bobby decided to run for the Senate in New York. At that time, Bobby was carrying on an affair with Fifi Fell's twenty-six-year-old daughter Natalie who was married to producer Fred Cushing. Fifi Fell was the socialite who had hosted a party in which both Marilyn and Jack were in attendance on April 14, 1962. The same party where Milt Ebbins notoriously helped a nude Marilyn Monroe fit into a tight dress before they arrived a couple hours late.

Like many of the young "Boiler Room Girls" for his later presidential campaign, Bobby asked Natalie to tag along. Natalie lied to Fred and told him she would be traveling with Ethel Kennedy. Steve and Jean Kennedy Smith knew Bobby was sleeping with Natalie. The affair was soon discovered and subsequently the Cushings divorced. Aide to Jack Kennedy and long-time friend Kenneth O'Donnell told Heymann what he learned from Steve Smith, "Stephen was managing Bobby's senatorial campaign and he became increasingly concerned that if word of the affair spread, it would impact on RFK's political future. Ironically, Bobby had faced the same problem while overseeing Jack's various campaigns."

Bobby Kennedy was sleeping with yet another actress before Marilyn Monroe: 28-year-old Kim Novak. This was in late 1961 according to his best friend Mort Downey, Jr. who knew him since Bobby was twenty-five or twenty-six. Mort, Jr. said to Heymann, "Bobby didn't need sex as a daily fix the way Jack did, but he knew how to get it. It was more of a macho thing with Bobby, as if he had to prove himself. This macho business extended to other areas as well… Kim represented Bobby's answer to Jack's affair with

Angie Dickinson, except Novak was better-looking." Near the end of 1961, Bobby went out of his way to get the necessary documents for Novak's visit to Russia. When she came back, Kennedy and Novak resumed their tryst at her room in New York's Plaza Hotel.

Joan Braden was cochairman of Bobby's 1968 presidential campaign in California. She was also a close friend of both Ethel and Bobby. Hours after Martin Luther King, Jr. was shot on April 4, 1968, Bobby met Joan in a motel room and said to her, "It could have been me."

She relayed in an earlier proposal for her book *Just Enough Rope*, "My heart wrenched from complicated tugs of emotion. He had never seemed more vulnerable. When he asked me to go upstairs, I went. On the bed, we kissed. Then he got up to take off his tie. But I could not go through with it. He was hurt, silent and angry. I watched his straight back under the streetlights as he walked toward his car. Why hadn't I done it?... Tom would have understood, even if Ethel would not have." Later, after wanting to retract the proposal because her ghostwriter was focusing more on her sex life, Braden said in a *New York Times* article, "The incidents did happen, but I didn't feel they were germane to what I wanted to write about."

JFK's former press secretary Pierre Salinger arrived at his home one night to a real surprise. Salinger asked biographer Seymour Hersh, "What do you know about Robert Kennedy?... In 1967, I came home and found him in bed with my wife." Later, Pierre divorced Nicole Gillman Salinger. The former Mrs. Salinger said to Hersh, "It's true that Robert Kennedy had affairs. Unfortunately, not with me." I had always wondered why Pierre Salinger's contribution was absent from Pat Kennedy Lawford's book *That Shining Hour*. It was a 1969 private family publication remembering her brother Bobby a year after he had been assassinated.

On August 2, 2007, documentarian Keya Morgan told the *New York Daily News* he spoke to Los Angeles police contacts that stated they were at the Beverly Hills Hotel on the night Bobby Kennedy was assassinated. Morgan related what one of the sources told him, "He said his job was to keep Ethel away from where Bobby had a call girl waiting at the Beverly Hills Hotel." Morgan continued that the call girl "was crying when he was killed. Very upset."[53]

Was Marilyn Monroe Pregnant with Bobby Kennedy's Child?

R. Graham of Bethesda, Maryland, posed the following question to Walter Scott's *Personality Parade* on July 4, 1971, "Is it true that the late Marilyn Monroe was impregnated by a prominent member of the Kennedy Administration and had the pregnancy aborted in Los Angeles at the Cedars of Lebanon Hospital?" Scott readily denied such an allegation yet it merits further study. Regarding July 27 – 29, 1962, an anonymous close friend of Sinatra reflected, "Frank... said that he wanted Marilyn at Cal-Neva so he could keep an eye on her, because he'd heard that she had had an abortion in the last couple of weeks. He didn't know whose kid it had been – his, Bobby's, Jack's – and he wanted to find out what was going on."

According to Natalie Trundy, she heard from her future husband Arthur Jacobs that Marilyn told him she had miscarried. At a time when the procedure was illegal, it probably was not smart to tell anyone about an abortion, especially if you're the most famous woman in the world. Miscarriage sounds better. Marilyn's real-estate friend Arthur James told Anthony Summers, "It was obvious the poor girl was in trouble even by her standards... Marilyn said she had lost a baby, and I thought there had been a miscarriage." James believed it was Robert Kennedy's child.

Many of Marilyn's close associates at the time were concerned that on July 20, 1962, Marilyn had secretly checked into Cedars of Lebanon Hospital to get an abortion presumably with the assistance of Marilyn's long-time gynecologist and dear friend Dr. Leon "Red" Krohn. Sinatra's valet George Jacobs relayed, "Marilyn's gynecologist was Red Krohn, who also treated the doctor-phobic Mr. S and performed all necessary abortions whenever Sinatra knocked someone up (never stars, but mostly one-night-stand waitresses and showgirls)."

Fred Lawrence Guiles wrote, "One of the Jacobs Office publicists said that on July 20, Marilyn was admitted to Cedars of Lebanon Hospital under an alias. He was told that she was having a pregnancy aborted... The cover story given out at the time by the Jacobs Office was that she had gone that weekend with the Lawfords to Lake Tahoe." Pat Newcomb readily admitted she only began to know Marilyn in 1961 (not including the few days she met Marilyn on *Bus Stop* in 1956). Newcomb told Spoto, "I took her to the

Marilyn Monroe: A Case for Murder

hospital once, a D & C... Here, at Cedars." I queried press agent Michael Selsman from the Arthur P. Jacobs Company regarding Marilyn Monroe's whereabouts in mid-July:

MARGOLIS: Were you aware of the abortion she had on July 20, 1962?

SELSMAN: Yes. It's in my book. She wasn't sure whether it was Jack or Bobby.

MARGOLIS: And she told Arthur Jacobs that she was pregnant weeks before?

SELSMAN: Yeah.

MARGOLIS: Where was the abortion performed?

SELSMAN: Cedars of Lebanon.

MARGOLIS: Do you think that her gynecologist Leon "Red" Krohn would have been involved?

SELSMAN: Yeah. He would have been.

Spoto claimed Dr. Krohn's records proved Marilyn never had an abortion in her life. No sensible doctor would keep a record of an illegal activity conducted in his hospital. Keith Badman wrote, "One Marilyn book [not sourced by Mr. Badman] even claimed that she went into Cedars for a 'D & C' (Dilatation and Curettage), a procedure to scrape and collect the tissue (endometrium) from inside the uterus, used both as a means of ameliorating certain gynecological conditions and as a method of abortion."

Marilyn's friend reporter George Carpozi, Jr. relayed, "Jack dumped her and gave her over to his brother. He said to Bobby, 'Take care of her. Get her out of my hair.' So Bobby, in order to get her out of his brother's hair, all of a sudden found himself infatuated with Marilyn that now he's taken over. She's like a hand-me-down. So she was going to have a baby. She thought Bobby was going to divorce Ethel and marry her. Of course that was a wild-eyed dream... It was Bobby's baby."

Brown and Barham wrote, "Other clues included a vial of morphine capsules with a Cedars of Lebanon label and a frantic telephone call from Monroe to her former gynecologist, Leon Krohn. The actress told Krohn's nurse that she needed 'an emergency appointment.' " Marilyn's close friend Rupert Allan related, "I heard that she was pregnant and that it was Bobby's child. She told Agnes there was an abortion and that she had checked into the hospital incognito. But this is the sort of thing Marilyn wouldn't have shared with me." Long-time hairdresser Agnes Flanagan relayed to studio maid Hazel Washington, "Marilyn's looking so poorly because she had an abortion."

Rupert Allan explained, "Nineteen sixty-two was a long time ago. If word that Marilyn had aborted a child by one of the Kennedys reached the press – in those pre-tabloid days – everyone connected with it would have been ruined." Peter Lawford and his wife Pat fronted the "Lake Tahoe" story. By taking care of it early, the potentially disastrous situation could be contained. Presumably out of respect for Marilyn's memory, Peter Lawford continued to front the Lake Tahoe story to C. David Heymann in 1983. Peter mentioned two trips to Lake Tahoe in July of 1962 to hide the fact Marilyn had an abortion that month. Peter related to Heymann:

> During July, Pat and I took her along on two junkets to Cal-Neva Lodge at Lake Tahoe. On the first we were all drinking pretty heavily, but Marilyn was also taking sleeping pills, which none of us realized until it was almost too late. She became so violently ill she had to be taken to Reno and from there flown back to Los Angeles aboard Frank Sinatra's private plane. The second visit ended just as abruptly when Joe DiMaggio suddenly showed up. Somebody evidently told him that Marilyn had been kidnapped and was being held at Cal-Neva against her will. There were always call girls around the lodge and sex and drugs and parties. But Marilyn certainly wasn't there against her will. DiMaggio wanted her to go home with him. They argued. She became upset and once again she had to leave early and return to Los Angeles aboard Sinatra's plane. [54]

Marilyn's last weekend at Cal-Neva has indeed frustrated many a biographer.

Marilyn Monroe: A Case for Murder

What Really Happened to Marilyn at the Cal-Neva? ✓

During Marilyn's second to last weekend alive, Peter and Pat Kennedy Lawford took Marilyn to the Cal-Neva Lodge from July 27 to 29 (Friday – Sunday). Below I rearranged Peter Lawford's interview with Heymann to describe one trip to Cal-Neva, not two, which makes more logical sense:

> During July, Pat and I took her along to Cal-Neva Lodge at Lake Tahoe… Joe DiMaggio suddenly showed up. Somebody evidently told him that Marilyn had been kidnapped and was being held at Cal-Neva against her will. There were always calls girls around the lodge and sex and drugs and parties. But Marilyn certainly wasn't there against her will. DiMaggio wanted her to go home with him. They argued. She became upset… We were all drinking pretty heavily, but Marilyn was also taking sleeping pills, which none of us realized until it was almost too late. She became so violently ill she had to be taken to Reno and from there flown back to Los Angeles aboard Frank Sinatra's private plane.

Anthony Summers wrote in his Frank Sinatra biography that there was proof from an FBI agent Bill Roemer and photographer William Woodfield that gangster Sam Giancana had sex with Marilyn Monroe at the Cal-Neva that last weekend. Roemer's only "proof" of this is he said he heard Giancana's lieutenant Johnny Rosselli over wiretap asking Giancana, "You sure get your rocks off fucking the same broad as the brothers [Kennedy], don't you?" Summers then argued Giancana may have been referring not to Marilyn but to Judy Campbell who also slept with Giancana in July 1962. Giancana could not have been referring to Judy Campbell because Rosselli mentioned *both* Kennedy brothers and it has never been suggested that Judy had an affair with Bobby Kennedy.

I asked Gloria Romanoff whether Giancana was sexually involved with Marilyn, "She was always Frank's guest and Giancana, whatever you may think of him, would not have violated his friendship with Frank, not for one moment… She never had a better friend than Frank Sinatra. He was very protective about her." Otash confidant Raymond Strait relayed to me, "Frank was sleeping with her and I don't think he wanted Giancana to sleep with her." Giancana's friend Tommy DiBella said, "No way. And I'll tell you why: because he knew how Sinatra felt about her, and Sam never screwed with

101

another man's girl… Screwing her right under Sinatra's nose at Cal-Neva? No way."

Bobby Kennedy told Peter Lawford to get Marilyn out of Los Angeles since he was coming there to give a speech and to stop by Twentieth Century-Fox to meet with producer Jerry Wald on Kennedy's film *The Enemy Within*. At Bobby's request, Peter and Pat Kennedy Lawford brought Marilyn up to the Cal-Neva for that last weekend. At this point, the Attorney General was keeping his distance from what he considered Marilyn's unpredictable and volatile demeanor. The truth of the matter is, had Bobby acted more civilly instead of avoiding her, she might have responded differently. Bobby's tactics of drop-n-ditch and duck-n-avoid weren't going to work with Marilyn. [55]

In fact, Bobby had promised her he would be there that weekend at the Cal-Neva. George Carpozi, Jr. related, "Peter Lawford picks her up and he says to her, 'I got word to Bobby that you got rid of the baby and he's going to be here next weekend. Do you want to see him?' and she says, 'Boy, do I!' " Breaking his promise, she was furious. The next few days were nothing but disaster for Marilyn.

Photographer William Woodfield told Anthony Summers that shortly after Marilyn's last weekend at Cal-Neva, Frank Sinatra gave him a roll of film to process. These pictures had been taken with Sinatra's camera without his knowledge and he wanted to see what was on the film. Woodfield recalled, "I developed the film and some of the pictures, about nine frames, showed Marilyn, on all fours. She looked sick. Astride her, either riding her like a horse or trying to help her up – I couldn't make out which – was Sam Giancana… Frank asked me what I thought he should do with the pictures. I said I'd burn them. He took out his lighter, burned them, and that was the end of it." By most accounts, Sam Giancana was fully clothed and trying to help Marilyn up off the floor. If Sam Giancana did not have sex with Marilyn then what really happened?

Joe DiMaggio found out from Fred Otash that Marilyn was at the Cal-Neva that weekend. After querying Bell Captain Ray Langford, in general, DiMaggio restricted himself to the perimeters of the Lodge. A Cal-Neva employee remembered Marilyn's gaze up a hill and DiMaggio looking right back at her. Ralph Roberts related to Anthony Summers, "She told me it was a nightmare, a dreadful weekend. She said she didn't want to go particularly and when she got there she found Joe there. She couldn't go out of her room without the conflict of Sinatra. Joe was terribly jealous of Sinatra."

Sinatra's valet George Jacobs relayed, "Because Johnny Rosselli was also there that weekend, there was talk of an S&M Mafia orgy to teach Marilyn a lesson for bestowing her famous favors on the Kennedys. She was *their* girl, not those Micks'. But I was the one who drove Marilyn to the plane that would take her back to L.A. In the car, the thing that bothered her most was that her drugged-out behavior had offended the strait-laced Mr. Sam, who was united with Mr. S in a hatred of drugs (this despite the mob's supposedly making a fortune in the narcotics trade). Marilyn had total respect for Sam, and he always treated her like a lady. That was his Old World style. To her Sam was no fearsome killer figure but a statesman of his own peculiar country. She liked him a lot."

Keith Badman described a similar scenario, "Before the night was over… Sinatra was discreetly handed a roll of film… Within minutes Sinatra was reeling in shock at nine freshly processed images of a semi-unconscious Marilyn, in complete disarray, being sexually fondled in the presence of mobsters [John] Rosselli and [Paul 'Skinny'] D'Amato. Reports soon came to light claiming that Sam Giancana was seen in one of the pictures. But, considering how respectful he was of the actress, I suspect he was an innocent bystander in the proceedings and was seen only at the tail end of the incident, attempting to haul Marilyn up off the floor. Sinatra immediately ordered the pictures and negatives to be destroyed." However, one of the nine pictures did survive. Badman noted, "One image was dispatched to Dorothy Kilgallen." On August 3, 1962, Kilgallen wrote in her column:

> Marilyn Monroe's health must be improving. She's been attending select Hollywood parties and has become the talk of the town again. In California, they're circulating a photograph of her that certainly isn't as bare as the famous calendar, but is very interesting. Marilyn's dress looks as if it was plastered to her skin and the skirt is hitched higher above the knees than any Paris designer would dare to promote in the fall showings. And she's cooking in the sex-appeal department, too; she's proved vastly alluring to a handsome gentleman who is a bigger name than Joe DiMaggio in his heyday. So don't write off Marilyn as finished.

Otash confidant Raymond Strait saw the same picture, "She was kind of sprawled out like she passed out. She had her clothes on but her dress was up. It was white. A couple of guys were trying to lift her up. I saw that a long time ago. Fred showed me that." Even though the two were known to be on friendly terms with the actress, it is this biographer's conclusion that Paul "Skinny" D'Amato and Johnny Rosselli raped Marilyn Monroe once she became unconscious.

In addition, through the nine photographs, Sinatra found out about the incident with D'Amato and Rosselli *after* he and Peter had helped her through

Jay Margolis

another sleeping pill overdose. The night following the rape, Marilyn nearly overdosed. Ignorant of what had transpired the evening before, Sinatra was instead disgusted by her excessive use of drugs and he didn't want her on the premises any longer. Sinatra told Marilyn to leave. She left. As much as he loved her, she was becoming quite a liability.

Skinny D'Amato met Joe DiMaggio for the first time in nearly 20 years after a falling out. Biographer Jonathan Van Meter wrote, "In New Jersey, Jimmie McCullough, the publicist for the 500 Club, was honored with the Super Sportsman Award at the Atlantic City Country Club for having attended every game of fifty-three consecutive World Series. Joe DiMaggio and Monte Irvin were the guest speakers. Skinny and Joe, estranged for seventeen years, were reunited that evening, and Joe finally forgave Skinny for the disastrous Marilyn Monroe weekend at Cal-Neva." [56]

✓ Pills, Pills, and More Pills

Gloria Romanoff was familiar with Marilyn's nightly routine, "Typically, Marilyn started taking pills at about eight o'clock. She'd time it. Eight o'clock. Nine o'clock. Ten o'clock. Eleven o'clock she was gone for the evening. Everyone thinking they were going to have a late night and she was just gone because she had gone to sleep." The incident with Rosselli and D'Amato humiliated Marilyn to the point where she did almost overdose that weekend but was miraculously saved at the last minute. On the night of July 28, Marilyn began taking more sleeping pills than usual. Before midnight, after hearing labored breathing coming from a phone line connected to the main switchboard, Frank Sinatra and Peter Lawford broke down the door to Chalet 52 and found Marilyn lying naked on the floor.

A member of the Cal-Neva kitchen staff, Ted Stephens related to Sinatra biographer Taraborrelli, "All I know is this: We got this call from Peter Lawford. 'We need coffee in Chalet 52,' he screamed into the phone, then hung up. He sounded frantic. No less than two minutes passed and it was Mr. Sinatra on the phone screaming, 'Where's that goddamn coffee?' I learned later that they were in 52, walking Marilyn around, trying to get her to wake up."

Frank Sinatra hated "Brother-in-Lawford" as he used to chide him but put up with him that weekend at Cal-Neva because he knew Peter was Marilyn's friend. An anonymous confidant reflected that Sinatra "had deep feelings for her, which is why she was there. Lawford was with her. However, Sinatra

104

ignored him and refused to have anything to do with him. The only reason he even allowed him on the premises was because he felt Lawford could help Marilyn, that she trusted him. He was willing to suppress his animosity for Peter if it meant helping Marilyn. He told me, 'I care about this woman more than she cares about herself.' I think she reminded him of what he had been with Ava, self-destructive."

When Bobby Kennedy failed to show at the Cal-Neva as promised, Marilyn resumed her threats to go public. The first of the two flights aboard Sinatra's private plane took Marilyn, Peter and his wife Pat to San Francisco where Pat took a regular plane back East. On the second flight, Peter and Marilyn returned to Los Angeles sometime after midnight. Peter got a ride from the pilot while Marilyn took a limousine back to her residence.

In his car, the pilot became irritated when Peter insisted on stopping at a pay phone for thirty minutes. Afraid that his own home had been bugged, Peter informed Bobby Kennedy over the public phone that Marilyn Monroe intended to live up to that press conference. She would not only reveal what was in her diary, she would also play for reporters taped phone conversations with herself and the Attorney General. Studio maid Hazel Washington told Brown and Barham that Bobby Kennedy would often call Marilyn and it was like "making love over the phone. And I do mean making love." [57]

Keya Morgan and the Million-Dollar Marilyn Monroe Sex Tape

Memorabilia collector and documentary filmmaker Keya Morgan brokered the sale of a Marilyn Monroe oral sex tape on April 14, 2008. The sale was made for $1.5 million to a New York businessman who has wished to remain anonymous. While conducting interviews and research with police, CIA, and FBI agents for his upcoming documentary, *Marilyn Monroe: Murder on Fifth Helena Drive*, Morgan said an agent led him to the sex tape.

The original film was in the hands of the son of a former informant working for the FBI. Morgan acted as intermediary for the sale to the New York businessman. On April 15, 2008, Keya Morgan appeared in a CBS News article entitled "Marilyn Monroe Sex Film Is 'Graphic,' Someone Who's Seen It Addresses Speculation Man In It Was A Kennedy." Morgan claimed that the male in the oral sex video may be either Jack or Bobby Kennedy.

In another interview for MSNBC, Keya Morgan told Dan Abrams that he doesn't know who the male on the tape is and that J. Edgar Hoover was obsessed with finding out. Morgan relayed, "I am producing a documentary

Jay Margolis

about Marilyn Monroe. I have interviewed many police officials. My documentary will prove once and for all that she was murdered and that there was a massive cover-up... I interviewed an FBI agent who was sitting outside of Marilyn's home on the night she died, was murdered, and he told me about it. First time he told me about it, I didn't believe it. It was very hard for me to believe. I thought he's embellishing this story to make it sound more interesting... I looked into it. Under Freedom of Informations Act, I pulled up the documents from the FBI. I had my lawyer work on it. We pulled up several pages that verified many of the things the FBI agent was saying like the involvement of –"

Dan Abrams interrupted Morgan at this point and after asking if Morgan's seen the tape, Abrams then asked, "In the most sanitized version, tell us what's on the tape." Morgan recalled, "The tape is around fifteen minutes long. There's no audio. It's black-and-white. You can see Marilyn Monroe, how do you put it, according to the FBI documents, performing a perverted act. In today's standards, you would say she's giving him oral sex. You cannot see the man's head at any time... It's from the neck and below."

Abrams next asked, "How do you know it's her?" Morgan relayed, "I know 100 percent it's her. First of all, it was verified by the FBI agent. And many other agents. Nine agents back then in the sixties. Second of all, Joe DiMaggio saw it and he verified its authenticity and he offered $25,000 back then. Now, Joe DiMaggio is no fool. Everyone tries to dupe him back then but he's not gonna get duped and then I saw it. It's 100 percent Marilyn Monroe. She has the mole, the hair, everything else. And the FBI agents. J. Edgar Hoover himself was completely fascinated by it."

Dan Abrams said, "Let me read from the FBI file. Letter to J. Edgar Hoover in 65: 'While in his office, the name blacked-out ran an 8 or 16 mm "French-type" movie which depicted Marilyn Monroe, deceased actress, in unnatural acts with an unknown male.' " Morgan conceded, "I don't know who the man is. J. Edgar Hoover was obsessed with trying to determine if that was JFK or not. There's a lot of crazy stories about that. He brought in prostitutes who allegedly had been with President Kennedy and tried to have them verify his phallus which is pretty bizarre." [58]

The male on the tape was Bobby Kennedy. Renowned lawyer Clark Clifford was chairman of the foreign intelligence advisory committee under President Kennedy. During the first month of 1966, J. Edgar Hoover rang Clifford who was now working for President Johnson. Heymann said Clifford was invited into Hoover's office to watch "a silent... black-and-white film showing deceased actress Marilyn Monroe committing a sexual act upon a man whose face was just out of range of the camera." Clifford told Heymann, "There was no question in my mind that the woman on her knees performing fellatio was Marilyn Monroe. I had no idea as to the identity of her partner."

Clifford explained that Hoover had said to him he was certain the man on the tape was Bobby Kennedy because she was not seeing Jack at that time. In 1965, a former Hoffa aide gave the tape to the FBI and now Hoover had his hands on it. As recollected by Clifford, the exchange between Hoover and Clifford was as follows:

> HOOVER: My guess is that Hoffa meant to blackmail Robert Kennedy in order to get the Justice Department off his back. We also know that Joe DiMaggio offered Hoffa a large sum of money for the film, but the transaction never took place. I called you in because I thought you might want to discuss the matter with your friend, President Johnson.
>
> CLIFFORD: What does Lyndon Johnson have to do with it? Even assuming it's Robert Kennedy in the film, why would the President want to become involved?
>
> HOOVER: I'm not sure. All I know is that the President has his own grievances against Senator Kennedy. He ought to be apprised of the film's existence, don't you think?

Clifford then told Heymann that during a Manhattan party the former First Lady suddenly approached him, "At one point in the evening, Jackie took me aside. She looked me straight in the eye and asked if I knew anything about a 'certain film' involving Marilyn Monroe and Bobby Kennedy engaging in a sexual act. I have no idea how she'd gotten wind of it or if she knew that J. Edgar Hoover had shown me the film. I imagine she had her spies throughout Washington, and very little escaped her scrutiny. In any case, I wasn't going to implicate myself in the affair. I told her I knew nothing about it. I don't think she fully believed me, but she let it slide, and we returned to the dinner table. She never brought it up to me again, and I have no specific knowledge of what became of the film."

What then happened to the other sound recordings on Marilyn Monroe and Bobby Kennedy, including those running during Marilyn's last night? On December 15, 1966, the District Attorney's Office in New York took possession of notorious wiretapper Bernie Spindel's tapes. Three days later, Spindel relayed to *World Journal Tribune* that the government raiders had stolen "my confidential file containing tapes and evidence concerning circumstances surrounding, and the causes of the death of Marilyn Monroe, which material strongly suggests that the officially reported circumstances of her demise are erroneous."

Government officials later claimed no such material existed on the confiscated tapes. Even though Spindel lost his recordings for the day of August 4, Fred Otash slyly evaded authorities threatening to confiscate his copy of the same material by allowing close friends to store the tapes in their homes until his death in 1992.

A close friend of his since the early 1970s, Raymond Strait was someone Otash could trust. In 1976, he gave Strait a sealed box with eleven hours of tapes recorded the last day of Marilyn Monroe's life, including what transpired during her death. Otash never said what was in the box and Strait never opened it. Ten years later, Otash told him to bring the box one night to his place. Together in Palm Springs, they listened to all eleven hours.

Strait confirmed for me that "the circumstances of her demise" were "erroneous" to use Spindel's words. Clark Clifford agreed the Mafia did in fact have compromising material on the Kennedys and that it was not simply a bluff by surveillance expert Bernie Spindel. [59]

What Reason Would Greenson Have for Killing His Patient?

Besides the exposure of a sexual affair that would obliterate his already burgeoning psychoanalytic career, Dr. Ralph Greenson had an alternative motive. Apparently, Greenson was at his wits end treating his star patient. Weeks after her death, he would later complain to his friend and colleague Dr. Marianne Kris that he was becoming a victim of countertransference while treating Marilyn Monroe. Greenson explained that countertransference "is an inappropriate reaction of the therapist to his patient." An analyst's "difficulty with empathy disrupts their timing and dosage of interpretation so that their interventions feel tactless and inaccurate. They have great difficulty in keeping their patients in treatment.

"Usually these analysts have patients who are predominately masochistic... These analyses go on interminably, usually seven years or more, and are interrupted only by some external event... Anger, sexual feelings, boredom, sleepiness, restlessness and uncontrollable laughter" on the part of the analyst "are all indications of the possibility of countertransference... One of the most frequent signals of countertransference reaction is the analyst's reaction to the patient's transference feelings or behavior. Finding oneself unduly enjoying the positive transference or reacting sexually or narcissistically to the transference manifestations may be an indication of a countertransference reaction."

According to Greenson, all people have transferences. However, in the analytic session, a transference is a patient's "experiencing of feelings, drives, attitudes, fantasies, and defenses toward a person in the present" such as the analyst "which do not befit that person but are a repetition of reactions originating in regard to significant persons of early childhood, unconsciously displaced onto figures in the present."

Greenson wrote about the maddening frustrations he experienced while treating his star patient, "If I behaved in a way which hurt her she reacted as though it was the end of the world and could not rest until peace had been re-established, but peace could be reconciliation and death. As a consequence I became aware that any negative transference required instant handling, with the result that she would call me at all hours of day and night, whenever any negative transference cropped up.

"I saw her 7 days a week because she was terribly lonely, the more so as she began to get rid of a lot of people around her who only took advantage of her." Strangely, Greenson decided who was taking advantage. He told Marilyn she should try to make friends outside the people she worked with at the studio.

After he saw little or no improvement in his patient, Greenson even questioned his own method with her, "I have some misgivings about how correct was I in my form of treatment and how much was I being led by countertransference feelings," which, according to Greenson, are "inappropriate reaction[s] of the therapist to his patient."

I mentioned to Gloria Romanoff these comments made by Greenson on Marilyn and she said, "He's a real prize. He couldn't even be gracious. He had every right to withdraw from the case." Perhaps his ego wouldn't allow him to do that. However, after Marilyn's death, Greenson took on other patients and continued to see them even if he knew countertransference feelings were present within him while treating them.

Money was more important than referring a patient to another therapist. The countertransference described in the following case is the therapist's annoyance with his patient. In a letter Greenson penned to his dear friend Anna Freud on September 26, 1975, he refers to his patient Mrs. Lita Hazen who is also their biggest monetary donor. In fact, Mrs. Hazen's estate valued at $200 million in 1986 money or $375 million in 2007 money.

Greenson wrote, "I am slowly but surely getting Mrs. Hazen out of my life. I hope she will continue to support the Anna Freud Archives and the Hampstead Clinic but I can no longer tolerate her possessiveness and I have refused to accept any money from her. The moment I do, I am her servant – not her helper. Also, I am moving out of Beverly Hills to a more modest office." Almost a year earlier, on November 19, 1974, Greenson sent a letter to Anna Freud notifying her that Mrs. Hazen had cut a check for $10,000, which is equivalent to $42,000 in 2007 money.

Interestingly, when Anna Freud was in need of clients who would support the Hampstead Clinic, a source suddenly and unexpectedly surfaced. Biographer Elisabeth Young-Bruehl wrote, "No millionaires materialized, but, ironically enough, the Clinic did get a sizable portion of the tardily settled estate of Marilyn Monroe. The actress made the bequest to her New York analyst, Marianne Kris, in a will she had made while she was with her Los Angeles analyst, Romi Greenson… Dr. Kris was instructed to give the money to the charity of her choice, and she chose the Hampstead Clinic… Marilyn Monroe's bequest came to the Hampstead Clinic just while the Clinic was adjusting to the tremendously influential work that Anna Freud had undertaken outside the Clinic – work in which the plight of children, like the young Marilyn Monroe, who had been bounced from one foster home to another, was central." [60]

From several accounts, it is clear Greenson was getting very tired of playing "surrogate father" to Marilyn Monroe. Dr. Robert Litman of the Suicide Prevention Team related, "There was a real washing out of the usual doctor boundaries… I would never suggest that there was anything wrong in the relationship. He virtually adopted a person. There was a danger when someone gets that involved."

On one of Marilyn's free-association tapes, John Miner recalled hearing her say, "Ever since you let me in your home and I met your family, I've thought about how it would be if I were your daughter instead of your patient. I know you couldn't do it while I'm your patient, but after you cure me maybe you could adopt me. Then I'd have the father I've always wanted, and your wife, whom I adore, would be my mother, and your children my brothers and sisters. No, Doctor, I won't push it. But it's beautiful to think about it. I guess you can tell I'm crying. I'll stop now for a little bit." Adding another member to his family was too much for Greenson to handle especially since Marilyn contacted him at all hours, several days a week.

Contrary to what Donald Spoto claimed in his book, the murder rumors did not start with Frank Capell, Norman Mailer, and author Robert Slatzer. On January 5, 1964, the *Oakland Tribune* noted, "Following her death, Dr. Greenson was flooded with mail from haters who denounced him as a 'criminal so-and-so… a Communist quack… a Hollywood murderer.' There were so many threats to his life that Dr. Greenson was compelled to turn them over to his lawyer."

Greenson wrote to Dr. Kris more than two weeks after Marilyn died, "And on top of it all, the notoriety, the press all over the world writing

Marilyn Monroe: A Case for Murder

about it and constantly linking my name with this tragic event, and often so wrongly... I was besieged by phone calls from all over the world. I received many terrible letters from people, accusing me of being a murderer or going after her money." Capell's controversial red pamphlet indeed was released two years *after* the threats to Greenson's life. According to Greenson himself, these threats began within days of Marilyn's death.

Professor Douglas Kirsner ominously noted, "Greenson told his colleagues that he decided to offer his family as a substitute for the family Monroe never had because she would have killed herself sooner if he had committed her to a mental hospital." On August 15, 1962, Greenson penned a letter to Marilyn's poet friend Norman Rosten, "I should have played it safe and put her in a sanitarium, but that would only have been safe for me and deadly for her." Greenson's son Danny agreed that after Payne Whitney, "He felt that therapy as he knew it wasn't working, he couldn't hospitalize her, because everyone came to stare and gawp at her, which was awful, and medication wasn't helping in her case." Milt Ebbins said Greenson "made a statement that Marilyn was doomed and eventually she would've done it anyway."

During the last month of Marilyn's life, Greenson felt she couldn't go one day without a crisis. Even his brother-in-law Mickey Rudin agreed. Rudin, who was Frank Sinatra and Marilyn Monroe's attorney, told Donald Spoto that Greenson's relationship with Marilyn "helped kill him... 'Don't get yourself all emotionally involved.' That should have been a rule for a psychoanalyst but Romi was an unusual man I must tell you. While he was my brother-in-law, my relationship to him was closer than my wife's relationship to him... He involved her *totally* beyond what he should have with the family... he totally involved her where he was worried about her all the time... I loved him dearly. I was concerned about him. He was not in the greatest of health. All of the strain on him."

Rudin complained about the great difficulty Greenson experienced months earlier before departing on May 10, 1962 for his much-anticipated five-week vacation, "When he went to Europe, I was delighted. He needed a week. Some time. Just needed it. There wasn't a crisis just with the picture [*Something's Got to Give*]. There was a crisis every day." Even a year earlier in July 1961 after Marilyn had recovered from gall bladder surgery, Greenson expressed his great frustrations, "I saw her at that time seven days a week, mainly because she was lonely and had no one to see her, nothing to do if I didn't see her."

Rudin said to Taraborrelli, "She could have a crisis over what she was having for lunch, she was that emotional and high-strung. She could have had an imagined crisis." In 1961, Diane Stevens, who worked for publicist John Springer in New York, related one of these imagined crises, "Once, during a late night at the office, we sent out for Chinese food. Marilyn and Joe were there. When the food came, Marilyn refused to eat it. She and Joe got into a big fight about it. 'If it was poisoned, I'd be dead now because I just ate some,' Joe told her. 'So, what the hell is going on with you?' Marilyn looked at him very seriously and said, 'I'm the one they want to poison, Joe. Not you.' "

Another night, Marilyn was having dinner with actress Maureen Stapleton when suddenly Marilyn "thought the waiter was reading her mind. At first, she said he was a secret agent or something, she said, 'He's one of the bad guys,' and then she said, 'He knows what I'm thinking now, we have to leave.' "

Ironically, the sleeping pills often kept Marilyn awake. The drugs would compound both her insomnia and paranoia, acting together to induce a state of unreality. Mickey Rudin reflected to Spoto, "She was terribly paranoid… I knew that her paranoia was such that she would not know the truth from what was her imagination, so as a lawyer, you couldn't work with it… She was not sane. Nobody seems to accept that fact… Marilyn should have been declared incompetent. She was incompetent… Institutionalizing Marilyn would be worse than death. It would be torture to her… She would call me at night with stories that were horrendous about what they did to her on the set. I called [producer and good friend of Greenson's] Henry [Weinstein]. He would tell me what was true and what wasn't true… We pushed him into that position hoping that whatever had to be done to protect Marilyn could be in a sense done by Henry."

Joan Greenson relayed, "She had visions of all kinds of crazy people climbing over her fence, or coming to her door at all times of day or night." Her last publicist Pat Newcomb told Spoto, "She was paranoid… Sometimes the paranoias turn out to be real and sometimes they don't." Producer Henry Weinstein reflected on Greenson's treatment of Marilyn, "He might have been able to keep her propped up. She was a very, very frightened, paranoid person." Spoto told Rudin, "I have her phone records. She called you not only at the office but she called you at home five, six, eight times a day at night constantly." Rudin said, "That's right and I wasn't impatient with her… It was time-consuming as hell. It was a pain in the ass."

I asked press agent Michael Selsman if Marilyn was paranoid, "Well, to the extent that every actor or actress is paranoid because their careers are absolutely perched on the knife's edge. She looks around at age 36 and she sees my wife at the time Carol Lynley. She was 19 and had the next dressing room to her. Then of course, Fox had hired Jayne Mansfield as a threat to Monroe. So every actor is paranoid that they'll never work again. They always think that their last job *is* their last job."

Rudin said to Spoto, "The problem faced with Marilyn having to do the picture is that she needed money. She didn't have any money." Gloria

Marilyn Monroe: A Case for Murder

Romanoff reflected, "She never had any real money. The house she died in was the first home she ever owned. It was a very simple house but it was everything to her. Marilyn was just very genuine. She had so little money and now it pains me that these people who are in charge of her estate are making fortunes, money she could have used."

George Jacobs described Mickey Rudin as a "combination bag man, hit man, and Hollywood hustler." Raymond Strait told me Rudin "was a scumbag and everybody knew it. He was Sinatra's man. Any dirt Sinatra wanted done, the one guy who got his hands dirty was Mickey Rudin." Mickey Rudin's ex-wife Elizabeth Greenschpoon, Greenson's sister, who played the cello in Ella Fitzgerald's band and knew Sinatra since the early 1950s, relayed to biographer Kitty Kelley how unscrupulous Rudin was, "I've known Frank a long time. He was a patient of my brother, who was a psychiatrist – Dr. Ralph Greenson… Mickey always left the house to find a pay phone to talk to Frank about certain things. When we got divorced, I found out that Mickey had put everything in my name, including Jilly's restaurant and Frank's house in Palm Springs. I had to sign about forty quit claims and that's when I decided to take back my maiden name so Mickey couldn't borrow against any of my property or use my name for whatever reason." [61]

Mickey Rudin told Spoto why Greenson was so insistent on going on his five-week vacation, "His wife was Swiss. This was an annual pilgrimage to her family. He'd probably beat his head if he didn't. How much exhaustion can a man who had a coronary condition take?" In a 1974 paper termed "On Transitional Objects and Transference," which was compiled along with others in his 1978 book called *Explorations in Psychoanalysis*, Greenson discussed his frustrations with Marilyn Monroe during the last months of her life.

He wrote what he did before he left for his trip in May, "I told an emotionally immature young woman patient, who had developed a very dependent transference to me, that I was going to attend an International Congress in Europe some three months hence. We worked intensively on the multiple determinants of her clinging dependence, but made only insignificant progress. Then the situation changed dramatically when one day she announced that she had discovered something that would tide her over my absence. It was not some insight, not a new personal relationship, it was a chess piece. The young woman had recently been given a gift of a carved ivory chess set.

"The evening before her announcement, as she looked at the set, through the sparkling light of a glass of champagne, it suddenly struck her that I looked like the white knight of her chess set. The realization immediately evoked in her a feeling of comfort, even triumph. The white knight was her protector, it belonged to her, she could carry it wherever she went, it would look after her, and I could go on my merry way to Europe without having to worry about her… I must confess that despite my misgivings, I also felt some relief. The patient's major concern about the period of my absence was a public performance of great importance to her professionally [President Kennedy's Birthday Gala]. She now felt confident of success because she could conceal her white knight in her handkerchief or scarf; she was certain that he would protect her from nervousness, anxiety or bad luck."

Then on May 10, 1962, Greenson dashed to Europe for a little rest and relaxation before his scheduled lectures. Joan explained, "Father was to give a lecture in Israel for the International Psychoanalytic Society, and from there they planned to visit my mother's family in Switzerland." Greenson wrote that a little more than a week later, "I was relieved and delighted to learn, while in Europe, that her performance had indeed been a smashing success. Shortly thereafter, however, I received several panicky transatlantic telephone calls from her. The patient had lost the white knight and was beside herself with terror and gloom, like a child who has lost her security blanket."

Mrs. Murray remembered, "Marilyn took a handsome chess piece from the set she had bought in Mexico – one knight to wrap in her handkerchief while she sang. A friend [Dr. Greenson] had suggested she take it and pretend he was right there with her to lend her courage. Marilyn took the chessman with her, but lost it somewhere in New York."

Hildi Greenson related, "That vacation we had, it was constant telephone calls. We were in Israel and we got phone calls from Marilyn and from the studio. Finally, when we got to Switzerland, my husband said, 'I promised them I'd come back and we'll save the picture.' That was the idea." Greenson wrote more than two weeks after his patient's death, "I left Marilyn in the hands of a colleague [Milton Wexler] whom she knew and I told her that I would return if it was necessary. As you know, after three weeks my colleague called me, and finally she called me, and I returned to Los Angeles [late on the night of June 6]. She was depressed, but within 24 hours of my return she had bounced up again and I reported to the movie studio that she would return to work within 48 hours. They, however, in their fury at Elizabeth Taylor, decided to fire Marilyn, which they did."

As for June 2, Joan relayed, "Danny and I did get a call after her birthday. She had sounded really druggy. Her thick-tongued-ness usually was a sign that she had taken lots of sleeping medication but still couldn't sleep… Danny and I went to her house. Her room was dark. The black-out drapes were pulled shut, and not a drop of light was let in. Marilyn was in bed with just a sheet pulled up around her. Her bed looked like she had had a bad night. It was totally disheveled. She asked Danny to come sit next to her bed and talk to her…

"What a sad picture, to have Marilyn in that darkened cave of a room so terribly unhappy. And there seemed that there was little, if anything, anyone could do to help her. What a terrible feeling of helplessness and hopelessness. My father didn't seem to be able to help her. I knew she had been talking to him on the telephone. Nothing seemed to be able to help... She seemed like such a contrast. In a sense she was so childlike herself yet she was so streetwise and suspicious of things and could see the ulterior motives. She'd had such a rotten childhood, and now she had made it and it felt like if there was any fairness in the world, Marilyn should have it easy and good now."

Hildi added, "She was bright and lovely and interesting, but there was something really very schizzy about her." Mrs. Murray relayed, "Marilyn didn't want to interrupt the psychiatrist's trip with her problems. His son had made a point of requesting that Marilyn let him get through the speaking engagement in Switzerland and a side trip to Tel Aviv without calling him home... A Dr. Wexler was on call for Dr. Greenson's patients. When he came out to visit Marilyn, he took one look at the formidable array of sedatives on her bedside table and swept them all into his black bag. To him, they must have seemed a dangerous arsenal."

Joan recalled, "It was clear that there was really no way Marilyn was going to make it through that picture without my father here or without some massive help... Father flew from Switzerland to New York, New York to L.A. He took a cab home. I remember greeting him at about 10 P.M. at the front door. He looked really tired. I took his suitcase into the house, and he found his car keys and went straight to the garage. He said he would just stop by and see Marilyn and would be back shortly."

Greenson continued in his 1974 paper, "A colleague of mine [Milton Wexler] who saw her in that interval said that all his interventions were to no avail and he reluctantly suggested that I cut short my trip and return. I hated to interrupt my vacation and I doubted whether my return would be beneficial. Surprisingly, it was. I no sooner saw her than her anxiety and depression lifted. It then became possible to work... on how she had used me as a good luck charm rather than an analyst. The talisman, the chess piece, served her as a magical means of averting bad luck or evil. It protected her against losing something precious." [62]

By June 22, 1962, Greenson expressed to colleagues and friends that he was fed up with Marilyn Monroe. Greenson wrote a letter to his friend Lucille Ostrow describing in detail how Marilyn Monroe ruined his summer vacation. Greenson complained how he missed professional commitments with his best friend Leo Rosten, producer Dore Schary and even his own publisher in New York. Not only that but when he returned, much to Greenson's chagrin, the studio fired her. Realizing that the end result would have been the same either way, he now viewed his early return home as a tremendous waste of time. During this period, Marilyn was not Greenson's only patient. In fact, in addition to others, he was treating actress Janice Rule months before Marilyn died and even soon after her death by Rule's own account.

On the same date in late June, Greenson complained to Anna Freud and wrote, "I had to interrupt my trip and return home because of the difficulties of one of my patients. Since I returned home she felt much better and was able to resume work. Nevertheless, the studio fired her the day after I returned for a variety of other reasons. This was a most frustrating experience, since now I was back home and she was feeling fine, but she no longer had to work and therefore I was free to return to Europe, which was impossible." On July 2, 1962, Freud replied, "I have tried to follow your fate in the newspapers and I saw that your patient was acting up. But I did not realize that this would interrupt your holiday and I do feel sorry for this. I wonder what will happen to her and with her. There must be something very nice about her from what I understood from Marianne Kris." Marilyn Monroe was a constant form of gossip among the world's leading psychoanalysts.

Per the Freud family maid, Paula Fichtl, Anna Freud briefly treated Marilyn Monroe. During the shooting of *The Prince and the Showgirl* in 1956, Freud actually spent a few days with the most famous woman in the world:

> For one week, Marilyn Monroe didn't show up for shooting. No one knew where she was. Daily, she rode her car to Maresfield Gardens [Anna Freud Centre] where she disappeared into Anna Freud's consulting room.
>
> Anna Freud took her to the nursery of the hospital. Here Monroe was relaxed, joking and playing with the kids. She was immensely impressed by the work of Anna Freud… Freud noted that Monroe had a tendency to exaggerate. She is "emotionally unstable, impulsive, cannot bear being alone, and is prone to depression and rejection; a paranoid schizophrenic with withdrawal symptoms."
>
> Anna Freud played a game of marbles with Marilyn Monroe. At a table, the two faced each other, a few glass balls between them. The analyst waited to see what she would do with the marbles. Monroe rolled one ball after Anna Freud's. Freud's interpretation: "desire for sexual contact." In fact, her next analyst [Greenson] will attest to Marilyn's "homophobia": fear of same-sex attractions.

He is the last person to phone the night of her death. Later it is even claimed that he had killed Marilyn Monroe. In 1985, the Swiss newspaper "Blick," which reprinted this allegation was sentenced to a fine – of which 10.000 Swiss francs went to the Anna Freud Centre in London.

Hildi Greenson reflected to Cathy Griffin, "That felt very good, winning my suit." "That was the story that she was shot in the heart?" "Yeah, and they had to pay and I sent it to the Anna Freud Clinic in London. They had to give $20,000 to them, and they had to pay me for my lawyers in Switzerland and the lawyer here, and I think I came out with the travel fare for going to Switzerland to be there at the trial." [63]

Was Greenson Obsessed with Marilyn Monroe?

Hildi Greenson welcomed her husband's idea to allow Marilyn Monroe into their home. But according to her, it was not all fun and games. Hildi relayed, "You always treaded on eggshells with Marilyn. You always had to be careful about what you'd say and how you'd say it." Greenson's son Danny conceded, "Until she came along he was assiduous in not saying anything about who his patients were. She was the only person I ever met who was in treatment with him at the same time. It was very much a thought-through process – to have her hang out with us – and we'd do things together and go places."

Joan wrote, "I glanced at my watch. It was almost time. I hastened to the curtained window and peered out. I knew any minute that the long black car would pull into the driveway which curved around the house. The scene had become a familiar one – one that was repeated almost daily." She remembers what it was like when she first met Marilyn Monroe, "Out of the car emerged a petite girl, her blond hair wrapped in a scarf. She all but almost disappeared into a huge black fur coat. Peeking out from under the coat were black, shiny silk pants and flat shoes. I couldn't really see her face clearly, but she seemed to wear no makeup." Greenson's friend author Leo Rosten said, "Romi was furious with me because I didn't want to come down and meet her. I just stayed upstairs in Danny's room."

Pat Newcomb relayed to Spoto that Greenson "was always on her side against everybody else… She let herself get really involved with his children and his family. Therapists I know didn't do that… Even then, I didn't know anybody who had that relationship and then to send Mrs. Murray down to Mexico with her… I can understand if she was in that much trouble. I mean it was like spying."

Greenson's alarmingly possessive nature would be in full bloom when Marilyn's hairstylist Sydney Guilaroff visited her home one day shortly after Marilyn had been fired on June 8. Guilaroff observed, "She crossed the lawn with some difficulty, leaning on a dour middle-aged man. When she introduced him as Dr. Ralph Greenson, I moved up to get a better look. His gaze was withering, betraying a deep hatred for me. His resentment became almost violent when Marilyn threw her arms around me." Eventually pulling her away from Guilaroff, Greenson snapped at Marilyn as they returned to the house, "You're under treatment with me. You must never see this man again." It was the last time Guilaroff would see her alive.

As for all of Marilyn's so-called advisors, Gloria Romanoff sadly reflected, "She wasn't deceptive with people. She was almost childlike in that respect and as a result, many people took advantage of her. Fame comes quickly. Her first instinct always was to think well of people and to think in a kind fashion about most people." Greenson told Zolotow in October 1973, "She was afraid of people… She was still a waif. She was still, inside her, the rejected orphan girl of her childhood. She needed supportive therapy rather than deep psychoanalysis until her ego was built up. She had never had a real home and known any continuing family life. She had never fully grown up emotionally."

Greenson wrote to a colleague, "I suggested to her that she look for a little house which she could buy so that she could have a place of her own, a piece of ground which was hers and she could therefore stop being an orphan and a waif and homeless. Slowly this idea began to be more appealing to her and the biggest spurt in her treatment came when she began to furnish such a house which in many ways was similar to mine… so that after a few months I was able to say to her some time in January that she was now well enough to go back to having just a regular session with me and she did not need to spend all that extra time at my home."

Hildi Greenson said that her husband "thought she was a waif who needed a home… She would tell me that she liked to help in the kitchen, which she did. She liked peeling potatoes. She liked doing the dishes. She said, 'That I'm good at. I had to do it in the foster homes all the time…' She would have no plans whatsoever for an evening." Joan wrote, "After the dishes were done, Marilyn usually went home. The task of driving her home fell to either my mother or me. She had once told me that people would run into her on purpose, just to meet her. I learned to believe her…

Marilyn Monroe: A Case for Murder

"One evening in driving her home, I needed gas, and I pulled into a gas station in my little Hellman. I suddenly began to realize that we were getting lots of help with the car: one person was pumping gas, one checking the hood, two were washing the windows – they were all staring at us. I know they didn't know who was in the car sitting next to me. She had on her usual outfit: a scarf on her head, over her hair, tied under her chin, a sporty car coat of black mink, pants, and flats. She had on no makeup at all... There was almost something animalistic in the way they took care of the car. I found myself getting a little worried and scared... Somehow there was an aura about her."

Joan reflected to Chris Turner, "It was a two-way street. It was sort of like having a very bizarre sister that I never had. It was always complex – partly because she was complex, her moods up and down, but also because of her fame: everything became complicated." Joan wrote, "Whenever Marilyn had feelings about a subject, it was always with a great deal of intensity... Her intensity of feelings made it at times difficult to have discussions. She liked to have everything black or white, right or wrong, good or bad. It was very hard for her to see, at times, all sides to a question."

Hildi told Cathy Griffin, "I was awfully sorry for her in many, many ways. She had an intensity in every direction. If she felt angry about something she would pound her chest. You heard it like a drum when she did it... She was a person of many moods and it could be that one day, the mood was very good and another time you had a feeling that she wasn't paying much attention to you. She'd be very preoccupied with herself. You could see these changes in mood but I wouldn't say that I could see her getting better or worse.

"Marilyn considered herself a liberal... She wanted to learn a great deal and had very little background to go on. She had a curious mind... Marilyn wanted to be pals with Joanie, to sort of adopt her as a younger sister. She was very charming and of course it delighted my daughter... Marilyn loved our house and since Eunice Murray had built it, she came in very handy. They went house-hunting together and Eunice went with her to Mexico and they bought tile because they wanted tile like in this house."

Studying the psychological problems of famous people fascinated Greenson. Other famous patients of his included Tony Curtis, Peter Lorre, Celeste Holm, Vincente Minnelli, Vivien Leigh, Mario Lanza, Kim Stanley, Oscar Levant, Janice Rule, and the aforementioned Inger Stevens. On the advice of his brother-in-law and best friend Mickey Rudin, Greenson took on Frank Sinatra as a patient in 1953. Greenson began treating him for a time after Sinatra reportedly attempted to commit suicide following his break-up with actress Ava Gardner, which devastated him. Later, Sinatra was immediately alleviated from his insecurities when he won his only Oscar for *From Here to Eternity*. Subsequently, he curtailed his therapy.

While treating the most famous patients, Greenson became obsessed with their problems. His colleague and best friend Milton Wexler remembered, "Greenson himself was a dramatic individual and undoubtedly would have made a splendid actor. He was intelligent, extremely articulate, almost a spellbinder on the platform. None of the tenets of psychology, psychiatry, psychoanalysis, even of ordinary social relationships were sacred to him.

"He questioned everything, dared everything, violated whatever rule displeased him and attracted many fascinating people to his side where he would ignore any social convention and run the ship his own way." Professor Kirsner noted that Greenson followed none of the principles in his 1967 book while treating Marilyn Monroe. On her father's unorthodox methods, Joan Greenson reflected, "It may have been foolhardy but he was willing to take a risk." [64]

Greenson simultaneously found Marilyn "pathetic" and "delightful" to use his own words from a letter to a colleague, "First of all she was a patient and I felt responsible for her. Then she was so pathetic, such a perpetual orphan that I felt even sorrier and she tried so hard and failed so often, which also made her pathetic... but there was something very lovable about this girl and we all cared about her and she could be delightful." Milton Wexler claimed he introduced Greenson to the idea of inviting Marilyn over to meet his wife and children. After a few meetings, Wexler asserted she was a borderline paranoid schizophrenic.

Wexler told Taraborrelli, "One misconception about her treatment is that it was Dr. Greenson's idea that she move in with his family. She never moved in with the Greensons. Instead, it was my suggestion that she spend as much time there as possible in order to create the environment that she lacked as a child... Also, I felt it would alleviate her separation anxiety if she knew she had a place to return to." Greenson's son Danny related, "My father's heart was in the right place, but his mind wasn't. I think he was backed into a corner and he couldn't give up on the idea that he could help her, but then the whole thing came down. The fact is, it didn't work. I mean, she killed herself."

Greenson became so enamored with the life of Marilyn Monroe that he lost all discretion with her. He once told his producer friend Henry Weinstein, "Don't you pay any attention to these fantasies of hers. She has a lot of them – one that is a typical fantasy of girls, for example, is that they want to go to bed with their fathers. That was her fantasy." She may have had this fantasy because she never met her father Charles Stanley Gifford. He worked as a film cutter at Consolidated along with her mother Gladys who at that time was a very attractive woman. Gifford would not recognize Marilyn Monroe as his offspring during her lifetime.

Before he died in 1965, his minister Dr. Donald Liden remembered that

Gifford had said to him, "My daughter was Marilyn Monroe." Liden relayed, "My jaw dropped. But I didn't doubt the truth of it. He said that he felt the mother had been unfair. She had cut him off and didn't allow him to see the child. When he married again, it got difficult. His wife was a fine woman and he didn't want to hurt her by acknowledging he'd had a child out of wedlock. I detected it was a sorrowful thing for him."

Leo Rosten was the author of the 1956 book *Captain Newman, M.D.* based on Greenson's own World War II experiences in a convalescent hospital. As his best friend, Greenson couldn't help but tell Rosten all about the different patients; hence the book. In fact, *Captain Newman, M.D.* later became a hit movie in 1963.

Gregory Peck played the Greenson role under the name Newman. Greenson himself removed his name entirely from the credits for fear that one of his patients would sue him for portraying them onscreen. Singer Bobby Darin received a Best Supporting Actor Oscar Nomination for playing Gregory Peck's colorful patient. The film itself also earned two additional Oscar Nominations, including Best Adapted Screenplay.

Rosten related, "I would bring him to dinner parties, and he began to get patients among the movie people. Greenson was a remarkable storyteller – a real ham – and he would describe his cases in great detail. As an analyst he had to keep quiet all day, and that frustrated him. Soon he was telling his stories all over Hollywood." Greenson was not a man known for his discretion. [65]

When he returned early from his summer vacation on June 6, Greenson realized he couldn't escape the deep countertransference that had engulfed him while treating Marilyn Monroe. He told a colleague more than two weeks after Marilyn died, "I had become a prisoner now of a form of treatment which I thought was correct for her but almost impossible for me… I was her therapist, the good father who would not disappoint her and who would bring her insights, and if not insights, just kindness. She was making progress, but at times I felt I couldn't go on with this, particularly since so often it became 6 or 7 days a week. Yet by this time I had become the most important person in her life and there was nothing I could do except hope that as she improved still more she would become more independent. I also felt guilty that I put a burden on my own family."

If Peter Lawford is correct, Greenson participated in the conspiracy of three to murder Marilyn Monroe. Greenson would later tell his family he thought his patient's death was a suicide but that it had been an "accident." Danny Greenson relayed, "Marilyn was dead when my father arrived at her house. He felt so awful that a patient of his killed herself. It really hurt him terribly on a personal level." Yet Noguchi relayed that the 64 pills Marilyn allegedly took were "too many to swallow 'accidentally.' " In addition,

Greenson told several people including colleagues, reporters, and the Suicide Prevention Team that one of his primary goals was to reduce Marilyn's intake of drugs in the last two months. Had this been true, her primary physician Engelberg would've known about the plan as well. [66]

Did Greenson Have a Sexual Affair with His Patient?

Marilyn Monroe didn't believe in monogamy. As a letter to Greenson proved dated March 2, 1961, she was simultaneously carrying on trysts with Frank Sinatra and her former co-star Yves Montand, a French actor, although according to Marilyn, Montand eventually begged off. Hildi Greenson addressed the rumors that her husband had bedded his star patient, "It's just ludicrous. It's so dumb." But Peter Lawford said Greenson *was* sleeping with her. This is something Peter claimed he didn't know until after Marilyn's death when he heard Mafia-Teamster tapes and listened to "sounds of their lovemaking." If this is true, one of the places where Marilyn and Greenson had sex was in her home.

John Miner once tested private investigator Cathy Griffin. After getting to know her, he asked, "Do you think Marilyn Monroe was having an affair with Dr. Greenson?" "Yes, I do." "You're a bright lady." This encounter and many others led Jeanne and C. David Heymann to conclude, "According to Griffin, there may well have been a sexual relationship between Marilyn and Dr. Greenson and this information may be on tapes. Griffin revealed that she had become friendly with John Miner… Griffin indicated that with further meetings with Miner, she could elicit further information from Miner regarding tapes. There was also the inference that Greenson's daughter Joan didn't want to release the tapes during her mother's lifetime – her mother is about 80 – because they would embarrass her in so far as they would reveal a sexual relationship with Marilyn… Tony Summers wasn't even able to get out of Joan Greenson the fact that there had been tapes made by Marilyn Monroe."

Ralph Roberts related to John Gilmore that Greenson "was having her get rid of people who loved her and were devoted to her. No one sees a psychiatrist for hours and hours at a time and practically lives in the psychiatrist's *home*. It's sick and abnormal. He's a Svengali who's taking Marilyn away from everything so that he'll have her exclusively for himself in a bizarre mental association. It is as if he's getting into her head completely and replacing her will with his own."

Marilyn Monroe: A Case for Murder

Mansfield's press secretary Raymond Strait told me, "Women like that who are very lonesome and feel like they've been abandoned are always trying to find some man that will love them and they think that sex is the way they do it. Nine times out of ten, they're looking for a father image. Jayne Mansfield, same way. She was three years old when her father died of a heart attack. The difference between Jayne and Marilyn is Marilyn was used by men while Jayne used men. Just a reverse."

George Jacobs relayed, "She was the ultimate Girl Who Can't Say No. In view of a deeply unloved childhood, if a man showed interest (it was rarely mere interest; it was usually rabid passion) she was so flattered that she thought it would be terribly rude to turn him down. Marilyn was nothing if not polite." Biographer Barbara Leaming noted how Greenson "recognized that she was painfully alone in the world, and admitted he had a weakness for damsels in distress." But this damsel in particular was the quintessential sexy woman.

Greenson's daughter Joan remembered how everything Marilyn did unconsciously radiated sex like a force in her body. The way she sat was sexy. The way she walked was sexy. Anything she did was sexy. Certain sexual mannerisms had become natural to her. Marilyn gave Joan a risky birthday present. She turned 22 on July 19, 1962. Joan recalled, "I must admit, I don't really remember what everyone gave me, except for Marilyn, because her present stole the show. She gave me the collected works of Arthur Miller, and she inscribed it. She said that I could share with her that part of her life. She also knew I loved the theater.

"But the real show-stopper was the tiny little night gown that she gave me. It was very short, and very sheer, dusty pink lace and lavender chiffon. It was a knock-out. My father's reaction was a knock-out, too. He couldn't believe it. He couldn't believe that anyone would wear it. And above all, he couldn't believe that his daughter would wear it, and that somebody would have given his daughter something like that to wear."

Joan was also intrigued by Marilyn's natural sexiness, "Why was it that no matter what she did she was striking? Why was it that she could just sit still on a bench, or in a chair, and you would end up staring?... There have been many sexy ladies in Hollywood but nothing like Marilyn. I was fascinated to see the way she sat. She would cross her legs at the knees, and lean forward; her left elbow was on top of her knee; her right elbow in the palm of her hand; her chin resting on her right palm.

"This seemed like a very natural and easy pose for her. She often would listen in that position. I had a chance to watch someone move around who was totally at home with their body. And I never tired of watching... Marilyn wore nothing under her clothes. She didn't wear underpants or stockings or bra for the most part. I must admit when I first realized this, I found it shocking. Marilyn really hated to have anything that restricted any of her natural movements... She could also be extremely exhibitionistic."

Greenson once told a candidate in training, "In addition to the problem of motivation in the beginning when you assess the patient, there is the problem of a change in motivation that happens when, for example, the patient develops an acute sexual transference. Now instead of coming for treatment because they want to get rid of symptoms or neurosis, they come out of love for you. Now the reasons a patient is coming is neurosis, schmeurois, it's 'Doctor, I love you, and if you want me to come I'll come, but the hell with this Freud stuff, let's go to the couch,' and they don't mean for free-association. God knows, this happens almost routinely with women patients."

Some of Greenson's colleagues bitterly called him on what seemed like reckless actions on the psychiatrist's part. Dr. Leo Rangell, a rival of Greenson's said, "This was seductive behavior, not therapeutic behavior... We all have very needy, traumatized patients. Very few of them end up in our families the way she did. She did because she was Marilyn Monroe! Even 'family therapy' doesn't mean therapy in the analyst's family... His earlier writings would never condone what he did."

Dr. Melvin Mandel relayed, "If it was true that she came from a tremendously deprived background, you couldn't go on with her in a strictly analytic way. It wouldn't work. I can imagine that's how he perceived it. You can never be sure of one's motivation in such a situation. He liked having people like that around. And maybe she needed it. But how much did he need it too? If an analyst is enthralled with stardom and himself has an unconscious wish to be on stage (and Greenson *was* a superb performer), he may seek to identify himself with prominent people."

In fact, one psychoanalyst Charles William Wahl has seen several cases of countertransference in his practice that involved famous persons and their analysts. Wahl wrote that problems tend to arise in psychoanalysis "if the person of celebrity is a movie personality or a 'sex symbol' of the opposite sex. Here, for the analyst to be especially chosen by such a patient may sometimes initiate in him a sexual countertransference of special puissance" which "can produce an overly-strong oedipal and incestuous transference in the patient."

An analyst often falls into a trap where he "promises more of himself as a personal resource to the patient than he can or should deliver. It is tempting to proffer to such patients, especially those who have had a deprived and alienated childhood, oneself, one's house, one's time, or one's family, as a surrogate resource. It is easy to forget that what can be a gift in friendship, can be a burden or impediment in a therapeutic relationship… No classical transference can develop in such a position of being 'just one of the family.' "

Greenson's friend *New York Times* journalist Lucy Freeman interviewed a psychoanalyst who wrote that Marilyn never really felt beautiful because "only a person who feels loved feels beautiful. Men liked her fragility. That activates all the rescue fantasies of men. It is more attractive than a beautiful body. These are the women who try to seduce their therapists not through desire but their own needs." [67]

Peter Lawford mentioned to Heymann that Marilyn's free-association tapes made for her psychiatrist referenced the affair as well. John Miner heard the following on one of the two tapes he listened to, which is overtly sexual, "What I told you when I first became your patient is true. I had never had an orgasm. I remember well when you said an orgasm happens in the mind, not the genitals… You said an obstacle in my mind prevented me from having an orgasm and that I felt so guilty about something that happened early in my life, I didn't think I deserved to have the greatest pleasure there is. It had to do with something sexual that was very wrong, and my getting pleasure from it caused my guilt. You said it was buried in my unconscious. Through analysis we would bring it to my conscious mind where we could get to the guilt and free me to be orgasmic.

"Well, we sure worked at it and got nowhere. I'd go home and cry and vomit from the frustration. Then you said we'd try a different approach to the orgasm problem: You would tell me how to stimulate myself, and when I did exactly what you told me to do, I would have an orgasm. And after I did it to myself and felt what it was, I would have orgasms with lovers. What a difference a word makes. You said I *would*, not I could. Bless you, Doctor. What you say is gospel to me…

"What wasted years. How can I describe to you, a man, what an orgasm feels like to a woman? I'll try. Think of a light fixture with a rheostat control. As you slowly turn it on, the bulb begins to brighten, then it gets brighter and brighter and finally, in a blinding flash, is fully lit. As you turn it off it gradually becomes dimmer and at last goes out.

"It is so good, Christ, I am doing it now. *(sounds of yipping and moaning for at least two minutes ending in a prolonged ahh)* Wow! You don't mind, do you? You shouldn't. Better than anything, that tells you what you have done for me. Doctor, I worship you." [68]

Marilyn Monroe's aggressively seductive behavior is documented in full bloom in a paper Greenson wrote on January 12, 1964 entitled, "Drugs in the Psychotherapeutic Situation." It is safe to assume Greenson was writing about his star patient in this work because the descriptive characteristics fit her perfectly. He wrote, "Sometimes all that is necessary is time; just waiting without interfering will give the patient the opportunity to recover his reasonable ego. Sometimes it may be necessary to interfere quite drastically, psychologically or even by introducing drugs… For example, an hysterical-depressive-impulsive woman patient became furious with me when she felt I was rejecting her sexual wishes and stormed out of the office. She was an intelligent woman… with a history of promiscuous behavior prior to her unhappy marriage to an austere academician [Arthur Miller]. [69]

"The above incident occurred during the fourth month of her analysis with me… She was impulsive and there was a history of some acting out in her adolescent spitefulness and defiance. Her motivation for treatment had been strong, since she had depressive moods, was sexually frigid, and was unable to work effectively in her job… She did return the following day… She still felt angry about my supposed cruel rejection of her, but by the middle of the hour I was able to work on this material to try to find past events in her life when she felt similarly rejected…

"About one year later, a similar constellation of events occurred, and again she fell into a rage. She refused to work on this but vented her fury on me by silence, nail biting, and leaving the hour early… That evening her husband had to leave her alone to attend a meeting, and she reacted to this unforeseen event as if it were another *maternal rejection*… The pre-oedipal hatred for the mother, which had been stirred up, plus being deserted by her husband unleashed primitive anger, spite, oral sensual desires, and a powerful need to be punished, which she could not contain."

Hildi remembered one time after an analytic session at the Greensons', her husband later learned she had taken in a taxi cab driver, who had driven her home. From March 1962 until her death, Marilyn was living on 12305 Fifth Helena but would occasionally drop by her old apartment on 882 Doheny Drive.

Sinatra's valet George Jacobs who lived in the same apartment complex explained, "Marilyn… was masochistic. She would get fat just to see if men would still like her, just as she would put on black wigs and glasses and go down to the bars on Santa Monica Boulevard, just to see if she could fail to be picked up… 'Nobody even looked at me. Not once all night,' she moaned to me after an abortive bar hop." Greenson said he took action against this self-destructive type of behavior by allowing Marilyn to become one with the family.

She would often join in, politely offering to clean the dishes after supper with the Greensons. Hildi reflected, "My husband said, when he wanted to bring her into the house, 'This is just not a case that one can analyze. She has to work through a great deal more before she can be analyzed.' She needed to become a whole person again." Greenson once told his patient-friend actress

Celeste Holm, "Celeste, this woman has no concept of family life. She was with Marianne Kris for years, but not one thing has touched her. So I'm trying to give her a model. I'm trying to give her some concept of the way it ought to be."

Soon, Marilyn became a member of Greenson's family and at one point, wearing dark glasses, a wig and scarf, joined his son Danny to help him find an apartment while he was going to UCLA. She was even showing up to Greenson's lectures in this disguise as well. Joan wrote, "Father liked to give lectures, and he was an excellent public speaker. He would wait for the last few stragglers and latecomers to settle into their seats. At this moment I looked around, and I saw one of the stragglers was Marilyn in disguise. She looked incredible. She had on a brown, dowdy wig, with a scarf over it, tied under her chin. She had on her sporty mink coat, under which she had this terrible, brown Pucci dress – the color was drab and dead. On her feet, without socks, thank God, were loafers.

"Marilyn sat in the seats just behind Mother and myself. When most of the auditorium was emptying, I watched as Marilyn got up and started to walk out. I watched the faces turn around and follow her with their eyes as she slowly made her way up the aisle. I knew no one recognized her, and only a few close friends of the family knew who that person was. But just her movement up the aisle made people stop and take notice and watch her as she exited. I told her that I thought her disguise was great, and we both thought it was pretty funny."

Hildi recalled, "When we'd have chamber music, my husband would invite her to come and listen. She'd sit in a corner and she'd turn away from the people and the musicians – just listening very intently, all huddled up." Greenson's patient actress Janice Rule became jealous when she learned that Marilyn had been invited to his living room recitals. Janice snidely remarked, "You knew I love music. How come you never invited me?" "You were never that ill." Greenson participated in these recitals albeit as a lousy violinist.

Joan reflected, "She would sit in the living room in the big wing-backed chair. As Mozart, Schubert, or Vivaldi would start to be played, Marilyn would get totally lost and absorbed in the music. Slowly, she would start to move with the music, her arms and her torso. Her eyes would remain closed. Her movements were so beautifully sensual, and so seemingly private and personal." During the spring of 1962, an excited Marilyn invited her poet friend Norman Rosten and his wife Hedda to the Greensons' on several occasions.

Greenson detailed in his 1964 paper what happened when he announced to his star patient that he would have to depart for his European vacation on May 10, 1962. He wrote, "When I left for a five week summer vacation I felt it was indicated to leave her some medication which she might take when she felt depressed and agitated, i.e. rejected and tempted to act out. I prescribed a drug which is a quick acting antidepressant in combination with a sedative, Dexamyl®. I also hoped she would be benefited by having something from me to depend on...

"When I returned she told me that she carried a supply of the tablets with her at all times in a silver pill box, which she had bought especially to hold them. She never became severely depressed during my absence and felt that the possession of the pills had been a safeguard, a magical protection for her in my absence.

"A dream in which the silver pill box turned green just like the pills (that is, *everything turned into Greenson*) seemed to explain the unconscious meaning... *I felt it was indicated to prescribe drugs for her.* I can condense the situation by saying that, at the time of my vacation, I felt she would be unable to bear the depressive anxieties of being alone. The administering of the pill was an attempt to give her something of me to swallow, to take in, so that she could overcome the sense of terrible emptiness that would depress and infuriate her... *Drugs may aid in the interval between visits.*" [70]

Greenson's friend and colleague Milton Wexler conceded that not all meaningful treatments of psychoanalysis are successful, especially the unorthodox ones. Wexler wrote in his book referring to his and Greenson's ideas, "Our own experience and the experience of many well-known psychoanalysts with whom we discussed the issue indicated to us that somehow these magical interpretations, this recovering of the dark secrets of the unconscious, did not seem to produce the wonderful changes promised.

"Over the course of time, Greenson began to write more and more about the importance of the real relationship between the analyst and the patient. He began to emphasize the importance and therapeutic impact of that real relationship. My own thinking went in a somewhat different direction... Once the symptoms were imbedded in that characteristic way of responding to the world, no amount of interpretation, enlightenment or bringing the unconscious into consciousness would do any good."

In Greenson's 1964 paper, he made it clear that Marilyn Monroe tried to come onto him during their first four months of analysis. When he rejected her sexual wishes, she saw it as another rejection and became very angry with him. A year later, she tried to come onto him again and he claimed he rejected her again. The psychiatrist wrote that she "fell into a rage." Peter Lawford said, to his great surprise no less, that Greenson finally succumbed to the seduction of the world's ultimate sex goddess.

Peter told Heymann he heard Mafia-Teamster tapes of Marilyn and Greenson making love. Greenson himself admitted in his writings that she was very seductive and that because of her, he had fallen victim to countertransference. Greenson wrote, "One of the most frequent signals of countertransference reaction is... reacting sexually... to the transference manifestations" of the analysand. In other words, when a therapist has sex with his patient. [71]

Did Marilyn Monroe Keep a Little Red Diary?

Marilyn, a member of SANE (Committee for Sane Nuclear Policy), once told a reporter, "My nightmare is the H-bomb. What's yours?" Marilyn had an interest in learning and tried her best to verse herself on national issues since she was always the first to admit she felt undermined by not completing her high school education at the young age of sixteen. But she read plenty of books and was always buying new ones that caught her attention mainly from classic authors like James Joyce (*Ulysses* in particular as noted by photographer Eve Arnold and subsequently John Miner through Marilyn's two tapes). She enjoyed the poetry of Heinrich Heine. She liked art and once she was reading a book on Goya.

In 1955, Twentieth Century-Fox laughed at Marilyn Monroe when she made known to reporters that she wanted to play the lead role in Dostoyevsky's *The Brothers Karamazov*. She was always quick to deliver some deliciously witty comebacks. When one reporter asked her why she wanted to play *The Brothers Karamazov*, she replied, "I don't want to play the brothers, I want to play Grushenka." Almost immediately, the man snapped, "Spell that name, Grushenka." She quipped, "Look it up." Marilyn wanted to change what she viewed as the general perception of her: "the dumb blonde."

She was no dummy and she was going to prove it to the world since they were always watching her. After analyzing FBI documents, Anthony Summers relayed, "We see clear evidence that she had met with one of the Kennedy brothers in the first week of July and discussed 'the morality of atomic testing...' Anything said by either of the Kennedy brothers... would have been of great interest to either Soviet or Cuban or any Communist intelligence... Marilyn Monroe and her contacts with the Kennedy brothers were perceived as a real security risk... in those crucial weeks right before her death."

Ralph Roberts told Susan Strasberg for her Marilyn Monroe book, "On that last July Fourth, [Bobby] Kennedy was visiting Pat Lawford and Peter, and Paula [Strasberg] was giving a big party at the beach. You were still in

Italy. Marilyn was very torn. She told me, 'I don't know what to do.' She went to the Lawfords'. And though she'd promised your mother she'd come there after, it was just down the beach, she never showed up." Thus, according to the FBI documents discussed by Anthony Summers and the testimonial of Ralph Roberts, we can now place Bobby Kennedy and Marilyn Monroe together at the Lawford home on July 4, 1962.

Fred Otash said the CIA, the FBI, and the Mafia had bugged Marilyn's home as well as Peter's. Thus, when Bobby Kennedy was talking to Marilyn Monroe on that date about "the morality of atomic testing," many were listening in and at this point, without a doubt, Marilyn Monroe was considered a national security risk especially if she had threatened within weeks to "tell all" at a press conference the Monday morning of August 6, 1962.

It had been Joe DiMaggio's idea for Marilyn to write everything down in her little red diary. After Marilyn was murdered, Joe probably felt terrible knowing he suggested she keep the book. DiMaggio's old friend Morris Engelberg related, "Bobby would... call her up every night and tell her what was happening. 'We're getting Giancana: we're getting this one.' Joe was a very funny guy; he wrote everything down. He said to her, 'Write it down in this red book. Just keep track of what he's saying.'"

In his DiMaggio biography, Engelberg explained he learned a lot of this information from DiMaggio's son. Engelberg said Joe Jr. "was willing to disclose what Marilyn had told him about Bobby Kennedy. She said she spoke with RFK three or four times a week, and he told her about the work he was doing... Marilyn would pass on some of those tidbits to Sinatra, according to Joe Jr... Big Joe knew about Marilyn's red-cover diary, and among the first things he did when he arrived at her home was to frantically look for it. He didn't find it... Nothing has been heard about that diary since." Another best friend of DiMaggio's Dr. Rock Positano agreed, "Everything that everybody wants to know was in this little book I called the red diary."

Biographer Richard Ben Cramer provided additional support from a third friend that DiMaggio was well aware of the red diary's existence. Cramer wrote, "Joe and Harry Hall went to Marilyn's house on Fifth Helena Drive... Later, he would complain to Harry that 'her book' was missing. 'It was her personal notes,' as Hall remembered... 'Joe kept looking for her book,' Hall said. 'But it was gone. He was hot about that.'" Then-Deputy Chief Tom Reddin told Brown and Barham, "If you've been intimate with the President and the Attorney General of the United States, as Monroe was, and if you have overheard high-level, sometimes top-secret, conversations – learning things you shouldn't know – what else do you need to be perceived as a threat?... She absolutely could have been in terrible danger."

Deputy Coroner's Aide Lionel Grandison saw Marilyn's diary and flipped through it. He said, "I had an occasion to look through the diary again. And it had some pretty bizarre information in there that no one had spoken about at that time. But I do know that these notations were in that book and I know that book only lasted around the Coroner's Office one day." Mike Rothmiller provided additional corroboration that Marilyn's diary did exist. In 1978, he worked as a detective for the OCID.

At that time, he said he saw a copy of the diary, not the original, in the OCID file rooms where there were stacks of confidential documents that were never publicly released or even known to exist. Rothmiller told Wolfe, "It was more like a journal. The majority of the entries were notes about conversations Marilyn Monroe had with John F. Kennedy and Robert Kennedy. The subject matter ranged from Russia and Cuba to the Mafia and Sinatra. I remember she referred to Castro as 'Fidel C.' "

Had Marilyn gone to the media with her diary on Monday morning, Skinny D'Amato said it would have ruined Bobby Kennedy's reputation. D'Amato told Anthony Summers, "There was more to what happened than anyone has told. It would've been the big fall for Bobby Kennedy, wouldn't it?" Mansfield's press secretary Raymond Strait said to me, as for that last weekend at Cal-Neva, Marilyn had also told Johnny Rosselli about her plans to get back at the Kennedys.

D'Amato who learned this information at the same time relayed that the "big fall" was the press conference where Marilyn would reveal sensitive political information she heard from the brothers. The Kennedys had used her as a sex object and then dumped her like yesterday's trash. Bobby's cavalier attitude more than ever reinforced the image of the dumb blonde and Marilyn's feelings were extremely delicate to start. It was terribly painful for her. She felt helpless and humiliated.

Childishly, she wanted revenge and she wasn't going to allow them to laugh it off and get away with it. Marilyn was going to humiliate them just as they had humiliated her. Her career was at stake and she may have been willing to take down the Kennedy brothers with her. In fact, D'Amato's friend Joe Del Raso relayed, "Skinny told us, way back, right after Jack Kennedy died, that her biggest problem was Bobby, it wasn't Jack. It was Bobby who she really fooled around with. Jack, back in those days, had an eye for Angie Dickinson." Raymond Strait confirmed to me that Jack Kennedy indeed had his sights set on Ms. Dickinson. [72]

Sam Giancana and the "Double Cross"

In 1992, Sam and Chuck Giancana, the godson and half-brother of the notorious Mafia boss Sam Giancana ("Mooney"), released their controversial book *Double Cross*. They said Giancana wanted to have Marilyn killed as a "double cross" against the Kennedys. He felt the Kennedys had crossed him by not getting the FBI off his back. After all, Giancana had helped Jack Kennedy get elected president by stealing critical votes in Illinois. In addition, he helped the Kennedys yet again in his attempts to have Castro killed, albeit a failed mission. The Giancanas wrote, "With Marilyn Monroe, Mooney would show them just how truly vulnerable they were."

The authors claim Robert Aime Maheu, a former FBI agent then covertly working for the CIA, agreed to organize operations to bug Jack and Bobby Kennedy on orders from Sam Giancana himself. They wrote, "For the task of tailing the Attorney General and the President, Mooney selected his CIA coconspirator Bob Maheu, telling him to put together a team of detectives that would eventually include Fred Otash and John Danoff."

Sam Giancana said Maheu was "workin' for our Teamsters' attorney friend Williams." Michael Carlson of the *Guardian* explained how "the legendary Washington fixer Edward Bennett Williams introduced [Maheu] to Johnny Rosselli, the mob's frontman in Las Vegas. Maheu and Rosselli became close friends." Maheu himself said the year of this meeting was 1958. Rosselli's FBI files, referring to a document dated July 13, 1961, read: "Rosselli admitted that he has known Robert Maheu for approximately five years."

Though he was a gangster, Maheu thought Rosselli was a nice and charming man, "All my children fell in love with him. He had that ability to make children feel important." Biographer Larry Hancock said the relationship between the two men lasted even after Jack Kennedy had been assassinated, "The FBI continued to monitor Rosselli during 1964 and 1965. Rosselli in turn connected with his old friend Robert Maheu and brought in Joe Shimon to perform counter bugging and surveillance against the taps on both he and Sam Giancana."

Known to be a confidant of the Kennedys, Robert Maheu helped bug them nevertheless on behalf of Giancana through Rosselli. Maheu then recruited private eye Fred Otash and his assistant John Danoff for the bugging. In the winter of 1990, Otash told Brown and Barham, "It was a game. In fact, I put in one system and, at a crucial point, sent tape copies to three sources – for which, of course, I was paid thrice." Maheu most likely had divided loyalties between the President, the FBI, the CIA, and the Mafia!

When asked by the CIA on orders from the brothers Kennedy to help

Marilyn Monroe: A Case for Murder

overthrow Cuba's Fidel Castro, Maheu contacted Giancana's lieutenant John Rosselli. In the documentary *Say Goodbye to the President*, the narrator said, "The idea that emerged later was for the American Mafia to assassinate Castro on behalf of the CIA. In return, they would get back the Cuban casinos they had run before the Revolution."

However, before organizing negotiations to follow through on the Castro hit, Maheu did a petty favor for Sam Giancana. He helped Giancana bug the home of comedian Dan Rowan to see if Giancana's girlfriend Phyllis McGuire was in fact cheating with Rowan. Carlson wrote, "When Maheu's operatives were caught in the act, they claimed they were worried McGuire would reveal 'national security' secrets about the Castro plan."

Hersh explained, "The case was turned over to the FBI, whose agents were told in late April 1961 that the CIA was working with Sam Giancana and the mob... Sheffield Edwards, director of the CIA's office of security, spent the winter and spring of 1961 – 62 trying to convince the FBI and Justice Department to drop the case and keep what they knew secret." When the case reached Bobby Kennedy, he oddly decided not to prosecute Giancana and those involved in the bugging operation.

Claiming ignorance to his own involvement in hiring gangsters to kill Castro, Kennedy told the CIA's general counsel Lawrence Houston, "I trust that if you ever try to do business with organized crime again – with gangsters – you will let the Attorney General know before you do it." When Giancana finally agreed to help kill Castro, he was paid the surprisingly small sum of $150,000.

From bugs in Marilyn's home he helped install, Fred Otash recorded the activities that occurred during her last hours and the aftermath. Mansfield's press secretary Raymond Strait told me Fred Otash "knew that Giancana's people did it. He knew that. He knew who paid the money. Who held it in escrow and he was paid $100,000 to keep his mouth shut... I know who put up the money, when it was put up, and it was long before he ever became president. Marilyn Monroe just became a circumstantial incident... It could've been Angie Dickinson." Additionally, Strait relayed, "I don't think the FBI was on the site at the time all this stuff happened. They stayed as far away from that as they could get." In his book, Wolfe revealed transcripts from ABC Television's 1985 20/20 program. Broadcast journalist Sylvia Chase interviewed Fred Otash:

> CHASE: Were these tapes recorded at Marilyn's house right up until Marilyn Monroe's death?

OTASH: They were recorded the day of her death – the night of her death.

CHASE: A conversation with Kennedy?

OTASH: A conversation with *Bobby* Kennedy.

CHASE: And what were they talking about?

OTASH: They had a very violent argument. She was saying, "I feel passed around! I feel used! I feel like a piece of meat!"

CHASE: And this conversation took place on the day of her death?

OTASH: That's right.

Afraid for his life by possessing these tapes, Otash discussed with biographer Ted Schwarz only a sanitized version, transcripts of which convinced Schwarz that Marilyn had committed suicide. Raymond Strait however is certain that the eleven hours of tapes he actually listened to prove without a doubt that Marilyn was murdered. Strait told me, "I had all those tapes in my garage in a sealed-up box for ten years... I never opened them. Fred called me one night in Palm Springs and he says, 'You still have that box?' 'Well, of course!' 'You bring it down to the Springs. I want to show you something.'"

Strait told Brown and Barham, "Fred was afraid of the tapes. And he was so afraid that he planned to release a far less graphic version in his upcoming autobiography." Strait assured the two biographers that Marilyn had been murdered, "It was obvious that she was subdued – probably with a pillow – while the drugs were administered." I asked Strait if he could make out the men's voices by listening to the tape and he said, "Not at all. No. They didn't have too much to say. They had a job to do and they went in there and did it." We discussed this further:

STRAIT: Giancana in Chicago is the one who ordered the direct hit on her. Two of his people were there in the bedroom with her. I talked about this on Joan Rivers' show [on January 7, 1993].

MARGOLIS: So that *Double Cross* book [first released in 1992] is correct?

STRAIT: Who did the *Double Cross* book?

MARGOLIS: Sam Giancana [SG's nephew and godson] and Chuck Giancana [SG's half-brother].

STRAIT: And what did they say in it?

MARGOLIS: They said the men gave her a chloral hydrate and Nembutal enema [actually they claimed it was one suppository containing a mixture of both Nembutal and chloral hydrate].

STRAIT: They also smothered her with a pillow. They told the truth! That's the facts as I know them. Just plain facts.

I mentioned enema and Strait agreed. He then told me, "That Newcomb, she hid in the closet and as soon as it was over, they shipped her out to Hyannis Port and then off to Paris." The Mafia did-it theory seemed to explain Newcomb's alleged hysterical words during the night as later reported to Florabel Muir. The neighbors claimed Newcomb screamed, "Murderers! You murderers! Are you satisfied now that she's dead?" According to this theory, Newcomb was screaming at the movie star's murderers who were departing the house.

Strait related to me on Bobby and Marilyn, "The last words he ever said to her were 'Go take another sleeping pill' and he slammed the door and left." Regarding *Double Cross*, Milt Ebbins told Spoto, "I read the book yelling at the book. I finally threw the book on the floor… Number one, he [Giancana] never would've killed Marilyn because Frank was in love with Marilyn!" Actress Terry Moore concurred and said, "Giancana was very nice to her. I think the Kennedys didn't want him to be friends with her any longer."

The Mafia theory is very slick but there are several holes that must be addressed. The authors of *Double Cross* wrote in their book that as for the notorious Sam Giancana, "What he didn't tell Chuck was that he'd soon have her life." So, already, Chuck Giancana admitted he heard it from someone else and this person he says was Chuck Nicoletti who worked as a hitman for Sam Giancana. Proceeding with this dubious hearsay, the authors claimed that Leonard "Needles" Gianola and James "Mugsy" Tortorella along with two other men went to Marilyn's home and murdered her hours later after "the Attorney General and the doctor [Kennedy's] left" in the afternoon. Oddly, there is no mention of Peter Lawford on this visit.

The authors of *Double Cross* assumed Marilyn died in the main bedroom where she was later discovered. As we will see, two reliable witnesses, Marilyn's handyman (also Eunice Murray's son-in-law) Norman Jefferies and Schaefer Ambulance attendant James Hall, will both independently say Marilyn expired in the guest cottage and then was subsequently moved to her own bedroom.

Raymond Strait, who agreed with Fred Otash that the Mafia killed her, told me he believed Marilyn died in the main bedroom. He mentioned two Mafia killers not four, "There were two of them in the house. The others were Freddy Otash and Peter Lawford... I knew Peter was there because Fred told me... Peter was drunk and hysterical. Fred slapped the shit out of him because of the way he was so hysterical at Marilyn's house. He was just like a hysterical woman, crying and carrying on. Fred didn't have much patience with that."

Strait told me as for Peter Lawford and Pat Newcomb, "I know that they were both there. I do not know that they arrived together." Strait remembered how Otash and Peter arrived at Marilyn's home before midnight:

> Fred was there in the house as she was dying... He told me in great detail everything that happened that day... Fred's job was to clean the mess up... Peter got scared and hysterical so he called Fred... Fred says, "You meet me at Marilyn's house." And Fred showed up with his soundman and Peter met him there and the Sergeant I interviewed told me that Fred was leaving the house when he arrived on the scene.

The authors of *Double Cross* claim the four men waited until the timing was right and then murdered Marilyn Monroe; however, the purported method of execution is highly unlikely, "Calmly, and with all the efficiency of a team of surgeons, they taped her mouth shut and proceeded to insert a specially 'doctored' Nembutal suppository into her anus... Indeed, within moments of insertion, the suppository's massive combination of barbiturates and chloryl hydrate [sic] quickly entered her bloodstream, rendering her totally unconscious." Donald Spoto made an excellent point, "As for Nembutal suppositories (sometimes fancifully suggested as the cause of death), these would only have reached about ten centimeters into the rectum: but in Marilyn's case, the entire sigmoid colon, a section very much higher, was grossly discolored."

Author Robert Slatzer provided the most persuasive argument against Mafia involvement in Marilyn Monroe's demise:

> Not long after Chuck and Sammy Giancana broke the above story on national television, however, Giancana's daughter,

Marilyn Monroe: A Case for Murder

Antoinette, disputed their entire account of Mob complicity in Marilyn's death. She also disputed Chuck Giancana's claims to have been a member of Mafia inner councils. Instead, she said, her father never trusted Chuck, who had held only a minor position within the organized crime hierarchy. If her father had been involved in Marilyn's death she implied, Chuck would have been one of the last to know about it. Her father considered Marilyn far more valuable to the Mob alive, Antoinette claims. Alive, she constituted a continuing threat that could be used against Bobby Kennedy. In fact, Marilyn's planned press conference gave Sam Giancana more reason to want her alive. If Marilyn had lived to carry through with the conference, Bobby would have been publicly disgraced and driven from office without Giancana or the Mob having to involve themselves at all.

Nevertheless, Anthony Summers argued there is reason to believe that Mafia boss Sam Giancana, acting on orders from the CIA, had Marilyn Monroe murdered by Gianola, Tortorella, and two other men from Chicago. In 1993, Summers said the Justice Department "believed that the mob had been involved in her death and that the whole thing had been an attempt to set up Robert Kennedy. *That* is what Justice Department officials were saying right back then. The whole thing hangs together." Later, Summers claimed that former FBI Assistant Director Courtney Evans "said to me, 'Yes, there was an attempt by organized crime to bring pressure on the Kennedys.' When I asked him to go into detail, he declined. He simply pointed me towards Sam Giancana."

The narrator of the same documentary stated, "It's not hard to imagine a hardened killer like Giancana murdering Marilyn to destroy RFK. And at least partial corroboration comes from the Chicago Crime Commission. They confirm the hitmen named in the [*Double Cross*] book Leonard 'Needles' Gianola and James 'Mugsy' Tortorella were both made members of the Chicago Mafia. And further corroboration comes from the Justice Department… Even the FBI seems to corroborate a Giancana-backed hit. Summers cited the statements of Former FBI Assistant Director Courtney Evans… The book also alleges a CIA connection. In fact, Chuck Giancana charges that CIA operatives actually requested that the hit be put on Marilyn." Raymond Strait told me, "The CIA was not in on it. I will go to my grave saying the CIA was not in on it." [73]

Jay Margolis

Who Gave Marilyn the Enema of Nembutal and Chloral Hydrate?

Per Anthony Summers, while Peter was high one night, his third wife Deborah Gould "said she asked Lawford whether he knew anything about how Marilyn had died. His only response, Gould told me – during an interview in which enemas had not been mentioned – was, 'Marilyn took her last big enema.' " Mrs. Murray was washing the sheets after the effects but this does not mean she herself was the one who administered it.

Several biographers including Anthony Summers and J. Randy Taraborrelli noted Marilyn Monroe was no stranger in the use of enemas throughout her life. She often took enemas daily. The fact that, in Noguchi's words, "the colon shows marked congestion and purplish discoloration" is curious since John Miner was of the opinion that Eunice Murray administered a fatal Nembutal enema to Marilyn.

As newsreel footage showed with reporters walking in and out, John Miner relayed, "The Sergeant who was the first police officer on the scene should have declared the residence a *crime scene* – everybody be kicked out. A complete inventory would be made of every item in there. That's the *minimum* that would be done in a proper investigation." Brown and Barham concurred, "By not summoning the crime lab – with its evidence experts, crime scene photographers, chemists, and fingerprint technicians – the LAPD deliberately refused to establish a 'crime scene' at the Brentwood house. No fingerprints were taken; the veritable pharmacopoeia of drugs on the bed table were not accurately inventoried, nor was the bedroom examined for signs of a struggle... All the while, Mrs. Murray flew through the house washing load after load of linens, and hauling off a dozen sacks of garbage – not to the trash receptacles, but to a pickup truck. Mrs. Murray's son-in-law, Norman Jefferies, allegedly drove the bulging sacks to the county dump." [74]

Donald Spoto claimed Greenson ordered Mrs. Murray to give Marilyn a chloral hydrate enema containing 17 pills. Arnold Abrams, M.D. related to Spoto, "The odds that she took pills and died from them are astronomically unlikely... I have never seen anything like this in an autopsy. There was something crazy going on in this woman's colon." Abrams said as for suicide by enema, "You don't know what the necessary fatal dose will be, and you have no guarantee that it's going to be absorbed before it's expelled. Look: if you're going to kill yourself with barbiturates, you do it with pills and glasses of water." Miner agreed on this point, "If she administered it, the fluid would have been absorbed as it came in. An effect of Nembutal, when it absorbs is to render the user unconscious and – *whammo!* – she would have no more control over the equipment of her body. So she would have been unconscious with all this stuff running out of her before enough of it was absorbed to kill her."

John Miner told Spoto, "Dr. Curphey in one of his more exuberant moments said, 'Oh, she gobbled 40 pills all at one time.' That's not possible... Why in the hell under these circumstances would the housekeeper be doing laundry at midnight makes *zero* sense unless the bed clothing had become soiled as a result of the administration of these drugs?... Contact with a noxious substance such as the barbiturates, which is an organic acid would account for the discoloration in the large intestine we saw at the autopsy." According to Wikipedia.org, "An organic acid is an organic compound with acidic properties... Chloral hydrate is produced from chlorine and ethanol in acidic solution." Thus, it is this biographer's conclusion that Marilyn's colon turned purple when an outside party administered to her an enema containing 13 – 19 Nembutals and 17 chloral hydrates.

Wolfe is adamant that Marilyn couldn't have had an enema because she was a victim of colitis, which in his mind accounted for the colon's discoloration found at the autopsy. Engelberg *claimed* Marilyn experienced diarrhea during those last days and Wolfe concluded it triggered her colitis. Wolfe argued that in the company of two men, Bobby Kennedy watched as Marilyn was injected with a combination of chloral hydrate and Nembutal.

It's important to note that chloral hydrate injections are not medically practiced. According to http://www.ncbi.nlm.nih.gov/pubmed/1614272, as part of an experiment, Syrian hamsters were given chloral hydrate injections, "Autopsy [of the Syrian hamsters] revealed severe peritonitis [ie. vomiting] and adynamic ileus [which hinders bowel movements]." However, an injection of chloral hydrate would have required that Marilyn's murderers obtain liquid chloral hydrate. Not only is this highly unlikely, it's far less convenient than simply breaking down actual pills into an enema.

John Miner rightly reasoned to Brown and Barham that administering a drug-laced enema to Marilyn Monroe was an "almost perfect crime" and "an easy one to cover up." Many, including Miner, have pointed the finger at Mrs. Murray but that would only be an assumption. [75]

A Surprise Visit from Bobby Kennedy

Norman Jefferies, who had seen Bobby and Peter earlier in the afternoon, said he accompanied his mother-in-law Eunice Murray to watch television with her later that night. Jefferies was surprised when Bobby Kennedy and two men ordered him and Mrs. Murray out of the house "between 9:30 and 10:00 P.M." The eyewitness account of an FBI agent interviewed by documentarian Keya Morgan provided additional corroboration.

The agent "saw Bobby Kennedy and other men go inside the house." Jefferies explained to Wolfe, "We were told to leave. I mean they made it clear we were to be gone. But this time Eunice and I didn't leave the neighborhood. We went to a neighbor's house. I had no idea what was going on. I mean, this was the Attorney General of the United States. I didn't know who the two men were with him. I assumed they were some sort of government men. We waited at a neighbor's house for them to leave." Wolfe noted that the men with Bobby Kennedy were later identified as "two detectives assigned to Kennedy as security officers."

Anthony Summers said after 9:30 P.M., Marilyn was happily chatting away with her friend and sometimes lover José Bolaños, presumably on the private line in her main bedroom. Marilyn may have been reading from her red diary when Bolaños would later claim during their last call that Marilyn told him "something that will one day shock the whole world."

Then there was a crash. Telling Bolaños she would be right back, she went to investigate the noise she heard coming from the guest cottage. Summers wrote, "Marilyn ended the conversation by simply laying down the phone – she did not hang up while he was on the line." She immediately went toward the guest cottage and found Bobby Kennedy and the two men with him rifling through the contents of her large filing cabinet. It had been forcibly broken into and the men were looking for the red diary, which was now in her main bedroom. Feeling her privacy was being violated, Marilyn screamed at the men to get out of her house.

John Miner said he heard the following on one of Marilyn's free-association tapes, "But, Doctor, I don't understand this big taboo about enemas. Most of the actresses I know use them, even some who won't admit it... I asked my gastroenterologist. He said it's true that constipation can cause pimples – something about intestinal toxins getting into the blood. So there you are... Yes, I enjoy enemas. So what? Sometimes I have them for sex play, sometimes medically for constipation. They sure beat the cramps and diarrhea you get from laxatives."

Spoto's book noted that Marilyn had many receipts for enema paraphernalia (most likely located in more than one of her bathrooms). When the police later discovered her body, only ten of fifty 500-mg chloral hydrate pills were remaining in the prescription bottle. According to biographer Gary Vitacco-Robles, "The guest bedroom near the pool shares a bath (at left) with the third bedroom. The middle door accesses a closet. The door to the far right leads to a hallway and a linen closet." Therefore, the water for the enema had been easily accessible and so were the linens later used to dry off her body after the enema had been expelled.

Once Marilyn entered the guest cottage to see what was going on, the two men with Kennedy threw her on the bed then according to Raymond Strait, covered her face with a pillow to keep her from screaming, held her down, and using one of the enema bags already in the guest cottage bathroom, the men forcibly administered an enema containing 17 broken-down chloral hydrates and between 13 – 19 Nembutals.

It is unknown whether Marilyn's Nembutal and chloral hydrate prescriptions were already in the guest cottage or if one of the security officers had to run to Marilyn's main bedroom to retrieve them while the other officer held her down. Keya Morgan told the *New York Daily News* that the FBI agent who was in a van spying in front of her house heard commotion from the guest cottage. Morgan relayed that the agent "heard them screaming and yelling in the guest cottage. They were in the guest cottage, not in her bedroom where her body was found."

Marilyn's young friend Jimmy Haspiel believed wiretapper Bernie Spindel and what Spindel heard on those tapes regarding Marilyn's last night, which indicated that the movie star had been murdered. Haspiel subsequently wrote in his first Marilyn book, "Suddenly without thinking further, the politician [Robert Kennedy] grabbed for a pillow across the bed and placed it over her tear-stained face."

Not even a minute after the enema had been given to her, Bobby Kennedy and the men preoccupied themselves again, frantically searching for the red diary. At this time, Marilyn grabbed the only phone, the public line from the guest cottage, to call her best friend Ralph Roberts. She reached his answering service. It was 10:00 P.M. The woman on the other end noted that Marilyn's was a "slurred voice." She asked for Ralph but the lady told her he was out for the evening. Then Marilyn hung up the phone. I asked Dr. Amador, "As a cry for help, she called her best friend and thought she was going to get through to him. Presumably I would think that minutes after she was given the drugs, she would be passing out, right?" "I would think so. Chloral hydrate will put a person to sleep."

She would shortly thereafter lose consciousness, leaning on the phone, a position in which Jefferies and Mrs. Murray would soon find her. Years later Mrs. Murray asserted that Marilyn had accidentally overdosed. This is in fact what it would truthfully appear to have happened when she discovered her employer. Mrs. Murray related, "I believe that Marilyn did *not* commit suicide purposefully. I think it was an accident. It's the only reasonable or logical conclusion that I would have." The question then becomes, why would Bobby Kennedy risk his career to be directly involved in such a strange turn of events? The fact that Kennedy was actually in Los Angeles from 11:00 A.M. (as seen on Stage 18 of the Fox lot by studio publicist Frank Neill) until after midnight proved he was willing to take that risk.

At 10:30 P.M., Jefferies said that Kennedy and the men left. Because of Maf's incessant barking, Jefferies and Mrs. Murray discovered Marilyn in the guest cottage. Mrs. Murray relayed to Slatzer, "I saw that the telephone was under her. She was lying on it." Jefferies told Wolfe, "I thought she was dead. She was facedown, her hand kind of holding the phone. It didn't look to me like she was breathing, and her color was awful – like she was dead. Eunice took the phone and called an ambulance. Then she put through an emergency call to Dr. Greenson, who was someplace nearby and said he would be right over. He told Eunice to call Dr. Engelberg. I went to the gates to wait for the ambulance, but before the ambulance got there Peter Lawford and Pat Newcomb arrived. Pat became hysterical and started screaming at Eunice. I had to take Eunice into the house. She was a basket case. I think the ambulance arrived before Dr. Greenson."

Jefferies took Mrs. Murray away from the guest cottage and into the living room. Detective Sergeant Robert Byron, who wrote the official police report, relayed to Anthony Summers, "Engelberg told me he'd had a call from the housekeeper who said Marilyn was either dead or unconscious. He came over and found Marilyn dead."

Matthew Smith interviewed Tom Reddin who was William Parker's Deputy Chief. Smith concluded that Chief Parker most likely protected Robert Kennedy from being implicated in any controversy surrounding Marilyn's death simply by association, in other words, being present at the scene. Parker's wife Helen told Anthony Summers that her husband relayed to her days later, "This thing has to be straightened out in more ways than one."

Parker sought to it that Kennedy was shielded from anything that would damage his career. After all, the Police Chief had a more selfish motive. For *The Marilyn Files* documentary, Sergeant Jack Clemmons relayed that Parker "was a very ambitious man and he wanted to be head of the FBI... He went to the point of trying to plant false stories about J. Edgar Hoover." On the same documentary, former Mayor Sam Yorty concurred, "I know that he would have liked to take the head of the FBI and he certainly would've been good at that. And of course to get that job you have to have Bobby Kennedy."

This seemed within reach considering Kennedy and Parker were close friends since they first fought organized crime together in 1956, alongside Captain James Hamilton. If Parker had been listening in on his own bug in Marilyn's home during the time she died, Otash confidant Raymond Strait confirmed to me that the voices on tape were too indistinguishable to make out. Therefore, from the tapes alone, one could not easily place Robert Kennedy at the scene simply by listening in.

Behind closed doors, Parker couldn't possibly know all the details. Summers wrote, "Weeks later, when his wife asked how the Monroe case was going, Parker was uncharacteristically vague. 'It seemed to be a big question mark,' Helen Parker recalls. 'I remember him just doing this' – and she draws a big question mark in the air." First husband Jim Dougherty wrote in his second book on Marilyn Monroe, "Did someone know she was in trouble? Robert Kennedy? Peter Lawford?... And were they so terrified about losing their careers, their reputations that they did nothing? If this is true, then they are accountable."

Biographer Ted Schwarz believed Marilyn committed suicide yet he told Brown and Barham what he heard from Fred Otash, who per Strait was at the scene with Peter, "Otash thought Bobby and Lawford knew what was happening and let her die... Otash viewed the death as a 'case of negligent homicide' and confided that 'the Kennedy brothers had already murdered her emotionally.' " [76]

Schaefer Ambulance Attendant James Edwin Hall Told the Truth

Based on rigor mortis, Westwood Village Mortuary employee Guy Hockett estimated Marilyn's death to be somewhere between 9:30 to 11:30 P.M. on August 4. Sergeant Jack Clemmons and Dr. J. DeWitt Fox agreed the two drugs that killed Marilyn were not taken orally. As Deputy Medical Examiner Dr. Thomas Noguchi noted in his official autopsy report on Marilyn Monroe, "The stomach is almost completely empty. The contents is [sic] brownish mucoid fluid. The volume is estimated to be no more than 20 cc. No residue of the pills is noted. A smear made from gastric contents and examined under the polarized microscope shows no refractile crystals... The contents of the duodenum is [sic] also examined under polarized microscope and shows no refractile crystals... The colon shows marked congestion and purplish discoloration." In the documentary *Marilyn Monroe: A Case for Murder*, former New York coroner Dr. Sidney Weinberg discussed discrepancies in the autopsy report that bothered him:

> WEINBERG: Let me tell you about the doubts that were raised in my mind. The most pressing thing in the whole report was the lack of finding of barbiturates in the stomach.

> FEMALE REPORTER: As an expert, what does it tell you that there was no residue in her stomach?
>
> WEINBERG: It tells me that the barbiturates that were analyzed in the liver and blood had entered her body in some other manner. Now what other manner could they possibly have entered? One would be by injection.

Another would be by enema. In October 1985, for ABC's *Eye-Witness News*, Noguchi said not to discount the possibility of foul play:

> NOGUCHI: She had a bruise, on her back or near the hip that has never been fully explained. There is no explanation for it, and it is a sign of violence.
>
> INTERVIEWER: Murder?
>
> NOGUCHI: Could be.

Milt Ebbins hypothesized to Spoto, "When there's an overdose of drugs, the first thing the doctor would give her was a shot of adrenaline." Now we come to the story of Schaefer Ambulance attendant James Edwin Hall. He first phoned the District Attorney's Office on August 11, 1982. Paranoid that he may be killed for giving his testimony, Hall telephonically communicated under the codename "Rick Stone." Refusing to give them his actual telephone number, Hall said *he* would always call them. Hall first talked to Deputy District Attorney Ronald "Mike" Carroll:

> CARROLL: One of the things I'm concerned about. You mentioned the man in the business suit used a needle in the heart.
>
> HALL: That's correct.
>
> CARROLL: That must have left a mark, right?
>
> HALL: I'm sure it left a mark in the flesh.
>
> CARROLL: Because as I look over the autopsy report, I don't see a needle mark.

HALL: Yeah, well, he put a needle in her heart. I guarantee it. I was looking right at it… He was wearing a business suit and a tie.

CARROLL: And you were there how many minutes approximately?

HALL: Oh maybe fifteen… I know this woman was hysterical when I got there. She was standing outside screaming, "She's dead! She's dead! I think she's dead!" In my opinion, she was either a heck of an actress or it was quite a shock to her.

CARROLL: How was Monroe dressed?

HALL: She was nude.

CARROLL: Was there any phone around her?

HALL: There was a telephone on a nightstand or a little table alongside the bed. The phone was *on* the hook. It was not off.

CARROLL: When did you next hear about the case?

HALL: I heard it on the radio and the TV and they said pills were scattered all over the floor and the phone was off the hook like she was trying to call somebody. That's not how that room was. Those pills were all in the bottles. All lined up perfectly on the nightstand and the phone was on the hook.

CARROLL: What was the time to the best of your twenty-year memory?

HALL: I'm gonna say between four and six in the morning but that's a long time ago. I know I'd seen the pictures when they carted the body out. It was daylight. When they took her out, it was the morning. I might be wrong on the time. I don't know.

CARROLL: Is there any way you'd be willing to come forward and talk to one of our investigators?

Jay Margolis

HALL: I'm gonna be very candid with you. I'm very afraid because of people getting shot. I'm not doing this as a good Samaritan. Quite frankly, on a financial basis, it would require expense money.

CARROLL: What kind of expense money?

HALL: I don't know, pal. I'm starving to death and my family is, too. That's the only reason we've been doing this.

CARROLL: Is there anybody working for the ambulance company that would remember you?

HALL: Absolutely. Let me give you a few names. There was a man by the name of Joe Tarnowski and a guy named Tom Fears.

CARROLL: Was that bought out by some other company?

HALL: Well, California Ambulance Services was at that time owned by Walt Schaefer.

Admittedly, James Hall didn't note the time when he arrived. All he was concerned about was helping a comatose Marilyn Monroe, whom he said he immediately attended to upon arrival. If Hall didn't carry a watch, he certainly may not have known what time it was when all this happened. In addition, Hall told Wolfe that back in 1962, he worked a 24-hour shift, which could further fog his perspective of the time element.

Unbeknownst to him, to confuse things further, the principles at the scene waited more than four and a half hours to call the police! Hall assumed they "carted the body out" very soon after she was dead. How was Hall to know this wasn't a reasonable assumption? Further corroborating his story, Anthony Summers interviewed the two Schaefer employees mentioned by Hall to Carroll: Joe Tarnowski and Tom Fears, who were both informed that an ambulance from their company had been dispatched to the Monroe residence that night. Days later, when James Hall phoned back, Carroll put Hall in communication with his investigator Alan B. Tomich. Hall described what happened when he arrived:

HALL: You go in and you turn to the left and the bed was

facing longways as you're looking at it. To the left of the bed was the table that had all the pills on it. She was laying across the bed with her head hanging over the edge of the bed. I threw her on the floor and proceeded to give close-chest heart massage.

TOMICH: She's on her back or on her stomach?

HALL: When she was laying on the bed, she was laying on her back.

TOMICH: Who else was present at the time you arrived?

HALL: A woman.

TOMICH: Then someone else arrived sometime after that?

HALL: The person with me went out to get the resuscitation equipment and walked back in the door. Right behind him in walked the gentleman in the brown business suit.

TOMICH: And what did he do?

HALL: He said he was her doctor. He said, "Give her positive pressure," which we did. Then he proceeded to open up his little bag and pulled out a loaded hypodermic syringe and injected the fluid into her heart.

TOMICH: And then what did he do?

HALL: He gave more closed-chest heart massage then said, "I'm releasing you. She's dead."

Regarding his account, James Hall explained to Tomich, "There will be no financial transaction until I take your polygraph to prove what I'm saying is true. At that time, you would pay right there on the spot when it's proved to be true… That thing happened twenty years ago. It's a long time. Now I gave you information on the phone that nobody has that you can check out and prove. I'm not just doing it because I'm Joe Goodguy. I'm doing it because of the economy and what's happened financially." Tomich eventually told Hall he wouldn't pay him beyond the initial expenses and Hall said that was fine. He would simply go to the tabloids, allowing them to give him their own polygraph tests. Tomich chuckled, "Well then we'd be getting our information for free, wouldn't we?"

Hall said in the documentary *Marilyn Monroe: A Case for Murder*, "We did what we could to save her. And I believe we could have saved her if we would've had the opportunity to take her to the hospital... We ascertained that her breathing was very shallow, her pulse was very weak and rapid and she was unconscious at that time." According to *The Marilyn Files* documentary, Pat Newcomb was the first person Hall saw. "I said, 'What's wrong?' She says, 'I think she took some pills.' " Newcomb then led Hall to a tiny bedroom where Marilyn was laying unconscious faceup on the day bed. Hall relayed, "She was naked. She had no sheet, no blanket... There was no water glass. No alcohol."

Noting Hall's observations, Spada wrote, "Marilyn was in the guest bedroom, not her own room, and she was comatose but still alive." To Spoto, a remarkably defensive Newcomb countered James Hall, "Whoever the writer was who said I leaned over the body screaming, 'She's dead! She's dead!' I never saw the body. So what is he talking about, this ambulance driver?... How can he say he saw me? I never saw an ambulance."

In the previous section, Norman Jefferies' statements regarding Mrs. Murray calling the ambulance shortly before Newcomb arrived at the scene casts doubt on the publicist's account. In fact, beginning with Fred Lawrence Guiles in 1969, Newcomb consistently claimed she didn't learn of Marilyn's death until 4:00 A.M. the next morning from a phone call by Marilyn's attorney Mickey Rudin. Later, we will learn she had surprisingly concocted a rather weak alibi.

Then on November 23, 1982, just weeks before the District Attorney's Office concluded their re-investigation into Marilyn Monroe's death, John Blackburn, Chuck Orman, and Dan McDonald of *Globe* publicly released James Hall's account for the first time: Hall said he saw Marilyn Monroe murdered by her psychiatrist Dr. Ralph Greenson. *Globe* gave him $40,000 for his testimony. After undergoing hypnosis by a professional experienced in police investigations, Hall was able to flesh out more details of his account:

> My driver and I had just dropped a patient off at a hospital, chatted with the medical staff for a few minutes and were returning to the office in our ambulance. Suddenly, we received a radio message to go to an address in Brentwood, 12305 Fifth Helena Drive. When we arrived, there was a hysterical woman standing outside in a robe, screaming: "She's dead! She's dead!" I told her to calm down that we'd do the

best we could. That's our standard response to distraught friends or relatives. My partner and I dashed into the house, saw a light, turned left in the hall and entered a smallish bedroom.

And there she was, lying on her back in the bed, her head hanging over the side. I recognized her immediately. "Oh my God," I thought, "Marilyn Monroe." I was absolutely stunned. I got to her side as quickly as I could – in the emergency ambulance business, just a few seconds can spell the difference between life and death. At the same time, I glanced at Marilyn's bedside table. I could not believe my eyes. It was simply loaded with bottles of pills, 10 or 12 of them. "Someone is sure over-prescribing," I remember thinking. However, all the bottles were lined up in neat little rows, and all of them were properly capped. Not what you'd expect if someone was hellbent to overdose. And that's not all. There was no telltale white froth around her mouth, a sure sign of an OD. Nor was there any odor of drugs around her mouth. But there was something terribly wrong. Miss Monroe's face had started to turn blue – so I knew we had to get her off that soft mattress and onto a surface hard enough for us to work on so we could get her breathing.

The bedside table Hall saw was delivered that morning according to Mrs. Murray's book! Noguchi mentioned to Brown and Barham bruises not documented in the original autopsy report, "I did find evidence which indicated violence. There were bruises on her lower back area – a very fresh bruise – and bruises on the arms." James Hall pulled her outside the guest cottage bedroom and onto a hard surface. Hall told Slatzer there were two bruises he was responsible for, "One was on her upper arm – that's my fingerprints. One was on her fanny – that's where we dropped her. Dead bodies don't bruise. She was still alive." Hall next told *Globe*:

So, my partner and I rolled her off the bed and dragged her across the carpet into the hall. We certainly weren't worried about a few rug burns or bruises – just in saving her life. Now, I'm not a doctor, but I knew my business. I had received intensive Red Cross training. Today, I'd be what they call a paramedic. And I knew instinctively that Marilyn was still alive. She didn't have that "gray" look of death on her face.

And her body didn't "feel" dead. Believe me, I've picked up enough dead bodies in my day to know what I'm talking about. Marilyn Monroe was still alive. That's why I didn't punch her in the heart, which is what I normally did to shock a stopped heart back into working. There was no need for it in this case. But I did tell my partner to get the resuscitator out of the ambulance – quick.

Meanwhile, I placed a plastic tube called an airway down her throat and, when the mechanical breathing equipment was brought in, I attached it to the airway. Well, as soon as I started to work on Miss Monroe by applying external heart massage, her color started coming back. And I was just about ready to get her in the ambulance and on the way to the hospital, when a man entered the house. He was fortyish, tall – almost six foot – and slender, with dark hair, longish sideburns and a moustache. "I'm her doctor," he said. But he certainly didn't look like a doctor to me. I should know – my father's a physician. He had dirty fingernails. He didn't act like a doctor either – because the first thing he did was order me to remove the resuscitator and try to get her breathing manually by blowing air in and out of the airway with my mouth.

That was the WRONG thing to do. You do that only when you don't have a resuscitator. But I was in no position to argue. He was supposedly a physician. I was just a 22-year-old ambulance attendant who had been told time and time again by his superiors: "Never, never argue with an M.D." All he had to do was report me and I was out of a job. My wife was pregnant, so I kept my mouth shut. After a few minutes of his charade, he pushed me aside with the comment: "I've got to make a show of this." I don't know what he meant, but he massaged her heart for a few moments. Then, he reached into his medical bag, pulled out a syringe with a long heart needle, filled it with a brownish fluid and injected it into Miss Monroe's heart. Strange, but when he was trying to find her heart, he had to count down her ribs – like he was still in premed school and had really never done this before.

Immediately after the injection, Miss Monroe started to lose her color again. Then, just a few moments later, he announced:

Marilyn Monroe: A Case for Murder

"I'm pronouncing her dead. You can go now." I couldn't believe it. Maybe I shouldn't second-guess the guy, but I'm sure that if I had gotten her to the hospital, Miss Monroe would be alive today. Her color was coming back. Resuscitation was working. Then this "doctor" comes in and – whammy – all of a sudden she's dead. If he had really wanted to save her life, he could have worked on her in the back of the ambulance as we were on the way to the hospital. But he didn't. And Marilyn Monroe died.

Just as we were packing up our equipment, two men dressed as police officers arrived. They didn't ask us any questions – which I thought was strange – just gave us a slip we could submit later to the county to get paid for the ambulance run.[77]

Globe wrote on page 5, "Incredibly, when Hall was shown a photograph of Eunice Murray as she looked at the time, he shook his head and declared: 'This is not the woman who was screaming hysterically outside the house and hovered over us the entire time we were working on Marilyn. Believe me, when I arrived, there was no one at that house but the hysterical woman.'"

Mrs. Murray and Jefferies by their own independent accounts were in the living room. Hall continued, "No door was locked. No window pane was broken. Miss Monroe was not facedown on the bed. But more important, there was absolutely no indication that Miss Monroe had ingested a massive overdose of barbiturates. I've seen enough ODs to know that for sure. The whole story was a tissue of lies. And I knew it." *Globe* noted, "Hall says he discussed his role in the case with friends over the years, 'but never went public because I had been warned "important people" didn't want anyone rocking the boat. Marilyn Monroe was a suicide – and that was that.'" When his family was hungry, a paranoid Hall took a chance and went public.

Hall told Spada he later identified the hysterical woman as Pat Newcomb, "Just as Marilyn started coming around, this doctor arrived. I believe it was Dr. Greenson. He had a bag with him and he looked legitimate. He said, 'I'm her doctor,' and Pat Newcomb didn't say he wasn't, so I figured everything was okay because she never would have allowed anyone near Marilyn who didn't belong there. I yielded to him and he leaned over her, pushed her breast to one side, and gave her an injection in the crease of her breast… For years I've felt that she had been given an Adrenalin shot in an attempt to save her and it had failed. But now I don't believe it was an accident. I think the shot was intended to kill her."

Hall told Slatzer, "I absolutely believe that Dr. Ralph Greenson murdered

Jay Margolis

Marilyn Monroe… He opened his bag and pulled out a hypodermic syringe with a heart needle already affixed to it." Learning of Cathy Griffin's findings after her investigation into Marilyn Monroe's death, Jeanne and C. David Heymann wrote in their notes, "One of the possible scenarios offered by Griffin was that Dr. Greenson murdered Marilyn Monroe by injecting her in the heart with some substance, brown. And Griffin suggested that he was working for the studio. He had dealings with many studio people at Fox who had been involved with making Marilyn Monroe's last movie *Something's Got to Give*."

Hall told *Globe* the liquid from the pharmaceutical bottle Greenson had was a "brownish fluid." Per www.sinoapi.com/Pharmacopoeia/jp15/JP56287-74-2.pdf, "Adrenaline Injection is a colorless, clear liquid. It changes gradually to pale red and then to brown on exposure to air and light." Adrenaline starts out clear so it's not adrenaline. The brown liquid James Hall saw had to be Nembutal, which was the only other drug found in Marilyn's body besides chloral hydrate. This does not mean, however, that the high level of Nembutal in Marilyn's body came from Greenson's shot. Rather, the high level came from the afternoon injection and the evening enema.

According to the following link: www.ummz.umich.edu/rep_amph/herp-prep.html, "There are two types of Nembutal, a clear, thin liquid, and a dark brown, syrupy liquid (elixir). The clear type is preferable. Nembutal must be diluted with water before using." In any event, Hall's account proved Greenson did not dilute the brown solution before injecting it into Marilyn's chest.

I asked Dr. Amador, "Is it true that since Dr. Greenson did not dilute this solution before he gave it to Marilyn in the heart, that that would kill someone regardless of what's in the solution?" "I would assume so. It goes up the brain stem and it paralyzes the respiratory center." Dr. Amador then said regarding the undiluted heart needle to the chest, "If that's true, that's murder. That is point-blank murder. That's never done for any reason except to kill."

In Melvin B. Bergman's documentary *The Marilyn Files*, the narrator reported, "In 1982, James Hall claimed that he and his partner Murray Liebowitz drove one of the ambulances to Marilyn's house that night." Hall related, "When they brought me out of hypnotism, we did a police identi-sketch. At that time, one of the reporters walked by and he says, 'Hey, I know that guy' and they pulled out the pictures of Marilyn's psychiatrist Dr. Ralph Greenson and that's who it was… He just shoved it right into her heart… At about this time, two men came in. The one man [Sergeant Marvin Iannone] was wearing a Los Angeles police officer's uniform. The other was in civilian clothes. The guy in the civilian clothes went up to Patricia Newcomb, put his arm around her and calmed her right down. She was really distraught… He went right over to her and calmed her right down. Subsequently, I've identified him, too and that was Peter Lawford."

When asked why Marilyn was later found in her own bedroom, Hall explained, "They moved her and they put her into the master bedroom. When Jack Clemmons, the first officer at the scene got there, he said she looked exactly like what she was: a dead body that had been laid in that position on the bed in the master bedroom, facedown covered with a sheet. There was the two I thought were police officers and the doctor and the publicist; they could've picked her up." In 1993, to Donald Wolfe, Hall identified one of the two police officers as Sergeant Marvin D. Iannone. [78]

In the 1982 *Globe* article, on page 5, Blackburn wrote, "Private investigator John Harrison… had been conducting polygraph examinations for 40 years." Harrison told *Globe*, "When I was first brought into this, I thought the whole thing was a fairy tale, but now I'm thoroughly convinced Hall is telling a true story. He was given a total of six polygraph tests, including control tests, and there was no evidence of any deception."

Blackburn continued, "Hall was interviewed while under hypnosis by Henry Koder, a professional forensic hypnotist with more than 20 years of law-enforcement experience and veteran of hundreds of major crime investigations." Koder told *Globe*, "Hall was a good subject. I was able to take him back to the night of Marilyn Monroe's death under hypnosis and listened to his step-by-step description of his involvement.

"He was able to vividly recall that night and pointed out details to me that he hadn't even remembered in earlier questioning. When wakened, Hall was able to give us a very thorough description of the injection doctor for our Identikit composite. Also, I implanted a post-hypnotic suggestion that Hall must be truthful. It would have been impossible for him to lie during the next polygraph without the machine showing a reaction."

The doctor Hall identified in his Identikit composite looks like Marilyn's psychiatrist and Greenson did have a moustache. Hall said the man referred to himself as "her doctor." Engelberg, Marilyn's other doctor, certainly didn't have a moustache.

In addition, Wolfe interviewed polygraph examiner Donald E. Fraser who gave James Hall more polygraphs on August 10, 1992. Fraser relayed, "There's no question that James Hall is telling the truth. His story regarding the scene and circumstances of Miss Monroe's death is absolutely true. He passed every question in several exhaustive polygraph examinations."

For the October 1993 issue, Number 12, Donald Wolfe wrote an article for fan newspaper *Runnin' Wild: All About Marilyn* entitled, "The Ambulance Chase." Fraser told Wolfe that one of the questions posed to Hall was, "Did you witness man who claimed to be Marilyn Monroe's doctor give her an injection into the left side of her chest?" Wolfe wrote, "Lack of line movement indicates Hall was being truthful." In fact, in the newspaper, Wolfe reproduced the actual polygraph test given to James Hall by Don Fraser. As for Hall, Fraser concluded, "His story and the conversation produced during the polygraph examination would hold up in court."

Greenson's son Danny told Spada, "I hate all this speculation, and especially that guy who says he saw my father plunge a needle into Marilyn's heart. That's ridiculous, and I've got to say that it hurts me." Hildi Greenson relayed to Cathy Griffin, "I sometimes have a feeling that this ambulance driver went on a call that night somewhere else and kind of managed to get these things into a different order."

In 1982, investigator Al Tomich from the District Attorney's Office asked Engelberg, "Would you have noticed any fresh needle marks on her at that time if there were any in the chest area?" "I would have noticed any gross things. I didn't notice any such thing." As for James Hall, Anthony Summers noted how his father, ex-wife, and sister all confirm they were told of his account at Marilyn's home right after it happened.

Wolfe said Marilyn's body displayed indicators of cyanosis, consistent with a needle injection. An actual witness to the cyanosis was *Life* magazine photojournalist Leigh Wiener who said he saw strange signs of blue all over her when he photographed Marilyn Monroe hours after her death. For a late 1980s documentary, Leigh Wiener said to his interviewer, "They'll look like a frozen cube of ice. You'll see little streaks of blue running through the body… That's how Monroe looked to me when I saw her."

Marilyn's friend reporter James Bacon relayed, "I stayed there long enough to get a good view of the body before the real coroner's staff arrived – then I made a quick exit… She was lying facedown on the bed, face slightly turned to the left on a pillow. Her legs were straight… I noticed that her fingernails were dingy and unkempt." Her nails had changed color because of the cyanosis.

In the documentary *Marilyn Monroe: A Case for Murder*, John Miner said, "Her body was examined minutely by both of us under magnification to see if we could find any needle mark of any kind anywhere on her body. And her body was observed and there were no needle marks."

After the John Belushi case, Noguchi conceded in his book that he almost missed a needle mark on Belushi's left arm. Noguchi wrote, "The very fact that the fresh punctures had been so difficult to discover worried me. Apparently a tiny medically clean needle had been used, and the injection had been made right into the vein, so that only drops of blood revealed them." In Marilyn's case, according to pathologist J. DeWitt Fox, M.D., "The blue post-mortem lividity occurred over the front part of the body. This might have masked or covered up any injection which she might have had in her chest."

Marilyn Monroe: A Case for Murder

Using Fox's expertise, Slatzer noted in his second Marilyn Monroe book that had she been moved, in this case facedown on the bed then "the bruise-like discolorations of post-mortem lividity" would hide an injection site on her chest, the needle Hall saw Greenson put into her heart. To quote the 1982 District Attorney's Report on the re-investigation of Marilyn Monroe's death, "Lividity, as described to our investigators, is a process by which blood drains to the lowest point in a deceased person after death due to the joint effect of the pull of gravity and the cessation of the blood pumping mechanism of the body... In addition to the rigor mortis observed in Miss Monroe's body, Noguchi and others observed a pattern of lividity on her face and chest." Sergeant Jack Clemmons, the first policeman officially at the scene, agreed with Dr. Fox's explanation of post-mortem lividity and believed James Hall's account.

Coinciding in all major points with the District Attorney's Office explanation of lividity noted by their medical professionals, Clemmons told Slatzer, "It was obvious to me, apparent to me, I should say, that Marilyn had been placed in that position. I felt at the time that the position of the body had to do with post-mortem lividity. When a person dies, their heart stops beating; the gravity will pull the blood to the lowest part of the body. Marilyn being facedown, all the blood came forward. As a matter of fact, the coroner's report particularly noted lividity, reddishness around the face and the chest area. I felt at the time that she was placed in that position to disguise needle marks." Miner conceded to Brown and Barham, "A cursory examination of Monroe's kidneys found them to be clear of drugs. This should have indicated that the stomach may have been bypassed. And the only way that could have happened was by injection."

The 1982 District Attorney's Report attempted to discredit James Hall's testimony by stating: "According to Hall, the doctor ultimately plunged a giant syringe filled with a brownish fluid into her heart, after which she quickly died while on her back on the floor... Minor streaks of lividity were... found on her back. These minor traces disappeared upon touch. This finding is consistent with the normal practice of transporting bodies from the death scene to the mortuary or Coroner's Office... If the mysterious 'doctor' had given Miss Monroe a fatal shot of pentobarbital, leading to her rapid death as described by Hall, the level in her liver would not have been as high as it in fact was because her body would not have had time to metabolize the 'hot shot.'" Marilyn died shortly before midnight and Noguchi began the autopsy after 9:00 A.M., leaving plenty of time for post-mortem lividity to hide the needle mark.

Marilyn did die on her back. Regarding the drugs found in her body, the District Attorney's Report did not consider the possibility that the high

Nembutal concentration in the liver was due to three factors: some oral intake throughout the day, the pentobarbital shot in the afternoon, and an enema containing 13 – 19 Nembutals. Indeed, the liver did not reach 13 mg. percent of pentobarbital right away but over a period of hours, a chance to be absorbed, at which point she died slowly. As for Greenson's shot to the heart, Dr. Amador told me that an undiluted injection would kill someone regardless of what's in the syringe and regardless of the amount injected into the body.

Marilyn Monroe was murdered by Dr. Ralph Greenson's undiluted Nembutal injection to the heart. Sergeant Clemmons said that when he arrived on the scene, Greenson was "cocky, almost challenging me to accuse him of something." Clemmons' suspicions were on target as Greenson's guilt was immediately apparent.

Peter Lawford relayed to Heymann, " 'Marilyn has got to be silenced,' Bobby told Greenson – or words to that effect. Greenson had thus been set up by Bobby to 'take care' of Marilyn." The Nembutal injection to the chest was exactly the way Greenson did it. In his mind, what better way for any witnesses to assume it couldn't have been anything but an adrenaline shot? This was a common way to save patients from an overdose.

When Hall and Liebowitz left the scene, her body was moved from the guest cottage to the master bedroom because this is where Clemmons found the body when he arrived at 4:45 A.M. As Greenson gave Marilyn the shot that killed her, Hall noticed it was obvious that Greenson had never done this before.

He was a psychiatrist and rarely do they carry medical bags containing large syringes with heart needles already attached to them. If Bobby arranged to have Greenson kill her, Bobby easily could have provided him with a syringe from his doctors, including the one who accompanied Bobby and Peter to Marilyn's earlier in the afternoon.

Referring to the afternoon pentobarbital shot, Dr. Sidney Weinberg concluded, "Knowing the results of the toxicology examination and the negative findings in the stomach, one must seriously consider the possibility of an injection. If I had handled the case, I would have been remiss in my duties if I did not refer it to the district attorney for investigation."

Later in the evening, Donald Wolfe claimed, "In the presence of Bobby Kennedy, she was injected with enough barbiturate to kill fifteen people." Wolfe is wrong. Miner relayed to author Robert Slatzer, "The amount of drugs found in Marilyn's body was so large that had it been administered by injection [containing high dosages of Nembutal and chloral hydrate], the star would have died almost immediately. The body would have only had minutes in which to begin absorbing all those drugs and a large, visible swelling containing the unabsorbed drugs would remain just beneath the surface of the skin." Rather, in the presence of Bobby Kennedy, two men accompanying him subdued Marilyn by throwing her on the guest cottage bed. The men then used a pillow to place over her mouth to keep her from yelling. Next, using paraphernalia already available, they forcibly administered an enema containing Nembutal and chloral hydrate. The drug enema didn't kill Marilyn within minutes as a lethal injection would, but it made her unconscious.

The last thing Bobby wanted was a hysterical Marilyn fighting him to get out of her house and away from her filing cabinet, located in the guest cottage. As James Hall attempted to revive her later, Greenson came in with a black medical bag, "pulled out a syringe with a long heart needle" then "filled it with a brownish fluid and injected it into Miss Monroe's heart." [79]

Who the Hell is Ken Hunter?

In December 1982, weeks after Hall's story to *Globe*, a man by the name of Ken Hunter would claim to the District Attorney's Office that he accompanied *his* partner Murray Liebowitz and that they, *not* James Hall, had gone to Marilyn's home during "the early morning hours of August 5, 1962." This is odd since Marilyn died *before* midnight. Nevertheless, Hunter told the District Attorney's Office they were in and out within minutes.

Anthony Summers wrote, "The D.A.'s staff talked to a former ambulance driver called Ken Hunter... He said he attended Marilyn's home with an assistant 'in the early morning hours.' He said – to the D.A.'s man at any rate – that Marilyn was already dead... He had told the District Attorney that he thought his assistant that night had been an employee named Murray Liebowitz... In 1985, I talked on several occasions to the late Walter Schaefer, who was then still running the ambulance company he founded. He confirmed, with utter certainty, that a Schaefer ambulance was called to Marilyn's home. Asked whether Murray Liebowitz was one of the crew, he said, 'I know he was.' " On December 14, 1982, the District Attorney's Office conducted the following tape-recorded interview with an unconvincing Ken Hunter:

TOMICH: What happened?

HUNTER: What do you mean?

TOMICH: Well, I mean, what occurred?

HUNTER: Well, I don't know. Nothing really occurred. She was dead and they wouldn't let us take her.

TOMICH: Well –

HUNTER: The coroner came and took her.

TOMICH: Did you go into the house?

HUNTER: Yeah, I believe so.

TOMICH: Did you see Monroe's body?

HUNTER: Yeah.

TOMICH: Where was it at the time?

HUNTER: She was on the bed, hanging off the bed or something.

TOMICH: Do you recall whether she was on her back or her stomach?

HUNTER: Side.

TOMICH: She was on her side?

HUNTER: Yeah, I believe she was on her side. Let's see, yeah, it seems to me she was on her side.

TOMICH: Did either one of you touch her body?

HUNTER: No, I didn't. I don't know if he did.

TOMICH: Did you know if your partner did?

HUNTER: Seems to me he did.

TOMICH: Do you know what he did?

HUNTER: Checked her just to see if – dead or what not. I

Marilyn Monroe: A Case for Murder

think she was. I think she was pretty cold at that time. Well, she was blue, the throat, you know, like she had settled, like she had been laying there a while. You know what I mean?

TOMICH: She was blue in any particular portion of her body?

HUNTER: I think – I don't really remember if it was her neck or her side that she was laying on or what. It was – But it seemed to me like – Well, let's put it this way. I could stand across the room and tell that she was dead.

TOMICH: Let me relate a story to you that we've received information from a person that an ambulance attendant was summoned to the residence. That when the ambulance attendant and his partner arrived the only person there was a female [Newcomb] standing outside screaming. And that the attendant went in and found Marilyn Monroe on the bed, removed her from the bed and began CPR or closed-chest massage. And that in the process of doing this that she started to come around, you know, to regain consciousness and the doctor came in and plunged a needle into the area of her heart and thereafter pronounced her dead. Does that sound familiar at all?

HUNTER: That's bullshit.

As written on page 16 of the District Attorney's Report, Ken Hunter stated that upon arriving at her home, he and Murray Liebowitz noticed that Marilyn was already dead and left a few minutes later. This scenario, if it were to be believed, makes it nearly impossible for Marilyn's neighbors Mr. and Mrs. Abe Landau to claim to have seen an ambulance when they arrived home late. They would have had to see it within the few minutes Hunter said he was on the scene, which is highly unlikely. That gives the Landaus approximately five minutes to spot the ambulance before it's gone.

A confidential source allowed me to listen to the full Alan Tomich/Ken Hunter interview. Quoting from earlier portions of the recording, Hunter volunteered to Tomich, "I know that Hall wasn't there. Period." Tomich asked if Hunter could remember the name of his partner, "I'm almost positive it was Liebowitz." Addressing Hall's story, Hunter is adamant, "The doctor wasn't even in the room!" then shortly thereafter he concluded, "It just looked like an accidental suicide." Regarding the extent of his employment with Schaefer, Hunter told Tomich a vague and sketchy recollection:

TOMICH: When did you start with Walt Schaefer?

HUNTER: I don't know. I don't remember.

TOMICH: How long would you say you've been on this job before Monroe's death?

HUNTER: Not long.

TOMICH: Months.

HUNTER: Months. Maybe two months.

TOMICH: Have you been with an ambulance service prior to that time?

HUNTER: I was in Long Beach.

TOMICH: And how long did you work there?

HUNTER: Four or five months.

From the evidence presented, we can safely conclude that James Hall and Murray Liebowitz were the Schaefer Ambulance attendants that went to Marilyn's home, *not* Ken Hunter who incidentally didn't work for Schaefer Ambulance in 1962.

On September 11, 1993, Donald Wolfe interviewed Carl Angelo Bellonzi (Vice President of Schaefer Ambulance for over 40 years) who stated that Ken Hunter only started working for Schaefer in the mid-1970s and even then never in the Los Angeles area but in Orange County! According to James Hall's Social Security number and his employment records, as shown in plain view in *The Marilyn Files* documentary, Hall did in fact work for Schaefer in August 1962 as the records from January to December 1962 indicated.

Wolfe tracked down a *Santa Monica Evening Outlook* photo of James Hall in his Schaefer Ambulance uniform dated October 4, 1962. *Runnin' Wild: All About Marilyn* displayed the same photo of Hall. See Donald Wolfe's article in the October 1993 issue, Number 12, entitled, "The Ambulance Chase." So, who was Ken Hunter, who took it upon himself to lie to the

District Attorney's Office? The Kennedys hired Hunter to discredit James Hall's account. [80]

The Santa Monica Hospital "Story"

For the documentary *Marilyn Monroe: A Case for Murder*, a female reporter noted that the President of Schaefer Ambulance Walt Schaefer "is now dead but in a 1985 interview, he said an ambulance did go to the scene that night but it was *not* driven by James Hall." Schaefer related, "We took Marilyn Monroe in on an overdose and of course she succumbed at the hospital. She was alive when she was picked up, yes."

Schaefer told a similar story to author Robert Slatzer, "I guess I can tell it. I came in the next morning and found on the log sheet we had transported Marilyn Monroe. I understood that she had overdosed. She was under the influence of barbiturates. They took her on a Code Three, an emergency, into Santa Monica Hospital, where she terminated." Asked how Marilyn could possibly have been brought back to her home in Brentwood, Schaefer replied, "Anything can happen in Hollywood."

Years later, Hall's partner Murray Liebowitz would change his last name to Leib. I interviewed Murray Leib's wife Sylvia. Mrs. Leib said Murray is now deceased but confirmed to me that her husband had told her that James Hall was indeed Murray's partner, *not* Ken Hunter.

However, Mrs. Leib also relayed that throughout the years Murray had told her Marilyn Monroe was taken to the hospital then brought back to her home after she was dead. Clearly, Murray Leib was following to the letter Walt Schaefer's original testimony:

> MARGOLIS: Were Murray Leib along with James Hall the ambulance drivers the night that Marilyn died?
>
> LEIB: Murray was the ambulance driver. He was always the driver when he worked for Schaefer. Generally, when there were celebrity problems, they always called on him... She was dead when he got there but they still had to take her to the hospital. That's the law. They can't do anything until an M.D. pronounces them dead. I think they took her to St. John's Hospital. Murray was always of the opinion that she took the pills herself. They took her to the hospital. When they got

there, the doctor came out and said she was gone. Murray says to him, "Well, what do you want me to do with her?" because the hospital won't take a body… Then they took her back.

MARGOLIS: It was James Hall who was his partner?

LEIB: When we saw it on television, Murray did approve that he was there. That he was with him.

MARGOLIS: That James Hall was with him?

LEIB: Yes. He was with him but he wasn't the driver.

MARGOLIS: Murray talked to Donald Wolfe the biographer, right?

LEIB: Yes.

MARGOLIS: You were in the room with Donald Wolfe at all times when he was talking to Murray?

LEIB: I don't know what Donald Wolfe was telling Murray on the other end of the line because he was talking to him on the phone.

MARGOLIS: James Hall was given grueling polygraph tests in which he was proven to not be lying about the guest cottage.

LEIB: Murray always referred to her as "at home" so I can't say whether "at home" was a guest cottage.

MARGOLIS: The autopsy report said that there were no pills in Marilyn's stomach, which means she did not swallow the 64 pills they said she swallowed.

LEIB: That the table next to her was loaded with pills.

MARGOLIS: That is correct but they were all "neatly-capped" just like James Hall said. This was not someone who was "hellbent to overdose" to put it in his own words.

LEIB: What are they trying to do now, to prove that she was murdered?

MARGOLIS: She made her last call at 10:00 P.M. and died before midnight. Why are there no pills in her stomach? Dr. Thomas Noguchi who performed the autopsy and Dr. John Miner who oversaw it with him, they both believed she was murdered. They do not believe she accidentally or intentionally took her life... James Hall's account correlates with the fact that she was killed.

LEIB: I don't think the Mafia was involved with this... There was a lot going on. She was involved with the Kennedys. They passed her down from one brother to the next. I do believe they had to get rid of her and she was really in the way... If she was really murdered, somebody needs to pay for that.

Runnin' Wild: All About Marilyn printed Walt Schaefer's retraction to his original hospital statement in the October 1993 issue, Number 12. Soon before he passed away in 1988, Schaefer told Slatzer why he lied about Marilyn Monroe being taken to the hospital, "Eighty percent of my business came from the County and government agencies." Slatzer later wrote in his 1992 book, "Schaefer admitted he'd lied to Clemmons the first time and confirmed his story to me... The Kennedys were involved and he knew his business would be ruined if he talked." Taking Schaefer's retraction into consideration, we can conclude that Marilyn Monroe was never at any time taken to Santa Monica Hospital.

Sylvia Leib, the late Walt Schaefer, and the District Attorney's Office all agree that Murray Leib went to Marilyn's home that night under the name Murray Liebowitz. In 1985, a frantic Murray Leib told Anthony Summers over the phone, "I don't want to be involved in this... I wasn't on duty that night. I heard about it when I came to work next morning... I'm not worried about anything, there's nothing to worry about. Don't bother to call me anymore."

Publicly, for over thirty years, Murray Leib didn't rock the boat and simply followed Walt Schaefer's initial story: Hall was not there that night and Marilyn was taken to the hospital where she died then she was brought back to her home in Brentwood. The important point to note here is how Sylvia Leib remembered her husband Murray admitting that James Hall *was* his partner when they both saw Hall on television. Mrs. Leib could not have mistaken

Hall for Hunter because Hunter was never at any time circulated in the media. In fact, no one has ever taken his picture for this investigation. [81]

Beverly Hills Police Officer Lynn Franklin Connects the Dots

Marilyn's neighbor Abe Landau told Slatzer, "My wife and I were out to a party. We came home quite late. It must have been close to 1:00 A.M. There was the ambulance. There was a police car and quite a few other cars." For the documentary *Marilyn Monroe: A Case for Murder*, Landau reiterated a similar account but placed the sighting closer to midnight:

> FEMALE NARRATOR: Then there's the story of this man, Abe Landau. He was Marilyn's next-door neighbor. Tonight, he breaks a 26 year-long silence to tell of a mysterious midnight traffic jam in front of Marilyn's house the night she died. When he asked what was going on, no one would say.
>
> LANDAU: We had been out to a party. We came home and the place was like Grand Central Station. The cars were all the way up the alley... Some limousine was here. I don't who it was. And of course, police cars and the ambulance.
>
> FEMALE REPORTER: After you went inside your house, what happened?
>
> LANDAU: Someone knocked on the door and wanted to know what we knew about Marilyn Monroe and we told them nothing.
>
> FEMALE REPORTER: Did the visitor describe himself as a reporter? Did he identify himself as a police officer?
>
> LANDAU: He didn't identify himself at all.

Officer Lynn Franklin placed the ambulance at the scene even sooner than Landau. In 1992, Franklin said he talked to James Hall and Fred Otash at around the same time (during and after the filming of *The Marilyn Files* TV Special, respectively). The two men made remarkably similar observations.

They each independently placed Sergeant Marvin Iannone at the scene with Peter Lawford. After speaking with Otash, Franklin noted in his book how "at about 11:45 P.M. on the night of her death, the place had been bustling with activity. An ambulance was at the scene."

Franklin wrote that in addition to Fred Otash, "I got another witness to verify Iannone's presence at the Monroe residence, well before he was officially dispatched. James Hall, who had been an attendant with Schaefer Ambulances that night, told me that Sgt. Iannone and Peter Lawford had been present in the home when Dr. Greenson injected Marilyn with the fatal heart needle...

"Fred Otash... told me that he had bugged the homes of Peter Lawford and Marilyn Monroe... 'I've got something you must hear, Lynn,' he told me. 'Iannone is dirty as hell.' That got me interested. In 1992, Iannone had been chief of police in Beverly Hills for four years, his highest rank on the career ladder. Shortly after August 1962, he had become captain of LAPD's Internal Affairs unit. He was later appointed chief of police in Beverly Hills... It was Otash's conclusion that the promotions of Iannone and others came as a reward for participating in the cover-up of Marilyn Monroe's death."

At 12:10 A.M. on August 5, Officer Lynn Franklin pulled over an inebriated Peter Lawford for speeding as high as 80 M.P.H. along Olympic Boulevard. After hitting the intersection at Robertson, Peter's Lincoln Continental sedan soon came to a stop. The others in the vehicle were a stone-silent Ralph Greenson in the front seat and a nervous Bobby Kennedy in the back seat. Placing Greenson, Peter, and Bobby within miles of the death scene, Franklin obviously had a lot of interest in what private eye Fred Otash and ambulance attendant James Hall had to say years later.

Franklin relayed to Brown and Barham, "I was thinking that maybe one of the others should take the wheel. Peter was so polluted – trembling and slurring his words." Regarding Greenson, Peter told Franklin, "He's a doctor. He's just riding along with us to the airport." Franklin remembered, "When I saw the coverage of the funeral, I knew that Greenson was definitely the man sitting next to Lawford in the front seat. But the man never said a word." As for Bobby Kennedy, Franklin observed, "He was wearing chinos and a tattered dress shirt."

Iannone's presence at the house around 11:45 P.M. suggests he was stationed at the Monroe residence as a guard for the Attorney General. Minutes after Greenson injected the heart needle into Marilyn's chest, James Hall saw Peter Lawford and Sergeant Marvin Iannone enter the guest cottage. Iannone had done that kind of detail for the Kennedys several times before. Wolfe noted, "Iannone was known to work for Hamilton in Intelligence, and whenever the President or the Attorney General visited the Lawfords', Iannone

Jay Margolis

received the special duty assignment from Hamilton to work the Lawford beach house." Iannone was now working the Monroe home. Bobby Kennedy needed to be protected. By this time Kennedy had returned and was waiting outside in his limousine. Greenson and Peter Lawford would join Kennedy shortly in Peter's nearby Lincoln Continental sedan. [82]

Strange Remarks Attributed to Strange Men

On August 20, 1962, Greenson sent a letter to his good friend and colleague Anna Freud discussing his feelings about the death of Marilyn Monroe, "This has been a terrible blow in many ways. I cared about her and she was my patient. She was so pathetic and she had had such a terrible life. I had hopes for her and I thought we were making progress. And now she died and I realize that all my knowledge and my desire and my strength was not enough. God knows I tried and mightily so, but I could not defeat all the destructive forces that had been stirred up in her by the terrible experiences of her past life, and even of her present life. Sometimes I feel the world wanted her to die, or at least many people in the world, particularly those who after her death so conspicuously grieved and mourned. It makes me angry."

The "present life destructive forces" were her "sexual" relationships with government men "at the highest level" as Greenson told the Suicide Prevention Team without mentioning the Kennedys specifically. "Those who after her death so conspicuously grieved and mourned" was a sarcastic reference to the Kennedy brothers who did *not* conspicuously grieve and mourn after Marilyn died.

Oddly, Greenson wrote to a colleague, "I am amazed how deeply people seem to be affected by this death. Everybody felt sorry for her and so many felt guilty… It is a sad, sad story and it will take me some time to get over. I shall probably go to New York for a few days, just to get away from this atmosphere here. It will give me a chance to talk to Max Schur [Greenson's analyst and colleague], where I can say certain things which I cannot say to anybody here."

Greenson excluded Marilyn Monroe from his own definition of immortality because he believed narcissists could not love other people. He gave two separate lectures on October 18, 1960 and October 11, 1961 pertaining to this subject: "I think the only kind of immortality that there is any evidence of is the immortality of being remembered by people. This is all. No other immortality exists, only the immortality of being remembered. I think anything more than this is an illusion, if not a delusion…

"There is only one kind of immortality that I believe in and that is to be remembered as a person who mattered and that people who matter to you remember you. But that kind of immortality is only for those people who care about others, not only themselves. For that you must be committed and, above all, you must be involved not only with your own circle of friends, but with the next generation, the children, the pupils, the students, the young. I think if one does that, one has achieved some form of immortality. It is only a small consolation, but it is realistic."

On January 20, 1963, Anna Freud responded to Greenson's letter, "I am terribly sorry about Marilyn Monroe. I know exactly how you feel because I had exactly the same thing happen with a patient of mine who took cyanide two days before I came back from America a few years ago. One goes over and over in one's head to find out where one could have done better and it leaves one with a terrible sense of being defeated. But, you know, I think in these cases we are really defeated by something which is stronger than we are and for which analysis, with all its powers, is too weak a weapon."

On October 24, 1973, in an article entitled, "Marilyn Monroe's Psychiatrist Speaks Out In Her Defense," Greenson told Ken Sandler of the *Medical Tribune* why he used unorthodox methods to treat Marilyn Monroe when he brought her into his home to live like one of the family. Greenson relayed, "It is controversial, I know that. Nevertheless, I have practiced for some thirty-five years, and I did what I thought best, particularly after other methods of treatment apparently hadn't touched her one iota… I did it for a purpose. My particular method of treatment for this particular woman was, I thought, essential at that time. But it failed. She died." Arguing against Norman Mailer's murder suspicions, Greenson concluded to Sandler, "I think it is wrong to connect her death with any sort of political intrigue. It is fantastic and not true." [83]

However, Greenson would act smug in front of the press in late 1962 when he told more than one reporter the following, "We made some mistakes at the end. And, if you really want to know what happened to Marilyn, why don't you ask Robert Kennedy." Brown and Barham interviewed a member of the Greenson family to elaborate on the quote, "I think he meant there was serious concern about her attachment to the Attorney General and that this might have been why she was upset at the end of her life."

Yet Greenson's "Ask Robert Kennedy" statement contradicted what he later told Maurice Zolotow for his October 13, 1973 article, "Marilyn did not have any emotional involvement with Robert Kennedy or any other man at this time." If Marilyn didn't have any involvement with Bobby Kennedy then why would Greenson mention him at all? Greenson told the Suicide Prevention Team days after Marilyn's death that she was having a "close relationship with extremely important men in government," plural not singular. That the relationship was "sexual" and that the men were "at the highest level." [84]

In the documentary *Say Goodbye to the President*, William Woodfield shared his recorded 1964 telephone call to Marilyn's psychiatrist in which Greenson discussed only what he said he could of Marilyn's last night. Oddly, two years after his star patient's death, he is still deferring all inquires to the Attorney General, "I can't explain myself or defend myself without revealing things that I don't want to reveal. I feel I – I can't, you know – you can't draw a line and say well I'll tell you this but I won't tell you that. It's a terrible position to be in to have to say I can't talk about it because I can't tell the whole story… Listen, you know, talk to Bobby Kennedy."

Although Greenson was caught off guard, Woodfield asked him what happened on Marilyn's last night. He could have said it was an accident that she killed herself as he allegedly told his family. When I mentioned the recorded "Talk to Bobby Kennedy" statement to Gloria Romanoff, she said, "It is unbelievable to see that kind of behavior in a professional man." As for his father's remark, Danny Greenson relayed to Chris Turner, "I don't know why he said that. I certainly don't think he felt that Bobby Kennedy killed her." Turner wrote, "Others suggest that he might have killed her by accidentally administering an overdose, or at her boyfriend Robert Kennedy's specific request." [85]

Greenson's cryptic remark to William Woodfield strikingly resembles the 5th Amendment, where it is better to say nothing at all than to face incrimination. What is it that he wants to defend against? Why can't he "explain himself" if it was just a suicide, plain and simple? If Greenson can't discuss what happened to Marilyn on her last night, why does he think Bobby Kennedy would be better at explaining it? What's the "whole story"? With these odd quotes by Greenson in mind, Peter Lawford's admission to knowledge of a conspiracy to murder the movie star cannot be dismissed lightly.

Greenson's Guilt After Marilyn's Death?

In a therapy session with Greenson, actress Janice Rule mentioned Marilyn's death shortly after it had happened and he weirdly remarked, "There's no way in my lifetime I will ever be able to answer any of this. I only worry how it will affect you as my patient." Greenson noted varying reactions from his patients after Marilyn died. He said, "Some of them saw no reaction in me, and were furious at me for being so cold and impersonal. They asked how could I come and work the next day, and how could I have taken such a patient anyway, and they were angry. Other patients felt sorry for me, and were sympathetic, and were crying. With some of them, I had tears in my eyes, and I couldn't hide it, and they saw it. And with some, I had tears in my eyes, and they didn't see it." *New York Times* journalist Lucy Freeman who was also a friend of Greenson's said, "He was never the same guy after she died. The death profoundly affected him; he blamed himself even though it was hardly his fault."

After his star patient passed away, Greenson met with a panel from the American Psychoanalytic Association (APA) who had summoned him before them. The subject at issue was his unorthodox treatment of Marilyn Monroe by bringing her into his home to meet the family. With his ego larger than ever, Greenson defensively stated, "Well, I think she deserved a psychiatrist who had experience. Where should she go? To a beginner?" Challenging those who criticized his idea of becoming emotionally involved with his patients, Greenson explained, "You can't sit there like a computer, or like a note-taker, or like a historian or a research worker… I've seen more patients driven mad by that than by anything else."

With guilt, Greenson reflected on Marilyn Monroe, "She was a poor creature, whom I tried to help and ended up hurting." A colleague said, "The fire went out in Greenson when Marilyn Monroe died. He never really recovered. He went on but he turned inward after that… He became a bit strange." In 1960, Julian Blaustein unsuccessfully tried to produce a film adaptation on Sigmund Freud's life, a film his friend Greenson didn't want made because Anna Freud disapproved of the project. When asked after his star patient's death why he didn't keep his moustache and had grown a beard in its place, Greenson replied to Blaustein, "I wanted to be somebody else." [86]

Does Greenson's Official "Story" Check Out?

In late 1973, Greenson publicly stated that on August 4, after he left Marilyn's house, he then went to dinner with his wife to the residence of a Mr. and Mrs. Arnold Alberts. However, a confidential source revealed to me that Greenson actually went to the home of actor Eddie Albert and his wife Margo. Albert

Jay Margolis

starred in 1962's *The Longest Day* and Greenson's own movie in 1963 called *Captain Newman, M.D.*

Greenson said he did not return home until "around midnight." The psychiatrist claimed he was tempted to call Marilyn but he "didn't want to wake her." The Greenson family has for years told biographers that Ralph Greenson did not get a call from Marilyn's home until at least 2:00 A.M. on August 5. Per the police report, Greenson arrived minutes after 3:30 and Engelberg pronounced Marilyn dead at 3:35 or at 3:50 A.M. depending on whether one reads the first or the follow-up report, respectively.

Interestingly, Mrs. Murray blurted out to the first policeman officially at the scene Sergeant Jack Clemmons that the discovery of Marilyn's body was around midnight. Clemmons said the two doctors present Greenson and Engelberg did not disagree with Mrs. Murray. In 1982, investigator Al Tomich from the District Attorney's Office asked Engelberg, "Someone told the first policeman there that you were called at midnight." "That I was called what?" "At midnight. That you had been there four hours before you called the police." "Nonsense. Absolute, utter nonsense."

Later, Clemmons noticed how the three principles told Detective Sergeant Robert Byron a different story: Mrs. Murray had called Greenson at 3:30 A.M. Living less than two miles away, Greenson told her he would be right over but instructed Mrs. Murray to call Engelberg. Greenson arrived before Engelberg and using a fireplace poker, he said he broke the only unbarred window to Marilyn's bedroom because he claimed her door was locked.

Al Tomich asked Engelberg, "Do you recall Greenson telling you how he got into the room and how the body was discovered?" "I recall this. I don't know if Greenson or Mrs. Murray told me but the door was locked to the bedroom. Mrs. Murray first looked in through the window and saw her and the way they got in was I guess through the window. Either they smashed a pane or turned a lock or were able to push it open. I don't recall which."

A photograph still exists of a man's hand pointing at the broken window proving a person could not reach in to undo the latch without cutting his fingers on the glass. After the 3:30 A.M. call from Mrs. Murray, according to the official police report, Engelberg said he got dressed then drove to Marilyn's home all within five minutes, pronouncing Marilyn dead at 3:35 A.M., which is impossible in light of what the physician would say twenty years later.

Engelberg relayed to the District Attorney's Office, "I was parked in the basement of the parking area of a small apartment house and somebody parked in back of me and I had to get that car moved. That must have delayed me about ten or fifteen minutes… I was living in an apartment on Beverly Boulevard between, just west of Doheny, so it must have taken me ten, twelve minutes. There's not much traffic at that hour of the morning." Therefore, it was impossible for Engelberg to arrive at Marilyn's house within five minutes as he relayed to Detective Sergeant Byron. [87]

Contrary to the official police report, Joan Greenson said a call came in to the Greensons' alerting her mother and father that Marilyn was in trouble, *not* at 3:30 A.M. as she told Anthony Summers, but "in the middle of the night." Joan relayed, "My parents were going to a dinner party, and were not having dinner at home and I decided that I really would rather just go to bed early, and that I wasn't very hungry. I went to bed around 8:00… I fell asleep fairly quickly, and didn't hear my parents come home, but I was awakened sometime in the middle of the night, by the phone ringing. Then I heard my father, a few minutes later, head down the stairs, and I knew something was up. Mother followed, and I heard the car drive away." Hildi added, "I was very worried, and my daughter was here and we immediately stayed up. We just went downstairs and sat around until my husband called me and said that Marilyn was dead."

Yet Joan wrote in her manuscript that she retired to her room to sleep, "I finished my snack, and went back to my parents' bedroom and told my mother I was going back to bed. I must have been in my bed for maybe 5 minutes when I heard the phone ring, and I got out of bed and went back to my mother's bedroom, and I knew it was Father on the phone. Mother turned to me and said, 'It's all over.' " [88]

Greenson, Engelberg, and Mrs. Murray told police Marilyn's door was locked. Hildi relayed to Cathy Griffin, "Her room was locked and with a bolt lock. It wasn't a lock that you could go through with a credit card and open it or undo it. It was locked and my husband had to break the window to get in." Griffin asked, "Did she keep her door locked usually when she went to bed?" "I don't think so but it was locked that night."

Her door couldn't have been locked since Marilyn did not have an operating lock on any of the doors except the ones from the outside. Los Angeles secretary Cherie Redmond wrote to Marilyn's close friend and New York secretary Hedda Rosten, "There isn't one door in the place that locks." David Marshall noted, "Linda Nuñez, who moved into the 5th Helena home after Marilyn's death, explained… that no one in her family ever had a key to any of the locks on any of the interior doors of the home. She expanded that to explain that the locks were old-fashioned skeleton key deadbolts but no keys had been turned over to the new owners when her family moved in. She emphasized that no one in her family ever locked any doors other than the front and back for that reason. The locks were very old and she doubted if they still worked."

Also, if what Brown and Barham say is true, that Mrs. Murray had a skeleton key attached to her own keychain there would be even more reason to believe Greenson wouldn't need to break the window to gain entrance to Marilyn's bedroom. Besides, after the terrible experience at the Payne Whitney Psychiatric Clinic in early February 1961, Marilyn was not eager to practice locking her door. In fact, on February 9, 1987, genealogist Roy Turner asked his friend Mrs. Murray if Marilyn's door was locked that night and she replied, "No." [89] An August 5, 1973 article detailing the psychiatrist's account stated:

> When Dr. Greenson called on Marilyn during the afternoon of Aug. 4th, he saw no Nembutals. He remained with her for 2 ½ hours, then left, telling her he had a dinner engagement, but that she could reach him by phone. He then drove home to shave and dress for his dinner at the Arnold Alberts [actually Eddie Albert]... While he was shaving, Marilyn rang up:
>
> MARILYN: I have some good news. I just had a talk with Joe Jr. (Joe DiMaggio's son) and he's broken up with that girl I never did like, and I feel real good.
>
> GREENSON: That's great. What are you going to do tonight, Marilyn?
>
> MARILYN: I don't know. Maybe I'll take a drive to the beach. I don't know.
>
> GREENSON: Don't forget to drink a large Coke. And if you need me, you know where I'm going to be. Mrs. Murray has my number. If anything happens you know where to get in touch with me.

The article concluded, "That was the last conversation Greenson had with Marilyn Monroe. It was Saturday Aug. 4th, 7:30 P.M. After dinner with the Alberts [Eddie and Margo Albert], Dr. Greenson returned to his home in Brentwood around midnight. He called his exchange and was told no one had phoned. He was tempted to phone Marilyn but didn't want to wake her. He then went to sleep. At 3 A.M. his phone rang. It was Mrs. Murray, Marilyn's companion-housekeeper."

Joe DiMaggio, Jr.'s call to Marilyn was at 7:00 and it lasted until 7:15 P.M. Spoto noted, "Joe DiMaggio, Jr. was able to fix the time of his conversation. In his subsequent police interview, he said that Marilyn picked up the phone while he was watching on television the seventh inning of a baseball game: the

Baltimore Orioles against the Anaheim Angels, being played in Baltimore that Saturday evening. The game began just after seven-thirty Eastern Daylight Time, which would have put the seventh inning at about ten o'clock (or seven o'clock Pacific Daylight Time)." Joe DiMaggio, Sr. said, "They spoke for about fifteen minutes and Marilyn seemed quite normal and in good spirits."

Greenson wrote to a colleague, "When I left at 7:15, she seemed somewhat depressed but I had seen her many, many times in a much worse condition… A half hour later she phoned me at home to tell me she had gotten some good news and she seemed quite pleasant and more cheerful… At any rate, she sounded pleasant on the phone, although somewhat depressed, but by no means acutely so.

"About an hour later, someone [Mickey Rudin] called the housekeeper and said that Marilyn had sounded funny on the phone, but the housekeeper said that Dr. Greenson had just been there and she did not want to disturb Marilyn. At midnight, the housekeeper awakened and saw that there was a light on in Marilyn's room, which was most unusual. The housekeeper was afraid to awaken Marilyn who would have become enraged, and so she fell asleep again."

Yet Mrs. Murray conceded in her own book, "I knew that the new white wool carpet filled the space under the door. The surface wool had piled up as a result of contact with the swinging door. This I remembered later, but not until after I had agreed that I saw a light under the door. Such are the pitfalls of demands under pressure when accurate reporting is desired." Now that Mrs. Murray retracted her own account, Greenson's version is highly suspect.

This added twist about Mrs. Murray falling "asleep again" resolves the discrepancy of the "midnight" discovery of the body as told to Sergeant Clemmons. Hildi Greenson countered, "People say that there were four hours before it was reported, and I think Eunice did that out of a kind of unconscious guilt. She wished she had awakened at midnight and called but she didn't… Eunice Murray awakened at midnight and saw the proverbial description, the light under the door, and wondered about it but fell asleep while wondering. She didn't get up. She saw the door I think from her bedroom or something and said, 'I wonder why she has the light on,' because she usually didn't go to sleep with the light on… The if then was, if she hadn't fallen asleep at midnight, she probably still could have been saved. By the time she called, which was somewhere between two and three, it was too late… He said, 'Eunice called and Marilyn's door is locked and she can't get in.' "

Joan relayed, "He had gone over to Marilyn's house after he had gotten the call from Mrs. Murray. Her bedroom door was locked, there was a light, and a telephone cord under the door. He knew Marilyn never liked to sleep that way. So he took a poker from the fireplace and went to the side window of her bedroom and broke the glass and reached in to let himself in. He could see that she had been dead for some time. He said she felt cold, but she was clutching the telephone in her hand, and he had trouble getting it out of her hand to hang it up… Father never believed for a moment that she meant to kill herself. He felt sure it was an accident. It must have been a terrible sight. They had struggled for such a long time, and now all was for nothing. What a terrible tragedy."

For a man who admitted to not having a great memory that night, Engelberg told a remarkably similar story to the District Attorney's Office, "I thought that at the time she took the pills, it was a suicide attempt. That was my opinion… That particular line about being called at midnight, I remember Mrs. Murray telling us clearly that she went to sleep around midnight and she saw the light on under Miss Monroe's door. And she woke up a few hours later and felt a little uneasy and the light was still on and that's when she knocked and didn't get a response and that's when she went outside and looked in and saw her sprawled over the bed. Because that's what she told us."

Greenson continued to his colleague, "At 3:30 the housekeeper awakened and saw the light and phoned me. I was there in five minutes, broke the window in the bedroom, found Marilyn lying dead, clutching the phone in her hand so strongly that I could not remove it. It seems she had died around midnight. I do not think she consciously wanted to die at this moment but expected to be rescued; this time, however, it failed."

Going against the official police report, Greenson's brother-in-law and best friend Mickey Rudin conceded to Donald Spoto that Greenson was at Marilyn's home *before* midnight, contradicting Greenson's account to police and unwittingly adding corroboration to James Hall's story. Mickey Rudin gave the following interview to Spoto on October 31, 1992:

> RUDIN: I got a call from my exchange from Milt Ebbins telling Marilyn had made these distress calls to Milt, looking to talk to Bobby [Kennedy] or some kind of calls which gave them a feeling of alarm that she had committed suicide. I did not call Romi [nickname for Greenson]. He had had enough but I called the housekeeper. I said, "Do me a favor. Tell me if Marilyn is okay." I hang onto the phone for about four minutes… She came back to me and says, "She's fine…" It was like the boy who cried wolf too much… Milt Ebbins could be hysterical… The housekeeper tells me she's alright. That's the last I heard of it. I got home. I got a call from Romi. He was over there. Marilyn had been found dead.

LATER IN THE TAPE:

SPOTO: When you arrived at the house, Romi and Engelberg were already there?

RUDIN: I don't remember Hy being there. It was certainly Romi who called me and he was there.

SPOTO: And that was certainly before midnight.

Silence for thirty seconds.

RUDIN: It wasn't a particularly late dinner party [at Mildred Allenberg's]. I went home. I'm not sure the call came in just as I got home or got undressed then the call came in. If I think back, I'd have to say it was just as I got home because I remember now taking the call from the breakfast room, one of my favorite hangouts.

SPOTO: Was it then Romi who called you from the house?

RUDIN: Yeah.

SPOTO: Who called him?

RUDIN: I don't know. Maybe Mrs. Murray.

Mickey Rudin said after Greenson called him, he came right over.[90] According to the police report, Mickey Rudin's call to Mrs. Murray was 9:00 P.M. At this time, Marilyn was fine and not dying. In fact, Greenson came to the house while Marilyn was still alive as Mrs. Murray corroborated in the *Say Goodbye to the President* documentary, "When he arrived, she was not dead because I was there then in the living room." Jefferies complemented Murray's recollection, "I think the ambulance arrived before Dr. Greenson... I was in the living room with Eunice when Marilyn died, and we could hear Pat Newcomb screaming [from the guest cottage], and we knew Marilyn was dead."

Greenson's story to the police is that he arrived minutes after 3:30 A.M., found the door locked, and then proceeded to use a fireplace poker to break the only unbarred window in Marilyn's bedroom. However, Anthony Summers intriguingly noted, "Dr. Greenson confirmed privately, years later, that Robert Kennedy was present that night and that an ambulance was called."

Hildi Greenson relayed to Cathy Griffin, "We had been out at a dinner party and that was another if. Apparently Lawford called Mickey Rudin and said, 'Marilyn sounds kind of peculiar,' and Mickey said, 'Okay, I'll check into it,' and he called the house and said, 'Eunice, is Marilyn okay?' and Eunice said, 'Yes, she's fine,' or whatever, and so he didn't alert my husband either because he thought, 'The poor guy, he needs a day off,' so that's the other if. They all sort of came together."

The accounts of Officer Franklin, Mrs. Murray, Norman Jefferies, and Mickey Rudin negate Greenson's official version to police. His story about a fireplace poker is clearly a fabrication. Before calling Greenson, Mrs. Murray claimed she went around to the side of the house and used a poker to "part the draperies" yet Pat Newcomb recalled to Spoto, "Those were heavy curtains that had no middle-divider." [91]

At About 10:30 – 10:40 P.M. Natalie Trundy Learns Marilyn's in Trouble

Why would Greenson, Engelberg, and Mrs. Murray wait over four hours to call the police? Greenson told Sergeant Clemmons he stalled because he had to get permission from Twentieth Century-Fox's studio publicity department first, a statement Clemmons rightly considered a non sequitur. Deputy District Attorney Ronald "Mike" Carroll who led the re-investigation into Marilyn's death in 1982 said regrettably in 1986, "We would have looked further if we had known, back then, of the statement that some individuals knew Monroe was dead five or six hours before the police were called." There was obviously more to the story.

In the *Say Goodbye to the President* documentary, Jacobs' future wife Natalie Trundy reflected, "About three quarters of the way through the concert, someone came to our box and said, 'Arthur, come quickly. Marilyn is dead or she's on the point of death.'" [92] According to Norman Jefferies, after Mrs. Murray rang for an ambulance and called the two doctors around 10:30 P.M., Peter Lawford and Pat Newcomb arrived together. Seeing Marilyn facedown on the bed, Pat screams at the housekeeper. Jefferies takes Mrs. Murray into the living room. Newcomb then used the guest cottage phone to call the Hollywood Bowl putting through an emergency request for Arthur Jacobs. It was Natalie Trundy's twenty-first birthday and Arthur treated her to a Henry Mancini concert with additional music by Ferrante and Teicher.

Marilyn Monroe: A Case for Murder

Natalie was absolutely certain that Pat Newcomb placed the call to Arthur Jacobs. Newcomb maintained ever since 1969 when first interviewed by Fred Lawrence Guiles that she received news of Marilyn's death the next morning from her home. Guiles wrote, "Pat was awakened by a phone call at 4 A.M. It was lawyer Mickey Rudin. 'Something's happened to Marilyn,' he told her; then added, 'She's dead.' When she recovered from the initial shock, Pat got dressed and drove to the Brentwood house." Wolfe contradicted Newcomb by pointing to newsreel footage, which showed Pat entering the housekeeper's green Dodge that morning before Mrs. Murray drove away. To Spoto, Newcomb claimed she remembered Mickey Rudin telling her "his exact words" over the phone:

RUDIN: There's been an accident.

NEWCOMB: What happened?

RUDIN: Marilyn has taken an overdose of pills.

NEWCOMB: Is she okay?

RUDIN: She's dead. You'd better get over here.

Rudin vehemently denied ever making this call to Pat Newcomb at her home in his October 31, 1992 interview with Spoto:

SPOTO: You didn't call Pat?

RUDIN: I didn't have her phone number.

Milt Ebbins related to Spoto, "It's strange that Mickey called Pat Newcomb. That's the first time I heard of that." [93] In his Marilyn Monroe biography, Spoto wrote that it was Mickey Rudin who called Arthur Jacobs at the Hollywood Bowl even though Natalie Trundy Jacobs has consistently told biographers including Summers, Spada, Smith, and even Spoto himself that it was indeed Pat Newcomb who made this call:

JACOBS: I didn't see him for days.

SPOTO: Where was he?

JACOBS: There with Pat Newcomb.

SPOTO: With Pat?

JACOBS: She chooses not to speak about it. I know Pat Newcomb was there that night.

SPOTO: Yes, she was.

JACOBS: Greenson, he was the first person that housekeeper called.

SPOTO: That's right… Did Arthur ever mention to you because he did to somebody else about Bobby Kennedy being there?

JACOBS: Yes. Yes, he did… Why am I lowering my voice?

SPOTO: Apparently, when Arthur arrived, Bobby was already there. Pat was there.

JACOBS: Yeah.

SPOTO: It was Pat who called Arthur obviously.

JACOBS: It had to be because she worked for Arthur.

SPOTO: The thing is that the Kennedys put him in a terrible position.

JACOBS: Arthur said, "I cannot speak. I cannot say anything."

Natalie Jacobs told Spada, "Pat Newcomb was the first one at the house." She relayed to Summers, "We got the news long before it broke. We left the concert at once and Arthur left me at our house. He went to Marilyn's house, and I don't think I saw him for two days. He had to fudge the press." I discussed Natalie Jacobs' recollection with press agent Michael Selsman from the Arthur P. Jacobs Company:

MARGOLIS: Natalie Trundy Jacobs is absolutely certain that Pat Newcomb called Arthur Jacobs at the Hollywood Bowl. What is your knowledge of this?

SELSMAN: That's exactly true. Pat called Arthur at the Bowl when he was with the LeRoys, Mervyn LeRoy and his wife. Arthur got a call from Pat saying, "Marilyn is dead. Come on over." So he did.

MARGOLIS: Arthur Jacobs arrived at Marilyn's house at approximately 11:00 P.M., is that right?

SELSMAN: Yeah, of course.

MARGOLIS: Did you get any impression on what he saw there?

SELSMAN: He wouldn't speak. He wouldn't talk about it... He called me around 4:45 A.M. to get to Marilyn's house and I got there at six.

Hildi Greenson countered to Cathy Griffin, "One thing that puzzles me very much – I've forgotten now who the people were who went to a concert in the Hollywood Bowl... Someone came and said Marilyn was dead or something. It just doesn't seem to add up and I don't understand how that ever happened."

Who else but Pat Newcomb would know *that quickly* where Arthur Jacobs was *that night*? Mickey Rudin denied having Pat Newcomb's number. Michael Selsman told me, "Of course Mickey had Pat's phone number but it didn't happen that way. Pat called Arthur when he was at the Bowl." [94] To Spoto, Rudin showed his dislike for Pat Newcomb: Greenson "couldn't tell her *not* to associate with Pat Newcomb so they can exchange pills." Also, Rudin revealed his close relationship with Engelberg: "I've known Hy since he was an intern. Hy was a damn good doctor... Hy was an excellent doctor." This was the old boy's club.

Incidentally, Natalie and Pat were next-door neighbors at the time (Pat at 150 South Canon Drive and Natalie at 152 South Canon Drive). When she got home, Natalie knew Pat's car was gone all night and wasn't back until late Sunday. Wolfe noted that Pat left her car at Peter's house. As for Arthur Jacobs, Milt Ebbins confirmed, "Pat Newcomb knew where he was every minute."

Author Robert Slatzer interviewed Newcomb. Slatzer relayed, "I told her that Mrs. Murray stated that she had dropped Pat off at the corner of Carmelina and Sunset, a short walk from Marilyn's house." Newcomb told

Slatzer, "I had my own car. Why would she drive me there?... I drove to Marilyn's that morning. There were a lot of press people there, and I was awfully upset because of the event itself, as anyone would be... Arthur Jacobs was there, too. Then I left and went home and talked to four or five hundred journalists all over the world who were calling my home."

In Mrs. Murray's book, her co-author Rose Shade wrote that as for Pat Newcomb, "The police practically had to forcibly evict her. But first she was allowed to telephone her psychiatrist and arrange to have him pick her up at the corner of Sunset and Carmelina, a few blocks away. Eunice offered to drive her there."

Aware that Peter drove Pat to Marilyn's, for additional corroboration, I asked a guest of Peter's that night Dolores Naar if Pat got a lift from somebody. Dolores said she didn't recall that detail, "I have no idea. I was so young. None of that meant *anything* to me. I was a young new mother and all I wanted to do was to get home to my baby and so I don't remember *any* of that." I asked her if anyone else was at Peter's party and Dolores recalled, "All I remember is 'Bullets' Durgom. George Durgom. There were other people there but I don't remember."

Durgom told Anthony Summers with absolute certainty that Pat Newcomb arrived at Peter's house at 9:30 P.M. Durgom told Summers that after ten or eleven o'clock, Mickey Rudin who was "the lawyer and somebody else went over to the house... and it was too late." When Rudin arrived between eleven and twelve, Peter Lawford and Pat Newcomb had already beat him to the scene in Peter's Lincoln Continental sedan. As noted previously by Norman Jefferies: Peter Lawford and Pat Newcomb had arrived together when Marilyn was not dead. James Hall and Raymond Strait did not know whether Peter Lawford and Pat Newcomb had arrived together yet they did agree Pat and Peter were both present in her home before Marilyn died.

When Summers interviewed Juliet Roswell, a former Arthur Jacobs employee, she quoted Jacobs as saying, "I went out there at eleven o'clock." Natalie Jacobs told biographer Matthew Smith it wouldn't have taken Arthur more than half-an-hour past 10:30 to get from the Hollywood Bowl to Marilyn's house. Oddly, Spada said Dolores Naar and the Lawford maid Erma Lee Riley observed that during Peter's regular Saturday evening party, there was no worry over Marilyn on Peter Lawford's end. [95]

Marilyn Monroe: A Case for Murder
Officer Lynn Franklin Pulls Over a Very Drunk Peter Lawford

In the *Say Goodbye to the President* documentary, former Mayor Sam Yorty recalled, "Chief Parker told me confidentially that Bobby Kennedy was supposed to be north of Los Angeles. Some say he was making a speech. But that actually, he said he was seen at the Beverly Hilton Hotel in Los Angeles... on the very night that she died." Detective Thad Brown's brother Finis, also a detective, relayed to Anthony Summers, "I talked to contacts who had seen Kennedy and Lawford at the Beverly Hilton Hotel the day she took the overdose."

At 12:10 A.M. on August 5, 1962, a very drunk Peter Lawford, driving a Lincoln Continental sedan, was going east along Olympic Boulevard. His speed was estimated to be 70 – 80 M.P.H. Franklin flashed on his red light. After hitting the intersection at Robertson, the Lincoln soon came to a stop. Using Franklin's own book and his interview with Brown and Barham, the following was roughly the exchange:

> FRANKLIN: Pete, what the hell do you think you're doing?... Your headlights are off and you were traveling seventy-five miles an hour.

> PETER: I'm sorry. I have to get somebody to the airport.

> FRANKLIN: You're heading in the wrong direction. You should be headed west not east.

> PETER: But first I have to check my friend out of the Beverly Hilton Hotel.

> FRANKLIN: You're still headed wrong. The Hilton is two miles in the other direction.

> Franklin glances at Greenson in the front seat.

> PETER: He's a doctor. He's just riding along with us to the airport.

> After aiming his flashlight in the backseat, Franklin is surprised to see Bobby Kennedy.

FRANKLIN: Evening, sir.

Bobby nods.

PETER: We've got to get the Attorney General checked out of the Hilton, and there's only a few minutes before his plane leaves.

FRANKLIN: Well, you wouldn't have gotten there at all the way you were heading. The Hilton and the airport are both miles in the opposite direction.

Bobby gets mad at Peter.

BOBBY: I told you, stupid!

Bobby then turns to Officer Franklin.

BOBBY: Can we go now?

FRANKLIN: Sure. Just don't take it at seventy-five miles an hour.

Peter turns the car around and drives away.

At the time, Franklin did not correlate Bobby Kennedy with Marilyn Monroe as the news of her death would not be released until hours later. After seeing Marilyn's funeral footage and other pictures, Franklin would later identify the third man in the front seat as her psychoanalyst Dr. Ralph Greenson. If we look back at Peter's interview with Heymann, Peter mentioned himself along with Bobby Kennedy and Greenson as co-conspirators responsible for Marilyn's death. These were the same three men pulled over by Franklin!

Franklin reflected in his book, "The significant thing that might be related to the hit attack on me was that I was the only witness that I know of, certainly the only one wearing a badge, who could testify that the Attorney General of the United States, Robert Kennedy, had been in Los Angeles in the middle of that night, going in the wrong direction at high speed, trying to get out of town as fast as he could, in the company of a doctor who had treated Monroe that same night and who by some accounts may have been responsible for her death…

"I'm not trying to cover the case here, but for my money, she was murdered and Robert Kennedy at least knew about it, maybe ordered the killing, and certainly tried to cover it up. The Secret Service very definitely tried to cover up the fact that Kennedy was in town, together with Marilyn's physician [Greenson], the night she died." On September 26, 2010, retired OCID detective Mike Rothmiller called me back:

> MARGOLIS: Do you know what happened to Marilyn's diary?
>
> ROTHMILLER: No.
>
> MARGOLIS: Did Donald Wolfe quote you correctly regarding what you saw in the diary?
>
> ROTHMILLER: Yes.
>
> MARGOLIS: Do you think Lynn Franklin's for real?
>
> ROTHMILLER: I think he's for real.
>
> MARGOLIS: Do the police believe she was murdered?
>
> ROTHMILLER: Many do.
>
> MARGOLIS: Do you think she was murdered?
>
> ROTHMILLER: That's what it appears to be.

Joe Naar told me he answered a call from Peter Lawford at 11:30 P.M. He said the same to Donald Spoto. About 40 minutes later, Franklin pulled over Peter. When I interviewed Joe Naar, I mentioned Lynn Franklin's account. Taken aback, Joe had this to say about Officer Franklin, "He is so full of shit. That is the most insane thing I have ever heard. I've *never* heard that one. Bobby was in the backseat? Peter was driving? I was on the phone with Peter most of that night. How in the world could he be in the car driving and drinking? He hadn't had a drink. That's one-on-one with me at 11:30 at night. Now who's telling the truth?

"What asshole would believe that jerk-off cop who's trying to get his name in the papers? Don't even repeat that story. You say it once and it gets out there and somebody repeats it and ten times later someone thinks it's the truth. If they had any idea of the truth it's not even 1000% close. It's somebody's imagination. What are they, writers or something? I mean that's the most insane thing I've ever heard. You're giving them too much respect. You're interviewing the wrong people. They know shit about it. Why would you talk to these assholes?"

After I mentioned that Lynn Franklin was a well-decorated officer who had received the presitigious CHA Award, Joe said, "If you're the highest decorated officer, you don't need that kind of publicity. He wouldn't talk like that. And of course, they're gonna put medals after his name."

When the murder rumors started spreading days after Marilyn's death, Joe Naar told me, "People like Warren Beatty think I know exactly what happened. That I'm covering it up because I'm a friend of the [Kennedy] family and that what really happened is that Bobby came down and killed her. It's such bullshit. Warren heard all sorts of things. In those days, everybody was talking about how Bobby killed her. 'Bobby had her killed.' "

Perhaps Beatty felt this way but he quickly changed his mind by passionately embracing Camelot's idealism to help the needy and less fortunate. In 1963, Jack wanted Beatty to star in a movie called *PT-109* where Beatty would play the role of Kennedy in a semi-true story. He declined but he and Jack met and became fast friends. According to Beatty's Internet Movie Database entry at imdb.com: "Beatty and [Jack] Kennedy remained very good friends up until Kennedy's death in 1963.

"He [Beatty] became close to Robert F. Kennedy during his 1968 campaign for the Democratic presidential nomination. Beatty's relationship with Robert F. Kennedy was closer than the one Beatty had had with John F. Kennedy. Beatty was particularly valuable during the campaign in firing up volunteers for such mundane activities as door-to-door canvassing. Robert F. Kennedy was impressed by Beatty's thorough understanding of the issues. After the assassination of Robert F. Kennedy in Beatty's hometown of Los Angeles, Beatty became a vocal gun control advocate."

Going against Joe Naar's assessment that Peter wasn't drunk, Officer Lynn Franklin stated to Brown and Barham that Peter "appeared drunk, terrified, and coming apart at the seems." Fred Otash confirmed that Lawford "looked like hell, trembling in the manner of a junkie going through cold turkey withdrawal. He was drunk, stoned, and an emotional basket case."

Milt Ebbins recalled, "I spoke to Peter at his house at one-thirty that night. Bullets Durgom told me he was there until one-thirty. At three o'clock I called Peter and there was no answer. He always disconnected the phone when he went to bed. He was very drunk when I spoke to him at one-thirty, and he couldn't have driven in that condition. I'm sure he passed out and that was that... Peter was getting drunker by the minute... He'd be coughing then be silent."

As mentioned above, Joe Naar told me he talked to Peter most of the night yet Ebbins is adamant that Peter had his phone disconnected. In any event, a police officer (Franklin), a former police officer (Otash), and a best friend (Ebbins) all attest that Peter was inebriated that night. [96]

Bobby Kennedy and the Plane Back to San Francisco

In 1970, biographer Patte Barham interviewed Peter Lawford's mother Lady May Lawford, who relayed, "I already knew that a dark helicopter, like the one the Kennedy boys used, had been parked on the beach. And I knew that neighbors saw Bobby dashing in and out on Saturday." Peter's next-door neighbor Ward Wood, who was married to Lynn Sherman, recalled, "It was Bobby all right. He was in khakis and a white shirt open at the neck."

Mansfield's press secretary Raymond Strait who listened to eleven hours of Otash's tapes told me, "Bobby skipped out of town and said he was never there but everybody knew he was there. You cover your tail as best you can. He took a quick hop up to San Francisco and acted like he was 400 or 500 miles away... I know that he went straight to Santa Monica and went up north to the Bay area to his friends."

Wolfe noted that reporter Joe Hyams interviewed Peter's neighbors who were "upset that a helicopter had touched down on the Santa Monica shore behind the Lawford residence in the early hours of Sunday morning, August 5, blowing sand into their swimming pools." According to Summers' research, helicopters "were permitted to land on the beach during the Kennedy presidency." Hyams unsuccessfully tried to obtain the helicopter logs from Conners Helicopter Service in Santa Monica.

Then his friend William Woodfield went back and talked to the pilot claiming he was doing a story on celebrities who had recently used their service including Frank Sinatra. The pilot agreed on the basis of positive publicity for their company. Woodfield related to Summers that one log in particular displayed an entry for August 5.

Woodfield remembered, "The time in the log was sometime after midnight – I think between midnight and two in the morning. It showed clearly that a helicopter had picked up Robert Kennedy at the Santa Monica Beach." James Zonlick worked for Hal Conners' helicopter service as one of his main pilots.

Zonlick recalled, "Hal had picked Robert Kennedy up at the beach house and left him at Los Angeles International Airport... He was a little pleased that we'd handled that V.I.P. sort of person." Connor's daughter Patricia said her father Hal arrived later than usual on the night of Marilyn's death. She relayed, "Next morning, I remember saying, 'Did you hear Marilyn Monroe died?,' and he didn't really answer at all."

Four days after Marilyn's death, Hyams and Woodfield called the Attorney General's Office to "put the story to rest." A Kennedy aide replied, "The Attorney General would appreciate it if you would not do the story." Yet Woodfield and Hyams pushed the story forward to New York in the office of the *Herald Tribune*. The editor said flatly, "But although we're a Republican paper and it's an election year, the story would be a gratuitous slap at the President. He'd be guilty by association. So we're killing it." On the morning of August 5 at 9:30 A.M., Bobby Kennedy attended Mass with his wife Ethel and four of their children at St. Mary Parish in Gilroy, California, 79 miles south of San Francisco. [97]

What Happened to Marilyn's Diary Before Bobby Kennedy Got It?

In the early afternoon, after Marilyn recovered from the intramuscular Nembutal injection, Bobby and Peter were eventually screamed out of the house. They left without the diary. That's why Kennedy came back just before Marilyn died. Instead of going in her main bedroom again, he searched her guest cottage where one of her filing cabinets was located. He looked for the diary in vain, yelling in the guest cottage. He never did find it that night. He couldn't understand why it wasn't there.

Bobby needed to find it. On Monday morning, August 6, Marilyn had threatened to go public with its contents. Marilyn wrote about Frank Sinatra, her affairs with both Kennedy brothers, political discussions she had with Bobby including the plot to kill Castro, among other issues ranging from Jimmy Hoffa, Sam Giancana and the Mafia to Russia. As Anthony Summers noted, because of the Kennedys, Marilyn Monroe was now a national security risk. [98]

The following morning when the police had already arrived, Pat Newcomb resumed the search at Marilyn's house for the red diary Bobby and the two men couldn't find the previous night. Norman Jefferies and Eunice Murray curiously observed how Pat Newcomb didn't want to leave. Jefferies related to Wolfe, "She was looking through drawers and going into Marilyn's bedroom... The police had to control her. When they told us to leave because they were going to seal the house, she became unglued. They had trouble getting her out of the door. She kept trying to get back inside." Mrs. Murray said, "Pat Newcomb didn't want to leave. She was sitting in the third bedroom where she had so recently spent the night. She had quieted down from her previous hysterical state, but gave no impression of planning to move... The police practically had to forcibly evict her."

It's important to point out that Mrs. Murray wasn't an evil woman as Donald Spoto had liberally portrayed her. Quite simply, she acted as a spy for Greenson and did only what she was told. In fact, Clemmons noticed a frightened Mrs. Murray when he arrived. Out of respect for her now deceased employer, the housekeeper was being very protective of Marilyn's property that night. She had to get everything in order before reporters descended like "vultures" at the house as Pat Newcomb later called them. Mrs. Murray cleaned the bed sheets in the guest cottage that had become soiled because of the effects of the enema. She removed the food from the fridge so it wouldn't spoil. She packed away all her things into a basket that was hers and other such tasks.

On Monday morning August 6, while waiting for Marilyn's executrix Inez Melson, Norman Jefferies said he saw Mrs. Murray give the red diary and one of Marilyn's address books to a driver for the Coroner's Office. Wolfe wrote, "Jefferies couldn't explain when or how Murray obtained the diary." Former Deputy Coroner's Aide Lionel Grandison provided corroboration for Jefferies' recollection.

Grandison recalled for *The Marilyn Files* documentary, "I sent the drivers to her house to pick up any property or any information that would lead us to the next of kin. They came back with a book. The infamous little red book... I saw the book that Monday... It had a very interesting series of stories, of assessments, of evaluations of things that were apparently going on in her life. John Kennedy, Robert Kennedy, Mafia... We got the property back up in that safe Monday evening. That Tuesday, it was gone, never to be seen again at least in Los Angeles County Coroner's Office to my knowledge."

Mrs. Murray also believed she was protecting Marilyn's property by holding onto the red diary and one of her address books until she could give it to someone who wouldn't steal or sell them. She had nonchalantly placed these items in her basket and nobody was the wiser. If Bobby Kennedy had seen the diary, he most certainly would've taken it.

The address book got to the right person but once the little red diary hit the Coroner's Office that Monday, the next day it was missing. Wolfe noted, "According to Grandison only three others knew the combination of the safe. Phil Schwartzberg, the coroner's administrative assistant; Richard Rathman, who was in charge of administration; and Coroner Curphey." [99]

Jay Margolis
Did Chief Parker Cover Up Bobby Kennedy's Tracks in Los Angeles?

Anthony Summers learned that Detective Sergeant Robert "Byron was roused from his bed around 5:00 A.M., and it took him forty-five minutes to reach Marilyn's house. He said the only people present were the attorney, Milton Rudin, Dr. Engelberg, and Eunice Murray... 'The lawyer said very little. He didn't want to discuss much about it.'

"The psychiatrist, Dr. Greenson, was no longer at the house by the time Sergeant Byron arrived. Byron and his superior, Lieutenant Grover Armstrong, Chief of Detectives in West Los Angeles, conducted the main interviews. As the reports show, they had some difficulty reconciling the accounts of Mrs. Murray, Dr. Engelberg, and Dr. Greenson, especially with regard to timing. They felt strongly enough to write in one report that Mrs. Murray was 'possibly evasive.' Byron, a veteran policeman, had been a Homicide detective for five years.

" 'My feeling,' he recalls, 'was that she had been told what to say, that it had all been rehearsed beforehand. She had her story, and that was it.' As for Dr. Engelberg and Milton Rudin, Byron says, 'as far as those two were concerned it was a negative result... They were telling me what they wanted me to know. That was my feeling at the time. I was thrown by their attitude. All in all,' Byron remembers, 'I got some wild answers. There was a lot more they could have told us... I didn't feel they were telling the correct time or situation but we did not do what we'd normally do, and drag them into the station.'

"The investigation was not pursued further, Byron explains, because there were no signs of violence at the scene and because the autopsy clearly reflected barbiturate poisoning... Byron says he heard, from police sources at the time, 'that Robert Kennedy had come to see her...' "

Byron is correct that Greenson couldn't have been at the house by the time the reporters were there as newsreel footage proved. It would be nearly impossible for Greenson to escape their snapping cameras. In fact, no such photographs of Greenson on the scene have survived, which provided strong support that he did in fact leave the scene early. I called Dorothea Byron but she wouldn't let me talk to her husband Robert:

MARGOLIS: It was a completely empty stomach.

BYRON: You know, I just can't help you. I know nothing

about it. My husband is incapable of knowing about it. At this time in his life.

MARGOLIS: He just said that the principles involved were evasive.

BYRON: I can't tell you a thing, I mean, really. He was pretty closed-mouthed about the thing anyhow... There are so many people who have written books.

MARGOLIS: I'm trying to clear through the nonsense.

BYRON: I'll let them leave that to the police department if they're so interested in clearing that up but I want no part of it.

Chief William Parker liked Bobby Kennedy, especially his stance on organized crime, but at first, Parker was apprehensive. Biographer John Buntin observed, "Several months after the convention, Parker went to visit his younger brother Joe and his sister-in-law Jane. One evening after dinner, the topic turned to the Kennedys. Bill made a fleeting comment, that 'he would never believe' the things the Kennedys were involved in. Joe would later speculate that Bill spurned a job with the administration in Washington because he did not care to associate with the likes of the actor Peter Lawford and his good friend, Frank Sinatra. Sinatra, whom Parker regarded as being 'totally tied to the Mafia,' was clearly a sore point."

As for the Marilyn Monroe investigation, Parker's wife Helen told Anthony Summers that her husband "wanted special attention paid to this particular case by the investigators, and he tried to send the best men out there, including detectives from the downtown office, because there was so much talk that she was close to John or Robert Kennedy. And Mr. Parker was very fond of Robert, thought he was very intelligent, thought he would've been a better president than John. Robert and John were supposed to be Catholics, I think and Mr. Parker was a Catholic. And maybe he thought undue pressure would be brought, that possibly the Republicans would jump on it. And so he said, 'This thing has to be straightened out in more ways than one.' "

Brown and Barham explained, "With the stroke of a pen, Chief Parker began the coverup by refusing to assign a full-time detective team to the Monroe case. Even when the cops stumbled on something, such as the time Sgt. Robert Byron told superiors that 'Murray is obviously lying. She is evasive and her answers are obviously rehearsed,' they were told to forget about it. And

Parker was ever vigilant, apparently fretting over every detail that threatened the coverup. When columnist May Mann filed a series on the ineptitude of the probe, she got a call from Parker that night. 'He told me it would be bad for my health if I kept writing stories like that.' " Former OCID detective Mike Rothmiller informed Brown and Barham, "Since nobody really ever investigated this death – they only covered up. All the trails were allowed to turn cold."

In the late summer of 1992, Rothmiller released his book *L.A. Secret Police: Inside the LAPD Elite Spy Network*, exposing the corruption he viewed within the police department while he was working for the OCID. Brown and Barham wrote, "It was this unit [the OCID] which had undertaken the clandestine probe of Monroe's death. Organized by the dictatorial Chief Parker in 1959, the fifty-seven man unit apparently rampaged beyond the bounds of legality."

Rothmiller said the unit would "accumulate dirt on the movers and shakers of L.A.'s political and entertainment establishment. The intelligence chiefs were ruthless and corrupt… And they had the power to ruin lives and reputations – or to safeguard. This is precisely what they did with the Monroe investigation… they protected the name of the Kennedy dynasty." Brown and Barham concluded, "It was this circle of handpicked detectives who investigated Monroe's death three times (in 1962, 1975, and 1982). Every scrap of paper about the death wound up in the hands of these investigative power brokers."

One of the first to arrive at the scene, Detective Daniel K. Stewart told me he believed Marilyn's death was an accident in that she forgot how many pills she swallowed. However, he would not comment to me whether Bobby Kennedy was in town on the night Marilyn died or if a crime scene had been established the next morning. Stewart suggested I contact former Beverly Hills Police Chief Marvin D. Iannone for more information. I called several times but to no avail.

Most of the officers at Marilyn's saw no evidence of foul play and simply assumed she took her own life, intentionally or accidentally. Murder was neither discussed nor encouraged. Because they believed it was a suicide, standard procedures were not conducted because nobody considered it a crime scene. Brown and Barham agreed, "That fatalistic thinking apparently tainted the investigation from the start. And former intelligence captain Neil Spotts, who also reinvestigated the death in 1975, is typical of this 'suicide mind-set': 'It was such an obvious case,' said Spotts. 'Because she had most certainly killed herself; it was the Coroner's case from the start. They found Mrs. Murray, learned of the discovery, found the empty pill bottles, and saw her hand grasping the telephone. There was absolutely nothing suspicious at the scene. Marilyn died by her own hand.'

"Spotts noted that Chief Parker didn't even assign a full-time homicide team to the investigation. 'It was handled in the field – as a routine matter.' In fact, Sgt. Jack Clemmons, the first man on the scene, overheard a conversation, which typified the relaxed rules governing the Monroe investigation. 'Nobody cared,' said Clemmons. 'Should we call the lab boys?' a young patrolman asked the ranking lieutenant standing next to him. 'What for?' the uniformed officer shot back. 'It's just another Hollywood broad who killed herself.' " Marilyn's friend reporter George Carpozi, Jr. related to Joanne Green-Levine, "They never conducted a criminal investigation. What they did was they had a psychiatric study of a bunch of doctors who concluded that she killed herself either accidentally or deliberately."

Odd things began to happen even after Marilyn's body was removed from her home. Robert Dambacher told me, "I was a Deputy Coroner at the time. My partner's name was Cletus Pace. So Cleet and I were dispatched at eight in the morning to go out to Westwood Village Mortuary to pick up her remains. Westwood had gone to the residence. We brought her body back to the Coroner's Office in Downtown Los Angeles. In retrospect, she should have come in to the Coroner's Office right in the beginning, right from the residence to the Coroner's Office, but she didn't… I think she took a deliberate overdose of drugs. She had enough drugs in her to kill about three of us. You can't accidentally take that many pills."

In a photo by Keystone/Getty Images, young Bob Dambacher and Cleet Pace, the older man behind him with glasses, are shown removing Marilyn Monroe from the Westwood Village Mortuary, a building with window blinds to the left and right. Many have mistakenly stated that the men were taking the body away from Marilyn's home. Dambacher confirmed this was not true, "I never did go to the residence."

Others were becoming aware of suspicious occurrences. *New York Herald Tribune* reporter Joe Hyams relayed, "I had a source at the telephone company and my source came back and said the Secret Service has already been here and taken our records. Kind of weird… The fact that the Secret Service had impounded all those telephone tapes was really weird because that's very uncommon. That's the first time in my memory as a reporter that they ever, ever stepped in that fast to start a hush." Hyams told Anthony Summers he contacted the telephone company "the morning after her death." Columnist Florabel Muir wrote in the *New York Daily News* on August 8, 1962:

"Strange 'pressures' are being put on Los Angeles police investigating the death of Marilyn Monroe," sources close to the probers said last night.

Police investigators have refused to make public the records of phone calls made from Miss Monroe's home last Saturday evening, hours before she took an overdose of sleeping pills. The police have impounded the phone company's taped record of outgoing calls. Normally in suicide probes here, the record of such phone calls would have been made available to the public within a few days.

The purported pressures are mysterious. They apparently are coming from persons who had been closely in touch with Marilyn the last few weeks.

Los Angeles Times reporter Jack Tobin, who Hamilton had often confided in, relayed to Anthony Summers, "Hamilton told me he had the telephone history of the last day or two of Marilyn Monroe's life. When I expressed interest, he said, 'I will tell you nothing more.'"

The Kennedys also had to exercise damage control on an absolutely hysterical Pat Newcomb. Press agent Michael Selsman said, "I believe that the Kennedys were concerned that Pat, being a close friend of Marilyn's, would become very emotional and might at some point mention something to somebody about the extent of the relationship between the Kennedys and Marilyn." Joe Hyams said, "Eunice Murray, who was Marilyn's housekeeper and who had found the body, disappeared. And Pat Newcomb disappeared but she reappeared very hastily working for the Kennedys in Washington. It just began to look like a vast cover-up."

George Barris relayed to me, "I'll tell you about Pat Newcomb. When Marilyn died, they couldn't reach Pat. All the press, the newspapers, the radio, television, they couldn't find her. When my story came out in the *Daily News*, I get a phone call. I was at the *Daily News* office. She called me there. I said, 'Where are you? Everybody's looking for you.' 'I don't want to talk to anyone but I'd like to see you.' 'Where are you?' 'I'm at the Sherry-Netherland.' It's a big hotel opposite Central Park in New York. 'Can you come over?' I said, 'Sure.' 'I'll give you a name to call me.' She didn't want to have her name there because the press could find her. So when I got there, I said I'm here to see so-and-so and I was able to go to her room. 'Are you alright? Where are you? What's going on?'

"'George, I was invited to stay with Bobby Kennedy. I was at the

Kennedys'.' And nobody knew where she was. She said, 'I'm going to Paris.' I think the Kennedys paid for that trip. Where was she going to get the money? She wanted to get away from everything, same as I didn't want the press bothering me. 'Do you know anybody in Paris?' 'No.' So I gave her the name of a friend and I said, 'Look, if you're lonely and you want to see Paris, call this person I can trust and he won't tell the press you're there or anything. And he'll take you to dinner and show you Paris.' So I gave her the name and phone number of a friend so she could have somebody to meet.

"She thanked me and I left. But she called me one day and said, 'George, I'm working in Washington. I know you took a lot of these wonderful pictures of Marilyn and I knew she wanted some. Would you?' It was as a memento, something to remember Marilyn. At my own expense, I flew down. I met her at the office near Bobby Kennedy. She had a job working for motion pictures. We chatted a while. She had tears in her eyes. I then flew back to New York. So she had a collection of photos of Marilyn for her own personal use. She doesn't want to talk about Marilyn because she was so close to her." [100]

Bobby Kennedy Publicly Praises the FBI Director

J. Edgar Hoover knew Bobby Kennedy had Marilyn Monroe killed. Hoover's teenage neighbor Anthony Calomaris told Anthony Summers decades later, "He said she was murdered, that it wasn't a suicide, that the Kennedys were involved." However, Hoover would never think of having Bobby arrested. It was not in his character. Instead, he blackmailed the Attorney General to secure his current position as head of the FBI, reminding Bobby who was really running the country. Besides, exposing the Kennedys in this scandal could destroy the integrity the nation had in its own government in the Pre-Watergate days. It would be inconceivable that Hoover would make such a move.

When Bobby Kennedy saw Marilyn Monroe on February 1, 1962, not knowing that the Lawford home was bugged by the FBI Director, Marilyn told Bobby she knew Hoover was following her and she wondered when Bobby was going to fire him. Bobby said he wasn't in a position to do so at the moment. Anthony Summers wrote, "For Edgar, reading the transcript in Washington, Kennedy's words must have held some comfort. He now knew, for sure, from the mouth of one of the brothers, that the Kennedys were afraid to dismiss him – for the time being. That gave him all the more reason to go on watching to keep on piling up compromising information."

In 1961, after disagreeing with J. Edgar Hoover at a function for the Justice Department, Ethel Kennedy "put an anonymous note in the FBI's 'suggestions' box proposing that the Director be replaced by the Los Angeles Police Chief William Parker, whom Hoover loathed." The potential for blackmail resolved the discrepancy of why Bobby Kennedy publicly expressed his gratitude towards Hoover, a man he was known to hate. On August 7, at the Seattle World's Fair, Kennedy uncharacteristically supported J. Edgar Hoover in public and said something that must have made Parker cringe, "I hope Hoover will continue to serve the country for many, many years to come."

On September 18, 1965, Bobby Kennedy attended a ceremonial line-up for Mickey Mantle at Yankee Stadium. Joe DiMaggio was present and when Bobby reached out to shake his hand, Joe quietly turned around and walked away, heading towards the dugout. Not even a year later on July 16, 1966, Chief Parker died of a heart attack while in attendance at a military dinner where he was a guest speaker. [101]

THE KENNEDY VERSION: ✓

Was Peter's Call to Ebbins a Cry for Help or a Really Good Alibi?

Milt Ebbins, Peter Lawford's best friend and Vice President of his production company Chrislaw, *claimed* he got a frantic telephone call from Peter around 7:15 or 7:40 or close to 8:00 P.M., depending on which version of his account one chooses. He said Peter was worried that something was wrong with Marilyn. That maybe she took too many sleeping pills. As we've already seen, there was absolutely nothing wrong with Marilyn at 7:15 or 8:00 or even 9:30 P.M.

Brown and Barham noted that according to Rupert Allan "the master publicist, Lawford's story sounded as though it had been written for him by a public relations expert. It seemed more like an alibi than an actual event." Ebbins denied that Peter would have driven to Marilyn's the night she died. Ebbins reflected to Spoto, "I was a confidant of Peter's. Believe me, I was a confidant of this man. He would've dropped it to me in a minute… Others told him, '[Comedian] Mort Sahl will go with you…' " Ebbins then claimed he phoned Marilyn's house, "I called and got a busy signal. The operator said it was out of order. It's off the hook!" Now that we know Marilyn was not in trouble anytime before 9:30 P.M., it's easy to see right through Ebbins' story: he simply was not telling the truth.

Ebbins continued to Spoto, "Peter Lawford wanted to go badly. I said, 'Peter, don't do it. Please let me at least call Mickey Rudin and alert him and *then* if we do that then you can go…' I was badly criticized for this by the way but he eventually agreed I was right… I said, 'Peter, had we gone, Mrs. Murray would've talked us out of it in minutes. Nothing would've happened. I mean, look at her. She probably does this every night…' I called Mickey Rudin at Mildred Allenberg's house. I got him on the phone. And he said, 'Let me check it out and I'll get back to you.' And he called me back and he said, 'I talked to Mrs. Murray. She's fine. She looked through the crack in the window. She said, "She's fine. She does this every night. Every night she does this." ' He said, 'You don't have to go over there. Please don't go over there. You're just gonna cause problems...'

"I called Peter back. 'I still want to go over there!' 'Mickey Rudin is her manager and lawyer. Is he gonna do anything wrong to her?' 'I wanna talk to Mickey Rudin.' I say, 'Mickey, if you don't call, he's gonna go...' He calls Peter. He convinces Peter not to go. Peter continually calls me after that getting drunker by the minute. I could tell because he had a very peculiar thing when he was drinking. He'd cough then he'd be silent. Peter says, 'I think we should go over there.' I said, 'Go! You don't need me.' He said, 'I'm not going. I'm not going.' "

Spoto told Ebbins that at 11:30 P.M., Peter called his best friend Joe Naar saying, "Go over to Marilyn's house." Spoto then said, "Joe Naar puts his trousers on and gets ready to leave and the phone rings again and Peter says, 'I just had a call from the doctors. They're there. Everything's fine.' "

Ebbins countered, "That's a lot of crap... Number one, Peter never talked to Rudin that night because Rudin told me to tell him [about Marilyn's death]. He told me to tell him. I called Peter immediately and the phone was dead. And Erma Lee says, 'We don't answer the phone when Peter goes to bed. Nobody picks up the phones downstairs. Upstairs, he pulls it out of the wall...'

"Because I tried to get him many times and couldn't get him! He won't answer... Erma told me he never left the house... The maid was there. The maid was his mistress!... Mickey Rudin calls me to tell me at four... I said, 'What are you doing up at this hour?' He said, 'We've got some problems.' I said, 'How's Marilyn?' He said, 'Not good.' I said, 'What's the matter with her?' He said, 'Well, I'm here with Dr. Engelberg and Dr. Greenson and they just pronounced her dead and we just notified the police. And you're the first one that knows about it. The first one that knows about it.' That's what he said to me, quote on quote. And he said, 'You better tell Peter.' "

Regarding accusations that Bobby Kennedy had Marilyn Monroe killed, Ebbins told Spoto, "Come on!... Bobby Kennedy had more ways. He could've gotten rid of Marilyn Monroe with a phone call to Peter Lawford. A phone call!... Of course we noted she had a mental problem for years. Marilyn always thought she was going to wind up like her mother. She was scared to death of that."

Director Bill Asher relayed, "I heard from Peter at eight or nine... Then he called later, maybe midnight, probably one o'clock to go over with him." Peter's good friend producer George "Bullets" Durgom was a guest at his Saturday evening party on August 4. Durgom claimed Peter expressed concern to him about going over to Marilyn's home. For the *Say Goodbye to the President* documentary, Durgom related, "He mentions maybe I ought to go up there and see if she's okay. I said, 'Well, I don't know, Peter, if you should do that at this time. I mean, I'm sure everything's all right. If we go up there and there is anything going on, who knows what kind of story this will wind up being.'"

Milt Ebbins told Spoto, "There were two numbers. Peter didn't have the other number... Rudin asked me to let him check it out – to see if there was any trouble." Rudin agreed to this account and said, "I did not call [Greenson]. He had had enough quite frankly. He had spent the day with her. But I did call the housekeeper."

On August 9, 1962, Ebbins told a reporter that Peter called him on that last night, "He said Miss Monroe told him she would like to come but that she was tired and was going to bed early. He said he noticed nothing unusual, except that she did sound tired."[102] This is odd: on August 9, 1962, there was "nothing unusual" but thirty years later to Donald Spoto there's a tremendous panic and "Peter Lawford wanted to go badly."

Peter's own mother Lady May Lawford once said of her son, "Peter was such a big mistake!" Here's what she thinks of his story on August 4, "The night that Marilyn died, I called Peter out at the Santa Monica beach house. The telephone lines were very busy, but I finally got through, 'I've been robbed!' I exclaimed to Peter, who could have cared less about my dwindling jewel and silver collection.

"In the background I thought I heard that awful Boston accent of Bobby Kennedy. 'Later' was Peter's one word solution to my concern over the third break-in and burglary. Then he hung up. The next day when I heard about Marilyn's last phone call to Peter, I realized that my call to Peter the previous night – about eight o'clock – was near the same time... He explained that both Milton Ebbins and Mickey Rudin called him and assured him that Marilyn was all right so that finally Peter gave up the idea of going to Marilyn's house.

"It all smells of fish to me... And I wonder about her press agent-friend Pat Newcomb who joined the Kennedy's staff immediately upon Marilyn's death. It was the next morning that I heard that she was dead. Reports said the body was found at 3:40 A.M., but a reader of any well-written English mystery could figure out a before-midnight death by rigor mortis... Then [Noguchi] said her stomach was as clean as a whistle... I knew that Marilyn was seeing Jack Kennedy. I also knew that Marilyn was seeing Bobby Kennedy. They often used Pat and Peter's beach house for their dalliances with Marilyn... Peter was so enamored with the Kennedy charisma that if Jack or Bobby asked him to, he would have done anything – legal or illegal. So it is with Marilyn's death – Peter had a part in the cover-up."[103]

On October 7, 1985, Milt Ebbins told his "story," which is riddled with errors. All the things he said didn't happen on Marilyn's last night actually *did* happen. Ebbins relayed, "I talked to Peter on the telephone several times that night. He never left his beach house in Santa Monica. Bobby definitely was not in Southern California that night and neither man went to Marilyn's house. Forget about the ambulance. It just couldn't have happened. Peter called in the afternoon and asked me to dinner with Bullets Durgom and Joe Naar and his wife – and Marilyn. I declined. He called again to say Marilyn couldn't come and that she was anxiety-ridden. He was upset and wanted to go to Marilyn's house in Brentwood. I told him not to. We all knew Marilyn took too many pills and was drinking heavily."

Unembalmed blood sent out for testing later showed no alcohol was consumed that last day. Ebbins continued, "I suggested we call Mickey Rudin, Marilyn's attorney, and her psychiatrist, Dr. Ralph Greenson, Mickey's brother-in-law, and ask them to go to her house. I got Mickey and told him about Peter's apprehension.

"Mickey called me about 7:30 to say he had talked to Mrs. Murray, a psychiatric nurse hired by Greenson, who said she looked in on Marilyn. Murray told Mickey, 'She does this every night. She takes the pills, calls somebody and falls asleep. She's fine.' Mickey said Mrs. Murray had look through the drapery of an outside window and saw Marilyn lying on the bed asleep. The lights were on and the radio was going. I told Peter this and he insisted on talking to Mickey. Mickey called Peter and convinced him all was well but Peter was still apprehensive and wanted to go to Marilyn's. I told him Mrs. Murray would tell him the same thing she told Rudin.

"This was no conspiracy to kill Marilyn, you know, involving Mickey and Mrs. Murray, for God's sake. Peter called me twice more when he was getting a little drunk, expressing his fear that Marilyn was very ill. Peter called me once after midnight and he was bombed.

"By this time Mort Sahl had stopped by to talk to me. Mort was there when about five minutes to 4 A.M. Mickey called. And I asked him, 'How's Marilyn?' He said, 'Not good. I'm here with Dr. Greenson and Dr. Engelberg. We broke into her bedroom. They pronounced her dead. We just called the police.' I was stunned and told Mort. We were the first to know, except for Mickey and the two doctors. I tried to call Peter but he had pulled the phone jack from the wall – which he did every night – and I couldn't reach him. So I went to bed and later when I did reach Peter, he had already been told.

"Peter was guilt-ridden because he hadn't gone to Marilyn's house. I told him that Marilyn was doomed. She had tried to commit suicide five or six times previously. This time she made it. I never heard Bobby's name mentioned, much less about him arriving at Peter's house in a helicopter that night. Peter was my closest friend. He would have told me if Bobby had been here or if Marilyn had been taken away in an ambulance.

"That is the unadulterated story of the night Marilyn died. The rest of that stuff is pure fantasy. How could Bobby be in town that night? He was in Northern California with his wife and children. And he and Peter were never close friends. If Peter had bailed Bobby out of a jam, don't you think they would have been friends for life? But when Pat and Peter divorced, Peter became persona non grata with the Kennedys. Bobby never called Peter when he came to town, neither did Teddy or any other family member. The authorities are satisfied Marilyn committed suicide and died alone. The stories going around are circulated by people who want their names in the papers."

Ebbins clearly does not have a firm grasp of the time element that night. He said, "Mickey called me about 7:30 to say he had talked to Mrs. Murray." Rudin told police he called the housekeeper at 9:00! In 1975, Peter claimed to police that 7:30 was when Marilyn was going under. Fifteen minutes earlier at 7:15, Marilyn had happily finished her phone call with Joe DiMaggio, Jr. Also, Ebbins' account contradicts many of the things we know. We can now accept that an ambulance arrived at her home. After midnight, a helicopter did in fact bring Bobby from Peter's house in Santa Monica to Los Angeles International Airport. He subsequently took a private plane back to San Francisco.

Ebbins' story is further called into question in that he seems to have an answer for everything. He is either covering up what he knows or more likely he doesn't know anything of what happened that night and simply agreed to go along with a pre-packaged story he rehearsed many times. Why would the principles involved tell him anything? Besides, Ebbins by his own account stayed home all evening so he is a completely unreliable witness.

Milt Ebbins said Peter was "persona non grata with the Kennedys." As for Peter Lawford's relationship with Bobby Kennedy, a *People* magazine article dated January 14, 1985 called Ebbins' statement into question. Malcolm Boyes wrote that Peter Lawford "remained, however, on good terms with the Kennedys. In fact, presidential candidate Robert Kennedy, after winning the California primary in 1968, was headed for a Lawford-hosted party when he, too, was killed by an assassin's bullets."

Gloria Romanoff concurred with Ebbins that Bobby Kennedy was never Peter's good friend, "I don't think there was a lot of affection between Bobby Kennedy and Peter Lawford. I think Bobby Kennedy tolerated him because he was Pat's husband. I don't think he was terribly fond of Peter and Peter knew that." Officer Lynn Franklin noted a similar reaction. After getting the correct directions to the Beverly Hilton Hotel, Bobby chided Peter and said, "I told you, stupid!" Nonetheless, Bobby Kennedy and Peter Lawford continued to see one another but as many attest, Bobby clearly resented him and Peter took it. [104]

Jay Margolis

The Account of Peter Lawford's Friend Director Bill Asher

In 1992, according to Ebbins and Asher himself, Bill Asher's production company optioned the book *Double Cross* into a movie, the same book that accused Sam Giancana of having Marilyn Monroe killed. To Donald Spoto, Asher provided a similar account as Ebbins on Marilyn's last night but added a new twist: the possibility of seeking the advice of a very important man.

Asher's story to Spoto began like this: "I was so used to having dinner dates and appointments with Marilyn that never happened. I said, 'Peter, I'm not gonna sit around and wait for her, not that I don't want to be with you but I've got other things.' I went home. He called me about eight or nine I think. Said he couldn't get her on the phone. I might have been there when she called... No, I think I left. I don't think I was there then.

"When he called me, he said, 'I can't get her. She's not showing up.' He'd talked to her earlier and she signed off, I mean she'd fallen asleep on the phone... She had a couple of glasses of wine. It didn't take much but that's all. She's wasn't stressed at all. She was a little slurry. She had a couple of drinks but it wasn't anything that anyone would have been concerned about. There were times she would get incapacitated and you'd be worried about her... She had been sad... She was a sad gal.

"She was not taking good care of herself. She wouldn't really groom herself well at times. No one was obviously concerned. And when Peter called me and wanted to go over there later about midnight, it's the only thing I always felt badly about because we didn't go... I know he called Milt... He wanted somebody to go with him. I told him to call the old man, Joe. I said, 'If we go over there and find something, I don't know if you should be there.' I said, 'Call Mr. Kennedy and ask him what you should do.' I don't know if he called him or not. Marilyn's connection to the President was delicate at that time and the rumors about Marilyn and Jack. They were inside rumors. I don't think it was out at that time.

"I said, 'Your brother-in-law's the President of the United States! It might not be an appropriate thing for you to go over there.' So we didn't go. The next thing, he woke me up at four in the morning. He had gotten word that said she was dead. He knew by four or five... I'm not sure about the time. It could have been six."

Spoto's bright assistant Charlie relayed to Asher, "Joe Naar said he got a phone call but he's not sure when – late at night like you got. Instead of saying, let's go over, just ask him to go. Joe said he got up and was getting ready to go out and get dressed but just before he left to go out, he got another call from Peter saying 'Forget it. Everything's fine.' This would be eleven-thirty to midnight." Asher replied, "That's about right."

Charlie continued with an intriguing question, "Did you ever get a call from Peter saying, 'Somebody thinks she's fine?' " "No. No, that didn't happen to me... I remember being just a little bit irritated at this call in wanting to go over there and then of course, the tragedy may be that had I gone, it might've made a difference but who would've known?... Peter was close to her. Very protective of her."

If Asher and Naar are *not* lying about receiving these calls from Peter then there's a hole in Peter's story bigger than the Grand Canyon. Why would Peter call Joe Naar at 11:30 P.M. telling him to go by himself to check on Marilyn who lived just four blocks away from Joe's house and then call Joe back minutes later telling him not to go? *Then*, why would Peter call Bill Asher between 12:00 and 1:00 A.M. asking him to go over with him if he had already told Joe Naar not to bother? The story doesn't check out and nothing more needs to be said on the matter now that the discrepancy is noticed. [105]

Dolores Naar Claims Peter Said Greenson Gave Marilyn Sedatives

Before they arrived at Peter's party in the evening, Dolores told me, "We were to pick her up. Peter called our house and said, 'Don't pick up Marilyn. She's not coming.' " The Naars told biographer James Spada that this call from Peter was at about 7:30 P.M. According to Joe in his interview with Donald Spoto and in an interview with me, Peter called again at 11:30 P.M. but this time to check on Marilyn. In Spoto's interview with him, Joe quoted Peter as saying the following, "I just talked to Marilyn and I'm scared. I don't like the way she sounds. I think she's taken some pills. Will you go check up on her?"

Joe agreed to see about Marilyn. Two minutes later after he's done tying his last shoe, Peter called him back. Dolores relayed to Spada, "He said that he'd spoken to Marilyn's doctor and he had said that he had given her sedatives because she had been disturbed earlier and she was probably asleep, so don't bother going. He said, 'You'll just wake her up.' " In her first interview with me, I asked Dolores the following questions:

> MARGOLIS: How were you apprised of the conversation between Joe and Peter? Did Joe tell you that Marilyn had received sedatives from her doctor?

DOLORES: Well, I was there.

MARGOLIS: So, you were listening in on the phone with Joe while Peter was calling?

DOLORES: I was in the room.

In her second interview with me, we discussed this matter further. I told her, "As far as that last call from Peter goes telling you and Joe not to go around 11:30 P.M., Joe said to me in an interview that Peter told him that Dr. Greenson had said, 'She does this all the time. Don't go.' " Dolores agreed and said Dr. Greenson "had given her something to sleep and she's fine. That's what Peter told Joe. 'So you don't need to go.' "

MARGOLIS: That the doctor had given her something to go to sleep?

DOLORES: Right.

MARGOLIS: And this doctor was Dr. Greenson?

DOLORES: Right.

Perhaps Peter was alluding to Greenson's undiluted Nembutal injection, which would not only put Marilyn to sleep but allow her to never wake up. Even though she believes Marilyn died of an accidental suicide, Dolores still found Peter's actions more than a little suspicious. She told Spada, "Peter probably called Jack or Bobby and was told to take care of things – do whatever he had to do. And *do it yourself* – don't involve anybody else under any circumstances."

Spada made some chilling points, "These were an odd pair of telephone calls in an evening replete with oddities. Why did Peter, who had been worried about Marilyn since seven-thirty, wait until the Naars had returned home to indicate any concern to them over Marilyn? And why did he first ask Joe to go over to Marilyn's (after being told by Mickey Rudin that she was okay) and then, just a few minutes later, tell him *not* to go?" Remember, the Naars only lived four blocks away from Marilyn.

Dolores told Spada she believed Peter's two calls were "calculated to mislead us. Joe and I wondered, 'Why did he call us the second time and tell us not to go?' Maybe because by then he knew that Marilyn was dead." As Spada and I had reported, Dolores said that Marilyn's doctor had given her sedatives. She confirmed to me that Peter said this doctor was Greenson. Columnist Earl Wilson, whom Joe Naar told me was a "bullshit artist," documented the same in two of his books.

However, Wilson said the message of no worry over Marilyn was communicated from Greenson to Rudin instead of Greenson to Peter. In his book *The Show Business Nobody Knows* Wilson wrote, "Dr. Greenson told Rudin, his brother-in-law, that he felt confident that Marilyn was all right despite the goodbye message to Peter Lawford." Wilson noted in his next book *Show Business Laid Bare*, "Rudin began trying to locate Dr. Greenson. Rudin… eventually got to Dr. Greenson, who said he believed that she was all right because he'd been with her before and she seemed OK." Rudin claimed to Donald Spoto he didn't phone Greenson: he called Mrs. Murray. All this doesn't mean much as it relates to the death of Marilyn Monroe. Peter's calls to the Naars are simply nothing more than another part of his alibi that night. [106]

CONCLUSION:

Peter Lawford gave Joe and Dolores Naar a "story," subsequently confusing many a Marilyn Monroe biographer in the process. After the Naars left the party, Pat Newcomb arrived at Peter's at 9:30 P.M. according to George "Bullets" Durgom. Before Bobby and the security officers departed Marilyn's house, someone called Peter telling him to get over there and to hire a cleanup crew.

Peter then phoned Fred Otash and they agreed to meet at Fifth Helena. Next, Peter drove Pat Newcomb to Marilyn's and arrived around 10:30 P.M. soon after Bobby Kennedy and his men left. Had Schaefer Ambulance attendant James Hall and his driver Murray Liebowitz been allowed to take Marilyn to the hospital, she would be alive today. She was not yet dead when James Hall first arrived in the guest cottage. However, there was a premeditated plan to murder her by Bobby, Greenson, and Peter, a plan Peter said originated with Bobby.

None of the principles involved counted on Mrs. Murray calling an ambulance. After Marilyn died, Peter would express deep guilt over what really happened to her: she was murdered and he was involved. The British actor told his friends Marilyn took too many pills by accident. Joe Naar said to biographer Laurence Leamer, "I blame the changes in Peter and his final decline into the bottle on Marilyn's death. Peter kept saying, 'I should have let you go. I killed her.' " Peter's strange actions in front of his friends could best be explained if he was trying to come up with an alibi.

After I read sections from Heymann's interview with Peter, Dean Martin's ex-wife Jeanne said to me, "Let the woman alone. Just let the whole story alone. Everybody had a theory. Everybody knew who killed Marilyn and absolutely no solid proof of anything or any indication of it. It's the worst kind of journalism. It's just the trashiest kind of writing you could possibly find. I mean she's history now. I don't know who's starting this again."

I told Mrs. Martin, "As a researcher, I have to consider every possibility no matter how ridiculous. That's what a good researcher does. Because if he doesn't then he's not considering every possibility." She said, "Let me say something else to you. I would think that out of all the subjects in the world and you're a researcher and you're serious, how could you be going after the 'Marilyn Monroe Murder Mystery?' It's such yellow journalism. It doesn't speak well of you at all." Quite the contrary, to allow people to get away with murder does not speak well of any society.

Marilyn Monroe was not just a thing, something she feared she would become. She told Richard Meryman in her last interview with *Life* magazine in July 1962, "I never quite understood it – this sex symbol – I always thought symbols were those things you clash together! That's the trouble, a sex symbol becomes a thing. I just hate to be a thing. But if I'm going to be a symbol of something I'd rather have it sex than some other things they've got symbols of!" Not only was she "the symbol of the eternal feminine," as Lee Strasberg said at Marilyn's eulogy, she was a human being.

Former FBI agent Bill Roemer believed neither Bobby Kennedy nor the Mafia had anything to do with Marilyn's death. However, he answered in the affirmative to support the convening of a grand jury, "I would. Yeah. I think there have been so many questions now and there's so much conjecturing. It would be nice to put it all out in the open once and for all so there'd be no question to what exactly happened."

Luciano Mecacci deduced, "Marilyn's death was in the end a relief for everyone: for the Kennedys, who had been freed from the nightmare of a scandal; for the CIA and the FBI, who were reassured about a possible leak of secret material; and for Greenson, who had been released from a personal and professional commitment that was becoming too demanding."

Fred Otash said the FBI and the CIA had bugged Marilyn's home. Concerned about her "tell all" press conference, they wouldn't miss Marilyn if she suddenly died; however, this does not mean these organizations were directly responsible for her death. When the CIA and the FBI were both listening in over wiretaps as Marilyn was dying, they did absolutely nothing to stop it. In that respect, they are culpable.

Hoover was not a stupid man. His agents reported back to him that Bobby Kennedy was seen entering Marilyn's home shortly after 9:30. Before ten o'clock, Marilyn struggled and that struggle was recorded on wiretap. The agents then noted that Kennedy left at 10:30. Through cause and effect, Hoover knew the Kennedys were involved as he later told a neighbor. Bobby was fully aware that Hoover knew Kennedy had participated in the murder of a movie star.

In the years to come, the FBI Director would play games with Bobby Kennedy, always sticking it to him about Marilyn Monroe. On July 8, 1964, Hoover wrote to Bobby regarding Frank Capell's soon-to-be-released *The Strange Death of Marilyn Monroe*, "His book will make reference to your alleged friendship with the late Miss Marilyn Monroe. Mr. Capell stated that he will indicate in his book that you and Miss Monroe were intimate, and that you were in Miss Monroe's home at the time of her death."

According to Peter, Bobby had "convinced" Greenson that Marilyn would also publicly reveal *his* affair with her. If this wasn't true, Bobby had successfully manipulated the psychiatrist for his own ends. Once Greenson realized this, it was too late and he had experienced firsthand what it was like to be used by one of the Kennedy brothers. Therefore, Peter concluded that Greenson had been "set up" by Bobby to murder his star patient.

In fact, according to Heymann's hand-written notes, Peter told him, "Marilyn's affair with Greenson took on a far greater meaning at the time of her death. Marilyn, as everyone later discovered, had threatened Bobby with the prospect of holding a press conference at which she planned to announce her assignations with both the President and the Attorney General.

"Such an admission would no doubt have resulted in a major scandal. Bobby, on hearing of Marilyn's plans – and somehow knowing of her concomitant relationship with Greenson, called the good doctor and convinced him that his star patient also intended to disclose her romantic dealings with the psychiatrist."

If Greenson had been tricked into murdering Marilyn Monroe, his recorded deference to the Attorney General ("Talk to Bobby Kennedy") was indeed a bitter and illuminating remark. As for the movie star's last publicist, Heymann wrote in his notes what Peter told him, "After Marilyn's death, the Kennedys gave Pat a job in Washington and soon sent her off to Europe so the American press couldn't get a hold of her."

Everyone deserves the right to due process of law and that right was not afforded to Marilyn Monroe in 1962 and almost 50 years have passed since she died. Those involved in her death are now deceased and the only justice that can be afforded her is to name her murderers: Peter Lawford, Robert Kennedy, and the man who finally ended her life, Dr. Ralph Greenson. May Marilyn Monroe finally rest in peace. [107]

THE OTHER "MURDERERS" OF MARILYN MONROE:

Her "Secret Husband" Robert Slatzer (1927 – 2005)

Without documentation to support his claim, a man by the name of Robert Franklin Slatzer would say years after Marilyn Monroe's death that he was secretly married to her for less than five days on October 4, 1952. In 1974, Slatzer released his highly unconvincing book *The Life and Curious Death of Marilyn Monroe* (See the ridiculous chapter entitled, "Cotton and Gin.") Slatzer claimed first thing that morning in early October that he and Marilyn dashed off to Tijuana, Mexico to get married. Slatzer wrote, "We breezed toward San Diego, far ahead of the Saturday morning traffic build-up."

An incident mentioned nowhere in his book, Slatzer would later tell biographer Anthony Summers because of studio pressure from Darryl F. Zanuck days later, he then went back to Mexico to bribe the officials to undo the marriage. For his 1993 biography, Donald Spoto informed his readers he uncovered a Bank of America check in the amount of $313.13 written by Marilyn Monroe on October 4, 1952. Directly contradicting Slatzer's marriage claim, she had gone on a shopping spree in the afternoon to Jax on Wilshire Boulevard with drama coach Natasha Lytess.

Greg Schreiner, President of *Marilyn Remembered* since 1982, saw this check on exhibit and told me nowhere was Slatzer's name found in Marilyn's address books and she included everybody he said. Schreiner actually knew Robert Slatzer for years because Marilyn's real friends would often attend as guest speakers for the fan club and Slatzer tried to blend in but as time passed Schreiner said Slatzer was less and less convincing.

In fact, Schreiner said when Slatzer knew he didn't believe him anymore, Slatzer stopped inviting him over for dinner. But in the beginning, he told me Slatzer was often very clever about his lies and that he used to sell things Marilyn never really owned. He said it was pathetic. Schreiner can definitively state that Slatzer did not know Marilyn Monroe at all and only met her once on the set of *Niagara*.

In addition, I spoke with Slatzer's friend playwright Doral Chenoweth.

Jay Margolis

Under the pseudonym "Tom Wallace," he conceded to ghosting notes on behalf of Slatzer for the repugnant and disrespectful May 1957 *Confidential* magazine article displaying Slatzer's then-outdated pictures with Marilyn from the set of *Niagara* in June 1952. Chenoweth did not tell me explicitly that his friend Slatzer was a liar but it is suggested from his conversation with me.

Chenoweth said that a Mr. Fred D. Pfening, Jr. had arranged for Slatzer what would become his only pictures taken with Marilyn Monroe. Chenoweth said, "The famous picture with Bob and Marilyn was used many times in books about Slatzer and Monroe. That was taken by a guy named Fred Pfening, Jr., editor of a magazine called *Bandwagon*. He was a historian and an authority on the American circus. Pfening is the one who took that picture at Niagara Falls and he describes it in great detail in a video I produced here. Fred, Jr. contends that he introduced Bob to Marilyn Monroe."

"So he introduced them?" "He introduced him because he had access to get on the set with Joseph Cotten and Marilyn Monroe." Slatzer claimed in his book to have dated actress Jean Peters before she became Mrs. Howard Hughes in 1957. I asked Chenoweth, "Slatzer was a friend of Jean Peters, wasn't he?" "No. Through Pfening if that's what you wanna call it... So Pfening took Bob to Niagara Falls and they shot these things on the roof of the hotel."

Marilyn's friend reporter George Carpozi, Jr. trusted Slatzer for close to thirteen years since the publication of Carpozi's first Monroe biography in 1961. During that period of time, Carpozi wrote a total of three books on her. A fourth called *Confidentially Marilyn: The Most Intimate Monroe Ever – The Real Story of Her Life, the Murder and the Cover-Up*, a project he seriously began working on in the early 1980s, remained unfinished when he died on May 14, 2000. Carpozi was ready to point the fingers at Bobby Kennedy, Peter Lawford, and Dr. Ralph Greenson.

The three books Carpozi wrote had nothing on Slatzer but a mishmash of the same information. How Slatzer allegedly reunited with Marilyn Monroe at a Niagara Falls restaurant and how he claimed to have known her since 1946. In 1962, Carpozi came out with his second Monroe biography and in 1973, Carpozi released his third. However, Carpozi would one year later stop believing Slatzer was a friend of Marilyn Monroe. Slatzer had by now claimed for the first time to everybody's surprise that he was once married to the legendary actress, something Slatzer had never told Carpozi in all those thirteen years.

Carpozi related to Deborah Chiel, "Back in 1974, I had a call from Andy Ettinger, who was then the Editor-in-Chief of Pinnacle Books in New York. Andy had done several of my books. My last big one was the Alice

Marilyn Monroe: A Case for Murder

Crimmins book *Ordeal by Trial* and he said, 'I've got a big job for you to do. Come down to the office.' So I went down to see him and he shows me this 300-page manuscript. It's *The Life and Curious Death of Marilyn Monroe* by Robert Slatzer and he says to me, 'This is unreadable. You've got to put it in shape. Rewrite it.'

"I take it home with me and you just could not believe how horribly he'd written it and the claims that he made, that he had married Marilyn Monroe... Andy says, 'Please don't upset the applecart. Put everything in there that he has but write it in English. We paid him a lot of money and we want this book to come out.' So I did and ever since then he's been living off this book. He's made a fortune out of it... I had someone speak to his wife at the time [Kay Eicher who was married to Slatzer from 1954 to 1956] and she said, 'He was right here. He couldn't have been marrying Marilyn.' "

Initially, Marilyn's first husband Jim Dougherty was fooled into believing Slatzer knew Marilyn so Dougherty had allowed him to write a tribute in his first book *The Secret Happiness of Marilyn Monroe*. Dougherty became wise to Slatzer's game years later and wrote in his second book at how furious he was when he discovered Slatzer was a fraud:

> The individual who claims to have been married to her after our marriage, I consider absolutely bogus. I won't even mention his name here. He was never married to her, but has managed to cleverly "prove" that he was and to perpetuate his story. How odd it is that the engraved old watches "To XXX with all my love Marilyn" show engraving that is very fresh and new looking. How convenient that all the suppressed records of that Mexican marriage have managed to have "been destroyed." Right. Well, there are some people who will always be willing to feed themselves from the dead body of someone else. You know, the way Buzzards feed from corpses.

Oddly, the foreword in Slatzer's 1974 book was credited to Marilyn's makeup man Whitey Snyder. In David Marshall's *The DD Group: An Online Investigation Into the Death of Marilyn Monroe*, Italian TV director Claudio Masenza wrote the following in a letter to DD Group member Peggy, "A few days later I met Allan Snyder and, after the interview, I asked him how well he knew Slatzer when Marilyn was alive. His reply came as a surprise. He didn't know him at all and never even heard of him until the day Slatzer asked him to write an introduction. Then he also said that he always trusted people and Slatzer had told him that he had been close to Marilyn for many years and since he didn't know all of her friends, he had believed it."

Jay Margolis

In the fan newspaper *Runnin' Wild: All About Marilyn* in the April 1994 issue, Number 14, Slatzer pathetically defended himself against Whitey Snyder's accusations regarding his "relationship" with Marilyn Monroe. Slatzer said, "Although Whitey states that he does not believe Marilyn and I were married, his statements are in direct contradiction to various inscriptions that he wrote on books and on a photograph. With regards to Whitey writing that I have mentioned 'two different versions' of my marriage to Marilyn, I have no idea what he is talking about. First of all, I do not believe that Marilyn confided to him about *anything*...

"His claim that Marilyn had never mentioned me to him is also very contradictory... He is also mistaken when he claims the only picture of Marilyn and I together was taken at the *Niagara* location – and he certainly was not the person I handed my camera to!... In spite of what Whitey has written, or possibly said, I still regard him as a dear friend." In the October 1994 issue, Number 16, Roman Hryniszak and Michelle Justice, the writers of the same fan newspaper, followed up on the Whitey Snyder accusations. Hryniszak and Justice wrote, "In telephone conversations with AAM [*All About Marilyn*], Whitey has stated that Bob took the original draft of the Foreword and completely rewrote it; further, Whitey said he was unaware of such until he returned from his travels and saw the published book."

As for the entries in Marilyn's red diary, Slatzer most likely obtained this information from Deputy Coroner's Aide Lionel Grandison who actually *did* see the diary. Or he could've gotten the "entries" another way: in the *Say Goodbye to the President* documentary, the narrator conceded, "Slatzer could have got his story years later from published sources."

Beginning in the early 1990s, Robert Slatzer pushed his charade even further when at hundreds of dollars per photograph, Slatzer would continue to dishonorably profit from Marilyn by claiming to have taken photographs of her on the closed set of *Something's Got to Give*. These pictures were actually taken by James Mitchell (see *Los Angeles Times* article entitled, "The Right Photographer" dated June 27, 1993). According to Greg Schreiner, Marilyn's stand-in Evelyn Moriarty was in attendance at an exhibition where Slatzer was selling some of these same photographs. Moriarty stormed up to Slatzer and exclaimed, "Bob, you were never on that set! I never saw you once!"

Given all this information, I have used both of Slatzer's books in my research, not because he knew Marilyn Monroe, which he didn't, but because his recorded interviews were relevant to understanding how Marilyn died. Throughout this text, Slatzer was referred to as "the author" but I cannot thank him for his contribution because he shamelessly profited from Marilyn Monroe like no other individual before him or after. He fooled too many intelligent biographers and people from the general public into believing he was actually her closest intimate and that in itself was a grave disservice to Marilyn Monroe and to see it any other way is a violation to her memory.

Future biographers take note: <u>Robert Slatzer did not know Marilyn Monroe at all</u>. He met her for two or three days in June 1952. Photographer Fred Pfening, Jr. admitted to introducing Marilyn to Slatzer on the set of *Niagara*. The famous movie star and the sweaty, overweight man with the terrible cologne had at least six pictures taken together. They made some polite banter between the shots and that's it. Milton H. Greene was Marilyn's ex-business partner and a world-renowned photographer known to capture some of the most beautiful photographs. His son Anthony Greene once snapped at Slatzer, "C'mon Bob. You've got to stop somewhere. You've got to get back to reality." [108]

Her "Best Friend" Jeanne Carmen (1930 – 2007)

Another clown by the name of Jeanne Carmen would make similar claims of a long-lasting friendship with Marilyn Monroe. She said they met "during the early 1950's… at a bar near the Actors Studio in New York City" as told to Carmen's son Brandon James who wrote his mother's laughable "biography" called *Jeanne Carmen: My Wild, Wild Life*. The truth is the two women met in August 1961 when they were both living in the same apartment complex on 882 Doheny Drive. Jeanne Carmen lived in apartment 4 according to a June 31, 1961 Western Union telegram she showed to Anthony Summers.

Sinatra's valet George Jacobs said as for Jeanne Carmen and Frank Sinatra, "They stayed sexually friendly for many years… The building was called 'The Sinatra Arms,' because in addition to Marilyn and me were Sinatra's secretary Gloria Lovell and his longtime on-off bedmate Jeannie Carmen [sic], who became Marilyn's best girlfriend… In the early sixties, Jeannie, Marilyn Monroe, and I all ended up in the same apartment complex on Doheny Drive and had a different set of adventures."

I'd like to stress that having "a different set of adventures" means that George Jacobs and Jeanne Carmen didn't share any adventures *together* with Marilyn Monroe. They relayed different accounts: George Jacobs has his story about Marilyn and Jeanne Carmen has her "story" about Marilyn. Since Carmen and Marilyn *did* live next to each other and since nobody can know what people are doing all the time, I'm sure George Jacobs just believed it when Jeanne Carmen told him about her "friendship" with Marilyn Monroe.

However, Jacobs actually has several candid pictures of himself with

Marilyn. With all of Carmen's "adventures," I find it rather strange how she didn't even have one photograph together with the famous actress. Greg Schreiner, who also knew Carmen, told me she was nowhere found in Marilyn's address books. Marilyn's friend reporter George Carpozi, Jr. told Deborah Chiel, "Have you heard of the name Jeanne Carmen?... She doesn't exist as Marilyn's friend. She didn't know Marilyn from a hole in the wall."

Jeanne Carmen wasn't a very good liar either. In her son's book, Carmen claimed Marilyn first called her "early in the morning on August 4th" complaining about how she couldn't sleep because of harassing phone calls until 5:30 A.M. Then supposedly Marilyn asked Carmen for additional sleeping pills. Oddly, August 4 is Carmen's birthday and Carmen still denies the movie star's request, "Marilyn, I'm sorry but I can't do it today. I've got a bunch of things I have to do here in town. Your house is so far. I wished you still lived next door."

In a phone call she never told Anthony Summers about, Carmen claimed Marilyn rang her a second time at 8:00 P.M. and told her, "A messenger came up and said he had a package for me. I took it and he left. When I opened it up, there was this really cute little stuffed tiger inside… Then I noticed a letter hanging around the tiger's neck so I took it off and read it… 'Bobby loves me, not you. You're old, you're fat and you're ugly.' " The most egregious error here is that Marilyn was hardly fat at this time in her life. She was never this skinny before and she was very attractive. According to the autopsy report, Marilyn weighed 117 pounds when she died.

As for the stuffed tiger story, it was first officially documented in Anthony Summers' *Goddess*. A man named Don Feld related a story supposedly told to him by hairdresser Agnes Flanagan. Flanagan, he says, claimed that during her last day alive, Marilyn received a package with a stuffed tiger inside and then became very startled. Summers wrote, "Had some devastating note arrived with the tiger or – curious thought – was the tiger itself the message?" Carmen said there *was* a note but *didn't* tell Summers this story at all when he interviewed her many, many times for his book.

In the same phone call, Marilyn allegedly told Carmen that Greenson gave her the afternoon injection, not Kennedy's doctor. Carmen "quoted" Marilyn as telling her, "I had to call Dr. Greenson up and have him come over and give me something to calm me down. That's how angry I was." As mentioned before, Greenson was not qualified to give intramuscular injections. That's why he had hired Engelberg to be Marilyn's physician. In addition, when Greenson stuck the needle into Marilyn's heart later that night, Schaefer Ambulance attendant James Hall noted, "Strange, but when he was trying to find her heart, he had to count down her ribs – like he was still in premed school and had really never done this before." If he had trouble administering an injection to the chest, how could he competently give Marilyn an intramuscular injection in the afternoon without killing her?

Carmen claimed Marilyn relayed to her what Bobby Kennedy said that last afternoon, "You know damn well what I'm looking for. The fucking bug you used to record me with. Where is it? Are you recording everything right now as well?" Summers documented in his book that a confidential source told him, "RFK was saying words to the effect, 'We have to know. It's important to the family. We can make any arrangements you want, but we must find it.' " Summers then wrote, "Apparently he was still looking for the recording device. Then they apparently came close to where the transmitter was." This was a straight copy-paste job by Jeanne Carmen. I have already established in a previous section why Bobby was looking for the red diary, *not* a recording device. Marilyn couldn't have told Carmen that Bobby was looking for a bug because Marilyn knew Bobby was actually looking for her diary.

Carmen alleged she concluded the phone conversation, "I reminded her that my birthday was on the following day [actually it was August 4] and I thanked her for the card she'd sent me and the present, a wood driver, a 2 wood and a 3 wood." Okay, so Marilyn sends Carmen an early birthday card *and* a present yet Carmen still wants to remind her, in case she forgot, the date of her birthday, which even she can't get right! If Marilyn Monroe had really sent Carmen a birthday card, surely she wouldn't have thrown it away, right? How come nobody's ever seen it? What makes even more sense is that this alleged birthday card never made it into Carmen's personal collection because it doesn't really exist.

In a "third" phone call, Carmen relayed, "Marilyn called me again one last time at around 10 P.M. She said, 'Carmen, I'm having trouble sleeping. The minute I close my eyes I think that woman is going to call and start harassing me again. Are you sure you can't come over with some pills?' " *Then* Carmen claimed, "The phone rang again about a half hour later but I didn't answer it." As we've already seen, shortly after 9:30 P.M., Marilyn was on the private line with José Bolaños. Shortly before 10:00 P.M., Marilyn puts down the phone in her main bedroom to investigate a noise. After arriving in the guest cottage, two men with Bobby Kennedy forcibly administer an enema containing chloral hydrate and Nembutal to knock Marilyn out while they look for her red diary. Not even a moment later, feeling the immediate effects of the drugs, Marilyn made her very last call from the public line in the guest cottage to the answering service of her best friend Ralph Roberts at 10:00 P.M. In no way would it be possible for Marilyn to call Jeanne Carmen to say she wanted pills a half-hour *before* or a half-hour *after* this time.

Carmen's claims have naturally aroused deep skepticism. Quite simply,

Jeanne Carmen: My Wild, Wild Life should be renamed *Jeanne Carmen: My Wild, Wild Lie*. Her son Brandon James wrote a book where Carmen interjected herself further into Marilyn's story by plagiarizing most of Anthony Summers' own biography. Not surprisingly, she related that Anthony Summers "ended up writing the best book ever written on Marilyn and it was called *Goddess*."

I asked Marilyn's longtime friend Gloria Romanoff who knew Frank Sinatra very well, "Have you ever heard of this woman Jeanne Carmen who claims to be her best friend?" "Yes, I have to tell you, she came very late to the scene. They shared the same address on Doheny Drive for a period." "So, you've seen them together as friends?" "No, I never did see them together in truth. I heard Marilyn prattling on about this girl. She knew her because they all lived on Doheny Drive. Sinatra lived in the same apartment. I would never suggest to you she ever gave me a hint that this was a close intimate friend. Marilyn was not given to that sort of friendship in truth."

"So, she's exaggerating?" "Oh, enormously. I give no credit to anything she says. She makes all kinds of claims, this woman." "But she did know Marilyn?" "If you pay attention, it's all *after the fact*. You never heard from her before Marilyn died. And she had fifteen minutes of fame and she stretched it out as far as possible. She knew her because she had the same small apartment complex that they all lived in. They *had* to know each other. They were tripping over each other. As neighbors, I'm sure they probably had dinner for an evening but there was never any suggestion from Marilyn that this is my close pal." "What have you heard Marilyn say about Jeanne Carmen?" "Very, very, very little. But it wasn't until after Marilyn's death and we were seeing Carmen on television a great deal listening to her talk about her 'relationship' with Marilyn that I have a couple of times heard Marilyn bring up her name. I couldn't even recall what it was that she had to say about her but nothing to suggest they were *close*. Marilyn was a girl who attracted a lot of these people who would want to perhaps be her 'friends' or to be associated with her." [109]

Marilyn must have been terrifically jealous once she realized Frank Sinatra placed Jeanne Carmen in the Doheny apartment complex just to be his sex toy. At that point, there's absolutely no reason why Marilyn would want to have anything to do with that woman, even though Marilyn lived just next door in apartment 3.

Marilyn Monroe: A Case for Murder

Her "Flirtation" with Colin Clark (1932 – 2002)

In 1995, Colin Clark, the third assistant director on the 1956 film *The Prince and the Showgirl,* published his "diary" under the title *The Prince, the Showgirl and Me,* detailing his six months on the set of the film. Five years later, Colin Clark wrote a second book *My Week with Marilyn* (2000), this time including the "nine missing days" from his original error-ridden diary. He mentioned for the first time a week spent secretly with Marilyn Monroe. However, this new book proved to be an insensitive fabrication. Clark used Marilyn's miscarriage to her third husband Arthur Miller as a backdrop for his so-called flirtation, which upon careful introspection of Clark's two books never happened.

In his second book, Colin Clark told of "spooning" with Marilyn Monroe, an incident he claimed occurred on September 17. Clark wrote, " 'I'll set the alarm for seven o'clock. That gives us another four hours of sleep.' Marilyn giggled. 'Four hours! Aren't we going to make love, Colin? Will that give us enough time?' 'Oh, Marilyn, you are a naughty girl,' I said sternly. 'We are not going to make love, OK? It's bad enough me being here. You've got to be able to tell your husband that we didn't even think about sex – that it never even crossed your mind. You've got to be able to say that with your hand on your heart. Otherwise he jolly well will leave you forever. And you don't want that.' Marilyn sighed. 'I guess so,' she said. I gave her hand a squeeze. 'Just out of interest, though, would you have liked to make love?' 'Kinda.' 'Me, too. But now we're going to sleep.'

" 'I tell you what, we'll spoon.' 'Spoon?' 'Yeah, I used to do this with Johnny – Johnny Hyde – when he was sick. Pull off your trousers and get into the bed, Colin. Now lie very straight, with your face towards the edge. Hey it's good that you're thin like Johnny.' Marilyn turned off the light and lay down behind me. I could feel her stretching out her face towards the back of my neck, until her body ran the whole length of mine. This is getting dangerous, I thought. One thing could lead to another in the dark. But Marilyn was clearly enjoying herself, being in control. 'Now slowly bring your knees up, Colin, and curl your back forwards.' As I did so I could feel Marilyn doing the same, until I was completely enveloped in a soft embrace. 'See?' said Marilyn. 'Like a spoon!' I breathed out at last. 'Goodnight,' I said. 'Sleep well.' 'Mmm,' said Marilyn. 'This is great. I will.' " [110]

Colin Clark wrote in his first book that he heard of Marilyn's potential pregnancy from someone else on September 2. "I came back and told Tony there was no truth in the rumour about the pregnancy. Why give SLO [Sir Laurence Olivier] another worry when there is nothing we can do about it? If the rumour does turn out to be true, we will all simply have to adapt as best we can, or the film will grind to a halt." On September 6, clearly speaking as an outside observer, Colin Clark wrote, "Sure enough, at 10 A.M. we had an official message from Parkside to say MM was not well, and a doctor had been called. I reported this to SLO. He wanted to know which doctor. A local GP? A specialist in nervous diseases? There was quite a difference. I rang Plod [Clark's nickname for his own policeman to 'confuse the Yanks,' see page 52] and spoke to Hedda [Rosten]. AM [Arthur Miller] had found the name of a London physician from a friend and had recommended him over the phone. Hedda had arranged for him to call that afternoon. But whatever he says, Hedda thinks that MM will not return to the studio before next Wednesday (Sept 12th). As AM returns from NYC next Tuesday (Sept 11th) this seems a likely guess." [111]

On September 8, Colin Clark, still speaking as an outside observer wrote, "Plod called me over to Parkside for a chat. He could say nothing directly, but he hinted that MM had been pregnant but had now miscarried. The baby must have been no more than a month. This seems very young to be called 'a baby' but I know nothing about pregnancy, I must admit. Plod is very concerned. He adores MM now, even though she doesn't seem to notice that he exists…

" 'Does anyone else know?' I asked. 'Milton Greene, I suppose.' 'Does Arthur?' 'I don't think so, no.' So much for marriage! I went over to Tibbs Farm to check it out. When I arrived, Milton and Amy were in a dreadful state. Josh, their son, had fallen out of their car as they were going down the driveway. A doctor was with him, but, amazingly, he wasn't hurt, just very shocked. Poor little guy. For once Milton wasn't remotely concerned with MM. They assumed that I had heard the news about Josh, and come over to sympathise about that. So I said nothing about Plod's news and I never will. I just hope MM recovers. She must have had a pretty bad shock too, if Plod is right." [112]

The above entry is interesting in light of what Colin Clark was to write five years later in his second book as it pertained to his alleged journal entry for September 18. Clark wrote in his first book that Marilyn's miscarriage occurred on September 8 and he clearly wrote of himself as an outside observer hearing the rumors of Marilyn being pregnant and subsequently miscarrying from his policeman he nicknamed "Plod." But now in his second book, he wrote of actually being there with Marilyn when she tells him exclusively and no one else that she is pregnant and to not alert anybody else about it.

Instead of writing of Marilyn's miscarriage on September 8, Clark now wrote in his second book of Marilyn's miscarriage on September 18. Clark relayed, "Less than an hour later, she was awake again. 'Colin! Colin!' she cried. I sat bolt upright in the darkness and fumbled desperately for the light.

I had fallen asleep on top of the bed and, thank goodness, fully dressed. I had not even taken off my shoes. 'It hurts. It hurts.' Marilyn lay on her back, clutching her stomach. She was as pale as a ghost. 'What's the matter?' I reached out and put my hand against her cheek. She didn't seem to have a fever. 'What's the matter?' 'It's a cramp. I've got cramps. It's terrible. Oh no! Oh no! Oh no!' 'What is it, Marilyn?'

" 'The baby! I'm going to lose the baby!' 'The baby? What baby? Are you having a baby?' I simply could not comprehend what was going on. For the first time since I had known her, Marilyn began to weep. I had never seen so much as the sign of a tear in the studio, even when Olivier was at his worst. I suppose I thought of her as someone whose life had been such a struggle, who had known so much pain as a child, that she would never allow herself to cry again. 'Poor Marilyn,' I said, as gently as I could. 'Tell me about the baby.' 'It was Arthur's,' Marilyn said, between sobs. 'It was for him. He didn't know. It was going to be a surprise. Then he would see that I could be a real wife, and a real mother.' A mother – I could hardly believe it. 'How long have you been pregnant?' 'Just a few weeks, I guess. At least, my period is a couple of weeks late. And I didn't dare mention it to anyone, in case it wasn't true. Ow!' Another spasm gripped Marilyn's tummy. She was clearly in terrible pain. 'I'm going to lose the baby. Maybe it's a punishment because I've been having such a good time.' 'Nonsense, Marilyn. We didn't do anything wrong. Nothing at all. I'd better tell Roger to call a doctor right away. And he'd better tell Milton too – only you are not to take any pills. Shall I get Paula and Hedda too?' 'Don't tell them about the baby, Colin. I always have cramps when my period is due. They're used to that. This seems just much worse, that's all.' " [113]

Clark wrote in his first book that Arthur Miller had ordered by telephone a doctor especially for Marilyn but now in his second book, Clark wrote about a policeman named Roger calling a doctor over instead who has no knowledge of Arthur Miller, " 'Are you OK, Marilyn?' I called. 'Roger is talking to a doctor right now. He'll be here very soon.' Marilyn let out a cry. 'Ooh! I'm bleeding so much.' " Colin Clark claimed that later a doctor arrived and asked, " 'And what are you doing here, Mr. Clark, if I may ask, in Miss Monroe's house at two o'clock in the morning?' 'I'm working on the film Miss Monroe is making at Pinewood Studios, and I'm, er, a friend of Miss Monroe's as well.' 'And Miss Monroe's husband? I presume she has a husband?' 'He's in America. I think.' 'Oh, really? And how long has he been gone?' 'Oh, a week. Six days, to be exact. And the baby, doctor?' Milton looked completely stunned. 'Oh, you know about that, do you? Well, it's true. Miss Monroe was about three weeks pregnant, I would say. Not now, of course. But she can always try again. It isn't the end of the world. I must be off. Goodnight, gentlemen.' " [114]

217

If we examine these excerpts closely from both of Clark's books, we can see that Colin Clark penned conflicting accounts of what actually happened with Marilyn's miscarriage. In his first book, he wrote that with the knowledge of Marilyn's friend Hedda Rosten, Arthur Miller himself ordered over the phone a doctor to tend to Marilyn on September 6. In his second book, he said that Arthur Miller, Hedda Rosten, and Milton Greene had no knowledge of the pregnancy at all and Clark claimed Marilyn told him not to say anything to them.

Given these contradictions, Colin Clark's *My Week with Marilyn* (2000) is clearly nothing more than absurd trashy fiction. There is not a ring of truth to it. Donald Spoto's account directly contradicts Colin Clark's. Spoto wrote, "While she was performing some of her best scenes in late August, Marilyn learned she was expecting a baby. Later, the pregnancy was always doubted even by those close to the situation like Amy [Greene] and [Rupert] Allan, but Irving Stein's daily memoranda of telephone calls from London indicate that as of August 31, Marilyn's condition was confirmed by two London doctors. 'Milton told me [by telephone] that she was pregnant but she is afraid she will lose the baby,' noted Irving. He understood Milton's concern, for Irving too had seen, before his departure from London, that 'Hedda and Marilyn were drinking a lot. Hedda is not a good influence on Marilyn and encourages her evasiveness of truth… and says she and Arthur are neither of them ready for children… Marilyn weeps, saying that all she wants is to finish the picture.' Marilyn lost the baby the first week of September."[115] As shown above, Irving Stein's memoranda proved Clark was lying in his second book about having exclusive knowledge of Marilyn's pregnancy. In fact, according to Stein's notes, Milton Greene knew Marilyn was pregnant as early as August 31.

Biographer Barbara Leaming corroborated Spoto's account, "Marilyn didn't show up at the studio again on Thursday [August 30]. Instead she saw Arthur [Miller] off at the airport. The next day [August 31], Milton Greene telephoned Irving Stein in New York to report that Marilyn was pregnant. A gynecologist visiting Parkside House confirmed the pregnancy… Miller wasn't due back in London until September 12, but he returned suddenly on Wednesday the 5th, only six days after he left. By Saturday [September 8], word was out that Marilyn had miscarried."[116]

So, by September 5, Arthur Miller returned, by September 8, Marilyn miscarried and by September 18, it was old news. Colin Clark wrote in his second book that he was alone with Marilyn while Arthur Miller was away for one week. After all, it was called *My Week with Marilyn*. Since Miller returned on September 5, there was no room for Mr. Clark to be alone with Marilyn anytime after that date including September 18.

This makes it impossible for Colin Clark to be there with Marilyn when she had the miscarriage on September 8 even if Clark got his dates screwed up because Arthur Miller was by her side as Marilyn miscarried. Thus, when Arthur Miller called the doctor over the telephone on September 6, according to Clark's first book, Miller had already been back for one day in the company of his wife Marilyn Monroe.

Incidentally, Clark had Arthur Miller returning to England on September 19, not September 5, "Milton tells me that Arthur is returning from New York this afternoon. I'm sure that will help. Marilyn told me she's going to work especially hard every day from now on, like she did yesterday, and I think she's serious. Her relationship with Arthur was a bit frantic when they first arrived, and his departure gave her a terrible shock. I think she'll concentrate on her career for a while now. At least until this film is finished." [117]

On May 18, 2010, in an article entitled, "Forget Vampires ... Hollywood's Greatest Undead Is – Marilyn Monroe!," Liz Smith wrote about Colin Clark's *My Week with Marilyn*, "The other Monroe movie is a screen adaptation of Colin Clark's 'diary' based on his adventures with Monroe and Laurence Olivier on the set of 'The Prince and the Showgirl.' Colin was Olivier's assistant. This book, like so many written by people who claim to have known Marilyn, doesn't ring quite true, but nobody's alive to dispute it." Ms. Smith doesn't have to worry since Clark contradicted himself quite a number of times. As shown above, his account clearly does not stand tall; it falls short, desperately so. [118]

Colin Clark's own brother Alan Clark called him a liar. On December 18, 2002, Ion Trewin penned an article entitled, "Colin Clark, Writer and film producer in the shadow of his father and brother." Trewin wrote, "Nearly 40 years later he produced for publication the diary he had kept during the making of the film. One of the first publishers to show an interest was Weidenfeld & Nicolson, which also happened to be Alan Clark's publisher. Alan was incensed. The first volume of his own highly praised and hugely successful diaries had just been published (*Diaries*, 1995). Whereas Colin viewed his brother's objection as simple jealousy, Alan's reasoning was more complex: he foresaw confusion in the public's mind if the same publisher brought out both brothers' diaries.

"He even suggested that Colin's diaries had been fabricated at a later date. Colin denied this, but it was a manifestation of an antagonism that was to colour their final years... Colin later published a second book on Marilyn Monroe, *My Week with Marilyn* (2000), which filled in nine days of missing entries and led many of Clark's colleagues on the film to surmise (incorrectly, Clark would also insist) that he and Monroe had enjoyed a torrid affair. But neither this, nor his autobiography, enjoyed anything like the success of his original Monroe diary." Perhaps it was a blessing *My Week with Marilyn* wasn't as successful as his original book since out of all the people who had shamelessly profited from Marilyn Monroe, we wouldn't want to add one more to the list.

Colin Clark's diary very well could have been fabricated at a later date, as many of his entries seem to be embellished upon by any of the number of Monroe biographies already available to the general public. Marilyn didn't have time to have a little dalliance with Colin Clark as she was already having an affair with her producer Milton Greene (per Greene's close friend entertainer Sammy Davis, Jr.) at the same time that Colin Clark claimed his flirtation occurred. Even though Colin Clark wanted so desperately to insert himself into Marilyn Monroe's life, the saddest part of his story is that Clark was only the third assistant director. That's it. Colin Clark said he spooned with the most famous woman in the world, an event that happened only in Clark's ruptured and perverted imagination. [119]

Blonde, My Week with Marilyn, or Tarantino?

Future moviegoers note: *My Week with Marilyn* is not a true story. However, Joyce Carol Oates' *Blonde* is worse, a book which is filthy and disgusting. If Marilyn Monroe had seen what Oates had written, she would cry. If you recall, Jane Russell said Marilyn was very sensitive to someone's slightest offhand remark. The word "whore" appears thirteen times in Oates' book.

She wrote that Marilyn received a surprise in an envelope, "It was a square of white toilet paper upon which someone had carefully block-printed, in what appeared to be actual excrement, WHORE." And don't get me started on Oates' fictionalized CIA character known only as "The Sharpshooter" who, as you guessed it, "sank the six-inch needle to the hilt into her heart."

Ms. Joyce Carol Oates, you are a great writer but you need to go back and do your research so you can write a better work on Marilyn Monroe in its place. Your book is not highly regarded among the serious Marilyn Monroe fans and scholars. Now's your chance to write a classy work to make up for the "novel."

Readers, when you see Michelle Williams and Naomi Watts in *My Week with Marilyn* (2011) and *Blonde* (2012), respectively, just remember how these are two of the most talented actresses working in Hollywood right now. If anybody can save these movies, it's them. Naomi Watts and Michelle Williams, for last minute research, read my book right away to get an idea of what really happened to this mysterious woman who died so young.

I hope the information I have collected will add more depth to the artistic interpretation of the role you're playing: the most misunderstood woman of the 20th century. In order to fully understand her, you need to know how she died. "Suicide" made her life tragic but murder made it even more tragic. The point is, let's get two *good* Marilyn Monroe movies for a change.

I highly advise you stay away from the film *Norma Jean & Marilyn* (1996) based on Ted "Eddie" Jordan's book about his fake relationship with Marilyn Monroe. The relationship never happened. And the story in the film never happened. Ted Jordan wrote an even worse book than Robert Slatzer called *Norma Jean: My Secret Life with Marilyn Monroe* where he displayed a picture of actress Arline Hunter and claimed it was a photograph of Marilyn Monroe.

In *Norma Jean & Marilyn*, I give credit to Ashley Judd for bearing the strongest resemblance of any actress to the brunette Norma Jeane Mortenson before she became the movie star Marilyn Monroe. However, as for the way that same film described Marilyn's death, I can assure you the most famous woman in the world did *not* break down all the pills and swallow them in a glass of champagne. Marilyn's unembalmed blood showed no alcohol that last day. Also, make note: Norma Jeane is how the name appears on her birth certificate *not* Norma Jean.

To the manufacturers of Blu-ray, Marilyn Monroe fans would love to see the following films: *The Asphalt Jungle* (1950), *Clash by Night* (1952), *Don't Bother to Knock* (1952), *Gentlemen Prefer Blondes* (1953), *How to Marry a Millionaire* (1953), *Niagara* (1953), *The Seven Year Itch* (1955), *Bus Stop* (1956), *The Prince and the Showgirl* (1957), and of course, the 45-minute reconstruction of the incomplete movie *Something's Got to Give* (1962), cinematography of which would look brilliant on Blu-ray. On February 1, 2011, *All About Eve* (1950) became available for the first time on Blu-ray and impressively, *Some Like It Hot* (1959) and *The Misfits* (1961) were simultaneously released on May 10.

Lastly, take note of Quentin Tarantino's extraordinary epic *Pulp Fiction*. In the film, actress Susan Griffiths played a remarkably successful Marilyn Monroe look-alike at the Jack Rabbit Slim's restaurant, down to the mannerisms. Certainly, Tarantino could write and direct the best film about Marilyn Monroe's murder. I can't wait to see it. [120]

EPILOGUE:

Her Idol Was Lincoln and Carl Sandburg (1878 – 1967) Was His Biographer

After her persistent efforts to meet him, Marilyn Monroe and Carl Sandburg met while she was making *Some Like It Hot* in 1958. They saw each other again in 1960 on the set of *Let's Make Love*. At that time, Sandburg was doing work on the screenplay for *The Greatest Story Ever Told*, eventually released in 1965. Len Steckler, a personal friend of Sandburg's, took the first photographs of Marilyn Monroe and Carl Sandburg together. The pictures were taken in Steckler's New York apartment in December 1961.

According to Steckler, "Hours later I went to open the door and there I was face to face with Marilyn Monroe, and she looked more ravishing than on the screen. She said, 'I am sorry I am late. I was at the hairdressers matching my hair to Carl's.' " Steckler called the series of pictures he took that afternoon, "Marilyn Monroe: The Visit." In the photographs, her hair is perfect. Also, she's wearing dark sunglasses. After the pictures were taken, Steckler said everybody had a drink of Jack Daniels.

On September 11, 1962, an article appeared for *Look* magazine entitled, "Tribute to Marilyn, from a friend… Carl Sandburg." Poet and Pulitzer Prize-winning biographer Carl Sandburg had never met anybody quite like Marilyn Monroe. To him, she was not what he had expected: a pleasant surprise. He said, "She came up the hard way. She never talked about her husbands… She had a mind out of the ordinary for show people. I found her fairly well read. I gave her a book of my complete poetry. I wanted her to have it…

"She knew I had an appreciation of her from two angles… first as a personality and then as an actress… Many people came to love her as a woman, rather than as a stage artist. She had a genuine quality. She was good to know offstage… She was not the usual movie idol. There was something democratic about her. Why, she was the type who would join in and wash the supper dishes even if you didn't ask her. She would have interested me even if she had no record as a great actress."

Her love of life was everywhere apparent to Sandburg. He said, "It was as if she wanted to see me as much as I wanted to see her. We hit it off and talked long. Marilyn was a good talker. There were realms of science, politics and economics in which she wasn't at home, but she spoke well on the national scene, the Hollywood scene, and on people who are good to know and people who ain't. We agreed on a number of things – that Charlie Chaplin is beyond imitation, for instance… Too bad that I was 48 years older than Marilyn. I couldn't play her leading man."

Sandburg learned of Marilyn's notorious struggle with insomnia. "I think it entirely possible that Marilyn had a hard time with her sleep. She talked a lot about wanting a good sleep." On January 20, 1962 at the Los Angeles home of *Something's Got to Give* producer Henry Weinstein and his wife Irena, Arnold Newman took the second and last photographs of these two great national icons together. In one of the pictures, Sandburg bends down showing Marilyn an exercise to help her get a good sleep. In another she is happily dancing with him. A scarf covers her hair and this time she's not wearing sunglasses.

Joan Greenson recalled of that day in late January, "One of Marilyn's friends that we did get an opportunity to meet was Carl Sandburg. Marilyn told me how much she had enjoyed him. They were old friends. I would say there were about 12 people at the house and they were all clustered around Carl Sandburg. Everyone seemed to be hanging on his every word. I listened for awhile, but felt the conversation had gotten too specific for me.

"A little while later, when I passed by Carl Sandburg's chair where he was sitting, he asked me if I danced the Hoochie Coochie, and I said no, that I didn't. He seemed to really love to flirt, and to be obstreperous. He didn't seem like he was overly impressed with his own fame or erudition. I liked his approach and his directness. Also, I liked the fact that he liked Marilyn, and I think it would have been fun to see the two of them together. It would have been some kind of match up."

Sandburg says he often remembered Marilyn in many of her brighter moments, "She had vitality, a readiness for humor. I saw no signs of despondency when I talked to her. She gave me an impression of happiness… She sometimes threw her arms around me, like people do who like each other very much… She was very good company and we did some mock playacting, some pretty good imitations… Marilyn had a certain homeliness that made people like her. She wasn't the perfect cutie like some stars – there was a certain irregularity about her features. The definition of beauty is difficult."

Look magazine wrote, "That night, they talked of serious subjects too. Marilyn, sitting at her friend's feet, reached up now and then to squeeze his hand. She even spoke of death. She said that she thought herself too intelligent to commit suicide." Sandburg had no idea his friend had been murdered. He reminisced sadly, "Gosh, there were a lot of people who loved her. She had loyal fans. There were no pretenses about Marilyn Monroe… I wish I could have been with her that day… I believe I could have persuaded her not to take her life. She had so much to live for." Indeed she did as her good friends attested. "Too bad she had to go – too bad. I remember Marilyn sitting two or three feet from me on the sofa when we met in New York. I didn't rise and escort her to the elevator when it was time for her to leave. I've never been good at manners. But I am 84 years old. I hope she forgave me." [121]

Timeline:

Note: Estimated times are indicated with a ~ symbol.

AUGUST 4, 1962:

8:00 A.M.
Mrs. Eunice Murray arrives for work.

9:00 A.M.
Isadore Miller calls from New York. Mrs. Murray assures Miller that Marilyn will return his call after she finishes dressing. Mrs. Murray never communicates the message to Marilyn.

Miller is Marilyn's ex-father-in-law, one of her closest friends, and the kindest father figure she ever knew. To Marilyn, he is known as "Dad."

9:00 – 10:15 A.M.
Marilyn's best friend Ralph Roberts massages her back in her bedroom using his portable massage table. He notes she is "in wonderful shape and not tense."

~ 10:20 A.M.
Ralph lets himself out the front door while Marilyn enters the kitchen and says good morning to Mrs. Murray. Per Mrs. Murray, Marilyn pours herself a glass of grapefruit juice. She does not eat or drink alcohol for the rest of the day. Tests of her unembalmed blood later reveal she hadn't had a drop of alcohol that day.

~ 10:30 – 11:00 A.M.
Mrs. Murray noted, "Sometime during the earlier part of the day, the bedside table was delivered and Marilyn wrote a check for it. The citrus trees were also delivered that day and were placed in the rear yard." Presumably the deliverers placed the bedside table where it belonged: in the guest cottage. There was already a bedside table in Marilyn's main bedroom.

11:00 A.M.
Per Frank Neill, Twentieth Century-Fox studio publicist, he saw Bobby Kennedy arrive on the Fox lot, Stage 18, via helicopter. Bobby jumps out of the helicopter and quickly enters a car waiting for him with Peter Lawford inside.

Peter's neighbor Ward Wood would later spot Bobby in the afternoon noting, "It was Bobby all right. He was in khakis and a white shirt open at the neck."

12:00 P.M.
Pat Newcomb, who stayed overnight at Marilyn's, awakens and per Pat and Mrs. Murray and later Greenson, Marilyn gets angry with her because Marilyn had no sleep the night before. In 1985, Mrs. Murray would concede that Bobby Kennedy was the real reason Marilyn was upset that day, not her alleged lack of sleep.

2:00 P.M.
Per the police report, Joe DiMaggio, Jr., 20, who was in the Marines, calls from Camp Pendleton in San Diego. Joe, Jr. said he could hear Mrs. Murray telling the operator that Marilyn was not home. Mrs. Murray never communicates the message to Marilyn.

~ 2:00 P.M.
Bobby and Peter arrive at Marilyn's. Peter slips into her home to tell Mrs. Murray and Marilyn's handyman Norman Jefferies (also Murray's son-in-law) to get lost for an hour. Per Jefferies, Peter gives them money for Cokes and they leave in Jefferies' pick-up. Per Peter, Marilyn offers Bobby some food she ordered from Briggs Delicatessen the day before: mushrooms, meatballs, a magnum of champagne, etc. Uninterested, Bobby says he's here for one reason: to tell her she can't contact him or his brother again.

Bobby and Marilyn argue for several minutes before per Peter, Marilyn threatens a press conference to announce her affairs with both Kennedy

Marilyn Monroe: A Case for Murder

brothers. Later per Sydney Guilaroff, he learned from Marilyn that Bobby had responded, "If you threaten me, Marilyn, there's more than one way to keep you quiet." Per Peter, Marilyn then impulsively takes a kitchen knife lying next to the tray of food and lunges at Bobby. Peter joins in to help Bobby. They eventually knock her down to the ground and kick the knife away from her.

During their typical Saturday afternoon bridge party, Marilyn's unidentified neighbor at 12304 Fifth Helena and the neighbor's friend Elizabeth Pollard witness Bobby leave Marilyn's. They see him running back to the car to retrieve his doctor. From an upstairs window, they see Bobby and a man in a well-dressed suit return through Marilyn's courtyard back to Marilyn and Peter. The neighbors notice the man in the suit is carrying a little black case.

Regarding Bobby, one of the card-playing ladies shouted to the others, "Look, girls, there he is *again!*" Then, while Peter and Bobby restrain her, Bobby's doctor subsequently sedates Marilyn with a heavy intramuscular pentobarbital injection, the bruise later noted in the autopsy report on her "left hip."

While she's temporarily stunned and immobile on the ground from the drugs, Bobby and Peter enter Marilyn's home with the sole purpose of looking for her red diary, a potential basis for blackmail, where she documented highly sensitive political information.

Bobby keeps looking while screaming, "Where the fuck is it?" but can't find it. Peter meanwhile flips through Marilyn's address book and calls Greenson to come over and tend to his patient. The psychiatrist agrees to be there within the hour. At this time, Marilyn musters enough energy to enter her house and furious that her privacy is being violated, screams and chases both men from her home. They leave without the diary.

~ 2:30 – 2:45 P.M.
Marilyn calls her friend Sydney Guilaroff and relays to him much of what had happened. Per Sydney, she's hysterical and tells him she's having an affair with both Kennedy brothers and that Bobby had threatened her. She said Bobby left with Peter Lawford. Sydney tries to calm Marilyn down and promises her they will talk later in the evening.

3:00 P.M.
When Greenson comes out by the pool, per Pat Newcomb, the psychiatrist dismisses her so he can be alone with Marilyn.

4:30 P.M.
Per the police report, Joe DiMaggio, Jr. calls and again Joe, Jr. can hear Mrs. Murray tell the operator that Marilyn is not home. Mrs. Murray never communicates the message to Marilyn.

5:00 P.M.
Peter claimed he called Marilyn inviting her to his regular Saturday evening dinner party. She tentatively agrees.

~ 5:45 – 6:00 P.M.
Ralph Roberts calls Marilyn. Greenson answers the public phone in her main bedroom. Asking if he can talk to her, Greenson replies in two words: "Not here" before rudely hanging up.

7:00 P.M.
Peter claimed he called Marilyn and that this time she begged off saying she was tired.

7:00 – 7:15 P.M.
Per the police report, Joe DiMaggio, Jr. phones for the third time. Mrs. Murray answers again but this time summons Marilyn from her bedroom to take the call. Mrs. Murray overhears how ecstatic and joyful Marilyn is at this time. Joe, Jr. tells Marilyn he broke off his engagement. She says to him he's too young to get married anyway. Per Joe DiMaggio, Sr., Marilyn and his son "spoke for about fifteen minutes and Marilyn seemed quite normal and in good spirits."

7:15 P.M.
Greenson leaves Marilyn's. He goes home to prepare for dinner at the residence of actor Eddie Albert and his wife Margo.

7:30 P.M.
Peter calls Marilyn to see if he can still get her to come to his party. Those at the Lawfords' a half-hour later: Joe and Dolores Naar, producer "Bullets" Durgom, and Lawford maid Erma Lee Riley.

Instead of "Say goodbye to Jack..." private eye Fred Otash said he heard Marilyn say over wiretaps, "No, I'm tired. There is nothing more for me to respond to. Just do me a favor. Tell the President I tried to get him. Tell him goodbye for me. I think my purpose has been served."

~ 7:30 P.M.
Per Dolores Naar, Peter calls the Naars and tells them not to bother picking up Marilyn because "she's not coming."

7:30 – 7:40 P.M.
Per Greenson and Mrs. Murray, Marilyn calls Greenson while he is shaving. He notes she is in high spirits because Joe DiMaggio, Jr. won't be marrying Pamela Reis after all, a girl Marilyn didn't like.

~ 7:40 – 8:00 P.M.
Milt Ebbins alleges Peter phones him in a panic, worrying that Marilyn may have taken too many pills and that they should go over there. Ebbins says he warned him against it because he's the President's brother-in-law. Before going over there, Ebbins asks Peter to wait until he calls Mickey Rudin first. Ebbins later reaches Rudin at Mildred Allenberg's party.

8:00 – 9:00 P.M.
Sydney Guilaroff got a call from Marilyn who sounds better. She told him she had just met with her psychiatrist. Before ending the call, Marilyn relayed to Sydney she knows a lot of secrets in Washington, a reference to her red diary.

8:00 – 9:00 P.M.
Dress manufacturer and long-time friend Henry Rosenfeld calls Marilyn and he reports she sounded normal.

8:00 – 9:00 P.M.
Peter's friend Bill Asher claims Peter called him to see if he would go along with him to Marilyn's house to find out if she's okay. Asher advised against it because Peter is the President's brother-in-law and that maybe they should call "old man Joe" Kennedy to seek his advice.

9:00 P.M.
Per the police report, Mickey Rudin called Mrs. Murray who informed him that Marilyn was fine, which she was.

9:30 P.M.
Per George "Bullets" Durgom, Pat Newcomb arrives at Peter's party. She wears what appear to be pajamas and a dark coat over it.

~ 9:30 – 9:45 P.M.
Per Jefferies and an FBI agent interviewed by documentarian Keya Morgan, Bobby Kennedy and two men enter Marilyn's home. They instruct Jefferies and Mrs. Murray to leave. Bobby and the men then enter the guest cottage with the sole purpose of looking for Marilyn's red diary. They break into her large filing cabinet and make a loud ruckus.

~ 9:45 P.M.
At this time, Marilyn is busy in her main bedroom chatting happily on her private line with her friend and sometimes lover José Bolaños. Marilyn tells Bolaños to hold on a moment while she goes to investigate the noise. According to Bolaños, she doesn't hang up but never comes back on the line.

~ 9:50 P.M.
Marilyn storms into her guest cottage and she screams at Bobby. The two security officers with Kennedy throw her onto the bed and per Raymond Strait, who heard eleven hours of Otash's surveillance tapes, the men then shove a pillow over her face to keep her from making noise.

Marilyn often took enemas daily. Using water and enema paraphernalia already available in the guest cottage bathroom along with Marilyn's own Nembutal and chloral hydrate prescriptions, between the two men, they forcibly administer to Marilyn a drug enema containing 17 chloral hydrates and between 13 – 19 Nembutals to knock her out.

It is unknown whether Marilyn's chloral hydrate and Nembutal bottles were already in the guest cottage or if one of the security officers had to run to Marilyn's main bedroom to retrieve them while the other officer held her down with the pillow.

Note: Presumably Marilyn didn't enter the guest cottage in the nude. The security officers stripped Marilyn of her clothes before they gave her the enema.

10:00 P.M.
From the guest cottage, right after the enema had been given to her, Marilyn grabs the phone, the public line, and makes her last call to best friend Ralph Roberts. She reaches his answering service. When told he's out for the evening, she hangs up before lapsing into unconsciousness from the drugs.

~ 10:20 – 10:25 P.M.
Someone calls Peter and tells him to get to Marilyn's house, ordering him to hire a professional to remove any link with the Kennedys and the famous movie star.

10:30 P.M.
Per Jefferies, Bobby and the men leave. After his second search for Marilyn's red diary that day, Bobby is thoroughly frustrated that he and his men couldn't find it despite more than a half-hour search.

~ 10:30 – 10:35 P.M.
Jefferies and Mrs. Murray return. They hear Maf barking in the guest cottage and walk over. Per Jefferies and Mrs. Murray, they find Marilyn facedown leaning on the phone.

~ 10:35 – 10:50 P.M.
Per Jefferies, a frightened Mrs. Murray takes the phone from Marilyn and calls an ambulance then calls Greenson who tells her to call Engelberg. Engelberg claimed to the District Attorney's Office in 1982 that he went to the house "immediately" upon receiving the call; however, he was double-parked so he had to move his car first. Engelberg would later tell investigative journalist Sylvia Chase that when he was called, it "must have been around eleven or twelve" and that an ambulance is "pure imagination."

After Mrs. Murray calls the ambulance and the two doctors then per Jefferies, Peter Lawford and Pat Newcomb arrive together. Peter drove since Pat left her car at the Lawfords'.

Per Jefferies, Pat screams at Mrs. Murray, perhaps blaming her for Marilyn's current state. Jefferies says he then escorts Mrs. Murray into the main house. At that point, Mrs. Murray responsibly takes possession of Marilyn's red diary (in the main bedroom) and one of Marilyn's address books. She places them into her purse or basket of things. Then per Mrs. Murray and Jefferies, they wait in the living room and stay there until Marilyn is eventually declared dead in the guest cottage.

Per Strait, before arriving at Marilyn's, a worried and hysterical Peter had called private eye to the stars Fred Otash to meet him at Marilyn's house. Strait said, "Fred's job was to clean the mess up… Fred was there as she was dying."

Right after Mrs. Murray and Jefferies had left the guest cottage, Pat phoned the Hollywood Bowl. With his soundman, Otash arrives and Peter approaches them. Presumably, Otash immediately assigns the soundman to the main house to remove all bugging equipment. Per 24-year-old Jacobs press agent Michael Selsman and 21-year-old Natalie Trundy, the person who phoned the Hollywood Bowl was Pat Newcomb. Per Natalie, an usher tells her boyfriend-at-the-time Arthur Jacobs, Marilyn's publicist, that Marilyn's "dying or on the point of death."

Otash and Peter hurriedly take an unconscious Marilyn off the guest cottage bed. Per Strait, Peter "was just like a hysterical woman" and "Fred slapped the shit out of him" since they have to act quickly before the ambulance arrives on scene. Otash and Peter hastily remove the soiled sheets off the bed. Mrs. Murray is later told to do the laundry when the ambulance leaves.

After Marilyn is quickly cleaned and dried off from the expelled enema, Peter and Otash place Marilyn faceup back on the bed. The linens used to clean and dry her off were easily accessible from a nearby linen closet down one of the guest bedroom hallways.

Finally, Peter and Otash dash to her main bedroom and grab the rest of Marilyn's pill bottles and neatly stack them onto the bedside table in the guest cottage, which was according to Mrs. Murray, delivered that very morning. When they're done, they slip out of the room and return to the main house.

11:00 P.M.
Arthur Jacobs arrives on the scene but does not go into the guest cottage.

~ 11:00 P.M.
Schaefer Ambulance attendant James Hall and his driver Murray Liebowitz arrive. Per Hall, Pat Newcomb is the first person he and his partner saw. From the outside, still hysterical, she screams at Hall and Liebowitz, "She's dead! She's dead! I think she's dead!" When Hall asked her what's the matter Newcomb replied, "I think she took some pills." Pat then directs them into the guest cottage where they find a naked Marilyn lying faceup on the bed with her head hanging over the edge, still unconscious with no sheet or blanket underneath her. Hall noted no odor of pear from her mouth so Marilyn definitely did not orally ingest the 17 chloral hydrates.

~ 11:00 – 11:30 P.M.
With Liebowitz's help, Hall drags Marilyn away from the guest room and into the hallway where there's a hard surface. Next, Hall said he and Liebowitz

dropped Marilyn "on her fanny," taking credit for the bruise on the "left side of [her] lower back," which Noguchi noted was "a very fresh bruise." Hall therefore deduced years later, "Dead bodies don't bruise. She was still alive."

Hall tells Liebowitz to get the resuscitator from the van. When Liebowitz returns, Hall puts an airway down Marilyn's throat and per Hall, Marilyn's color is coming back and Hall believes they can safely take her to the hospital. Hall then tells Liebowitz, "Get the gurney."

11:30 P.M.
Peter's best friend Joe Naar and his then-wife Dolores claim Peter called (which could have only been from Marilyn's house), asking Joe, who lived four blocks from Marilyn, to go over and check on her. Two minutes later, according to the Naars, Peter calls back telling them not to go. Dolores thought the two calls, so close to each other were "calculated to mislead us."

~ 11:30 – 11:45 P.M.
Before Liebowitz returns with the gurney, only Pat Newcomb and James Hall are in the guest cottage with Marilyn when suddenly Greenson arrives and says he's "her doctor." Hall defers to him because he had always been told to never challenge an M.D. Greenson tells Hall to remove the resuscitator, which was in fact doing its job. Per Hall, Greenson then takes a syringe with a long heart needle already attached to it out of his medical bag and tells Hall, "I've got to make a show of this."

Presumably Bobby gave the medical bag and syringe with a heart needle to Greenson from his many resources. Next, Greenson fills the syringe with a "brownish fluid" (Nembutal) from a pharmaceutical bottle. Hall then notes something peculiar about Greenson: "he had to count down her ribs – like he was still in premed school and had really never done this before."

This makes sense since he's a psychiatrist who doesn't normally deal with needles. Then Greenson injects it into Marilyn's heart without diluting the solution first making the shot lethal regardless of what's in the syringe and the amount injected into the body. Within minutes, Marilyn dies.

Greenson then tells Hall he can leave because he's going to pronounce her dead. For years, says Hall, he believed the solution was adrenaline in an attempt to save her but now Hall thinks the shot was intended to murder her.

Greenson's brother-in-law and Marilyn's attorney Mickey Rudin would later claim on a recorded interview that he arrived sometime before midnight and that Greenson was the one who called him to say Marilyn was dead.

~ 11:45 – 11:50 P.M.
Marilyn's neighbor Abe Landau arrives home with his wife and sees several cars parked up the narrow street including a limousine (Bobby Kennedy's), a police car (per Hall and Otash, Sergeant Marvin Iannone's), and an ambulance (Hall and Liebowitz's). Kennedy waits in his limousine until Peter and Greenson leave Marilyn's to join him in the Lincoln Continental sedan (Peter's).

Minutes after Dr. Greenson injected Marilyn in the heart, James Hall saw Peter Lawford and Sergeant Marvin Iannone enter the guest cottage. Per Officer Lynn Franklin, Otash said that at 11:45 P.M. he "observed Sgt. Iannone, in uniform, in conversation with Peter Lawford."

In the early 1990s, Hall would identify the hysterical woman as Pat Newcomb and the man who comforted her as Peter Lawford. In 1992, to Officer Franklin, Hall identified the policeman as Sergeant Marvin D. Iannone. In 1993, Hall also identified him to Donald Wolfe.

Per Jefferies, not long after Marilyn's death, plainclothes officers orchestrated the "locked room" story. They broke the window Greenson would later claim to police he had to break in order to enter Marilyn's bedroom yet the movie star's inside doors, not including the front and back doors, had no operable locks many years before she owned the house.

Next, the principles at the scene move the pill bottles and Marilyn's body to the main bedroom, and lay her facedown on the bed. This was done so the post-mortem lividity could disguise the needle mark to the chest by the time the autopsy was performed a little more than nine hours later and it worked! No needle marks were discovered at that time. Perhaps this was another reason why there was a delay in calling the police: to give the needle mark time to disappear with the help of post-mortem lividity.

Further corroboration supporting the existence of post-mortem lividity is located in the autopsy report, which noted, "lavidity [sic] of face and chest… The fixed lividity is noted in the face, neck, chest, upper portions of arms and the right side of the abdomen." Years later, Noguchi would insist he saw no needle marks. John Miner, who was present at the autopsy, would also insist on the same.

AUGUST 5, 1962:

12:00 – 1:00 A.M.
Peter's friend Bill Asher claims Peter called him, saying they should go over there to check on Marilyn. Asher, admittedly irritated by this call, claims he again advised against it.

12:10 A.M.
Near the intersection of Robertson and Olympic Boulevards, Beverly Hills police officer Lynn Franklin pulls over an inebriated Peter Lawford in his Lincoln Continental sedan with the headlights off going 70 – 80 MPH with Greenson in the front seat and Bobby Kennedy in the backseat. Not eager to give Peter a ticket with Bobby in the backseat, Officer Franklin gives them proper directions to go to the Beverly Hilton Hotel since Peter, drunk and hysterical, was driving in the opposite direction. At the time of the stop, Franklin said he did not correlate Bobby with Marilyn Monroe as news of her death was still hours away.

- 12:30 – 2:00 A.M.
Bobby takes a helicopter from the Lawfords' to Los Angeles International Airport, boards a private plane, and is flown back to San Francisco.

4:25 A.M.
Norman Jefferies, Pat Newcomb, Mickey Rudin, and Engelberg are all at the scene when Greenson calls the police reaching watch commander Sergeant Jack Clemmons. In Greenson's own words (from a newspaper article on August 5, 1973), he claims to have said he wants to "report the death of a person, a sudden and unexplained death."

4:45 A.M.
When Clemmons arrives, he talks to a sarcastic Greenson, a frightened housekeeper Mrs. Murray, and a depressed Engelberg. Greenson tells Clemmons that Marilyn committed suicide. Greenson points to the empty bottle of Nembutal, which he implies speaks for itself. According to his initial suspicions, Clemmons believed Marilyn was murdered and that her body had been moved.

He asserts she did not die facedown on the bed in the soldier's position: her arms at her side and her legs perfectly straight. Clemmons would later reflect that Marilyn had been placed that way to disguise needle marks. He also found it strange how Mrs. Murray was running the laundry after Marilyn's death.

During this time, Jefferies, Newcomb, and Mickey Rudin hide in rooms Clemmons later admitted he didn't search, including the guest cottage. Clemmons reflected he should have looked since he had noticed quite a few cars in Marilyn's courtyard.

5:25 A.M.
Per the 1982 District Attorney's Report, Clemmons notifies Detective Sergeant Robert E. Byron of Marilyn's death.

~ 5:30 A.M.
Sergeant Marvin Iannone dismisses Clemmons from the scene.

~ 5:45 A.M.
By the time Detective Sergeant Byron arrives he notes Greenson is no longer at the house but places Pat Newcomb on the scene. Had Greenson still been there, he surely would have been hounded by reporters and couldn't have conceivably escaped their photographs, none of which have survived.

Westwood Village Mortuary employees Guy Hockett and his son Don arrive. The elder Hockett notes that rigor mortis is advanced and places Marilyn's death roughly between 9:30 to 11:30 P.M. on August 4.

~ 6:00 – 6:30 A.M.
Per reporter Joe Hyams, the Hocketts strap Marilyn into a gurney then lift the gurney into their Ford Panel truck and drive away.

~ 6:30 – 7:00 A.M.
Per Jefferies and Mrs. Murray, before the police seal the house, they notice that Pat Newcomb doesn't want to leave. Per Jefferies, he sees Pat "looking through drawers and going into Marilyn's bedroom. She had spent Friday night at the house and perhaps she was looking for something she left there. The police had to control her… They had trouble getting her out of the door." That's because she was looking for the red diary that Jefferies a day later said he saw in Mrs. Murray's possession, the same diary that Bobby Kennedy couldn't find the night before.

Note: On Monday August 6, Jefferies will witness Mrs. Murray give the red diary and one of Marilyn's personal address books to a driver for the Coroner's Office before executrix Inez Melson arrives. After a day at the Coroner's Office, per Deputy Coroner's Aide Lionel Grandison, the red diary was gone.

~ 8:00 – 8:45 A.M.
Per Deputy Coroner Robert Dambacher, he and his partner Cletus Pace brought Marilyn Monroe's remains from the Westwood Village Mortuary back to the Coroner's Office in Downtown Los Angeles.

~ 9:00 A.M.
Dr. Thomas Noguchi will perform the autopsy overseen by Deputy District Attorney John Miner. Noguchi noted what he later considered strange observations, "The stomach is almost completely empty. The contents is [sic] brownish mucoid fluid. The volume is estimated to be no more than 20 cc. No residue of the pills is noted. A smear made from the gastric contents and examined under the polarized microscope shows no refractile crystals... The contents of the duodenum is [sic] also examined under polarized microscope and shows no refractile crystals... The colon shows marked congestion and purplish discoloration."

9:30 A.M.
Bobby Kennedy attends Mass in Gilroy, California with his wife Ethel and four of their children at St. Mary Parish.

10:30 A.M.
Noguchi completes the autopsy, signing his report on Marilyn Monroe, reluctantly declaring her death a "probable suicide."

Autopsy Report:

OFFICE OF COUNTY CORONER
File# 81128
Date: Aug. 5, 1962
Time: 10:30 a.m.

ACUTE BARBITURATE POISONING
INGESTION OF OVERDOSE
(final 8/27/62)

ANATOMICAL SUMMARY

EXTERNAL EXAMINATION:
1. Lavidity of face and chest with slight ecchymosis of the left side of the back and left hip.
2. Surgical scar, right upper quadrant of the abdomen.
3. Suprapubic surgical scar.

RESPIRATORY SYSTEM:
1. Pulmonary congestion and minimal edema.

LIVER AND BILIARY SYSTEM:
1. Surgical absence of gallbladder.
2. Acute passive congestion of liver.

UROGENITAL SYSTEM:
1. Congestion of kidneys.

DIGESTIVE SYSTEM:
1. Marked congestion of stomach with petechial mucosal hemorrhage.
2. Absence of appendix.
3. Congestion and purplish discoloration of the colon.

EXTERNAL EXAMINATION:

The unembalmed body is that of a 36-year-old well-developed, well-nourished Caucasian female weighing 117 pounds and measuring 65½ inches in length. The scalp is covered with bleached blond hair. The eyes are blue. The fixed lividity is noted in the face, neck, chest, upper portions of arms and the right side of the abdomen. The faint lividity which disappears upon pressure is noted in the back and posterior aspect of the arms and legs. A slight ecchymotic area is noted in the left hip and left side of lower back. The breast shows no significant lesion. There is a horizontal 3-inch long surgical scar in the right upper quadrant of the abdomen. A suprapubic surgical scar measuring 5 inches in length is noted.

The conjunctivae are markedly congested; however, no ecchymosis or petechiae are noted. The nose shows no evidence of fracture. The external auditory canals are not remarkable. No evidence of trauma is noted in the scalp, forehead, cheeks, lips or chin. The neck shows no evidence of trauma. Examination of the hands and nails shows no defects. The lower extremities shows no evidence of trauma.

BODY CAVITY:

The usual Y-shaped incision is made to open the thoracic and abdominal cavities. The pleural and abdominal cavities contain no excess of fluid or blood. The mediastinum shows no shifting or widening. The diaphragm is within normal limits. The lower edge of the liver is within the costal margin. The organs are in normal position and relationship.

CARDIOVASCULAR SYSTEM:

The heart weighs 300 grams. The pericardial cavity contains no excess of fluid. The epicardium and pericardium are smooth and glistening. The left ventricular wall measures 1.1 cm. and the right 0.2 cm. The papillary muscles are not hypertrophic. The chordae tendieneae are not thickened or shortened. The valves have the usual number of leaflets which are thin and pliable. The tricuspid valve measures 10 cm., the pulmonary valve 6.5 cm., mitral valve 9.5 cm. and aortic valve 7 cm. in circumference. There is no septal defect. The foramen ovale is closed.

The coronary arteries arise from their usual location and are distributed in normal fashion. Multiple sections of the anterior descending branch of the left coronary artery with a 5mm. interval demonstrate a patent lumen throughout. The circumflex branch and the right coronary artery also demonstrate a patent lumen. The pulmonary artery contains no thrombus.

The aorta has a bright yellow smooth intima.

RESPIRATORY SYSTEM:

The right lung weighs 465 grams and the left 420 grams. Both lungs are moderately congested with some edema. The surface is dark red with mottling. The posterior portion of the lungs shows severe congestion. The tracheobronchial tree contains no aspirated material or blood. Multiple sections of the lungs show congestion and edematous fluid exuding from the cut surface. No consolidation or suppuration is noted. The mucosa of the larynx is grayish white.

LIVER AND BILIARY SYSTEM:

The liver weighs 1890 grams. The surface is dark brown and smooth. There are marked adhesions through the omentum and abdominal wall in the lower portion of the liver as the gallbladder has been removed. The common duct is widely patent. No calculus or obstructive material is found. Multiple sections of the liver show slight accentuation of the lobular pattern; however, no hemorrhage or tumor is found.

HEMIC AND LYMPHATIC SYSTEM:

The spleen weighs 190 grams. The surface is dark red and smooth. Section shows dark red homogeneous firm cut surface. The malpighian bodies are not clearly identified. There is no evidence of lymphadenopathy. The bone marrow is dark red in color.

ENDOCRINE SYSTEM:

The adrenal glands have the usual architectural cortex and medulla. The thyroid glands are of normal size, color and consistency.

URINARY SYSTEM:

The kidneys together weigh 350 grams. Their capsules can be stripped without difficulty. Dissection shows a moderately congested parenchyma. The cortical surface is smooth. The pelves and ureters are not dilated or stenosed. The urinary bladder contains approximately 150 cc. of clear straw-colored fluid. The mucosa is not altered.

GENITAL SYSTEM:

The external genitalia shows no gross abnormality. Distribution of the pubic hair is of female pattern. The uterus is of the usual size. Multiple sections of the uterus show the usual thickness of the uterine wall without tumor nodules. The endometrium is grayish yellow, measuring up to 0.2 cm in thickness. No polyp or tumor is found. The cervix is clear, showing no nabothian cysts. The tubes are intact. The openings of the fimbria are patent. The right ovary demonstrates recent corpus luteum haemorrhagicum. The left ovary shows corpora lutea and albicantia. A vaginal smear is taken.

DIGESTIVE SYSTEM:

The esophagus has a longitudinal folding mucosa. The stomach is almost completely empty. The contents is brownish mucoid fluid. The volume is estimated to be no more than 20 cc. No residue of the pills is noted. A smear made from the gastric contents and examined under the polarized microscope shows no refractile crystals. The mucosa shows marked congestion and submucosal petechial hemorrhage diffusely. The duodenum shows no ulcer. The contents of the duodenum is also examined under polarized microscope and shows no refractile crystals. The remainder of the small intestine shows no gross abnormality. The appendix is absent. The colon shows marked congestion and purplish discoloration. The fecal contents is light brown and formed. The mucosa shows no discoloration.

The pancreas has a tan lobular architecture. Multiple sections shows a patent duct.

SKELETOMUSCULAR SYSTEM:

The clavicle, ribs, vertebrae and pelvic bones show no refractile lines. All bones of the extremities are examined by palpation showing no evidence of fracture.

HEAD AND CENTRAL NERVOUS SYSTEM:

The brain weighs 1440 grams. Upon reflection of the scalp there is no evidence of contusion or hemorrhage. The temporal muscles are intact. Upon removal of the dura mater the cerebrospinal fluid is clear. The superficial vessels are slightly congested. The convolutions of the brain are not flattened. The contour of the brain is not distorted. No blood is found in the epidural, subdural or subarachnoid spaces. Multiple sections of the brain show the usual symmetrical ventricles and basal ganglia. Examination of the cerebellum and brain stem shows no gross abnormality. Following removal of the dura mater from the base of the skull and calvarium no skull fracture is demonstrated.

Liver temperature taken at 10:30 a.m. registered 89° F.

SPECIMEN:

Unembalmed blood is taken for alcohol and barbiturate examination. Liver, kidney, stomach and contents, urine and intestine are saved for further toxicological study. A vaginal smear is made.

T. NOGUCHI, M.D.
DEPUTY MEDICAL EXAMINER

TN:ag:G
8-13-62

Jay Margolis

REPORT OF CHEMICAL ANALYSIS
LOS ANGELES COUNTY CORONER
Toxicology Laboratory
Hall of Justice
Los Angeles, California

File No. 81128
Name of Deceased: Marilyn Monroe
Date Submitted: August 6, 1962
Time: 8 A.M.
Autopsy Surgeon: T. Noguchi, M.D.

Material Submitted	Blood X	Liver X	Stomach X
	Brain	Lung	Lavage
	Femur	Spleen	Urine X
	Kidney X	Sterum	Gall bladder
	Drugs X	Chemicals	Intestines X

Test Desired: Ethanol, Barbiturates

Laboratory Findings:

Blood: Ethanol   Absent
Blood: Barbiturates   4.5 mg. per cent
Phenobarbital is absent.

Drugs: (1) 27 capsules, #19295, 6-7-62, Librium, 5 mgm. #50
(2) 17 capsules, #20201, 7-10-62, Librium, 10 mgm. #100
(3) 26 tablets, # 20569, 7-25-62, Sulfathallidine, #36
(4) Empty container, #20858, 8-3-62, Nembutal, 1½gr. #25
(5) 10 green capsules, #20570, 7-31-62, Chloral Hydrate, 0.5 gm. #50 (Refill: 7-25-62 – original)
(6) Empty container, #456099, 11-4-61, Noludar, #50
(7) 32 pink capsules in a container without label, Phenergan, #20857, 8-3-62, 25 mg. #25

Examined by: Raymond Abernathy Head Toxicologist. Date: August 6, 1962

REPORT OF CHEMICAL ANALYSIS
LOS ANGELES COUNTY CORONER
Toxicology Laboratory
Hall of Justice
Los Angeles, California

File No. 81128
Name of Deceased: Marilyn Monroe   1st Supplement
Date Submitted: August 6, 1962
Time: 8 A.M.
Autopsy Surgeon: T. Noguchi, M.D.

Material Submitted   Blood X   Liver X   Stomach X
                      Brain   Lung   Lavage
                      Femur   Spleen   Urine X
                      Kidney X   Sterum   Gall bladder
                      Drugs X   Chemicals   Intestines X

Test Desired: Chloral Hydrate, Pentobarbital

Laboratory Findings:

Blood: Chloral Hydrate   8 mg. per cent
Liver: Pentobarbital   13.0 mg. per cent

Drugs: Correction – delete #7 on original report of August 6 and add:
(7) 32 peach-colored tablets marked MSD in prescription type vial without label.
(8) 24 white tablets #20857, 8-3-62, Phenergan, 25 mg. #25

(SEE ORIGINAL REPORT)

Examined by: Raymond Abernathy Head Toxicologist. Date: August 13, 1962

Re Death Report of Marilyn Monroe – L.A. Police Dpt.

Death was pronounced on 8/5/62 at 3:45 A.M., Possible Accidental, having taken place between the times of 8/4 and 8/5/62, 3:35 A.M. at residence located at 12305 Fifth Helena Drive, Brentwood, in Rptg. Dist. 814, Report # 62-509 463.

Marilyn Monroe on August 4, 1962 retired to her bedroom at about eight o'clock in the evening; Mrs. Eunice Murray of 933 Ocean Ave., Santa Monica, Calif., 395-7752, CR 61890, noted a light in Miss Monroe's bedroom. Mrs. Murray was not able to arouse Miss Monroe when she went to the door, and when she tried the door again at 3:30 A.M. when she noted the light still on, she found it to be locked. Thereupon Mrs. Murray observed Miss Monroe through the bedroom window and found her lying on her stomach in the bed and the appearance seemed unnatural. Mrs. Murray then called Miss Monroe's psychiatrist, Dr. Ralph R. Greenson of 436 North Roxbury Drive, Beverly Hills, Calif, CR 14050. Upon entering after breaking the bedroom window, he found Miss Monroe possibly dead. Then he telephoned Dr. Hyman Engelberg of 9730 Wilshire Boulevard, also of Beverly Hills, CR 54366, who came over and then pronounced Miss Monroe dead at 3:35 A.M. Miss Monroe was seen by Dr. Greenson on August 4, 1962 at 5:15 P.M., at her request, because she was not able to sleep. She was being treated by him for about a year. She was nude when Dr. Greenson found her dead with the telephone receiver in one hand and lying on her stomach. The Police Department was called and when they arrived they found Miss Monroe in the condition described above, except for the telephone which was removed by Dr. Greenson. There were found to be 15 bottles of medication on the night table and some were prescription. A bottle marked 1½ grains Nembutal, prescription #20853 and prescribed by Dr. Engelberg, and referring to this particular bottle, Dr. Engelberg made the statement that he prescribed a refill for this about two days ago and he further stated there probably should have been about 50 capsules at the time this was refilled by the pharmacist.

Description of Deceased: Female Caucasian, age 36, height 5.4, weight 115 pounds, blonde hair, blue eyes, and slender, medium build.

Occupation: Actress, Probable cause of death: overdose of nembutal, body discovered 8/5/62 at 3:25 A.M. Taken to County Morgue – from there to Westwood Mortuary. Report made by Sgt. R.E. Byron, #2730, W. L.A. Detective Division. Next of kin: Gladys Baker (Mother).

Coroner's Office notified. The body was removed from premises by Westwood Village Mortuary.

(8/5/62 11 A.M. WLA hf – J.R. Brukles 5829)

Los Angeles Police Department
FOLLOW-UP REPORT
Report # 62-509 463

Type Crime: DEATH REPORT
Date and Time Occurred: 8-4/5-62 8P/3:35A
Date and Time of this Report: 8-6-62 4:15P
Location of Occurrence: 12305 Fifth Helena Drive
Victim's Name: MONROE, Marilyn

Upon reinterviewing both Dr. Ralph R. Greenson (Wit #1) and Dr. Hyman Engelberg (Wit #2) they both agree to the following time sequence of their actions.

Dr. Greenson received a phone call from Mrs. Murray (reporting person) at 3:30A, 8-5-62 stating that she was unable to get into Miss Monroe's bedroom and the light was on. He told her to pound on the door and look in the window and call him back. At 3:35A, Mrs. Murray called back and stated Miss Monroe was laying on the bed with the phone in her hand and looked strange. Dr. Greenson was dressed by this time, left for deceased residence which is about one mile away. He also told Mrs. Murray to call Dr. Engelberg.

Dr. Greenson arrived at deceased house at about 3:40A. He broke the window pane and entered through the window and removed the phone from her hand.

Rigor Mortis had set in. At 3:50A, Dr. Engelberg arrived and pronounced Miss Monroe dead. The two doctors talked for a few moments. They both believe that it was about 4A when Dr. Engelberg called the Police Department.

A check with the Complaint Board and WLA Desk, indicates that the call was received at 4:25 A.M. Miss Monroe's phone, GR 61890 has been checked and no toll calls were made during the hours of this occurrence. Phone number 472-4830 is being checked at the present time.

RE – INTERVIEW OF PERSONS KNOWN TO MARILYN MONROE

August 6, 1962

G.H. ARMSTRONG, COMMANDER, WEST L.A. DETECTIVE DIVISION

Date and Time Reported: 8-10-62 8:30A

The following is a resume of the interview conducted in an effort to obtain the times of various phone calls received by Miss Monroe on the evening of her death. All of the below times are estimations of the persons interviewed. None are able to state definite times as none checked the time of these calls.

MILTON RUDIN

Mr. Rudin stated that on the evening of 8-4-62 his exchange received a call at 8:25P and that this call was relayed to him at 8:30P. The call was for him to call Milton Ebbins. At about 8:45P he called Mr. Ebbins who told him that he had received a call from Peter Lawford stating that Mr. Lawford had called Marilyn Monroe at her home and that while Mr. Lawford was talking to her, her voice seemed to "fade out" and when he attempted to call her back, the line was busy. Mr. Ebbins requested that Mr. Rudin call Miss Monroe and determine if everything was alright, or attempt to reach her doctor. At about 9P, Mr. Rudin called Miss Monroe and the phone was answered by Mrs. Murray. He inquired of her as to the physical well being of Miss Monroe and was assured by Mrs. Murray that Miss Monroe was alright. Believing that Miss Monroe was suffering from one of her despondent moments, Mr. Rudin dismissed the possibility of anything further being wrong.

MRS. EUNICE MURRAY

Mrs. Murray stated that she had worked for Marilyn Monroe since November, 1961, that on the evening of 8-4-62 Miss Monroe had received a collect call from a Joe DiMaggio, Jr. at about 7:30P. Mrs. Murray said that at the time of this call coming in, Miss Monroe was in bed and possibly had been asleep. She took the call and after talking to Joe DiMaggio, Jr., she then made a call to Dr. Greenson and Mrs. Murray overheard her say, "Joe Jr. is not getting married, I'm so happy about this." Mrs. Murray states that from the tone of Miss Monroe's voice, she believed her to be in very good spirits. At about 9P, Mrs. Murray received a call from Mr. Rudin who inquired about Miss

Monroe. Mr. Rudin did not talk to Miss Monroe. Mrs. Murray states that these are the only phone calls that she recalls receiving on this date.

Note: It is officers opinion that Mrs. Murray was vague and possibly evasive in answering questions pertaining to the activities of Miss Monroe during this time. It is not known whether this is, or is not intentional. During the interrogation of Joe DiMaggio, Jr., he indicated he had made three phone calls to the Monroe home, only one of which Mrs. Murray mentioned.

JOE DIMAGGIO – Miramar Hotel, Room 1035, Santa Monica

Mr. DiMaggio was informed of the rumor which quoted him as saying that he would not invite Mr. Lawford to the funeral services because he could have saved Marilyn's life and didn't. Mr. DiMaggio denied this, stating that he had not talked to any member of the press, nor had he said such a thing to anyone who might have repeated it to the press. He stated that the decision to limit the number of people was a mutual agreement, decided upon in order to keep from hurting the feelings of many of Marilyn's friends who might be accidentally overlooked.

JOE DIMAGGIO, JR. – Miramar Hotel, Room 1035, Santa Monica

Joe DiMaggio, Jr. was in his father's suite and interviewed immediately after the above interview. He stated that he had placed three collect calls to Miss Monroe on 8-4-62 and that the first call was about 2P. He could overhear the operator talk to Mrs. Murray who informed the operator that Miss Monroe was not in. The second call was placed at approximately 4:30P and again was answered by Mrs. Murray, and again he was unable to contact Miss Monroe. The third call was placed at approximately 7P and on this occasion Mrs. Murray stated that she would see if Miss Monroe was available and in a few moments Miss Monroe came on the phone and he held a short conversation with her. During the conversation, he told Miss Monroe that he was not going to get married. The time of the last call is estimated to be 7P, as he states it was during the 6th or 7th innings of the Angels-Orioles baseball game in Baltimore.

PETER LAWFORD

An attempt was made to contact Mr. Lawford, but officers were informed by his secretary that Mr. Lawford had taken an airplane at 1P, 8-8-62. It is unknown at this time the exact destination, however his secretary stated that she did expect to hear from him and that she would request that he contact this Department at his earliest convenience.

R.E. Byron #2730
W.L.A. Detectives

POLICE REPORTS ON MARILYN MONROE DEATH
8-5-62
L. Selby, OIC, Homicide Special Sec., R.H.D.
Date of Report: 8-27-74

At the request of Commander McCauley, an attempt was made to determine the number and type of police reports taken by this Department in connection with Marilyn Monroe's death which occurred in W.L.A. Div. on August 5, 1962. Commander McCauley also requested we determine if any of these reports were still available at this time.

In this regard, Sgt. Sturgeon, O.I.C., R. & I. Div., was contacted and requested to make a search of R. & I. files in an attempt to locate any reports we may have. He stated he could locate no records pertaining to the 1962 death of Miss Monroe. He further stated that all original crime reports that are controlled by R. & I. Div. are destroyed after a 10-year retention period. All reports, file cards, and DR blotters are included in the destruction.

Note: Attached is a copy of correspondence dated Sept. 4, 1973, to Assistant Chief D.F. Gates from Assistant Chief D.H. Speck pertaining to the "retention and destruction of crime reports."

The files at R.H.D. were checked for any records of the death of Miss Monroe. This division has no such records.

Investigators contacted W.L.A. Div. and were informed that they had no crime reports in their files pertaining to Miss Monroe's death. It was further determined from present W.L.A. investigators that the original W.L.A. detective who handled the case was Sgt. R.E. Byron, now retired.

Mr. Byron was contacted... He stated he was called to the scene of Miss Monroe's death. Lieuts. Gregoire and Armstrong also responded. Byron stated he completed a death report and believes that he classified it as "accidental." Byron believes that he subsequently made a follow-up report to the original death report but is not sure how that was classified.

Byron does not have copies of any of these reports nor does he know of any existing copies.

CONFIDENTIAL

Employees Reporting: L.A. Murray 6692 RHD

Bibliography:

Acacia, John. *Clark Clifford: The Wise Man Of Washington*. Kentucky: University Press of Kentucky, 2009.

Allen, Maury. *Where Have You Gone, Joe DiMaggio?* New York: Signet, 1976.

Arnold, Eve. *Marilyn Monroe: An Appreciation*. New York: Knopf, 1987.

Bacon, James. *Made In Hollywood*. Chicago: Contemporary Books, 1977.

-----. *Hollywood Is a Four Letter Town*. Chicago: Henry Regnery Company, 1976.

Badman, Keith. *The Final Years Of Marilyn Monroe: The Shocking True Story*. London: J.R. Books, 2010.

Banner, Lois W. *MM – Personal: From The Private Archive Of Marilyn Monroe*. New York: Abrams, 2011.

-----. *American Beauty*. Chicago: The University of Chicago Press, 1983.

Barris, George. *Marilyn: Her Life In Her Own Words*. New York: Birch Lane Press, 1995.

Belmont, Georges. *Marilyn Monroe And The Camera*. London: Schirmer Art Books, 2007.

Berthelsen, Detlef. *Alltag Bei Familie Freud: Die Erinnerungen Der Paula Fichtl. (Life Of The Freud Family: The Memoirs Of Paula Fichtl)* Hamburg: Hoffman Und Campe, 1987.

Blaine, Gerald, and Lisa McCubbin. *The Kennedy Detail: JFK's Secret Service Agents Break Their Silence.* New York: Gallery Books, 2010.

Braden, Joan. *Just Enough Rope: An Intimate Memoir.* New York: Villard Books, 1989.

Bradlee, Benjamin C. *Conversations With Kennedy.* New York: Norton Paperback, 1984.

Brashler, William. *The Don: The Life And Death Of Sam Giancana.* New York: Harper & Row, 1977.

Brodsky, Jack, and Nathan Weiss. *The Cleopatra Papers: A Private Correspondence.* New York: Simon & Schuster, 1963.

Brown, Peter, and Patte Barham. *Marilyn: The Last Take.* New York: Signet, 1993.

Buchthal, Stanley, and Bernard Comment, ed. *fragments: poems, intimate notes, letters by Marilyn Monroe.* New York: Farrar, Straus and Giroux, 2010.

Buntin, John. *L.A. Noir: The Struggle For The Soul Of America's Most Seductive City.* New York: Three Rivers Press, 2009.

Burke, Richard E. *The Senator: My Ten Years With Ted Kennedy.* New York: St. Martin's Press, 1992.

Buskin, Richard. *Blonde Heat: The Sizzling Screen Career Of Marilyn Monroe.* New York: Billboard Books, 2001.

-----. *The Films Of Marilyn Monroe.* Illinois: Publications International, 1992.

Capell, Frank A. *The Strange Death Of Marilyn Monroe.* New York: The Herald of Freedom, 1964.

Capote, Truman. *Music For Chameleons.* New York: Vintage International, 1994.

Carpozi, Jr., George. *Marilyn Monroe: "Her Own Story."* New York: Belmont, 1961.

Carroll, Ronald H., and Alan B. Tomich. "The Death of Marilyn Monroe – Report to the District Attorney." December 1982, pp. 1-29.

Chekhov, Michael. *To The Actor: On The Technique Of Acting.* New York: Harper & Row, Publishers, 1953.

Christie's. *The Personal Property Of Marilyn Monroe.* New York: International Flavors & Fragrances, 1999.

Churchwell, Sarah. *The Many Lives Of Marilyn Monroe.* New York: Metropolitan, 2004.

Clark, Colin. *My Week With Marilyn.* London: HarperCollins, 2000.

-----. *The Prince, The Showgirl And Me: Six Months On The Set With Marilyn And Olivier.* New York: St. Martin's Press, 1995.

Clayton, Marie. *Marilyn Monroe: Unseen Archives.* New York: Barnes & Noble Books, 2004.

Clifford, Clark M., and Richard Holbrooke. *Counsel To The President: A Memoir.* New York: Anchor, 1992.

Cockburn, Alexander, and Jeffrey St. Clair. *Whiteout: The CIA, Drugs And The Press.* New York: Verso, 2001.

Conway, Michael, and Mark Ricci, ed. *The Films Of Marilyn Monroe.* New Jersey: The Citadel Press, 1979.

Cramer, Richard Ben. *Joe DiMaggio: The Hero's Life.* New York: Touchstone, 2001.

Cunningham, Ernest W. *The Ultimate Marilyn.* Los Angeles: Renaissance Books, 1998.

Dallek, Robert. *An Unfinished Life: John F. Kennedy*. New York: Little, Brown and Company, 2003.

Davis, Sammy, Jr. *Hollywood In A Suitcase*. London: Granada Publishing, 1980.

De Dienes, Andre. *Marilyn: Mon Amour*. London: Bracken Books, 1993.

De La Hoz, Cindy. *Marilyn Monroe: The Personal Archives*. London: Carlton Books, 2010.

Demaris, Ovid. *Captive City: Chicago In Chains*. New York: Lyle Stuart, 1969.

De Toledano, Ralph. *J. Edgar Hoover: The Man In His Time*. New York: Manor Books, 1974.

-----. *R.F.K.: The Man Who Would Be President*. New York: Signet: 1967.

Dougherty, Jim. *To Norma Jeane With Love, Jimmie*. Missouri: BeachHouse Books, 2001.

-----. *The Secret Happiness Of Marilyn Monroe*. Chicago: Playboy Press, 1976.

Dunne, Dominick. *The Way We Lived Then: Recollections Of A Well-Known Name Dropper*. New York: Crown Publishers, 1999.

Editors of Life. *Remembering Marilyn*. New York: Time, Inc., 2009.

Ellroy, James. *American Tabloid*. New York: Alfred A. Knopf, 1995.

Engelberg, Hyman, M.D., and Henry F. Greenberg. *The Doctor's Modern Heart Attack Prevention Program*. New York: Funk & Wagnalls, 1974.

Engelberg, Morris, and Marv Schneider. *DiMaggio: Setting The Record Straight*. Minnesota: MVP Books, 2004.

Evans, Mike. *Marilyn Handbook*. London: MQ Publications Limited, 2004.

Exner, Judith, and Ovid Demaris. *My Story*. New York: Grove Press, 1978.

Fanta, J. Julius. *Sailing With President Kennedy: The White House Yachtsman.* New York: Sea Lore Publishing, 1968.

Farber, Stephen, and Marc Green. *Hollywood On The Couch: A Candid Look At The Overheated Love Affair Between Psychiatrists And Moviemakers.* New York: William Morrow & Company, 1993.

Federal Bureau of Investigation. *John Roselli: The FBI Files (Volume One + Two).* Filiquarian Publishing, LLC, 2009.

-----. *Marilyn Monroe: The FBI Files.* Filiquarian Publishing, LLC, 2007.

Feingersh, Ed. *Marilyn In New York.* Munich: Schirmer/Mosel, 2008.

Finn, Michelle. *Marilyn's Addresses: A Fan's Guide To The Places She Knew.* London: Smith Gryphon Publishers, 1995.

Fowler, Will. *Reporters: Memoirs Of A Young Newspaperman.* Malibu: Roundtable Publishing Company, 1991.

Franklin, Lynn. *The Beverly Hills Murder File.* Indiana: 1st Books Library, 2002.

Freeman, Lucy. *Why Norma Jean Killed Marilyn Monroe.* New York: Hastings House, 1993.

Gates, Daryl F. *Chief: My Life In The LAPD.* New York: Bantam Books, 1993.

Gentry, Curt. *J. Edgar Hoover: The Man And The Secrets.* New York: Norton Paperback, 2001.

Giancana, Sam, and Chuck Giancana. *Double Cross: The Explosive Inside Story Of The Mobster Who Controlled America.* New York: Skyhorse Publishing, 2010.

Gilmore, John. *Inside Marilyn Monroe.* California: Ferine Books, 2007.

Graham, Sheilah. *Confessions Of A Hollywood Columnist.* New York: Bantam Books, 1970.

Greenson, Joan. *Untitled 90-Page Marilyn Monroe Manuscript.* Greenson Papers, Special Collections, UCLA.

✳ Greenson, Ralph, M.D. *Explorations In Psychoanalysis.* New York: International Universities Press, 1978.

-----. *The Technique And Practice Of Psychoanalysis.* Connecticut: International Universities Press, 1967.

-----. "Drugs in the Psychotherapeutic Situation." January 12, 1964. Greenson Papers, Special Collections, UCLA.

Guilaroff, Sydney, and Cathy Griffin. *Crowning Glory: Reflections Of Hollywood's Favorite Confidant.* Santa Monica: General Publishing Group, 1996.

Guiles, Fred Lawrence. *Legend: The Life And Death Of Marilyn Monroe.* Michigan: Scarborough House, 1991.

-----. *Norma Jean: The Life Of Marilyn Monroe.* New York: Bantam Books, 1970.

Guthman, Edwin O., and Jeffrey Shulman, ed. *Robert Kennedy: In His Own Words.* New York: Bantam Books, 1989.

Hancock, Larry. *Someone Would Have Talked.* JFK Lancer Productions & Publications, 2003.

Haspiel, James. *The Unpublished Marilyn.* Edinburgh: Mainstream Publishing Company, 2000.

-----. *Young Marilyn: Becoming The Legend.* New York: Hyperion, 1994.

-----. *Marilyn: The Ultimate Look At The Legend.* New York: Owl Book, 1993.

Hays, Thomas G., and Arthur W. Sjoquist, and the Los Angeles Police Historical Society. *Los Angeles Police Department (Images Of America: California).* South Carolina: Arcadia Publishing, 2005.

Her Psychiatrist Friend. *Violations Of The Child Marilyn Monroe*. New York: Bridgehead Books, 1962.

Hersh, Seymour M. *The Dark Side Of Camelot*. New York: Back Bay Books, 1998.

Hethmon, Robert. *Strasberg At The Actors Studio: Tape-Recorded Sessions*. New York: Theatre Communications Group, 1996.

✱ Heymann, C. David. *Bobby And Jackie: A Love Story*. New York: Atria, 2009.

-----. *RFK: A Candid Biography Of Robert F. Kennedy*. New York: A Dutton Book, 1998.

-----. *A Woman Named Jackie*. New York: Lyle Stuart, 1989.

Hudson, James. *The Mysterious Death Of Marilyn Monroe*. New York: Volitant, 1968.

Israel, Lee. *Kilgallen*. New York: Delacorte Press, 1979.

Jacobs, George. *Mr. S: My Life With Frank Sinatra*. New York: HarperEntertainment, 2004.

Jaffe, Lee. *The Technique And Practice Of Psychoanalysis, Volume III: The Training Seminars Of Ralph R. Greenson, M.D.* New York: International Universities Press, 2004.

James, Brandon. *Jeanne Carmen: MY WILD, WILD LIFE As A New York Pin Up Queen*. Nebraska: iUniverse, 2007.

Johnson, Dorris, and Ellen Leventhal, ed. *The Letters Of Nunnally Johnson*. New York: Knopf, 1981.

Kahn, Roger. *Joe & Marilyn: A Memory Of Love*. New York: William Morrow & Company, 1986.

Kazan, Elia. *Elia Kazan: A Life*. New York: Da Capo Press, 1997.

Kelley, Kitty. *His Way: The Unauthorized Biography Of Frank Sinatra*. New York: Bantam Books, 1986.

-----. *Jackie Oh!* New York: Ballantine Books, 1979.

Kennedy, Edward M., ed. *The Fruitful Bough*. Halliday Lithograph Corporation. Privately printed, 1965.

Kennedy, Robert. *The Enemy Within*. New York: Popular Library, 1960.

Kessler, Ronald. *In The President's Secret Service: Behind The Scenes With Agents In The Line Of Fire And The Presidents They Protect*. New York: Three Rivers Press, 2010.

Kirkland, Douglas. *An Evening With Marilyn*. New York: Welcome Books, 2005.

Kirsner, Douglas. *Unfree-associations: Inside Psychoanalytic Institutes*. Maryland: Jason Aronson, 2009.

-----. (2007) " 'DO AS I SAY, NOT AS I DO': Ralph Greenson, Anna Freud, and Superrich Patients." Psychoanalytic Psychology, 24: 475-486.

-----. (2005) "Politics masquerading as science: Ralph Greenson, Anna Freud, and the Klein wars." Psychoanalytic Review, 92: 907-927.

Kotsilibas-Davis, James, and Joshua Greene. *Milton's Marilyn: The Photographs Of Milton H. Greene*. New York: teNeues, 1998.

Lawford, Lady May, and Buddy Galon. *Mother Bitch: Lady Lawford Exposes The Kennedys, The Royal Family & Her Own Son, Peter Lawford*. New York: S.P.I. Books, 1992.

Lawford, Patricia Kennedy, ed. *That Shining Hour*. Halliday Lithograph Corporation. Privately printed, 1969.

Lawford, Patricia Seaton, and Ted Schwarz. *The Peter Lawford Story: Life With The Kennedys, Monroe And The Rat Pack*. New York: Carroll & Graf Publishers, Inc., 1988.

Leamer, Laurence. *The Kennedy Women: The Saga Of An American Family.* New York: Ballantine Books, 1996.

Leaming, Barbara. *Marilyn Monroe.* New York: Three Rivers Press, 1998.

Luitjers, Guus. *Marilyn Monroe: in her own words.* London: Omnibus Press, 1991.

-----. *Marilyn Monroe: a never-ending dream.* New York: St. Martin's Press, 1986.

Mailer, Norman. *Marilyn.* New York: Warner Books, 1975.

Marshall, David. *The DD Group: An Online Investigation Into The Death Of Marilyn Monroe.* Nebraska: iUniverse, 2005.

Martin, Ralph G. *Seeds Of Destruction: Joe Kennedy And His Sons.* New York: G.P. Putnam's Sons, 1995.

McCann, Graham. *Marilyn Monroe.* New Jersey: Rutgers University Press, 1988.

Mecacci, Luciano. *Freudian Slips: The Casualties Of Psychoanalysis From The Wolf Man To Marilyn Monroe.* Scotland: Vagabond Voices, 2009.

Meyers, Jeffrey. *The Genius And The Goddess: Arthur Miller And Marilyn Monroe.* Chicago: University of Illinois Press, 2010.

Miller, Arthur. *Timebends.* New York: Grove Press, 1987.

-----. *After The Fall.* New York: Bantam Books, 1965.

Miracle, Berniece Baker, and Mona Rae Miracle. *My Sister Marilyn.* North Carolina: Algonquin Books, 1994.

Monroe, Marilyn, and Ben Hecht. *My Story.* Maryland: Taylor Trade, 2007.

Moore, Robin, and Gene Schoor. *Marilyn & Joe DiMaggio.* New York: Manor Books, 1977.

Morgan, Michelle. *Marilyn Monroe: Private And Undisclosed*. New York: Carroll & Graf, 2007.

Murray, Eunice, and Rose Shade. *Marilyn: The Last Months*. New York: Pyramid Books, 1975.

Nemiroff, Robert A., M.D., Alan Sugarman, Ph.D., and Alvin Robbins, M.D. *On Loving, Hating, And Living Well: The Public Psychoanalytic Lectures Of Ralph R. Greenson, M.D.* Connecticut: International Universities Press, 1992.

Newfield, Jack. *Robert Kennedy: A Memoir*. New York: E.P. Dutton & Co., 1969.

Noguchi, Thomas T., M.D., and Joseph DiMona. *Coroner To The Stars*. London: Corgi Books, 1984.

Novotny, Mariella. *King's Road*. New York: Manor Books, 1972.

O'Brien, Michael. *John F. Kennedy: A Biography*. New York: St. Martin's Press, 2005.

Oppenheimer, Jerry. *The Other Mrs. Kennedy*. New York: St. Martin's Paperbacks, 1995.

Otash, Fred. *Investigation Hollywood!* Chicago: Henry Regnery Company, 1976.

Parker, Robert, and Richard Rashke. *Capitol Hill In Black And White*. New York: Dodd, Mead & Company, 1986.

Peary, Danny, ed. *Close-Ups: The Movie Star Book*. New York: Fireside, 1988.

Porter, Darwin, and Danforth Prince. *The Kennedys: All The Gossip Unfit For Print*. New York: Blood Moon Productions, 2011.

Quirk, Lawrence J. *The Kennedys In Hollywood*. Texas: Taylor Publishing Company, 1996.

Rappleye, Charles, and Ed Becker. *All American Mafioso: The Johnny Rosselli Story*. New York: Doubleday, 2001.

Reeves, Thomas C. *A Question Of Character: A Life Of John F. Kennedy*. New York: Forum, 1997.

Reymond, William. *Marilyn, le dernier secret*. Paris: Flammarion, 2008.

Riese, Randall, and Neal Hitchens. *The Unabridged Marilyn: Her Life From A To Z*. New York: Bonanza Books, 1990.

Rollyson, Carl E., Jr. *Marilyn Monroe: A Life Of The Actress*. New York: Da Capo Press, 1993.

Rosten, Leo. *Captain Newman, M.D.* New York: Harper & Brothers, 1961.

Rosten, Norman. *Marilyn: An Untold Story*. New York: NAL/Signet, 1973.

Rothmiller, Mike, and Ivan G. Goldman. *L.A. Secret Police: Inside The LAPD Elite Spy Network*. New York: Pocket Books, 1992.

Russell, Jane. *Jane Russell, An Autobiography: My Path & My Detours*. New York: Franklin Watts, 1985.

Sakol, Jeannie. *The Birth Of Marilyn: The Lost Photographs Of Norma Jean By Joseph Jasgur*. London: Sidgwick & Jackson, 1991.

✽ Schlesinger, Arthur M., Jr. *Robert Kennedy And His Times*. New York: Mariner Books, 2002.

Schwarz, Ted. *Marilyn Revealed: The Ambitious Life Of An American Icon*. Maryland: Taylor Trade Publishing, 2009.

Schwarz, Ted, and Mardi Rustam. *Candy Barr: The Small-Town Texas Runaway Who Became A Darling Of The Mob And The Queen Of Las Vegas Burlesque*. Maryland: Taylor Trade Publishing, 2008.

Selsman, Michael. *All Is Vanity: Memoirs Of A Hollywood Operative*. California: New World Digital Entertainment, 2009.

Shaw, Sam, and Norman Rosten. *Marilyn: Among Friends*. Australia: Magna Books, 1992.

Shaw, Sam. *The Joy Of Marilyn: In The Camera Eye*. New York: Peebles Press International, 1979.

Shevey, Sandra. *The Marilyn Scandal*. New York: Jove Books, 1990.

Skolsky, Sidney. *Don't Get Me Wrong – I Love Hollywood*. New York: G.P. Putnam's Sons, 1975.

Slatzer, Robert. *The Marilyn Files*. New York: S.P.I. Books, 1992.

-----. *The Life And Curious Death Of Marilyn Monroe*. London: W.H. Allen, 1975.

Smith, Matthew. *Marilyn's Last Words: Her Secret Tapes And Mysterious Death*. New York: Carroll & Graf Publishers, 2005.

Smith, Dr. Paul A., and Richard E. May, ed. *Official Report Of The Proceedings Of The Democratic National Convention And Committee*. Washington, D.C.: National Document Publishers, 1964.

Spada, James. *Peter Lawford: The Man Who Kept The Secrets*. New York: Bantam Books, 1991.

Spada, James, and George Zeno. *Monroe: Her Life In Pictures*. New York: Doubleday, 1982.

Speriglio, Milo. *The Marilyn Conspiracy*. New York: Pocket Books, 1986.

Spindel, Bernard B. *The Ominous Ear*. New York: Awards Book, 1968.

Spoto, Donald. *Marilyn Monroe: The Biography*. New York: HarperCollins, 1993.

Stanislavski, Constantin. *An Actor Prepares*. New York: Theatre Art Books, 1948.

Steinem, Gloria, and George Barris. *Marilyn*. New York: Henry Holt and Company, 1986.

Stern, Bert. *Marilyn Monroe: The Complete Last Sitting.* Munich: Schirmer/Mosel, 1992.

Strait, Raymond. *Bob Hope: A Tribute.* New York: Pinnacle Books, 2003.

-----. *Here They Are Jayne Mansfield.* New York: S.P.I. Books, 1992.

-----. *The Tragic Secret Life Of Jayne Mansfield.* London: Robert Hale & Company, 1976.

✶ Strasberg, Susan. *Marilyn And Me: Sisters, Rivals, Friends.* New York: Warner Books, 1992.

-----. *Bittersweet.* New York: Putnam, 1980.

Sugarman, Alan, and Robert Nemiroff, and Daniel Greenson. *The Technique And Practice Of Psychoanalysis, Volume II: A Memorial Volume To Ralph R. Greenson.* Connecticut: International Universities Press, 2000.

Summers, Anthony, and Robbyn Swan. *Sinatra: The Life.* New York: Vintage Books, 2006.

✶ Summers, Anthony. *Goddess: The Secret Lives Of Marilyn Monroe.* London: Phoenix, 2000.

-----. *The Secret Life Of J. Edgar Hoover.* New York: Pocket Star Books, 1994.

Taraborrelli, J. Randy. *The Secret Life Of Marilyn Monroe.* New York: Grand Central Publishing, 2009.

-----. *Sinatra: Behind The Legend.* New Jersey: Carol Publishing Group, 1997.

Thomas, Evan. *Robert Kennedy: His Life.* New York: Simon & Schuster, 2007.

Van Meter, Jonathan. *The Last Good Time: Skinny D'Amato, The Notorious 500 Club & The Rise And Fall Of Atlantic City.* New York: Crown Publishers, 2003.

Victor, Adam. *The Marilyn Encyclopedia*. New York: The Overlook Press, 1999.

Vitacco-Robles, Gary. *Cursum Perficio: Marilyn Monroe's Brentwood Hacienda*. Nebraska: iUniverse, 1999.

✳ Wahl, Charles William. (1974). "Psychoanalysis of the Rich, the Famous and the Influential." Contemporary Psychoanalysis, 10:71-76.

Wallis, Brian, and John Vachon. *Marilyn August 1953: The Lost LOOK Photos*. New York: Calla Editions, 2010.

Warner, Silas L. (1991). "Psychoanalytic Understanding and Treatment of the Very Rich." Journal of the American Academy of Psychoanalysis, 19:578-594.

Weatherby, W.J. *Conversations With Marilyn*. New York: Mason/Charter, 1976.

Wertheimer, Molly Meijer, ed. *Inventing A Voice: The Rhetoric Of American First Ladies Of The Twentieth Century*. Maryland: Rowman & Littlefield Publishers, 2004.

Wexler, Milton. *A Look Through The Rearview Mirror*. Illinois: Xlibris Corporation, 2002.

Wiener, Leigh. *Marilyn: A Hollywood Farewell*. Los Angeles: Publishing Company, 1990.

Wikipedia on "The Death of Marilyn Monroe": http://en.wikipedia.org/wiki/Death_of_marilyn_monroe

Wilson, Earl. *Show Business Laid Bare*. New York: G.P. Putnam's Sons, 1974.

-----. *The Show Business Nobody Knows*. Chicago: Bantam, 1973.

Wolfe, Donald H. *The Last Days Of Marilyn Monroe*. New York: William Morrow & Company, 1998.

Young-Bruehl, Elisabeth. *Anna Freud: A Biography.* New York: Summit Books, 1988.

Zolotow, Maurice. *Marilyn Monroe: Revised Edition.* New York: Perennial Library, 1990.

-----. *Marilyn Monroe: An Uncensored Biography.* New York: Bantam Books, 1961.

DOCUMENTARIES:

"In Search of…" The Death Of Marilyn Monroe History Channel documentary, 1980.

The Death of Marilyn Monroe documentary with Donald Wolfe, Michael Selsman, Joe Hyams, Lynn Franklin, and George Barris, n.d.

History's Mysteries: The Death of Marilyn Monroe documentary, A&E Television Networks, 2000.

JFK: A Presidency Revealed History Channel documentary, A&E Television Networks, 2003.

JFK's Women: The Scandals documentary, Quickfire Media, 2006. Director/Producer Harvey Lilley.

KNBC Hard Copy 4/20 Edition on Marilyn Monroe, 1992.

The Legend of Marilyn Monroe documentary, 1964. Producer David L. Wolper, narrated by director John Huston.

The Marilyn Files documentary, KVC Entertainment, 1991. Producer Melvin B. Bergman.

The Marilyn Files Live TV Special, 1992. Hosted by Bill Bixby.

Marilyn: The Last Word (A Reenactment of the Events Leading Up to Her Tragic Death) Hard Copy documentary, 1993.

Marilyn's Man documentary, Viking Films, 2005. Director Schani Krug.

Marilyn Monroe: The Final Days TV documentary, 2001.

The Reporters Special Edition – Marilyn Monroe: A Case for Murder TV documentary, 1988, starring attorney Raphael Abramowitz, Krista Bradford, and Steve Dunleavy.

Say Goodbye to the President BBC documentary with Anthony Summers, 1985.

Something's Got to Give documentary, 1990. Henry Schipper of Fox-Entertainment News.

MAJOR NEWSPAPER ARTICLES:

Adams, Tim. "Michael Munn: the celebrity biographer reveals all." Guardian. 25 July 2010.

Barnes, Bart. "Washington Insider Clark Clifford Dies: Reputation of Adviser to Presidents Suffered in Bank Scandal." Washington Post. 11 October 1998.

Blackburn, John, Chuck Orman, and Dan McDonald. "I Saw Marilyn Murdered." Globe. 23 November 1982, Volume 29, Number 47, pp. 1, 3-5, 7-8.

Buchwald, Art. "Let's Be Firm on Monroe Doctrine." Washington Post. 19 November 1960.

Carlson, Michael. "FBI agent and CIA fixer who became Howard Hughes's bagman." Guardian. 20 August 2008.

Davis, Lisa. "The Right Photographer." Los Angeles Times. 27 June 1993.

"How Bobby Kennedy Silenced Marilyn Monroe." Star. (USA), 8 September 1998, Vol. 25, Iss. 36, pp. 6-7, 38.

Judis, John. "Political Affairs: A biography of Robert F. Kennedy focuses on his love life." New York Times. 3 January 1999.

Justice, Michelle, and Roman Hryniszak. Runnin' Wild: All About Marilyn. October 1994, Number 16.

-----. Runnin' Wild: All About Marilyn. July 1994, Number 15.

-----. Runnin' Wild: All About Marilyn. April 1994, Number 14.

-----. Runnin' Wild: All About Marilyn. October 1993, Number 12.

-----. Runnin' Wild: All About Marilyn. January 1992, Number 5.

Leigh, Wendy. "Jane Russell: My friend Marilyn did not kill herself." Daily Mail. 3 March 2007.

Luther, Claudia. "Actress [Jane Russell] redefined movie mores: She turned sexy image to comic effect." Los Angeles Times. 1 March 2011.

McLellan, Dennis. "John Miner, investigator of Marilyn Monroe's death, dies at 92." Los Angeles Times. 4 March 2011.

Nelson, Valerie J. "Psychiatrist Robert Litman dies; co-founded suicide prevention center." Washington Post. 14 March 2010.

Oliver, Myrna. "Fred Otash; Colorful Hollywood Private Eye and Author." Los Angeles Times. 8 October 1992.

O'Neill, Ann W. "Ex-Prosecutor Says Monroe Dumped Robert Kennedy." Los Angeles Times. 14 December 1997.

Pace, Eric. "Judith Exner Is Dead at 65; Claimed Affair With Kennedy." New York Times. 27 September 1999.

"Psychiatrist Breaks Silence In Defense of Marilyn Monroe." Yuma Daily Sun. 23 October 1973.

Schickel, Richard. "Jottings from an earnest soul." Los Angeles Times. 1 November 2010, pp. D1, D4.

Scott, Vernon. "Debunking MM murder rumors latest Hollywood industry." European Stars and Stripes. 7 October 1985.

Sherrill, Bob. "Busy Nights in Camelot." Washington Post. 11 October 1998.

Thomas, Evan. "The Woman Who Knew Too Much. A VERY PRIVATE WOMAN: The Life and Unsolved Murder of Presidential Mistress Mary Meyer." Washington Post. 11 October 1998.

Trueheart, Charles. "Joan Braden's Book Proposal: Kiss & Sell?; Memories of Rocky, RFK & Friends." Washington Post. 8 September 1987.

Turner, Christopher. "Marilyn Monroe on the Couch: To Dr. Ralph Greenson, Marilyn Monroe was more than just a patient. Now, for the first time, his family recall their favourite 'big sister.'" Telegraph. 23 June 2010.

Welkos, Robert W. "New Chapter in the Mystery of Marilyn: Her Own Words?" Los Angeles Times. 5 August 2005.

Widdicombe, Ben. "New Marilyn death docu is in the offing." New York Daily News. 2 August 2007, p. 20.

Wilson, Earl. "Marilyn Monroe Will Divorce Arthur Miller." Los Angeles Mirror. 11 November 1960.

Yarrow, Andrew L. "Washington Book Proposal Withdrawn." New York Times. 10 September 1987.

Zolotow, Maurice. "Monroe's last days: Drowsy death in a barbiturate darkness." Chicago Tribune. 14 September 1973.

-----. "MM's Psychiatrist a Troubled Man." San Antonio Light. 13 October 1973, p. 9-A.

MAJOR MAGAZINE ARTICLES:

Allan, Rupert. "Marilyn Monroe… A Serious Blonde Who Can Act." Look. 23 October 1951, pp. 40-44, 46.

Boyes, Malcolm. "The Passing of Peter Lawford Rekindles Memories of the Joys and Sadness of a Camelot Lost." People. 14 January 1985.

Carroll, Donald. "Conversation with Dr. Thomas Noguchi." Oui. February 1976, pp. 66-68, 74, 118, 120-122.

DePaulo, Lisa. "The Strange, Still Mysterious Death of Marilyn Monroe." Playboy. December 2005, pp. 76, 78, 82, 192, 194-196.

Donaldson, Martha. "One Year Later: Marilyn Monroe's Killer Still at Large!" Photoplay. August 1963, pp. 52-53, 74-75.

Gable, Kathleen. "Clark Gable As I Knew Him…" Look. 29 August 1961, pp. 68-72, 75-76.

Hersh, Seymour. "Secrets and Lies." Vanity Fair. November 1997, pp. 96, 100, 107-108, 110, 112, 114-115, 119-122.

Miner, John. "Marilyn Uncensored." Playboy. December 2005, pp. 80-81, 197-200.

Rebello, Stephen. "Somebody Killed Her." Playboy. December 2005, pp. 79, 186-188, 190.

Scaduto, Anthony. "Was Marilyn Monroe Murdered? Do the Kennedys Know?" Oui. October 1975, pp. 34-36, 42, 110, 112-114, 116, 118.

Scheer, Julian. "Carl Sandburg Talks About Marilyn Monroe." Cavalier. January 1963, pp. 12-15.

Schreiber, Flora Rheta. "Remembrance of Marilyn." Good Housekeeping. January 1963, pp. 30-32, 135.

Smith, Liz. "The Exner Files." Vanity Fair. January 1997, pp. 30, 32, 34, 37-40, 42-43.

"Tribute to Marilyn from a friend… Carl Sandburg." Look. 11 September 1962, pp. 90-94.

"Two Myths Converge: NM Discovers MM." Time. 16 July 1973, pp. 60-64, 69-70.

Wallace, Tom. "He Sure Made Time On That Couch With Marilyn Monroe!" Confidential. May 1957, pp. 20-23.

DONALD SPOTO'S INTERVIEWS:

Abrams, Arnold, M.D. Interview with Donald Spoto. 2 November 1992.

Allan, Rupert. Interview with Donald Spoto. 17 August 1991.

Asher, William. Interview with Donald Spoto. 25 September 1992.

Bernstein, Walter. Interview with Donald Spoto. 5 March 1992.

Ebbins, Milton. Interview with Donald Spoto. 22 September 1992.

-----. Interview with Donald Spoto. 6 August 1992.

Gurdin, Michael, M.D. Interview with Donald Spoto. 21 September 1992.

Guthman, Edwin. Interview with Donald Spoto. 29 October 1992.

Jacobs, Natalie Trundy. Interview with Donald Spoto. 28 February 1992.

Litman, Robert, M.D. Interview with Donald Spoto. 23 April 1992.

Maltz, Esther Engelberg. Interview with Donald Spoto. 23 October 1992.

Miner, John. Interview with Donald Spoto. 11 June 1992.

Naar, Joseph. Interview with Donald Spoto. 22 July 1992.

Newcomb, Patricia. Interview with Donald Spoto. 3 August 1992.

Roberts, Ralph. Interview with Donald Spoto. 2 March 1992.

Rudin, Milton "Mickey." Interview with Donald Spoto. 31 October 1992.

Snyder, Allan "Whitey," and Marjorie Plecher. Interview with Donald Spoto. 2 May 1992.

Springer, John. Interview with Donald Spoto. 3 March 1992.

JAY MARGOLIS' INTERVIEWS:

Amador, Elias W., M.D. Interview with Jay Margolis. 11 January 2011.

Barris, George. Interview with Jay Margolis. 7 January 2011.

-----. Interview with Jay Margolis. 29 November 2010.

Byron, Dorothea. Interview with Jay Margolis. 13 September 2010.

Chenoweth, Doral. Interview with Jay Margolis. 6 December 2010.

Dambacher, Robert. Interview with Jay Margolis. 9 March 2011.

Farberow, Norman, PhD. Interview with Jay Margolis. 17 January 2011.

Heymann, C. David. Interview with Jay Margolis. 13 July 2010.

Leib, Sylvia. Interview with Jay Margolis. 3 February 2011.

Martin, Jeanne. Interview with Jay Margolis. 11 November 2010.

Moore, Terry. Interview with Jay Margolis. 23 November 2010.

Naar, Dolores. Interview with Jay Margolis. 4 November 2010.

-----. Interview with Jay Margolis. 3 November 2010.

Naar, Joseph T. Interview with Jay Margolis. 2 September 2010.

Newcomb, Patricia. Interview with Jay Margolis. 5 January 2011.

Pepitone, Lena. Interview with Jay Margolis. 23 November 2010.

Romanoff, Gloria. Interview with Jay Margolis. 28 January 2011.

-----. Interview with Jay Margolis. 27 October 2010.

-----. Interview with Jay Margolis. 8 September 2010.

-----. Interview with Jay Margolis. 2 September 2010.

Rothmiller, Mike. Interview with Jay Margolis. 26 September 2010.

Russell, Jane. Interview with Jay Margolis. 29 November 2010.

Schreiner, Greg. Interview with Jay Margolis. 3 January 2011.

Selsman, Michael. Interview with Jay Margolis. 29 March 2011.

-----. Interview with Jay Margolis. 28 March 2011.

Stewart, Daniel K. Interview with Jay Margolis. 14 January 2011.

Stewart, Patricia S.L. Interview with Jay Margolis. 14 January 2011.

Strait, Raymond. Interview with Jay Margolis. 18 March 2011.

-----. Interview with Jay Margolis. 13 December 2010.

-----. Interview with Jay Margolis. 18 November 2010

MISCELLANEOUS INTERVIEWS:

Bellonzi, Carl Angelo. Interview with Donald Wolfe. 11 September 1993.

Carpozi, George, Jr. Interview with Deborah Chiel. 7 November 1992.

-----. Interview with Deborah Chiel. 6 November 1992.

Carpozi, George, Jr. Interview with Joanne Green-Levine. 21 January 1992.

Greenson, Hildi. Interview with Cathy Griffin. 4 June 1991.

Griffin, Cathy. Interview with Jeanne and C. David Heymann. 11 March 1991.

Hall, James. Interview with Ronald "Mike" Carroll. 1982.

Hall, James. Interview with Alan B. Tomich. 1982.

Endnotes

1. (SNYDER, ALLAN, AND MARJORIE PLECHER. INTERVIEW WITH DONALD SPOTO. 2 MAY 1992:

   SPOTO: This was not a woman who was about to commit suicide.

   MARJORIE: Not at all.

   WHITEY: No way. No.

   MARJORIE: She was so excited about going back to work.)

   (SPOTO 1993, p. 560: On August 2, "Around six o'clock, Marilyn invited Allan Snyder and Marjorie Plecher to the house for champagne and caviar. They recalled how happy and optimistic she was, radiating charm and wit and good health.")

   (MOORE, TERRY. INTERVIEW WITH JAY MARGOLIS. 23 NOVEMBER 2010: "The first time I met Marilyn I was with Natasha Lytess…")

   (SPOTO 1993, p. 137: "On their first meeting (March 10, 1948), Marilyn was captivated by Natasha's experience and erudition…")

   (SPOTO 1993, p. 132: During February 1948, MM met producer Joseph Schenck at a party.)

   (ROMANOFF, GLORIA. INTERVIEW WITH JAY MARGOLIS. 2 SEPTEMBER 2010: "Oh no. She was in one of her better moments…")

(ROMANOFF, GLORIA. INTERVIEW WITH JAY MARGOLIS. 28 JANUARY 2011: She planned to meet MM on Sunday evening August 5.)

(Scott, Vernon. "Death of Marilyn Monroe under investigation." <u>Redlands Daily Facts</u>. [Redlands, CA] 6 August 1962. No. 5.: Dean Martin said, "I'm sure it was an accident...")

(MARTIN, JEANNE. INTERVIEW WITH JAY MARGOLIS. 11 NOVEMBER 2010: "Marilyn was the sweetest woman. She was gentle, endearing and quite charming... She just OD'd, not surprisingly. Why anybody would wonder...")

(EBBINS, MILTON. INTERVIEW WITH DONALD SPOTO. 6 AUGUST 1992: "She didn't commit suicide. She OD'd.")

(NAAR, JOSEPH. INTERVIEW WITH JAY MARGOLIS. 2 SEPTEMBER 2010: "The truth is, I do think she died of an overdose. But your most important interview will be Pat Newcomb...")

(NEWCOMB, PATRICIA. INTERVIEW WITH JAY MARGOLIS. 5 JANUARY 2011: Pat Newcomb didn't want to talk about MM's "accidental suicide.")

2. (http://www.youtube.com/watch?v=wKHHv54fK_o:

REPORTER: Mrs. Robin, how did you come to work for Marilyn Monroe?

BETTY ROBIN: I was asked to do it by Mickey Rudin the attorney who knew of my work for David Selznick and Myron Selznick. He knew that if I could live with them I could live with Marilyn or I could help her get along with the studio.

REPORTER: How long were you with her?

BETTY ROBIN: Eight months... till she died.

REPORTER: [surprised] Until she died. The last eight months of her life.

BETTY ROBIN: But I wouldn't have taken the job except my husband thought she was so cute when she was sexy. He wanted me to take the job.

Marilyn Monroe: A Case for Murder

REPORTER: Awww... Could I ask you to sum up your impressions of her? If I asked you, "Who was or what was Marilyn Monroe to you?" Your impressions of that star, that lady, that woman.

BETTY ROBIN: I thought she was a friendless, wandering person. The only people that surrounded her were people that she paid. And she paid my salary. The only person who would come to see her would be Joe DiMaggio. He would come with love or his son. In New York, Carl Sandburg was a friend of hers but otherwise she was a very lonesome person.

REPORTER: Did she will that on herself or was this a set of circumstances that grew through the years?

BETTY ROBIN: I think it was a result of the way she had been mishandled by people for most of her life.

REPORTER: How had she been mishandled? Can you give us an example of what you mean by being mishandled?

BETTY ROBIN: I think she was used. People used her to further their own desires whether it was in a personal way or in work. I don't think they would think, "This is a great actress." They'd say, "Oh, she's good box office." And she was a great actress... I think she resented the people who abused her. Maybe that's too strong a word to use but they wanted her to grind out a picture. They didn't care if she wanted to do it; if she felt comfortable in the role; if it was going to do anything for her; if it was going to make several million dollars for Twentieth, that's all they cared about. Marilyn never had a white mink coat. She never wore dangling earrings. And she would wear one dress for six months wherever she went... It was a dress she liked. It was a [Norman] Norell and she didn't have a wardrobe that she changed into. She had a lot of jeans and blouses and pants but she had one dress that she wore when she went out except when she went to the Golden Globe Awards and then she was sewn into a dress as everybody could see.

REPORTER: In chatting with you, obviously these were her last months, but still was there a sense of humor that would come out in her dealings with you?

BETTY ROBIN: Not really. She was very –

REPORTER: Too far beyond that?

BETTY ROBIN: I'm not saying she was far beyond it. I didn't know her when she had it. But she was a quiet person. Very quiet. In New York, we'd eat dinner. It was always the same. There was never bread in the house. She'd be quiet. She liked the way I would arrange flowers for the table... We had New York steak. Thin. Well-done.

REPORTER: Did she read a lot?

BETTY ROBIN: She read. And she worked hard. She really did.

REPORTER: Did she go out much?

BETTY ROBIN: She stayed home most of the time... She went to see Carl Sandburg. She went to an opera and a play once. This was over a period of about a month. Most of the evenings were spent at home. Sometimes she'd have a few friends... And she did not drink.

REPORTER: She didn't drink?

BETTY ROBIN: No.

REPORTER: Did she smoke?

BETTY ROBIN: No.

REPORTER: Didn't smoke or drink?

BETTY ROBIN: No. No. She would sip on some champagne. But very little. She never drank any hard liquor that I saw. She had sort of a split personality. She had one voice when she would talk to me and another voice for the telephone, that cute little pip-squeak voice. But that's the actress in her.

REPORTER: She took lessons, didn't she? But that would be before your time?

BETTY ROBIN: No, she was going to –

REPORTER: The [Actors] Studio –

BETTY ROBIN: At the time. In New York. Oh, yes, conscientiously.

REPORTER: The Strasbergs... What did you say about suicide there?

BETTY ROBIN: She did *not* commit suicide. She did not voluntarily take her life.

REPORTER: Oh my gosh... So then, how did she die?

BETTY ROBIN: Well, I think doctors gave her pills. She had a bad habit. She had a very large table next to her bed. She had a stock of pills there... I assume if she took one or two, she might have been a little... and taken another one or two but voluntarily she did *not* commit suicide.

REPORTER: And you say that from the woman you knew?

BETTY ROBIN: Despite the fact that she was not a happy woman.

REPORTER: She had too much what, integrity and sort of inner-strength to take her own life?

BETTY ROBIN: I think she had so many knots in her life that she lived with that it wouldn't have occurred to her that that was the way to go away. She was extraordinarily beautiful. I don't think they ever caught that really radiant beauty on film. But she wasn't vain. She admired her body. She said, "Wasn't I lucky to have such wonderful grandparents?" Not parents. Grandparents... She I know did not commit suicide which is the only reason I'd like to talk to you is I'd like people to know it.)

(SUMMERS 2000, p. 415: "Dr. Greenson would later say he had brought in Dr. Engelberg to try to wean Marilyn away from sleeping pills...")

(SPOTO 1993, p. 586: "Chloral hydrate interferes with the body's production of enzymes that metabolize Nembutal.")

(*Marilyn Monroe: The Final Days* TV documentary, 2001: Engelberg related, "At the side of her bed, there was a lot of Seconal, which I had never given her. Also, the autopsy showed that her liver had a lot of chloral hydrate. I never gave her chloral hydrate and I don't think any doctor in the United States gave it to her. She must have bought it in Tijuana.")

(SPOTO 1993, pp. 497-498, 506, 581-582, 585-586, 590, 663: Greenson told biographer Maurice Zolotow and photographer William Woodfield that he had in fact written chloral hydrate prescriptions for MM.)

(SPOTO 1993, p. 581: "100-milligram Nembutal capsules" and "500-milligram chloral hydrate capsules.")

(SPERIGLIO 1986, p. 19: "The Hocketts arrived… Father and son first collected the pill bottles, establishing that there were fifteen.")

(MURRAY 1975, p. 42: Mrs. Murray relayed, "Under Dr. Greenson's guidance, she was taking only chloral hydrate pills for sleep.")

(Zolotow, Maurice. "Monroe's last days: Drowsy death in a barbiturate darkness." Chicago Tribune. 14 September 1973, sec. 2, p. 4: "Her psychiatrist, Dr. Ralph Greenson, was attempting to cut down her dependence on Nembutal by switching her to chloral hydrate as a sleep-inducer.")

(SPOTO 1993, p. 590: Greenson to Woodfield regarding the large chloral hydrate prescriptions, "Well, I've made a number of mistakes in my time.")

(CONFIDENTIAL SOURCE: District Attorney's Report dated September 27, 1982. Investigator Alan B. Tomich interviewed MM's physician Dr. Hyman Engelberg who relayed, "I don't know that I notified him [Greenson] about every prescription that I wrote for Marilyn. I'm not a little busboy, you know. I do know that we were limiting the amount and generally, I was following our mutual feeling about how much she should have… I didn't go over with him if I wanted to give her a vitamin B12 shot or if she had an infection but I did coordinate with her sleeping medication. In her last movie that she was making, she had a recurring sinus problem and liver and vitamins kind of boost resistance. They make you feel better and maybe have a psychological effect in getting an injection a couple of times a week.")

(HEYMANN 1998, p. 312)

(TARABORRELLI 2009, p. 378: "She was taking chloral hydrate to sleep, and Dr. Engelberg emphatically states that he never prescribed it to her, nor did Dr. Greenson. In fact, Engelberg would say that he was amazed at the number of drugs found in her system when she died – including the aforementioned chloral hydrate, which he now presumes she bought when she was in Mexico just before her death.")

(http://www.cbsnews.com/video/watch/?id=1533691n&tag =mncol;lst;1: September 27, 1982 recorded interview for the District Attorney's Office with MM's physician Dr. Hyman Engelberg, conducted by investigator Alan B. Tomich.

TOMICH: There were apparently quite a volume of pills that were discovered at her death, at her bedside.

ENGELBERG: Yes.

TOMICH: Do you recall looking at a list of those pills? And were they all prescribed by you?

ENGELBERG: No. Only *one* had been prescribed by me. I had prescribed Nembutal to help her sleep. But as I recall, to the best of my ability, I was surprised to see at the side of her bed a large number of *other* sleeping pills, which looked like Seconal, which she had apparently purchased on a recent trip to Mexico. To my understanding that in Mexico in those days you could walk into any pharmacy and buy, you know, any tranquilizers or sleeping pills you wanted. There certainly were lots of other pills I had not prescribed.

TOMICH: Chloral hydrate specifically?

ENGELBERG: I didn't notice that specifically. I know that the Coroner's rep – the Coroner told me after that they had found evidence of barbiturates and chloral hydrate. I knew nothing about any chloral hydrate. I never used chloral hydrate.

TOMICH: So you wrote her a prescription for Nembutal only?

ENGELBERG: That was it. That was the only prescription I wrote – for sedatives.

TOMICH: Did you go to her house?

ENGELBERG: Oh, sure.

TOMICH: Immediately?

ENGELBERG: Immediately.

TOMICH: Do you recall the time?

ENGELBERG: What?

TOMICH: Do you recall the time?

ENGELBERG: [Pause and long sigh] I didn't think, you know, of looking at the exact time. But I recall that it must have been in the general area of 3:00 A.M., maybe 2:30. Somewhere in that area.

TOMICH: The reason I'm asking is, as you probably know, is the discrepancies in the time that you were called. One person saying it was around midnight, and another one was saying it was around 3 A.M.

ENGELBERG: Dr. Greenson was called first. And he got there first. I think I was called around 2:30 to 3 o'clock.

TOMICH: It wouldn't have been around midnight?

ENGELBERG: Oh, no. No, no, no, no. Absolutely not.

TOMICH: Did you then go into Marilyn's bedroom?

ENGELBERG: Yes.

TOMICH: What did you see there?

ENGELBERG: She was sprawled over the bed. She was dead.

TOMICH: When you say sprawled, what position was she actually in?

ENGELBERG: I don't recall exactly what position she was in. I knew that I had to be since I was the internist. I took out my stethoscope and listened to make sure her heart wasn't beating. Checked her pupils because that's one of the sensitive ways to tell if a person is dead or not. I said she was dead. Which of course, Dr. Greenson knew anyway, but I had to go through the motions.

TOMICH: Was there a reason there was a delay of half hour or do you consider it was a delay?

ENGELBERG: We were stunned. We were talking over what happened, what she had said. Ordinarily, when you pronounce somebody dead, you don't call the police, you call the mortician. I was the one who I guess eventually said, gee, I think in this case, we'd better call the police.)

(Zolotow, Maurice. "Monroe's last days: Drowsy death in a barbiturate darkness." Chicago Tribune. 14 September 1973, sec. 2, p. 4: In an interview with Dr. Engelberg, Zolotow quoted him as saying, "The reason there was [a] delay [was because] normally you don't call the police. You call the mortuary to remove the body. Dr. Greenson and I discussed this back and forth. I strongly insisted that because of who she was and the possibility of suicide, we should call the police. I had been treating her for some time for an acute sinus condition. She got injections of liver and vitamins. She was, by the way, in excellent physical condition as far as her heart and all vital organs were concerned.")

(GREENSON, HILDI. INTERVIEW WITH CATHY GRIFFIN. 4 JUNE 1991: "The idea was that she was never to be said no to when she wanted a prescription…")

(TARABORRELLI 2009, p. 377)

(CONFIDENTIAL SOURCE: GREENSON, JOAN. UNTITLED 90-PAGE MARILYN MONROE MANUSCRIPT, p. 84: "Father had a policy that if Marilyn wanted to have sleep medication…" The complete work is located in Greenson Papers, Special Collections, UCLA, sealed from the public until January 1, 2039.)

(WARNER 1991, pp. 582-583: "Part of improving the patient's environment is prescribing 'proper' medication that will magically solve problems. This medication is either what has recently been reported in newspapers or magazines as new and effective or what other affluent patients report as 'doing miracles.' Again, the psychiatrist's authority is undercut because holding out against prescribing the medication on which the patient insists risks that the patient will not respond favorably to his or her own medication. The psychiatrist may then lose the patient and be bad-mouthed as stubborn and incompetent… This phenomenon is not found only in rich patients. The studies of Hollingshead and Redlich (1958) showed that undereducated psychiatric patients from lower socioeconomic strata always expected to be prescribed medication by a psychiatrist. If they only received psychotherapy, they felt cheated and would go to another psychiatrist and insist that medication be prescribed for them.")

(GREENSON 1964, p. 209: "The administering of a drug is a responsibility since it may cause physical side effects…" The complete work is located in Greenson Papers, Special Collections, UCLA.)

(CONFIDENTIAL SOURCE: Greenson wrote to Dr. Kris on August 20, 1962, "I later found out that on Friday night she had told the internist [Engelberg] that I had said it was all right for her to take some nembutal…" The complete letter is located in Greenson Papers, Special Collections, UCLA, sealed from the public until January 1, 2039.)

(SPOTO 1993, p. 586: How Greenson knew his star patient well enough to know on what prescription she was "somewhat drugged.")

(CONFIDENTIAL SOURCE: Greenson wrote to Dr. Kris on August 20, 1962, "I received a call from Marilyn at 4:30 in the afternoon. She seemed somewhat depressed and somewhat drugged." The complete letter is located in Greenson Papers, Special Collections, UCLA, sealed from the public until January 1, 2039.)

(GUILES 1970, p. 378: "She asked him to give her a new sleeping pill prescription. After he [Engelberg] was convinced that the drug she was taking – chloral hydrate – was not working, he agreed to prescribe twenty-five tablets of Nembutal.")

(MIRACLE 1994, p. 197: "Friday evening Pat Newcomb arrives at Marilyn's house to spend the night. Dr. Engelberg stops in, gives Marilyn an injection to help her sleep and, because the chloral hydrate has apparently not been working, writes her a prescription for twenty-five Nembutal capsules.")

(GREENSON, HILDI. INTERVIEW WITH CATHY GRIFFIN. 4 JUNE 1991: "In trying to help Marilyn get off the barbiturates she was on he was giving her a different kind of medication that is not quite as addictive…")

(MURRAY 1975, p. 42: MM told Mrs. Murray regarding chloral hydrate: "You know they used to give these to the soldiers in the war for sleeping. They're really very mild.")

(http://www.youtube.com/watch?v=YiGyyHf5R2I&feature=related: KNBC *Hard Copy* 4/20/92 Pt 2 of 4 Marilyn Monroe: For *Hard Copy*'s reenactment of MM's last day, Mrs. Murray's recollection of MM taking chloral hydrate and how mild MM thought it was.)

(ROMANOFF, GLORIA. INTERVIEW WITH JAY MARGOLIS. 27 OCTOBER 2010: I asked Mrs. Romanoff why MM would have 17 chloral hydrates in her body when she died after specifically requesting the stronger drug Nembutal the previous afternoon? Mrs. Romanoff replied, "It doesn't make sense...")

(CONFIDENTIAL SOURCE: On August 20, 1962, Greenson wrote to Dr. Kris, "At the end of the conversation she asked me whether I had taken away her nembutal bottle..." The complete letter is located in Greenson Papers, Special Collections, UCLA, sealed from the public until January 1, 2039.)

(BROWN AND BARHAM 1993, p. 423: Joan Greenson said Engelberg didn't tell her father about the Nembutal prescription the day before MM died because his wife was kicking him out of the house that day and he had a lot on his mind. However, this does not explain a bigger problem: Engelberg's original Nembutal prescription on July 25 just days before.)

(CONFIDENTIAL SOURCE: GREENSON, JOAN. UNTITLED 90-PAGE MARILYN MONROE MANUSCRIPT, p. 85: "That Saturday he had checked her medication..." The complete work is located in Greenson Papers, Special Collections, UCLA, sealed from the public until January 1, 2039.)

(GREENSON, HILDI. INTERVIEW WITH CATHY GRIFFIN. 4 JUNE 1991: "It happened on a bad day. A divorce either became final or he was moving out of his house...")

(SUMMERS 2000, p. 414: "An empty bottle, with a label indicating it had contained twenty-five Nembutal pills, would be among the medicines retrieved from Marilyn's room after her death. The label showed it had been prescribed on Friday, the day before her death.")

(SUMMERS 2000, pp. 432-433: A photograph in Summers' book proved Engelberg wrote an original Nembutal prescription for MM on July 25, 1962, which was subsequently refilled days later on August 3. Summers incorrectly assumed this was for chloral hydrate but as we have seen, Nembutal was the *only* sleeping medication Engelberg prescribed for MM.)

(SMITH 2005, p. 31: Quoting from the official police report #62-509 463: "Dr. Engelberg made the statement that he prescribed a refill for this about two days ago and he further stated there probably should have been about 50 capsules at the time this was refilled by the pharmacist.")

(NEWCOMB, PATRICIA. INTERVIEW WITH DONALD SPOTO. 3 AUGUST 1992: "She asked for some Nembutals. Engelberg was having problems with his wife...")

(LITMAN, ROBERT, M.D. INTERVIEW WITH DONALD SPOTO. 23 APRIL 1992: "I am stuck with the information that she went out and got pills from Siegel and Engelberg.")

(Carroll, Ronald H., and Alan B. Tomich. "The Death of Marilyn Monroe – Report to the District Attorney." December 1982, p. 25: Engelberg's refill and the alleged Nembutal prescriptions by Dr. Siegel.)

(SUMMERS 2000, p. 415: Dr. Lee Siegel from Twentieth Century-Fox denied seeing MM in the last weeks leading to her death.)

3. (http://www.youtube.com/watch?v=Za3ct_fha9g: 1980s documentary where George Barris and reporter discussed MM's last days.)

(SPOTO 1993, p. 554: "Marilyn was signed at a salary of $250,000, two and a half times the amount of her original contract.")

(STEINEM 1986, p. 181: George Barris took the last photograph of MM on July 18.)

(BARRIS 1995, p. 122)

(BARRIS 1995, p. 133: "She never seemed happier...")

(BARRIS, GEORGE. INTERVIEW WITH JAY MARGOLIS. 7 JANUARY 2011: "Why would she take her own life?...")

(BARRIS 1995, p. ix: "I had always wanted to work on a book with Marilyn Monroe, from the first time I met her on a freelance photographic assignment back in September 1954. At that time she was in New York City on location for *The Seven Year Itch*.")

(BARRIS 1995, p. ix: "What I particularly liked about Marilyn was that she didn't act like a movie star. She was down to earth...")

(BARRIS, GEORGE. INTERVIEW WITH JAY MARGOLIS. 7 JANUARY 2011: "When I arrived, she said, 'What are you doing here?! I heard you were in Rome with Elizabeth Taylor!...' ")

(BARRIS 1995, p. xv: "So, for the weeks from June 9 until July 18, I was busy working with Marilyn.")

(BARRIS 1995, p. 51: "I don't think anyone was ever more determined, and I never encountered a model who worked as hard as she did.")

(BARRIS 1995, p. xvi: "I will never believe that she took her own life. It will always be my conviction that she was murdered.")

(BARRIS, GEORGE. INTERVIEW WITH JAY MARGOLIS. 29 NOVEMBER 2010: "I'll never forget her because she was kind, and she was honest, and she was loveable...")

(RUSSELL, JANE. INTERVIEW WITH JAY MARGOLIS. 29 NOVEMBER 2010: "I met him one time after his brother had been killed...")

(http://www.dailymail.co.uk/femail/article-439026/Jane-Russell-My-friend-Marilyn-did-kill-herself.html: Leigh, Wendy. "Jane Russell: My friend Marilyn did not kill herself." Daily Mail. [MailOnline.com] 3 March 2007.)

(http://www.express.co.uk/posts/view/168607/Debbie-Reynolds-Marilyn-Monroe-was-at-risk: "Debbie Reynolds: Marilyn Monroe Was At Risk." Daily Express. 12 April 2010: "We knew each other because we attended the same church...")

(http://www.youtube.com/watch?v=MzQ27ElP9ik: *Marilyn Monroe: A Case for Murder* documentary, 1988, part 1 of 5 – Debbie Reynolds relayed, "Her life was very sad. And the ending was very sad indeed...")

4. (ROMANOFF, GLORIA. INTERVIEW WITH JAY MARGOLIS. 27 OCTOBER 2010: "You don't find it ludicrous of someone suggesting she swallowed...")

(http://southernwingsaircraft.com/howmarilyndied.html: "Marilyn was taking 500 mg capsules of CH [chloral hydrate]. A normal dose of CH is between 500 – 1000 mg. The lethal does is considered to be 10 grams, which is 20 capsules. Marilyn had roughly 80% of the lethal dose of 20 capsule amount in her blood so she would have had to take 17 capsules.")

(http://www.youtube.com/watch?v=njDgjium7yQ: "In Search of..." *The Death of Marilyn Monroe,* History Channel documentary, 1980, part 1 of 3: Dr. Sidney Weinberg, Sergeant Jack Clemmons, and Deputy Coroner's Aide Lionel Grandison.)

(Blackburn, John, Chuck Orman, and Dan McDonald. "I Saw Marilyn Murdered." Globe. 23 November 1982, Volume 29, Number 47, p. 3: Dr. Sidney Weinberg said, "From everything I see, these drugs were injected into Miss Monroe's body...")

(http://www.youtube.com/watch?v=ORac4GJKbqA&feature=related: "In Search of..." *The Death of Marilyn Monroe,* History Channel documentary, 1980, part 2 of 3: Deputy Coroner's Aide Lionel Grandison.)

(SMITH 2005, p. 55: Official Statement by Dr. Theodore J. Curphey dated August 17, 1962.)

(SLATZER 1975, p. 268: Q & A with Dr. Curphey.)

(BROWN AND BARHAM 1993, pp. 368-369: "From the very first, [Police Chief William] Parker classified Monroe's death as a suicide, plain and simple. He told his force to investigate it as a suicide, and gave the coroner similar guidelines. To make sure the point was made, he turned the case over to the new Suicide Prevention Team, which he knew by its definition could only determine *why* Monroe had killed herself. The team was not allowed to investigate *how* she had died.")

(SPOTO 1993, p. 582: "Litman and his colleagues submitted a verdict of suicide because that had been Curphey's initial judgment.")

(SUMMERS 2000, p. 416: MM called the answering service of Ralph Roberts at 10:00 P.M.)

(AMADOR, ELIAS, M.D. INTERVIEW WITH JAY MARGOLIS. 11 JANUARY 2011: "I am surprised that there are no capsules in the stomach…")

(http://www.youtube.com/watch?v=ayHRGXeSfq0: "In Search of…" *The Death of Marilyn Monroe,* History Channel documentary, 1980, part 1 of 3: Dr. Robert Litman said, "At the autopsy, her stomach was empty…")

(LITMAN, ROBERT, M.D. INTERVIEW WITH DONALD SPOTO. 23 APRIL 1992: "How do you explain how these pills got into her? That's my job. The coroner says we got a case here, which looks like they took fifty Nembutals and chloral hydrates and died. Now we want you to evaluate the mental state of the person from the standpoint, were these ingested intentionally or not intentionally?")

(SUMMERS 2000, p. 338: Farberow admitted the Kennedys were not questioned.)

(SUMMERS 2000, p. 455: Farberow and Pat Newcomb.)

(FARBEROW, NORMAN, PhD. INTERVIEW WITH JAY MARGOLIS. 17 JANUARY 2011)

(Carroll, Ronald H., and Alan B. Tomich. "The Death of Marilyn Monroe – Report to the District Attorney." December 1982, p. 3: "Officials of the Coroner's Office contacted the Suicide Prevention Center in Los Angeles and requested a report from a Psychiatric Investigative Team to assist the

Coroner's Office in determining whether or not Miss Monroe had accidentally or intentionally ingested the lethal quantities of drugs.")

(" 'Suicide Team' Probes Marilyn's Pill Death." Star-News. [Pasadena, CA] 6 August 1962: "A 'suicide team' of psychiatrists today began an investigation to determine if the apparent overdose of sleeping pills that killed actress Marilyn Monroe was taken on purpose or accidentally.")

("Marilyn." Winnipeg Free Press. [Winnipeg, MB Canada] 16 August 1962: Suicide Prevention Team contacts Dr. Marianne Kris and Payne Whitney doctors for MM's "state of mind.")

(SPOTO 1993, pp. 456-458: Dr. Kris admitted MM into Payne Whitney.)

(ROMANOFF, GLORIA. INTERVIEW WITH JAY MARGOLIS. 2 SEPTEMBER 2010: "When she was hospitalized in New York...")

(NEWCOMB, PATRICIA. INTERVIEW WITH DONALD SPOTO. 3 AUGUST 1992: "That was the worst experience...")

5. ("Quiet services for Marilyn Monroe." Redlands Daily Facts. [Redlands, CA] 8 August 1962: Peter Lawford told a reporter he may have been the last person to speak to MM on the phone.)

(CRAMER 2001, p. 419: "Peter Lawford came forward as the 'mystery caller' – he'd talked to Marilyn that Saturday night – and he quoted her last words to him (or maybe he wasn't really quoting): 'Say goodbye to Pat, say goodbye to the President, and say goodbye to yourself, because you're a nice guy.' ")

(SUMMERS 2000, p. 457: Peter and the 7:30 P.M. call to MM.)

(SUMMERS 2000, p. 421: Harry Hall said DiMaggio "held Bobby Kennedy responsible for her death.")

(SUMMERS 2000, p. 482: DiMaggio said to the funeral director, "Be sure that none of those damn Kennedys come to the funeral.")

(DePaulo, Lisa. "The Strange, Still Mysterious Death of Marilyn Monroe." Playboy. December 2005, pp. 194-195: Comments by DiMaggio's best friends Morris Engelberg and Dr. Rock Positano.)

(CRAMER 2001, p. 408: "Marilyn would muse about adopting a Mexican child.")

(ENGELBERG 2004, pp. 281-282: Joe DiMaggio told his son, "The Kennedys killed her...")

(ROMANOFF, GLORIA. INTERVIEW WITH JAY MARGOLIS. 8 SEPTEMBER 2010: "Not many people really got to know her...")

(ROMANOFF, GLORIA. INTERVIEW WITH JAY MARGOLIS. 2 SEPTEMBER 2010: On having girlfriends, "Marilyn was not given to that sort of friendship in truth.")

(SUMMERS 2000, p. 291: "Pat Lawford liked Marilyn and felt she needed help. It was her idea – according to Lawford – to start inviting Marilyn to the beach house in the months before John Kennedy's presidency.")

(SUMMERS 2000, p. 482: Peter Lawford said, "It seems to be a concerted effort to keep some of Marilyn's old friends from attending.")

(SPADA 1991, p. 330: DiMaggio privately responded, "If it wasn't for her so-called friends, Marilyn would be alive today.")

(FANTA 1968, p. 37: On August 12, 1962, four days after MM's funeral, "The President and his guests aboard the MANITOU on second day of Maine cruising," including Peter Lawford, Pat Kennedy Lawford, and Pat Newcomb.)

(WOLFE 1998, pp. 244-245: Same MANITOU photograph is located in the picture section between these two pages.)

(HEYMANN 1998, p. 325: "Three days after Marilyn's death, RFK left San Francisco on a camping trip to Oregon...")

(SLATZER 1992, p. 349: Quoting from the official police report # 62-509 463: "An attempt was made to contact Mr. Lawford...")

(LITMAN, ROBERT, M.D. INTERVIEW WITH DONALD SPOTO. 23 APRIL 1992: "Probable suicide" based on the "physical evidence" and "past history of having made overdoses.")

(SPOTO 1993, p. 582: Dr. Robert Litman related, "It was obvious to us, after speaking with Dr. Greenson about Marilyn's psychiatric history, that the only conclusion we could reach was suicide, or at least a gamble with death…")

(Rebello, Stephen. "Somebody Killed Her." Playboy. December 2005, p. 187: Miner discussed how MM would have been unconscious before she could finish taking 30 – 40 pills. As we will see later, she was still up and mobile shortly before 10:00 P.M.)

(Rebello, Stephen. "Somebody Killed Her." Playboy. December 2005, p. 187: Miner related, "I was called on a Sunday, and the techs wouldn't even have gotten to the specimens until the following day…")

(SUMMERS 2000, p. 432: Noguchi related, "For some reason I felt uncomfortable and shortly after the case was formally closed I called Toxicology…")

(*History's Mysteries: The Death of Marilyn Monroe* documentary, 2000: Noguchi said of Coroner Curphey, "He certified the manner of death to be 'probable suicide…'")

(*History's Mysteries: The Death of Marilyn Monroe* documentary, 2000: John Miner vehemently discounted the "probable suicide" verdict by Dr. Curphey: "What we really have is a coroner chief medical examiner…")

6. (BROWN AND BARHAM 1993, p. 338: Clemmons remembered a man with a European accent calling to notify him of the death of MM.)

(Rebello, Stephen. "Somebody Killed Her." Playboy. December 2005, p. 187: According to John Miner, Greenson did call the police, contrary to the official police report that said Engelberg called instead.)

("Marilyn." Independent Press-Telegram. [Long Beach, CA] 5 August 1973: Greenson himself admitted it was he who called the police.)

(WOLFE 1998, p. 5: " 'She committed suicide,' Dr. Greenson said. Then, gesturing toward an empty container of Nembutal on the nightstand, he added, 'She took all of these...' Clemmons recalled, 'She was lying facedown in what I call the soldier's position. Her face was in a pillow, her arms were by her side, her right arm was slightly bent. Her legs were stretched out perfectly straight.' He immediately thought she had been placed that way... 'Was the body moved?' Clemmons asked. 'No,' the doctors replied. Greenson, who did most of the talking, had a strange, defensive attitude. Clemmons recalled, 'I kept thinking to myself, What the hell's wrong with this fellow? because it just didn't fit the situation.' 'Did you try to revive her?' Clemmons asked. 'No, it was too late – we got here too late,' Greenson replied. 'Do you know when she took the pills?' 'No.' ")

(BROWN AND BARHAM 1993, pp. 340-341: Clemmons said of Greenson and Engelberg, "Liars, both of them." Clemmons was not impressed when he felt Greenson was being fresh with him, "I strongly disliked Greenson's attitude...")

7. (BADMAN 2010, p. 279: Badman incorrectly surmised, "At no time during the conversation did the sergeant remark to Dougherty he felt that there was a conspiracy going on at the home.")

(SLATZER 1975, p. 240: Clemmons waited until he returned to the police station to call Dougherty with the tragic news of MM's death.)

(SPERIGLIO 1986, p. 18: Out of respect for his good friend, Clemmons did not tell Dougherty about his murder suspicions.)

(*Marilyn's Man* documentary, 2005: Jim Dougherty said, "I thought about it. I firmly believe this was gonna happen, that she was gonna accidentally overdose because she'd done it before. They lose count. They want to sleep. They want to sleep. They want to sleep and they can't. They take an upper to get going and it takes too many downers to get them back to where they can sleep and they die.")

(DOUGHERTY 2001, p. 1: Dougherty received Clemmons' call in bed, *not* in a squad car as Badman incorrectly reported.)

(BADMAN 2010, p. 279)

8. (http://www.telegraph.co.uk/culture/film/7843140/Marilyn-Monroe-on-the-couch.html: Turner, Christopher. "Marilyn Monroe on the Couch: To Dr. Ralph Greenson, Marilyn Monroe was more than just a patient. Now, for the first time, his family recall their favourite 'big sister.' " Telegraph. 23 June 2010: Chris Turner interviewed the Greenson children Danny and Joan.)

(SUMMERS 2000, p. 422: Coming home after MM died, Greenson "kept repeating that he was sure it had been an accident.")

(GREENSON, HILDI. INTERVIEW WITH CATHY GRIFFIN. 4 JUNE 1991: "I think it was accidental suicide, like probably the others had been, too...")

(SPADA 1991, p. 326: Danny Greenson said, "Marilyn was dead when my father arrived at her house. He felt so awful that a patient of his killed herself. It really hurt him terribly on a personal level.")

(BERNSTEIN, WALTER. INTERVIEW WITH DONALD SPOTO. 5 MARCH 1992: To Bernstein's surprise, Spoto said he discovered that actress Inger Stevens died under Greenson's care as well.)

(ROMANOFF, GLORIA. INTERVIEW WITH JAY MARGOLIS. 27 OCTOBER 2010: "That's a very pat solution to the problem...")

9. (*Marilyn Monroe: The Final Days* TV documentary, 2001: Engelberg discussed MM's last night.)

(HEYMANN 1998, p. 320: Peter Lawford mentioned MM's "manic-depressive tendencies.")

(MARSHALL 2005, p. 199: MM told Meryman, "No kidding. They're making me take liver shots...")

(CONFIDENTIAL SOURCE: District Attorney's Report dated September 27, 1982. Investigator Al Tomich interviewed MM's physician Dr. Hyman Engelberg who relayed, "I saw her Friday evening...")

(HEYMANN 1998, p. 324)

(CAPELL 1964, p. 32: Engelberg's Creditor's Claim for an injection to MM on August 3, 1962.)

(CONFIDENTIAL SOURCE: Greenson wrote to Dr. Kris on August 20, 1962, "I had an internist [Engelberg] who would prescribe medication for her and to give her vitamin injections and liver injections…" The complete letter is located in Greenson Papers, Special Collections, UCLA, sealed from the public until January 1, 2039.)

(SPOTO 1993, p. 661: "Regarding the so-called 'liver and vitamin injections,' the first Mrs. Hyman Engelberg told DS [Donald Spoto] that she never heard of them.")

(MALTZ, ESTHER ENGELBERG. INTERVIEW WITH DONALD SPOTO. 23 OCTOBER 1992: "Dr. Greenson used Hy to sedate [Marilyn].")

(SPOTO 1993, pp. 540, 542: "According to invoices later submitted, Engelberg visited Marilyn at home every day but six during July: except for the fourth, the sixth through the ninth and the sixteenth, she received injections – liver and vitamin shots, she said. But these transformed her mood and energy with alarming rapidity. 'She asked to postpone our talk,' recalled Richard Meryman, who arrived late one afternoon [July 5, 1962] for the second of a series of interviews with *Life*. 'She was tired out, she said,' after meetings at Fox. But then they were interrupted by the arrival of Engelberg: Marilyn bounded out to the kitchen, received a shot and returned to Meryman – suddenly eager to talk on and on, which she did until midnight and after. That evening (unlike the other meetings) her speech was rapid and disjointed – hardly the effect of 'liver and vitamin shots.' ")

10. (Zolotow, Maurice. "MM's Psychiatrist a Troubled Man." San Antonio Light. [San Antonio, TX] 13 October 1973, p. 9-A: "Greenson insists, though she was depressed about the dismissal [from *Something's Got to Give*], though she felt her life was at a dead end, she was showing many signs of continuing recovery, in terms of being more outgoing, interested in meeting people, dining out, furnishing her new house, making plans for future film projects.")

(MAILER 1975, p. 341: "Dr. Thomas Noguchi stated for *Time* magazine that 'no stomach pump was used on Marilyn.' ")

("Two Myths Converge: NM Discovers MM." *Time*. 16 July 1973, p. 70)

("Psychiatrist Breaks Silence In Defense of Marilyn Monroe." *Yuma Daily Sun*. [Yuma, AZ] 23 October 1973)

(SUMMERS 2000, p. 337: "Dr. Litman says today that Greenson spoke to him of a 'close relationship with extremely important men in government,' that the relationship was 'sexual,' and that the men concerned were 'at the highest level.' Dr. Litman says that while Dr. Greenson did not actually name the Kennedys, he had 'no real doubt' whom he meant by 'important men in government.' Litman also felt Dr. Greenson had not been 'totally candid,' even with him.")

11. (MURRAY 1975, p. 156: Mrs. Murray said, "It's well known that Marilyn had a history of attempts at suicide. But at this particular time, she didn't seem to have a desperate need to end it all. Plans were being resolved and there were many promising, exciting possibilities for the future. I think her mind was hazy as a result of the sedation and there was no conscious desire to take her life, but only an automatic physical reaction that kept her downing pills in a semi-stupor.")

(WIENER 1990, p. 11: "Years later, in an interview, Mrs. Murray would change parts of her story, but not the belief that Marilyn's death was probably accidental. Marilyn might have taken some sedatives before her phone calls, Mrs. Murray speculated, and more when she finally went to bed. Twice during the night Mrs. Murray got up and walked to Marilyn's door. The light was on, the phone cord still led inside. But not until 3 A.M. did Mrs. Murray let her worry overcome standing orders not to disturb her employer under any circumstances. 'She was too quiet,' Mrs. Murray said. 'Her sedations were often spaced, and I think I had got in the rhythm of this. I expected her to get up every three or four hours, get some hot milk to take with the pills, wander around. When she didn't do this, I began to wonder if something was wrong. It was only then that I tapped at the door, called to her, tried the door and found it locked. It wasn't her practice to lock the door.' Then

Mrs. Murray called the psychiatrist, Dr. Ralph Greenson, who rushed to the house, broke a window in Marilyn's bedroom and found her dead… Was it an accident, as Mrs. Murray and others seemed to believe?")

(SLATZER 1992, p. 184: MM's neighbor Abe Landau was told by Mrs. Murray how MM took too many pills because she forgot that she had taken some earlier then died.)

("Two Myths Converge: NM Discovers MM." Time. 16 July 1973, p. 70: "It was not a case, says Noguchi, of 'automatism' – that gray area…")

12. (SUMMERS 2000, p. 442: John Miner "says he was asked by Dr. Curphey, the Coroner in 1962, to secure an interview with Dr. Greenson. He assumes he was picked because he had taught at the Institute of Psychiatry and knew Greenson personally.")

(WOLFE 1998, p. 38: John Miner relayed, "I knew Dr. Greenson personally. Dr. Curphey knew that, and so he asked me to interview Dr. Greenson.")

(TARABORRELLI 2009, p. 493: John Miner relayed, "I kept my promise to Dr. Greenson to respect the confidentiality of his interview with me and the contents of Miss Monroe's tapes. I kept that promise in spite of incredible pressures from reporters, authors, and official investigators to relate this information. It is only after Donald Spoto, Melvin Bergman, and others accused Dr. Greenson of being responsible in some way for causing Marilyn Monroe's death that I approached Dr. Greenson's widow to ask for a release from my promise to her husband. She wishes to do whatever is possible to clear his name and granted my request.")

(TARABORRELLI 2009, p. 494: Miner's theory regarding housekeeper Eunice Murray and a Nembutal enema.)

(BROWN AND BARHAM 1993, p. 427: Miner noted that MM's purple colon was very unusual in the couple thousand autopsies he had attended.)

(Welkos, Robert W. "New Chapter in the Mystery of Marilyn: Her Own Words?" Los Angeles Times. 5 August 2005: "It is Miner's theory that the actress took or was given chloral hydrate to render her unconscious – possibly in a soft drink –

and someone then dissolved Nembutal in water by breaking open 30 or more capsules and administered the lethal solution by enema.")

(SLATZER 1992, p. 259: Miner explained his theory, "If some of these drugs were taken orally and rendered the patient unconscious an enema could be administered to her without her knowledge that would put enough of the drugs in her to kill her. That she would do it that way to kill herself is highly unlikely.")

(SUMMERS 2000, p. 416: "At about ten o'clock, Ralph Roberts learned next day, a woman with a 'slurred voice' called his answering service. Told Roberts was out, the caller hung up.")

(GUILES 1970, p. 382: "Marilyn's last contact with a human being was the voice of an operator informing her that Mr. Roberts was out for the evening.")

(GUILES 1991, p. 438: "After Marilyn made her next call, which was to Ralph Roberts, who was unfortunately out for the evening and whose answering service reported that a fuzzy-voiced woman had asked for him, she fell into a fatal doze, her phone off the hook, the receiver in her hand.")

(MARSHALL 2005, p. 310: Marshall incorrectly labeled 8:30 P.M. as the time of this phone call based on Peter's initial testimony that MM was going under from pills after his 7:30 P.M. phone call to her. There is no evidence provided by Marshall or his DD Group to support such a theory. Marshall wrote, "An operator at Ralph Roberts' answering service takes a call from a 'fuzzy-voiced' woman at 8:30.")

(BADMAN 2010, p. 266: Badman provided no evidence for the call around 8:25 other than the suggestion that MM was going under after Peter's call. Badman wrote, "Shortly before 8:25 P.M. Marilyn mustered enough energy to call one other friend: Ralph Roberts.")

13. (MINER, JOHN. INTERVIEW WITH DONALD SPOTO. 11 JUNE 1992: Oddly, Greenson told Miner, "If at the end of our interview, you reach any kind of conclusion, I have no objection to you stating that conclusion to Dr. Curphey.")

(SMITH 2005, pp. 63-66: John Miner recollected his memorandum to Dr. Curphey, "After I attended her autopsy, you asked me to interview Marilyn Monroe's psychiatrist, Ralph Greenson, M.D. on the suicide issue...")

(SUMMERS 2000, p. 443)

(Say Goodbye to the President documentary, 1985: Miner said, "Based on the content of that conversation with Dr. Greenson, I wrote a memorandum in which I indicated at least that I did not believe Marilyn Monroe committed suicide... That was Dr. Greenson's opinion as well.")

(The Marilyn Files documentary, 1991: Miner said the stigma of suicide should be excised from MM's story.)

(BROWN AND BARHAM 1993, p. 419: Miner relayed that the Suicide Prevention Team did not have enough evidence when conducting their investigation.)

14. (Carroll, Donald. "Conversation with Dr. Thomas Noguchi." *Oui*. February 1976, p. 74: Noguchi said, "Our examination was coupled with what we call a psychological autopsy...")

(NOGUCHI 1984, pp. 80-81: After learning of John Miner's memorandum to Greenson, Noguchi considered the possibility of murder. He believed an oral accidental overdose of that many pills was highly improbable.)

(NOGUCHI 1984, p. 68: "I found absolutely no visual evidence of pills in the stomach or the small intestine...")

(STRAIT, RAYMOND. INTERVIEW WITH JAY MARGOLIS. 13 DECEMBER 2010: On how Noguchi never believed suicide but didn't rock the boat.)

(Scaduto, Anthony. "Was Marilyn Monroe Murdered? Do the Kennedys Know?" *Oui*. October 1975, p. 116: Negating oral ingestion of pills, Dr. Weinberg relayed, "One must seriously consider the possibility of an injection or the use of a suppository to account for the toxicological findings.")

(AMADOR, ELIAS, M.D. INTERVIEW WITH JAY MARGOLIS. 11 JANUARY 2011: Taking 64 pills is too many to take accidentally.)

(*The Marilyn Files* documentary, 1991: Dr. J. DeWitt Fox explained why death by oral ingestion of Nembutal was impossible in MM's case.)

(BROWN AND BARHAM 1993, pp. 372, 426: Shying away from oral ingestion of the pills, Noguchi considered the possibility of an enema infusion of the drugs by saying, "The drugs that killed Monroe entered her body another way.")

(NOGUCHI 1984, p. 82: "The remaining questions will go unanswered…")

15. (SUMMERS 1994, p. 340: "The predominately male press corps of those days liked Kennedy and somewhat envied his success with women. They believed that a politician's private life was his own business, not to be probed or written about. Secret Service agents [like Gerald Blaine] took the same view and protected him as best they could.")

(SUMMERS 2000, p. 468: Bates said, "Even Peter Pan would have had a hard time doing that. It's mind-boggling.")

(*Say Goodbye to the President* documentary, 1985: John Bates claimed Bobby couldn't have been in Los Angeles the day Marilyn died:

BATES: That afternoon we all hiked up to the top of the ranch and had a big touch football game, which of course is a typical family sport of the Kennedys. It was a full active day.

INTERVIEWER: Why do you think so many witnesses told us and told the police that Bobby Kennedy was in Los Angeles that day?

BATES: I just can't speculate on their misinformation or their bad information or what they think they saw or what they think they knew but there's just no way he could've been in Los Angeles unless he had a twin.

INTERVIEWER: Isn't it odd that key members of the police department of that time, that is the Police Chief [William Parker] himself and the Chief of Detectives [Thad Brown] were both of the view that Bobby was there if in fact there was no evidence?

BATES: I'd like to cross-examine them. I can't believe it.)

(SPOTO 1993, pp. 561-563: Testimony of the Bates family for the weekend of August 3, 1962.)

(SLATZER 1975, p. 227: Pat Newcomb claimed, "Bobby did not talk to Marilyn that night" but conceded that Peter did phone her.)

(WOLFE 1998, p. 94: Over wiretaps, Otash relayed MM's response to Peter's dinner invitation, "No, I'm tired. There is nothing more for me to respond to…")

(BADMAN 2010, p. 260)

(SUMMERS 2000, p. 457: On October 16, 1975, in his first interview, Peter told the police MM's "last words" at 7:30 P.M.: "Say goodbye to Jack, say goodbye to Pat, and say goodbye to yourself because you're a nice guy.")

(EBBINS, MILTON. INTERVIEW WITH DONALD SPOTO. 6 AUGUST 1992: "Peter, you're a wonderful man, you're a terrific guy. Pat is terrific and Jack is great. I just want you to know…")

(ROMANOFF, GLORIA. INTERVIEW WITH JAY MARGOLIS. 27 OCTOBER 2010: On MM's alleged last call to Peter where MM slurred, "Say goodbye to Jack…" as her last words: "It's fantasy.")

(SPOTO 1993, p. 570: Joe DiMaggio, Jr.'s 7:00 P.M. call to MM on August 4, 1962.)

(SLATZER 1975, pp. 225-226: Mrs. Murray remembered how happy MM was after Joe DiMaggio, Jr.'s phone call and claims MM subsequently called Greenson with the good news.)

(WOLFE 1998, p. 460: Joe DiMaggio, Sr. recalled how his son Joe, Jr. and MM "spoke for about fifteen minutes…")

16. (SUMMERS 2000, p. 408: On August 3, "During the day, Marilyn ordered food and liquor worth forty-nine dollars – a major purchase when translated into today's prices – from the Briggs Delicatessen.")

(CAPELL 1964, p. 13: "Don J. Briggs, Incorporated… Creditor's Claim No. P-458935" for August 3, 1962 in the amount of $49.07.)

(HEYMANN 1989, pp. 368-369: "In anticipation of [RFK and Peter Lawford's] visit Marilyn had set out a buffet of Mexican food – guacamole, stuffed mushrooms, spicy meatballs – which she had ordered from a nearby restaurant, and a chilled magnum of champagne.")

(HEYMANN 1998, pp. 321-322: Peter said, "They argued back and forth for maybe ten minutes...")

(HEYMANN 1989, pp. 368-369)

(SUMMERS 1994, p. 347: Peter relayed to Heymann, "Marilyn allowed how first thing Monday morning she was going to call a press conference and tell the world about the treatment she had suffered at the hands of the Kennedy brothers. Bobby became livid. In no uncertain terms he told her she was going to have to leave both Jack and himself alone – no more telephone calls, no letters, nothing.")

(SUMMERS 2000, p. 470: "Marilyn, says Gould, had refused to accept messages from Kennedy passed on through Lawford, and Kennedy now decided to confront her for the last time.")

(SUMMERS 2000, p. 470: Debbie Gould said RFK "came straight to see Marilyn at her home. Marilyn knew then that it was over, that was it, final, and she was very distraught and depressed.")

(NEWCOMB, PATRICIA. INTERVIEW WITH DONALD SPOTO. 3 AUGUST 1992: "I was at her house that afternoon until 3 and that's when Greenson came and told me to leave...")

(MURRAY 1975, p. 124: Newcomb, who had stayed overnight on August 3, slept until noon. Mrs. Murray suggested that Pat may have taken some of MM's Nembutal.)

(CONFIDENTIAL SOURCE: Greenson wrote to Dr. Kris on August 20, 1962, "Apparently she saw this girlfriend [Pat Newcomb] on Friday night and they continued quarreling but not very intensively. This girlfriend stayed over night in the house and I received a call from Marilyn at 4:30 in the afternoon. She seemed somewhat depressed and somewhat drugged. I went over to her place and talked with her for about 2 ½ hours. She was still angry with her girlfriend who had slept 15 hours that night and Marilyn was furious because she had such a poor sleep." The complete letter is located in Greenson Papers, Special Collections, UCLA, sealed from the public until January 1, 2039.)

(Zolotow, Maurice. "MM's Psychiatrist a Troubled Man." San Antonio Light. [San Antonio, TX] 13 October 1973, p. 9-A: Greenson's account of MM fighting with Pat Newcomb over getting more sleep than MM the night before.)

(CONFIDENTIAL SOURCE: Greenson wrote to Dr. Kris on August 20, 1962, "I finally asked the girlfriend to leave because this was Marilyn's request, and I asked the housekeeper to stay overnight..." The complete letter is located in Greenson Papers, Special Collections, UCLA, sealed from the public until January 1, 2039.)

(SLATZER 1975, p. 225: Mrs. Murray related, "Dr. Greenson asked me if I had planned on staying that night. He asked this in a rather offhand way, without any special reason for my staying at her home, for Marilyn felt secure...")

(*Say Goodbye to the President* documentary, 1985: Mrs. Murray conceded to Anthony Summers the real reason MM was upset that last afternoon: her row over RFK.)

(WOLFE 1998, p. 90: "When Summers asked Murray why she hadn't told the truth to the police in 1962...")

(SUMMERS 2000, p. 207: Pat Newcomb tried to steal a man MM was interested in.)

(NEWCOMB, PATRICIA. INTERVIEW WITH DONALD SPOTO. 3 AUGUST 1992: "I think she thought I was interested in a guy that she was interested in.")

(SPOTO 1993, p. 566: Newcomb claimed MM was angry at her for getting more sleep but admitted "something else was behind it all.")

(SUMMERS 2000, p. 412: Jeanne Martin on Pat Newcomb's infatuation with RFK.)

(BARRIS, GEORGE. INTERVIEW WITH JAY MARGOLIS. 7 JANUARY 2011: "That's the way she was, they both were interested in the same men.")

17. (CONFIDENTIAL SOURCE: Greenson wrote to Dr. Kris on August 20, 1962, "Marilyn wanted to go for a walk on the pier in Santa Monica, and I said she was too groggy for that but if she drank a lot of fluid I would allow the housekeeper to drive her to the beach." The complete letter is located in Greenson Papers, Special Collections, UCLA, sealed from the public until January 1, 2039.)

    (Zolotow, Maurice. "MM's Psychiatrist a Troubled Man." San Antonio Light. [San Antonio, TX] 13 October 1973, p. 9-A: Greenson claimed he warned MM against going to the beach: "Don't do that as people might recognize you, but why don't you go for a drive up the coast highway with Mrs. Murray?")

    (EBBINS, MILTON. INTERVIEW WITH DONALD SPOTO. 6 AUGUST 1992: "We were gonna have Mexican food at Peter Lawford's… Peter calls me. He said Marilyn had a little anxiety and her doctor told her to walk along the beach…")

    (ASHER, WILLIAM. INTERVIEW WITH DONALD SPOTO. 25 SEPTEMBER 1992: As for Saturday, August 4, Asher relayed, "Marilyn was there. Took a little walk on the beach… She wasn't too steady in the sand…")

    (MURRAY 1975, p. 130: MM told the housekeeper, "I don't think we'll take that drive after all, Mrs. Murray.")

18. (SUMMERS 2000, p. 461: Natalie Trundy Jacobs on MM's death.)

    (BROWN AND BARHAM 1993, pp. 352-353: Rupert Allan on MM's death.)

    (CARPOZI, GEORGE, JR. INTERVIEW WITH DEBORAH CHIEL. 6 NOVEMBER 1992)

    (HEYMANN 1998, p. 322: Peter on Mafia-Teamster tapes and MM's tapes.)

    (STRAIT 1992, p. 155: "I've listened to tapes in which Jayne and the President were the principal players. Lawford had copies of the tapes and once, during a bong-sharing session with Jayne in the pink palace, played them back for her. Later on, she prevailed upon Peter to play them for one of her lovers but he declined. Peter apparently owned quite a library of audio tapes of his famous brothers-in-law and their trysts with famous Hollywood sex symbols…")

(HEYMANN 1998, pp. 539-540: Heymann wrote, "Peter Lawford: The current author spoke to the actor in 1983, a year before his death, for a biography of Jacqueline Kennedy Onassis… At that time, Lawford described in full the details of the RFK-Dr. Greenson conspiracy to 'subdue' Marilyn." Heymann said he didn't print that section of the Lawford interview because he couldn't confirm the existence of MM's free-association tapes. A little more than a decade later, Heymann learned that Former Deputy District Attorney John Miner actually listened to two of these tapes. Heymann concluded by saying, "This biography contains Lawford's comments in toto.")

("How Bobby Kennedy Silenced Marilyn Monroe." Star. (USA), 8 September 1998, Vol. 25, Iss. 36, pp. 6-7, 38)

(JACOBS 2004, pp. 169, 172-173: When he learned there was no drug residue in MM's stomach, Sinatra started to think Lawford and the Kennedys had something to do with her death.)

(NEWCOMB, PATRICIA. INTERVIEW WITH DONALD SPOTO. 3 AUGUST 1992: "There's no way they could've done this. I resent it so much… I'd like to see Bobby exonerated from this…")

(GATES 1993, p. 165: Former Police Chief Daryl F. Gates conceded, "The truth is, we knew Robert Kennedy was in town on August 4…")

(ROTHMILLER 1992, pp. 113-114: "Airport detail. LAPD higher-ups wanted to know who was coming in and out of L.A., and this little intelligence activity was part of OCID's routine… Chief Gates once told Lew Wasserman, longtime chairman of the MCA entertainment conglomerate: 'We knew every time you boarded a plane for Las Vegas.' Gates claimed this surveillance was for the protection of people in the entertainment industry. The LAPD was watching over them to make sure they were not victimized by the Mafia, he explained. George Orwell's Big Brother also watched over all his citizens for their own good… The six to eight

OCID detectives detailed to LAX were a familiar sight to Western [Airlines] employees and they were given free run of the facilities. Western employees even trained them to use the airline's computer system so they could personally check names, flights, and other data.")

(SELSMAN, MICHAEL. INTERVIEW WITH JAY MARGOLIS. 28 MARCH 2011)

(MARTIN, JEANNE. INTERVIEW WITH JAY MARGOLIS. 11 NOVEMBER 2010: "If any of that were true, you would not know it. You would not know it at all and somebody would've said something years ago...")

19. (HEYMANN 1998, p. 316: Peter said, "You could hear the voices of Marilyn and JFK in addition to Marilyn and RFK...")

(SUMMERS 2000, p. 317: "Reports in files of the Los Angeles DA's Bureau of Investigation, covering 1961, refer to Peter Lawford raising funds to aid Cohen's associate, Candy Barr, then in jail on narcotics charges. Lawford was 'desperately attempting' to obtain compromising sound tapes of 'parties' he had attended in Barr's dressing room.")

(NAAR, JOSEPH. INTERVIEW WITH JAY MARGOLIS. 2 SEPTEMBER 2010)

(BADMAN 2010, p. 296: "Moreover, at that time, according to his former manager, Milton Ebbins...")

20. (STEWART, PATRICIA S.L. INTERVIEW WITH JAY MARGOLIS. 14 JANUARY 2011: MM and Peter were very close friends for more than ten years. Mrs. Stewart told me she had a collection of Peter's letters and notes to prove it.)

(KENNEDY 1965, pp. 225-226: Peter Lawford's written tribute to Joseph P. Kennedy, Sr.)

21. (MARTIN 1995, p. 383: "In a sworn deposition on the Monroe death, Robert Kennedy testified that he had gone to see her shortly before her death [with Peter on the afternoon of August 4] because she had been bothering his brother. He had taken a doctor with him and she had clawed at him when he held her so that the doctor could inject a tranquilizer." Presumably

pentobarbital (i.e. Nembutal) the other drug in her system besides chloral hydrate, an oral drug, not medically practiced by injection.)

(RIESE AND HITCHENS 1990, p. 248: "In a sworn deposition regarding Marilyn's death, [Bobby] Kennedy allegedly testified that he did indeed go to Marilyn's house on August 4 and that he was escorted by a doctor, who injected MM with a tranquilizer to calm her down.")

(CONFIDENTIAL SOURCE: GREENSON, JOAN. UNTITLED 90-PAGE MARILYN MONROE MANUSCRIPT, p. 46: "Marilyn found out that the neighbor who you could see from her property was a professor at the university." The complete work is located in Greenson Papers, Special Collections, UCLA, sealed from the public until January 1, 2039.)

(BROWN AND BARHAM 1993, p. 433: In 1978, former OCID detective Mike Rothmiller saw the deposition made by RFK, stored in the OCID building's secret filing rooms. On RFK, Rothmiller related, "He said he was involved with Monroe – but he wasn't...")

(ROTHMILLER, MIKE. INTERVIEW WITH JAY MARGOLIS. 26 SEPTEMBER 2010: Rothmiller saw a copy of MM's diary, not the original.)

(BARRIS, GEORGE. INTERVIEW WITH JAY MARGOLIS. 7 JANUARY 2011: "She said, 'Mr. Barris, I was a neighbor to Marilyn...' ")

(SLATZER 1975, p. 227: "Now, going back to late that afternoon, I would like to report a story told to me by a woman whose mother was at a card party with about a dozen other women, a weekly ritual in a house next to Marilyn's. One of the women looked out of the window toward Marilyn's newly installed Mexican gates and said, 'Look, girls, there he is *again.*' The other women went to the window and looked out. They didn't have to be told that the visitor was the younger brother of the President of the United States.")

(MURRAY 1975, p. 128: "In his recent book *The Life and Curious Death of Marilyn Monroe*, Robert F. Slatzer has related sensational rumors about Bobby Kennedy's arriving at the house that afternoon with a physician, reportedly to sedate an hysterical Marilyn. Slatzer's story stems from reports of a card party on Fifth Helena that afternoon at which the ladies were supposed to have looked out the window and seen Kennedy walking through Marilyn's gate with a man carrying a doctor's black bag.")

(SPERIGLIO 1986, pp. 118-120: "All the ladies were fairly elderly, but they threw down their cards and bustled to the window to see Bobby Kennedy entering Marilyn Monroe's residence with an unidentified man who was carrying what looked like a 'medical bag.' The D.A.'s men took great pains to prove that the card-playing ladies could not possibly have seen Robert Kennedy without a great deal of contortion and lucky timing... I was able to establish that from the upstairs card room one could look out and see who was going down Fifth Helena Drive. Marilyn's gates and front entrance were, indeed, highly visible.")

(SUMMERS 2000, pp. 469-470: "In 1982 the District Attorney gave cursory attention to a report that Kennedy was seen arriving at Marilyn's home during the afternoon. I recently tracked that story to its source, a woman called Betty Pollard. She says her mother [Elizabeth] was playing bridge at a neighbor's home [unidentified] that day, when her hostess drew the players' attention to a car parking outside. Kennedy, immediately recognizable, emerged from the car and went into Marilyn's house. The hostess mentioned that she had seen him visiting on previous occasions.")

(MARSHALL 2005, p. 92: "The basics of the story have a group of neighborhood women gathered at one of the homes facing 5th Helena for a Saturday afternoon game of cards.")

(BROWN AND BARHAM 1993, p. 335: "The Attorney General and another well-dressed man came to the house sometime late in the afternoon..." Brown and Barham mistakenly wrote that Slatzer interviewed Elizabeth instead of her daughter Betty.)

(SUMMERS 2000, pp. 520-522: On their trip to MM's home on August 4, 1962, Peter Lawford and RFK were looking, not for a listening device as Summers' source hypothesizes, but for MM's red diary.)

(SLATZER 1992, pp. 286-287: "Some journalists have speculated that Bobby Kennedy was looking for an electronic bug he felt was placed somewhere in Marilyn's house... A more likely explanation is that he was looking for Marilyn's red diary.")

(http://www.youtube.com/watch?v=OK5WFA5qOOc&feature =related: *Marilyn: The Last Word* documentary, 1993, part 4 of 6: Anthony Summers said the bugs in MM's home were active the very day she died and picked up the afternoon visit with RFK and Peter Lawford. Summers conceded it's very possible RFK was looking for MM's red diary, not a listening device.)

22. (SUMMERS 2000, p. 410: "During the morning Norman Jefferies, working on the kitchen floor, found himself looking at a pair of bare female feet. He looked up to see Marilyn wrapped in a huge bath towel, and was appalled.")

(WOLFE 1998, p. 455: Mrs. Murray relayed, "Oh sure, yes, I was in the living room when he [RFK] arrived. She was not dressed.")

(WOLFE 1998, p. 456: Norman Jefferies said MM was hysterical after RFK and Peter Lawford had visited her in the afternoon.)

(SUMMERS 2000, p. 340: Norman Jefferies related, "It was funny because Eunice and I were there with Marilyn, and we were to leave. She and I were to clear out before he [RFK] came, and that's what we did.")

(SUMMERS 2000, p. 410: Norman Jefferies said, "I will never forget the sight of her. She looked sick, desperately sick – not only in the physical sense – and I thought there must be something terribly wrong. She must have taken a lot of dope or something, or maybe she was scared out of her mind. I had never seen her look that way before.")

(SUMMERS 2000, p. 519: Otash's employee relayed, "Lawford said Marilyn had called the White House, trying to reach the President, saying, 'Get your brother away from me – he's just using me...' ")

(Miner, John. "Marilyn Uncensored." Playboy. December 2005, p. 200: MM said on a free-association tape, "But Bobby, Doctor. What should I do about Bobby? As you see, I have no room in my life for him. I guess I don't have the courage to face up to it and hurt him. I want someone else to tell him it's over. I tried to get the President to do it, but I couldn't reach him… Maybe I should stop being a coward and tell him myself.")

(GUILAROFF 1996, p. 166: MM recollected for Guilaroff: RFK told MM, "It's over." MM replied, "But you promised to divorce Ethel and marry me.")

(SUMMERS 2000, p. 512: Otash said he heard MM say to RFK on that last day, "I feel passed around – like a piece of meat. You've lied to me. Get out of here. I'm tired. Leave me alone.")

(SUMMERS 2000, p. 519: After RFK's visit in the afternoon on August 4, "Otash insists that from then on, rather than Marilyn reaching out to Kennedy that evening, *he* tried to get her to come to the Lawford beach house. Marilyn's response, Otash says, was 'Stop bothering me. Stay away from me.' ")

(SELSMAN, MICHAEL. INTERVIEW WITH JAY MARGOLIS. 28 MARCH 2011: "She was convinced that not Jack but Bobby would leave Ethel and all their kids…")

(WOLFE 1998, pp. 456-457: MM called Guilaroff in the late afternoon to say RFK was at her home and threatened her if she were to go public.)

(GUILAROFF 1996, pp. 165-167, 170: Curiously, MM's hairstylist and friend Guilaroff wrote the following in his 1996 book two years before Heymann released his book on RFK (1998): "But then and now I also believe that there was a conspiracy between the Kennedys and Dr. Greenson… I suspect we will never know all the details of the events that led to her death. But as far as I am concerned, John and Robert Kennedy, aided by Dr. Greenson, murdered Marilyn Monroe just as surely as if they had shot her in the head.")

(SUMMERS 2000, p. 513: Otash said Peter's friend "Bullets" Durgom told him, "Bobby was very worried about Monroe getting spaced out and shooting her mouth off. He told Peter, 'Get her to your place. She won't talk to me now, you get her to the beach.' ")

(WOLFE 1998, p. 460: According to Guilaroff, after Greenson's visit, MM was in a better frame of mind and called him one last time in the evening.)

(SUMMERS 2000, pp. 415-416)

(WILSON 1973, pp. 320-321)

23. (MARSHALL 2005, pp. 303-307: "The curious thing is how Peter's story changed between the publication of the first book and the second...")

(HEYMANN 1998, pp. 539-540: Why C. David Heymann withheld certain elements from his 1989 Jackie biography until his 1998 *RFK* biography.)

(HEYMANN 1998, p. 540: "John Miner: following MM's death, Ralph Greenson... played him excerpts from several of her tapes.")

(Welkos, Robert W. "New Chapter in the Mystery of Marilyn: Her Own Words?" Los Angeles Times. 5 August 2005: "Greenson's widow Hildegard told The Times this week that she didn't know if the tapes existed and never heard her husband discuss them. Still, she does not discount that Monroe may have given her husband such tapes and that he played them for Miner. 'That seems like something my husband would do,' she said. 'He might want to play it to show how she felt and what was going on with her.' ")

24. (http://www.highbeam.com/doc/1G1-56350823.html: Fee, Gayle, and Laura Reposa. "RFK Bio Author Throws Book At Trio Who Disavow Him." Boston Herald. 25 September 1998.)

(http://www.highbeam.com/doc/1G1-7184960.html: "Marilyn Monroe, Jackie Kennedy Had Conversation In Which Jackie Conditionally Agreed to Divorce JFK So MM Could Marry Him." Star. [Tarrytown, NY] 17 April 1989.)

(http://www.highbeam.com/doc/1P2-692986.html: Sherrill, Bob. "Busy Nights in Camelot." <u>Washington Post</u>. 11 October 1998.)

(http://www.highbeam.com/doc/1P3-1849455391.html: Carrington, Brenlee. "Bobby and Jackie Up In a Tree, K-i-s-s-i-n-g After JFK's Death?" <u>Winnipeg Free Press</u>. 30 August 2009: Heymann relates to Carrington, a Winnipeg attorney, "As a biographer, it has always been my conviction that sexual or personal behavior is integral to a fuller understanding of a person's life, particularly in the case of public personalities.")

(http://www.nytimes.com/1999/01/03/books/political-affairs.html: Judis, John. "Political Affairs: A biography of Robert F. Kennedy focuses on his love life." <u>New York Times</u>. 3 January 1999.)

(THOMAS 2007, pp. 192-193, 429: "A small publishing industry has grown up devoted to proving, or at least insinuating, that RFK not only slept with Marilyn Monroe, he then arranged to have her snuffed out – and covered up the sordid mess…")

(DUNNE 1999, p. 198: "The Kennedys were the root of Peter's problems… Further, Peter was ill-used by his famous and glamorous brothers-in-law…")

(HEYMANN, C. DAVID. INTERVIEW WITH JAY MARGOLIS. 13 JULY 2010)

(HEYMANN 1998, p. 230: "Jayne, whose marriage to Mickey Hargitay was floundering during this period, used to call Jack 'Mr. K…' ")

(STRAIT, RAYMOND. INTERVIEW WITH JAY MARGOLIS. 18 MARCH 2011: JFK "calls my house and said, 'Tell her Mr. K called.' That's the name he used with me to reach her…")

(HEYMANN 1989, p. 214: Peter said, "Joe Kennedy ran the campaign from an outdoor enclosure next to the swimming pool…")

(THOMAS 2007, p. 34: "Joseph Kennedy was a secretive man…")

(KENNEDY 1965, pp. 225-226: Peter wrote, "One of the best pieces of advice he ever gave me…")

(HEYMANN 1989, p. 214: Peter said, "Joe Kennedy was the world's greatest hypocrite…")

(CONFIDENTIAL SOURCE: Patricia Seaton Lawford Stewart was *not* dating or living with Peter Lawford at the time C. David Heymann interviewed him.)

25. (SPOTO 1993, p. 550: When MM died, she had "$2,200 in bank accounts; and $405 cash on hand.")

(CONFIDENTIAL SOURCE: Greenson wrote to Dr. Kris on August 20, 1962, "She was a Cinderella girl who did not live happily ever after." The complete letter is located in Greenson Papers, Special Collections, UCLA, sealed from the public until January 1, 2039.)

(HEYMANN 1989, p. 364: Peter related, "She was crazy about Jack…")

(BURKE 1992, p. 108: "In fact, I was gaining my own view of the late President, which was not the portrait the family painted…")

26. (HEYMANN 1989, p. 181: "A link between Sinatra and Kennedy had been established in 1955.")

(TARABORRELLI 1997, pp. 215-216: "Sinatra became immersed in Kennedy's presidential campaign in 1959, when it was first decided that Kennedy would be a candidate. Sinatra committed himself to John Kennedy because he respected his politics. They had become friends, and he wanted to see him in the White House. Jack's father, Joseph, the ambassador, was primarily responsible for campaign strategy.")

(TARABORRELLI 1997, p. 216: "Kennedy had spent the weekend of November 6 and 7, 1959, at Sinatra's home in Palm Springs after a Los Angeles fund-raiser. Afterward, Frank had a plaque mounted on the door with the inscription 'John F. Kennedy slept here November 6 and 7, 1960.' Sinatra got the year wrong on the plaque!")

(JACOBS 2004, p. 136: "Frank Sinatra controlled the one thing JFK wanted more than anything else…")

(TARABORRELLI 1997, p. 216: "John Kennedy had always looked forward to socializing with Sinatra, to whom he was introduced by Peter Lawford, because he liked Frank's wild antics, exciting women, show-business excesses, and Hollywood gossip.")

(HERSH 1998, p. 139: "Both before and after winning the presidency, Kennedy especially enjoyed weekend visits to Sinatra's home in Palm Springs, with its routine womanizing.")

(TARABORRELLI 1997, p. 223: A Kennedy aide remembered, "We were discussing Frank one day and all that he was doing for the campaign…")

(HERSH 1998, p. 138: Tina Sinatra relayed her father's response to Giancana, "I believe in this man and I think he's going to make us a good president…")

(TARABORRELLI 1997, p. 223: Jack Kennedy said to one of his aides, "Every night, before I go to bed, I pray to God that I don't wake up and read in the newspaper…")

(HEYMANN 1989, pp. 364-365: Peter said, "Then one day she told me she had telephoned Jackie at the White House…")

(JACOBS 2004, pp. 125-126: "Mr. S had an immediate mistrust of Joe's son Bobby…")

(JACOBS 2004, pp. 149-150: "Jackie couldn't stand him. She hated him without really knowing him, refusing to visit Palm Springs out of hand…")

(KELLEY 1986, pp. 290-291: Peter Lawford relayed, "It's true that Jack loved hearing about Frank's Hollywood broads. During one of our private dinners he brought up Sinatra and said, 'I really should do something for Frank.' Jack was always so grateful to him for all the work he'd done in the campaign raising money. He said, 'Maybe I'll ask him to the White House for dinner or lunch.' I said that Frank would love that, but then Jack said, 'There's only one problem. Jackie hates him and won't have him in the house. So I really don't know what to do.' We joked for a few minutes about stuffing Frank into a body bag and dragging him around to the side door so the gardeners could bring him in like a bag of reuse and Jackie wouldn't see him. We also talked about sneaking him in one of John-John's big diaper bundles. The President brightened up a few minutes later and said, 'I'll wait until Jackie goes to Middleburg, and I'll have Eunice be the hostess.' So that's what he did. When Jackie left, Evelyn Lincoln called Frank and invited him to the White House. He flew to Washington for the day and a car drove him up to the southwest gate. Even without Jackie there, the President still wouldn't let him come in the front door. I don't think he wanted reporters to see Frank Sinatra going into the White House. That's why he never flew on Air Force One and was never invited to any of the Kennedy state dinners or taken to Camp David for any of the parties there. He got to Hyannis once, but that was only because Pat and I invited him.")

(HEYMANN 1998, pp. 199, 233-234: RFK's affairs with actresses Kim Novak and Lee Remick.)

27. (HEYMANN 1989, pp. 365-366: Peter related, "Jack had planned on spending March 24th to the 26th, 1962, at Sinatra's Palm Springs home...")

(SUMMERS 2006, pp. 282-283: "According to [Sonny] King and George Jacobs, Frank kicked at a door, smashed photographs of the Kennedys, and pounded the concrete helipad with a sledgehammer. Lawford was once again expelled from the Sinatra magic circle.")

(KELLEY 1986, pp. 301-302: Peter Lawford relayed, "It had been kind of a running joke with all of us in the family that Frank was... adding cottages for Jack and the Secret Service... and building a heliport. He even erected a flagpole for the Presidential flag after he saw the one flying over the Kennedy compound in Hyannisport... He really expected his place to be the President's Western White House. When Jack called me, he said that as president he just couldn't stay at Frank's and sleep in the same bed that Giancana or any other hood slept in... I made a few calls, but in the end it was Chris Dumphy, a big Republican from Florida, who arranged everything at Bing Crosby's house... Bing Crosby, of all people – the other singer and a Republican to boot. Well, Frank never forgave me. He cut me off like that – just like that!... Frank was livid. He called Bobby every name in the book, and then rang me up and reamed me out again. He was quite unreasonable, irrational, really. George Jacobs told me later he went outside with a sledgehammer and started chopping up the concrete landing pad of his heliport. He was in a frenzy… Jack said, 'He's pretty upset, but I told him not to blame you because you didn't have anything to do with it… The Secret Service thought Crosby's place afforded better security.' That's the excuse we used – security – and we blamed it all on the Secret Service. We'd worked it out beforehand, but Frank didn't buy that for a minute, and with a couple of exceptions he never spoke to me again. He cut me out of all the movies we were set to make together and turned Dean and Sammy and Joey against me as well.")

(EBBINS, MILTON. INTERVIEW WITH DONALD SPOTO. 22 SEPTEMBER 1992: "Bobby Kennedy not letting Jack stay at Sinatra's house because Sam Giancana was a guest two weeks before, doesn't make sense!")

(JACOBS 2004, pp. 162-165: "Mr. S's total humiliation occurred in early spring 1962…")

(TARABORRELLI 2009, p. 418: George Smathers relayed, "JFK told me that they were talking about one thing or another and…")

(BADMAN 2010, p. 91: "Marilyn handed the President a gift, a Ronson Adonis chrome cigarette lighter…")

28. (http://www.jfklibrary.org/Historical+Resources/JFK+in+History/Jacqueline+Kennedy+in+the+White+House.htm: Jackie Kennedy in New Delhi, India on March 14, 1962.)

(http://www.youtube.com/watch?v=mOlNxPan0mo: On March 15, 1962, Jackie is still in New Delhi, India. She later sees the Taj Mahal, also in India.)

(http://www.youtube.com/watch?v=4O99kT8T_Is: "Jackie Kennedy in India 1962/3/22" riding on an eight-foot elephant with her sister Princess Lee Radziwill.)

(http://www.youtube.com/watch?v=ZQ8JPEW_jnw: Jackie Kennedy with President Mohammad Ayub Khan at the Shalimar Gardens, Lahore, Pakistan, March 22, 1962. Jackie's stay in Pakistan from March 22 – 25.)

(http://www.youtube.com/watch?v=4lCUVKwZS-o&feature=player_embedded: Jackie Kennedy's continued stay in Pakistan on March 26, 1962.)

(WERTHEIMER 2004, p. 263: Jackie Kennedy publicly addresses Pakistan, "I must say I am profoundly impressed by the reverence which you in Pakistan have for your art and for your culture…")

(http://www.youtube.com/watch?v=ZQ8JPEW_jnw)

(http://www.google.com/#sclient=psy&hl=en&q=jfk+library+jacqueline+kennedy+returns+home+march+29+1962&aq=f&aqi=&aql=&oq=&pbx=1&fp=83f87efc6f926f13: Jackie Kennedy and her return home to Washington on March 29, 1962: See first Google search, "Jacqueline Kennedy welcomed home to the White House, March 29, 1962.")

29. (BADMAN 2010, pp. vii-ix, 255: Badman used Heymann's interview with Peter Lawford without citing *A Woman Named Jackie*.)

(SUMMERS 1994, p. 563: "My book *Goddess, supra.*, was the main source for the Monroe material, but Peter Lawford's description of the affair came from David Heymann's book *Jackie, supra.*")

(SUMMERS 2006, p. 534: Heymann's *A Woman Named Jackie* is listed in his bibliography but curiously absent is Heymann's *RFK* biography, which has Peter discussing MM's free-association tapes and the RFK – Greenson plot to murder MM.)

(BROWN AND BARHAM 1993, p. 478: "Chapter 22 of Heymann's *A Woman Named Jackie*.")

(SPADA 1991, p. 483: Spada lists Heymann's *A Woman Named Jackie* in his bibliography.)

(OPPENHEIMER 1995, p. 664: Oppenheimer lists Heymann's *A Woman Named Jackie* in his bibliography.)

(TARABORRELLI 1997, p. 524: "I also referred to… *A Woman Named Jackie* by C. David Heymann…")

(TARABORRELLI 2009, p. 515: "I still found Lawford to be extremely charming and erudite. I also have never believed any of the quotes attributed to him after his death concerning Marilyn Monroe and the Kennedys. While interviewing Sammy Davis Jr. and Dean Martin for my biography of Frank Sinatra, I learned that both found it very difficult to imagine Peter ever implicating the Kennedys in Marilyn's death – *especially* if it was true... In fact, in a deathbed interview he gave to the *Los Angeles Times*, he was very clear that even if all of the rumors were true – he would certainly not be the one to confirm them. Some very skilled and respected reporters over the years decided that he was just covering for the Kennedys with that interview. Every reporter is entitled to his opinion, of course.")

(GENTRY 2001, p. 814: Gentry lists Heymann's *A Woman Named Jackie* in his bibliography.)

(BADMAN 2010, p. 87: "In June that year JFK penned a letter to the singer thanking him...")

(TARABORRELLI 1997, p. 268: "On June 4, 1962, more than two months after the visit to Crosby's, Kennedy wrote to Sinatra thanking him...")

(TARABORRELLI 1997, p. 268: "An August 28, 1962 telegram from Frank mentioned a film that Kennedy had urged him to make: 'United Artists representatives will contact you regarding *Manchurian Candidate*. Print will be available any hour day or night, for reviewing by the President.' ")

(BADMAN 2010, p. 87)

(JACOBS 2004, p. 174: On *Manchurian*, Sinatra told Jacobs, "I hope it pisses the shit out of them.")

(HEYMANN 1989, p. 365: Peter said, "He telephoned Bobby Kennedy and called him every name in the book...")

(JACOBS 2004, p. 3: "After all, one of the few times I ever saw the guy cry...")

30. (Donaldson, Martha. "One Year Later: Marilyn Monroe's Killer Still at Large!" <u>Photoplay</u>. August 1963, pp. 52-53, 74-75)

31. (Schreiber, Flora Rheta. "Remembrance of Marilyn." Good Housekeeping. January 1963, pp. 30, 32)

(Hyams, Joe. "Marilyn's Chauffeur Is Upset." Daily Times-News. [Burlington, NC] 25 September 1962: Almost two months after MM died, Ralph Roberts told Joe Hyams he visited MM on her last day and gave her a massage.)

(MURRAY 1975, p. 124: MM had a glass of grapefruit juice.)

(MURRAY 1975, pp. 124-125: Schiller couldn't have arrived at 9:30 or 10:00 because MM was inside with Ralph Roberts at this time.)

(DePaulo, Lisa. "The Strange, Still Mysterious Death of Marilyn Monroe." Playboy. December 2005, p. 192: Larry Schiller said he visited MM that last morning and found her working on her garden.)

(GUILES 1970, pp. 379-380: MM supposedly told Schiller while showing him the guest cottage, "Don't mind the doggy smell.")

(SLATZER 1975, p. 222: "Photographer Larry Schiller reportedly dropped by the house sometime on Saturday. However, neither Mrs. Murray nor Pat Newcomb have any recollection of seeing him there that day. When I asked if Schiller had visited the house very often, Mrs. Murray said, 'No. I never met him. Of course, he could have come while I was away.' ")

(GUILES 1970, pp. 362-363, 379-380: Schiller claimed a mystery person dropped off an unmarked envelope yet conceded that prior to her death, he had an agreement with MM to use her photographs *only* with her approval.)

(GUILES 1991, p. 435)

(BROWN AND BARHAM 1993, p. 353: "Photographer Lawrence Schiller, who unwittingly stumbled in to pick up release forms for the nude swimming photos, remembers much shouting about how to 'keep the Kennedys out of it all.' ")

(SELSMAN, MICHAEL. INTERVIEW WITH JAY MARGOLIS. 28 MARCH 2011: "Arthur and I and that was pretty much it because Pat was incommunicado at that time...")

(SELSMAN, MICHAEL. INTERVIEW WITH JAY MARGOLIS. 29 MARCH 2011: "Rupert wasn't even part of the Jacobs Office then... Release forms were never... As for the mysterious envelope or person...")

(http://www.youtube.com/watch?v=IVaVYw7zJrI&feature=related: *The Death of Marilyn Monroe* documentary, part 1 of 5. Arthur Jacobs' employee Michael Selsman related, "I received the call in the middle of the night or early Sunday morning from Arthur Jacobs, asking me to come to the office right away, that there was an emergency.")

(SUMMERS 2000, p. 452: "Lawrence Schiller... was out of town when he heard the news of Marilyn's death. He hurried back to Los Angeles, and that evening found himself sitting in the office of Arthur Jacobs... As he sat in the office, Schiller says, he overheard Jacobs talking with Pat Newcomb. Their great concern at the time, he says, was 'what would be revealed by the telephone records.'")

(MURRAY 1975, pp. 125-126: The morning of August 4, there were two sets of deliveries including MM's bedside table for her guest cottage.)

(SLATZER 1975, p. 220: Mrs. Murray said, "On the day before [Friday], Marilyn and I went to a small furniture store on Santa Monica Boulevard, and she bought a bed table. That was delivered on Saturday morning...")

32. (ROBERTS, RALPH. INTERVIEW WITH DONALD SPOTO. 2 MARCH 1992: Roberts said he learned from MM's secretary May Reis that MM often took about 6 Nembutals a day.)

(Carroll, Ronald H., and Alan B. Tomich. "The Death of Marilyn Monroe – Report to the District Attorney." December 1982, p. 3: Concentrations of chloral hydrate and pentobarbital found in MM's body at the time of her death.)

(http://southernwingsaircraft.com/howmarilyndied.html: "Marilyn was taking 500 mg capsules of CH [chloral hydrate]. A normal dose of CH is between 500 – 1000 mg. The lethal does is considered to be 10 grams, which is 20 capsules. Marilyn had roughly 80% of the lethal dose of 20 capsule amount in her blood so she would have had to take 17 capsules.")

(LITMAN, ROBERT, M.D. INTERVIEW WITH DONALD SPOTO. 23 APRIL 1992: "High content in the liver just means she died slowly…")

(AMADOR, ELIAS, M.D. INTERVIEW WITH JAY MARGOLIS. 11 JANUARY 2011)

(CARPOZI, GEORGE, JR. INTERVIEW WITH DEBORAH CHIEL. 7 NOVEMBER 1992)

(SLATZER 1992, p. 137: John Miner said as for the 13 mg. % of Nembutal, "It indicates that however the drugs were administered, hours and not minutes were involved before she died.")

(SPOTO 1993, pp. 581, 583-585: Dr. Abrams estimated that the 4.5 mg. % of Nembutal in the blood is equivalent to 40 – 50 pills.)

(SUMMERS 2000, p. 416: MM's last call to Ralph Roberts at 10:00 P.M.)

(SLATZER 1992, p. 257: John Miner said, "The amount of drugs found in Marilyn's body was so large that had it been administered by injection, the star would have died almost immediately…")

(SLATZER 1992, pp. 135-136: John Miner relayed, "There was a small quantity of liquid in the stomach but we did not detect any sign that would indicate it contained any heavy drugs or sedatives… The duodenum was felt all the way down to the ileum…")

(SLATZER 1992, pp. 258-259: Dr. J. DeWitt Fox and his assessment that the bruise on MM's hip may very well be an injection site.)

(BROWN AND BARHAM 1993, pp. 382-383: Noguchi relayed, "There were bruises on her lower back area – a very fresh bruise.")

(SUMMERS 2000, p. 542: Noguchi relayed "he could not be positive the actress was not murdered by injection.")

(SUMMERS 2000, p. 260: John Huston told Summers MM took as many as 20 Nembutals in one day.)

33. (SUMMERS 2000, p. 512: "It is claimed that tapes were made the very day Marilyn died, and there is no logical reason to reject the notion that the microphones were active that day. Otash says they showed that Robert Kennedy did visit Monroe in the afternoon, and that the couple made love, then began a violent argument. It led to an outburst in which Marilyn said in effect, 'I feel passed around – like a piece of meat. You've lied to me. Get out of here. I'm tired. Leave me alone.' Kennedy left.")

(Zolotow, Maurice. "Writer: Kennedy-Monroe Romance Just Rumor." Lima News. [Lima, CA] 10 September 1973: Noguchi relayed, "The examination I made included contents of vaginal passages which were made on a smear and studied under a microscope. There was no indication of sexual intercourse.")

("Two Myths Converge: NM Discovers MM." Time. 16 July 1973, p. 70: Noguchi agreed that "examination showed she had had no sexual intercourse on that final day, ending any speculation that she was in the arms of a lover on the night of her demise.")

(STRAIT, RAYMOND. INTERVIEW WITH JAY MARGOLIS. 18 MARCH 2011: "I know they had a long conversation that afternoon. Mostly it was just fighting back and forth…")

34. (HEYMANN 1998, p. 540: Peter said, "I certainly think Marilyn would have held a press conference. She was determined to gain back her self-esteem. She was unbalanced at the time – and Bobby was determined to shut her up…")

(http://www.youtube.com/watch?v=ogYy0IJ4d-Q&feature=related: *Marilyn Monroe: A Case for Murder* documentary, 1988, part 4 of 5: "Wiretapper John Danoff reports that Marilyn said [over wiretap] if Bobby Kennedy did not make a commitment to her, she would reveal her involvement with him and his brother John F. Kennedy. She threatened to make the announcement on August 6," two days after she died.)

(GILMORE 2007, pp. 203, 207: "Slatzer… elaborating on Mailer's fabrication as well the concocted tale of right-wing Capell's whose ruminations were the first to dump on the Kennedys… Yet Slatzer stayed busy, thrusting himself into the limelight like a sweaty wrestler struggling between the ropes, enlisting any support for his continued 'investigation into the mysterious murder death of Marilyn…' Any media source showing curiosity in Slatzer's theories and proclamations became fodder for the 'cause' – demanding a new investigation into the 'mystery' death.")

(MARSHALL 2005, p. 4: "It wasn't until after the publication of Norman Mailer's *Marilyn* and Robert Slatzer's *The Curious Death of Marilyn Monroe* that the possibility of the Kennedys having a hand in her death became accepted.")

(MARSHALL 2005, p. 17: "…the infamous press conference written up first by Robert Slatzer." This suggests Slatzer made up the press conference out of thin air, which is not true.)

(SPOTO 1993, pp. 599-611)

(SELSMAN, MICHAEL. INTERVIEW WITH JAY MARGOLIS. 28 MARCH 2011: "We had heard rumors but she was out of control…")

(BROWN AND BARHAM 1993, pp. 324-325: Close friend Rupert Allan on MM and the possibility of a press conference.)

(BADMAN 2010, pp. 244-245: On August 2, 1962, Judy Simms remembered MM threatening a press conference on TV, a segment later lost from record.)

35. (SUMMERS 1994, p. 350: "Later in the sixties, ranting on about the Kennedys during his California vacations, [J. Edgar Hoover] would rarely fail to bring up Monroe's name. Years later, at home in Washington, he would respond to a question about the case from a young neighbor Anthony Calomaris. 'He said she was murdered,' Calomaris recalled, 'that is wasn't a suicide, that the Kennedys were involved.' ")

(SUMMERS 2000, p. 465: Lawford's ex-wife Deborah "Gould, quoting Lawford, says the Kennedys ensured there would be no proper inquiry into Marilyn's death.")

(SUMMERS 2000, p. 452: Then-Deputy Chief Tom Reddin and how the Kennedys' affairs with Monroe were well known within the Los Angeles Police Department.)

(BROWN AND BARHAM 1993, p. 375: Tom Reddin said, "When I saw the report, it was so fragmentary...")

(WOLFE 1998, p. 37: "Litman, Farberow, and Tabachnick were all associates of Greenson, either as faculty of UCLA, as members and lecturers at the Psychoanalytic Institute, or as fellow committee members at the American Civil Liberties Union. Shortly after the Los Angeles Suicide Prevention Team was recruited, it received a sizable grant from the National Institute of Mental Health, under a government welfare program initiated by Robert Kennedy and administrated by his intimate friend of many years, David Hackett.")

(Nelson, Valerie J. "Psychiatrist Robert Litman dies; co-founded suicide prevention center." Washington Post. 14 March 2010.)

(LITMAN, ROBERT, M.D. INTERVIEW WITH DONALD SPOTO. 23 APRIL 1992. The Suicide Prevention Team "didn't consider the murder hypothesis.")

(*Say Goodbye to the President* documentary, 1985: Police Chief William Parker's successor Tom Reddin stated, "One of the reasons advanced for the highly secret nature of this investigation was that there could be some kind of national security problem in connection with the association between a national figure and a highly publicized entertainer... It was treated as an intelligence division operation. Logically, it could be so treated because there was the involvement of the Attorney General of the United States. They treated it as a 100% intelligence operation and those operations are highly secret... If there was a national security implication, [it was] certainly put under wraps. If there was none, I would see no reason for keeping it under wraps... I don't see any [national security implication].")

(SUMMERS 2000, p. 541: "National security implication.")

(BROWN AND BARHAM 1993, p. 453: "Through the Freedom of Information Act, Hoover biographer Anthony Summers found memos from Hoover to RFK which referred to copies of surveillance tapes involving Monroe...")

(BROWN AND BARHAM 1993, p. 331: Former Chief Tom Reddin related, "Chief Parker was close to the Kennedys...")

(BROWN AND BARHAM 1993, p. 375: "In the estate papers of homicide detective Thad Brown" there "were photocopies of Monroe's phone records – which Parker had always denied receiving.")

(MARTIN, JEANNE. INTERVIEW WITH JAY MARGOLIS. 11 NOVEMBER 2010: On Mike Rothmiller, "That shows just what a lousy guy he is...")

(ROTHMILLER 1992, pp. 105-106: Cross files of MM and the Kennedys.)

(ROTHMILLER 1992, pp. 108-110: "The index card file at OCID contained names and indicators to reports found in several rows of floor-to-ceiling shelves... The third set of OCID files was organized alphabetically into twenty-six sets – one for each letter of the alphabet. Each lettered file was transported to a public storage unit rented in the name of a detective and paid for in cash. There was also a plan in place to change storage units every year. This stuff would be impossible to trace unless one of these key detectives with the key to the kingdom rolled over on any of the locations... 'The one thing I dread is the day an ACLU attorney gets into the files,' [Captain Stuart] Finck said. 'That would be the day the entire lid is blown off the police department.' The captain gestured toward the departing files and explained that from now on, 'These don't exist. These are not files.' If just having this stuff in their possession was so frightening, why didn't these people just destroy the files? They wanted them in case they ever needed them for something in the future. These files so painstakingly put together over the years were hot potatoes... The money used to pay for the storage units was taken from a cash fund called the Secret Service Fund that was earmarked for incidental expenses and payoffs to informants... Because there was even a fourth set of intelligence files – kept by the chief. It consisted of notes and paper briefings that were not written on standard LAPD intelligence file forms. They were called, 'white papers,' not official LAPD documents, so how could anyone subpoena them? They would not be presented to a court because they were just scraps of paper, not files.")

(BROWN AND BARHAM 1993, pp. 431-434: Rothmiller related, "This was common practice. They just rented those anonymous storage lockers...")

36. (SUMMERS 2000, p. 439: "Thad Brown's adjutant, 'Pete' Stenderup, handled the Chief of Detectives' paperwork... 'I remember anything from three to eight pages a day for weeks and weeks. These were notes, what we called "fifteen/sevens," officers' memoranda. They were confidential, not part of the package that can be subpoenaed into court – the informal suspicions as to what might have happened. Robert Kennedy was mentioned frequently in those reports...' It was sent instead to another legendary figure, Captain James Hamilton, head of the Intelligence Division. He handled the matter in an atmosphere of secrecy that cut off his most trusted employees...")

(KENNEDY 1960, p. 13: "...my friends Captain Hamilton...")

(SUMMERS 2000, p. 451: "The Captain, and head of the Intelligence Division, was James Hamilton, who personally directed the Monroe work for Chief Parker... Kennedy admired Hamilton's intelligence-gathering system, and used his advice during his work in the Senate and at the Justice Department... Hamilton's son says, 'He had a relationship with the Kennedys independent of his professional function.' ")

(BUNTIN 2009, pp. 220, 223-224, 279: Parker and Hamilton formed a solid alliance against organized crime with RFK in 1956.)

(WOLFE 1998, p. 49: Former mayor Sam Yorty said, "Hamilton's Intelligence Division was Parker's version of the FBI. Parker believed that he was the man who would one day succeed J. Edgar Hoover, and Bobby and Jack Kennedy led Parker to believe he was their choice.")

(THOMAS 2007, pp. 76-79: RFK and the Select Committee hearings.)

(WOLFE 1998, p. 277: Gates related, "At the invitation of Chief William Parker, Bobby Kennedy set up his offices in the LAPD Intelligence Division. Their desks were next to Captain James Hamilton's. Bobby Kennedy and Hamilton became close friends...")

(WOLFE 1998, p. 277: "Two of Hamilton's most trusted officers, the detectives Archie Case and James Ahearn...")

(WOLFE 1998, p. 14: "Hyams and photographer William Woodfield noted that Captain James Hamilton of the LAPD Intelligence Division was there [at the death scene] along with several intelligence officers...")

(SUMMERS 2000, p. 439: Phillips relayed, "We knew about the inquiry...")

(WOLFE 1998, pp. 51-52: Thad Brown "knew Kennedy was in Los Angeles that night, and he told Chief Parker... Apparently, Thad Brown had done his job too well. Shortly after he relayed his information about Bobby Kennedy to Chief Parker, he was removed from the case. Finis stated that from then on the case was exclusively in the hands of Captain James Hamilton.")

(GATES 1993, p. 81: "Jim Hamilton, the captain of Intelligence, had been Parker's man in that position from day one...")

(GATES 1993, p. 81: Chief Parker told Gates, "Pete Rozelle thinks the mob's shaving points on football games and he wants to hire a director of security who knows organized crime...")

37. (SUMMERS 2000, pp. 442-443: "Marilyn, however, who purchased a tape recorder a few weeks before she died, may have offered her private outpourings to her psychiatrist. Miner says Greenson subsequently destroyed the recording.")

(MINER, JOHN. INTERVIEW WITH DONALD SPOTO. 11 JUNE 1992: Greenson told Miner, "If at the end of our interview, you reach any kind of conclusion, I have no objection...")

(SMITH 2005, pp. 64-65: Miner recollected his memorandum to Dr. Theodore Curphey. Miner wrote, "Dr. Greenson granted the interview on condition that I would not ever reveal what was said or heard during the interview, but I could make known whatever conclusion I reached on the suicide question...")

38. (WOLFE 1998, p. 72: "Disturbed by allegations in Donald Spoto's 1993 book, *Marilyn Monroe: The Biography*, that Dr. Greenson was responsible for the actress's death, John Miner obtained permission from Greenson's widow to reveal some of the things he had heard on the tapes Greenson played for him in 1962.")

(TARABORRELLI 2009, p. 493)

(SMITH 2005, pp. 181-182)

(O'Neill, Anne W. "Ex-Prosecutor Says Monroe Dumped Robert Kennedy." Los Angeles Times. 14 December 1997: Miner denied that MM was killed by Greenson and the Kennedys.)

(Welkos, Robert W. "New Chapter in the Mystery of Marilyn: Her Own Words?" Los Angeles Times. 5 August 2005)

(Rebello, Stephen. "Somebody Killed Her." Playboy. December 2005, p. 188: Miner says within hours he wrote down notes on tapes Greenson played in his office from MM's free-associations. Miner relates, "While I was writing I could hear her. It was almost a weird kind of experience to hear somebody's voice when that person is not there and can't be talking. But I heard her.")

39. (NOGUCHI 1984, p. 80: Miner "was allowed to listen to tape recordings of Monroe's own words in her sessions with Dr. Greenson.")

(FRANKLIN 2002, pp. 112, 127: Before midnight, Otash "observed Sgt. Iannone, in uniform, in conversation with Peter Lawford. This was four-and-a-half hours before LAPD was even notified of Marilyn's death.")

(*Say Goodbye to the President* documentary, 1985: "According to Debbie Gould, Lawford had already done a rough search of the house to remove any connection with the Kennedys...")

(STRAIT, RAYMOND. INTERVIEW WITH JAY MARGOLIS. 18 NOVEMBER 2010: Otash was with Peter at MM's way before midnight.)

(SUMMERS 2000, p. 517: "Fred Otash… is aware of the irony, that a man involved in bugging the Kennedys should now act on their behalf.")

(EBBINS, MILTON. INTERVIEW WITH DONALD SPOTO. 6 AUGUST 1992: "I know Peter Lawford better than anybody. If somebody says to me he called Fred Otash…")

(Oliver, Myrna. "Fred Otash; Colorful Hollywood Private Eye and Author." Los Angeles Times. 8 October 1992: "The colorful Otash, who had just completed a book titled 'Marilyn, Kennedy and Me' about the death of Marilyn Monroe, died Monday… A heavy smoker, he had been troubled for the last decade with emphysema and high blood pressure.")

(STRAIT, RAYMOND. INTERVIEW WITH JAY MARGOLIS. 13 DECEMBER 2010: "We were working on the book when he died.")

40. (NEWCOMB, PATRICIA. INTERVIEW WITH DONALD SPOTO. 3 AUGUST 1992: "No, she wasn't that organized.")

(SUMMERS 2000, p. 512: "There was talk of Robert Kennedy having failed to meet Marilyn at Lake Tahoe.")

(HEYMANN 1998, p. 320: MM threatened to go to the press with her affair with the Kennedy brothers and had taped phone conversations with RFK.)

(SUMMERS 2000, p. 513: Otash said Peter's friend "Bullets" Durgom told him, "Bobby was very worried about Monroe getting spaced out and shooting her mouth off. He told Peter, 'Get her to your place. She won't talk to me now, you get her to the beach.'")

(SUMMERS 2000, p. 512: Otash said he heard MM say to RFK on that last day, "I feel passed around – like a piece of meat. You've lied to me. Get out of here. I'm tired. Leave me alone.")

(HEYMANN 1998, p. 316: Peter said, "At the behest of Dr. Greenson, Marilyn was making 'free-association' tapes. Greenson had suggested she tape her daily thoughts while riding to and from appointments in the backseat of her limousine...")

(SUMMERS 2000, p. 519: After RFK's visit in the afternoon on August 4, "Otash insists that from then on, rather than Marilyn reaching out to Kennedy that evening, *he* tried to get her to come to the Lawford beach house. Marilyn's response, Otash says, was 'Stop bothering me. Stay away from me.' ")

(Miner, John. "Marilyn Uncensored." Playboy. December 2005, p. 200: MM said on a free-association tape for Greenson, "But Bobby, Doctor. What should I do about Bobby? As you see, I have no room in my life for him. I guess I don't have the courage to face up to it and hurt him. I want someone else to tell him it's over. I tried to get the President to do it, but I couldn't reach him... Maybe I should stop being a coward and tell him myself. But because I know how much he'll be hurt, I don't have the strength to hurt him.")

(BROWN AND BARHAM 1993, p. 271: Edwin Guthman said RFK "was a wonderful person to tell your troubles to. And Marilyn called him a lot during the summer of 1962. But then, so did Judy Garland and other ladies in trouble.")

(GUTHMAN, EDWIN. INTERVIEW WITH DONALD SPOTO. 29 OCTOBER 1992)

(HEYMANN 1998, pp. 316-317: According to Peter, RFK tried to help MM in her fight with MCA.)

(STRASBERG 1992, p. 250)

(BROWN AND BARHAM 1993, p. 148: William Travilla said, "He led her to believe that the White House was taking care of it. Her impression was that the nasty telegram had been rescinded...")

(BROWN AND BARHAM 1993, pp. 147-148: RFK's calls to Peter Levathes and Milton Gould.)

(SUMMERS 2000, p. 504: Milton Gould relayed, "He got very angry and abusive, and banged the phone down on me. He called me a 'no-good Jew bastard'... He made it clear to me in subsequent meetings that he resented what I'd done. He never forgot.")

(WOLFE 1998, p. 425: "The Attorney General's telephone records indicate a number of calls to Judge Rosenman just prior to Marilyn's being fired.")

(BADMAN 2010, p. 181: "Rosenman was sensitive to his pleas but told him the only person capable of doing such a thing was Milton S. Gould – a man instrumental in Marilyn's sacking and an individual whom Kennedy, just a month earlier, during the run-up to his brother's gala, had labeled a 'Jewish bastard.' The Attorney General was powerless to assist.")

(SUMMERS 2000, p. 380: MM's Western Union telegram to RFK dated June 13, 1962.)

(BROWN AND BARHAM 1993, p. 250: Regarding the telegram, Rupert Allan said that was a reference to a chat RFK and MM had on February 1, 1962, "She said they talked of how few really big stars remained...")

(CONFIDENTIAL SOURCE: GREENSON, JOAN. UNTITLED 90-PAGE MARILYN MONROE MANUSCRIPT, pp. 67, 75-76: "There was never a line in the paper or trade paper..." The complete work is located in Greenson Papers, Special Collections, UCLA, sealed from the public until January 1, 2039.)

(BROWN AND BARHAM 1993, p. 259: As for RFK, "Later she taught him how to dance the Twist. They moved about the floor as 'The Peppermint Twist' and 'Let's Twist Again' repeated on Peter Lawford's record player.")

(BROWN AND BARHAM 1993, pp. 252-253: Darryl Zanuck and Nunnally Johnson's mutual disappointment over MM being fired.)

(SPOTO 1993, pp. 536-537, 546-548: "The studio was caught short by Dean Martin's loyalty, his insistence on his contractual rights and his canny sense of the best casting... Thus, discussions for an eventual resumption of *Something's Got to Give* were resumed just a week after Marilyn's dismissal, as negotiations began for a complete script revision by Hal Kanter. At the same time, there were telephone calls and meetings to determine how Marilyn Monroe and Dean Martin could be brought back in October, after Martin had completed another scheduled picture… Darryl F. Zanuck was elected president of Twentieth Century-Fox, Levathes was booted out, and Milton Gould and John Loeb resigned from the board… Zanuck personally attended the meetings on the recommencement of *Something's Got to Give*.")

(MARSHALL 2005, p. 306: The Group suggests Lawford couldn't have access to MM's free-association tapes because Greenson had them locked up in his office. They don't consider the possibility that RFK and Peter stole them from MM's home.)

(STRAIT, RAYMOND. INTERVIEW WITH JAY MARGOLIS. 18 NOVEMBER 2010)

(STRAIT, RAYMOND. INTERVIEW WITH JAY MARGOLIS. 13 DECEMBER 2010)

41. (ROMANOFF, GLORIA. INTERVIEW WITH JAY MARGOLIS. 27 OCTOBER 2010: I discussed with Mrs. Romanoff some of Miner's recollections of MM's musings to Greenson on recorded tapes.)

(Miner, John. "Marilyn Uncensored." Playboy. December 2005, p. 199: MM talks about Frank Sinatra, Joe DiMaggio, and Arthur Miller.)

(Miner, John. "Marilyn Uncensored." Playboy. December 2005, pp. 81, 197: MM makes references to James Joyce which correlates with what Peter Lawford himself heard on MM's free-association tapes. She also said it was her idea to record herself, not Greenson's.)

(HEYMANN 1998, p. 316: Peter said, "In a kind of stream-of-consciousness mode…")

42. (SCHLESINGER 2002, pp. 161-162: Jimmy Hoffa quote about the pleasure of having RFK on wire-tap.)

(http://www.youtube.com/watch?v=OK5WFA5qOOc&feature =related: *Marilyn: The Last Word* documentary, 1993, part 4 of 6: Anthony Summers related that MM's home was bugged.)

(SUMMERS 2000, pp. 114-115, 351, 511: Arthur James said, "The request was that I should get Marilyn away from her house for a while...")

(BROWN AND BARHAM 1993, p. 453: Veronica Hamel and the bugs found in MM's roof in the 1970s.)

(HEYMANN 1998, p. 315: Peter said, "Marilyn's house was being bugged by everyone...")

(HEYMANN 1998, p. 316: Ted Schwarz relayed, "There would actually be five clients for the same tape...")

(BROWN AND BARHAM 1993, p. 452: Fred Otash explained, "It was a game. In fact, I put in one system and, at a crucial point, sent tape copies to three sources...")

(CRAMER 2001, p. 409: "Joe would meet with Otash, who'd give him his reports: Marilyn in meetings with the Kennedys at the Lawfords' beach house...")

(WOLFE 1998, pp. 92-93: Suppressed 20/20 Sylvia Chase interview with Fred Otash.)

(SUMMERS 2000, p. 352: "I tracked down John Danoff, a policeman at the Department of Defense facility, who had once worked for Fred Otash... In 1961, according to Danoff, the Otash team succeeded in wiring the rooms and telephone lines at both Marilyn's apartment and the Lawford beach house. They were also 'hooked into' Marilyn's answering service. Danoff's main part in the operation, he says, was to sit in a vehicle monitoring receiver equipment. The bug at the Lawford house, he claims, transmitted desultory conversation between the President and Marilyn, and the unmistakable sounds of lovemaking. Danoff's recollection is that this occurred 'around Thanksgiving' in 1961. As we have seen, the President was in Los Angeles that November, and did meet Marilyn.")

(SUMMERS 2000, p. 355: "Spindel told [his assistant] Jaycox that some of the information on Marilyn and Robert Kennedy came from a bug installed at the Justice Department in Washington. Spindel described the bug as transmitting through conductive paint from a device hidden in the baseboard of the Attorney General's Office. The 'product' was then collected by Spindel's contact in the Justice Department. Preposterous though this sounds, newly obtained FBI documents show that, from summer 1961 till the spring of the year Marilyn died, there was serious concern that Hoffa had 'two contacts in the Criminal Division of the Department.' One Hoffa infiltrator was identified and investigated; the second source of the leaks remains a mystery.")

(SUMMERS 2000, pp. 510-512: "The bugs at the home of Peter Lawford, says [Otash's] consultant, were installed before the interest in Marilyn. The devices had been planted earlier, when the consultant attended a large social occasion at the house... For the first time, Otash and others have described what the microphones picked up. 'There were more tapes made on Robert Kennedy and Monroe,' Otash says, 'than there had been on Marilyn and the President.' The tapes contained the sounds of love-making – and of quarrels. 'On one tape I heard,' Otash told me, 'she was screaming, just screaming on and on at him, because, according to her, he had promised to get divorced and marry her. She kept bringing that up, and it led to fights...' Spindel's technician Earl Jaycox, who had earlier admitted only to seeing tapes, now admits that Spindel played him recordings of Marilyn's 1962 telephone conversations with both Kennedy brothers. There were calls to the White House, and to Robert Kennedy at the Justice Department. 'When she was calling looking for Jack,' says Jaycox, 'there was a male secretary she spoke to quite frequently... Kenny was the name, I think.' President Kennedy's personal assistant was called Kenneth O'Donnell. 'Marilyn was almost always agitated on these calls,' says Jaycox, 'very agitated... She was acting like a betrayed woman.' There was talk of a rendezvous at a location in Virginia, and of Robert Kennedy having failed to meet Marilyn at Lake Tahoe. The calls to the President, Jaycox says, seemed designed to worm information out of him about his brother's intentions. 'Jack Kennedy would talk to her rather calmly,' Jaycox recalls. 'He covered pretty well for his brother.' Robert Kennedy, in contrast, 'would get infuriated and hang up on her.'")

(SUMMERS 1994, p. 343: "Peter Lawford had long since been under surveillance on the orders of someone else – Edgar. The sound specialist who installed the bugs is still operating today and has revealed his role only on the formal understanding that his name is not used. 'The job at the Lawford house,' the source said in 1991, 'was done for the Bureau, through a middleman. I installed the devices on FBI orders. They were in the living room, the bedrooms, and one of the bathrooms. An intermediary for Hoover came to me to arrange the installation, I guess at the end of the summer, in 1961. The formal reason given was that Hoover wanted information on the organized crime figures coming and going at the Lawford place. Sam Giancana was there sometimes. But of course the Kennedys, both John and Robert, went there, too. Hoover's intermediary told me that, as Attorney General, Robert Kennedy had given strict orders that the house was *not* to be bugged. But it was covered, on Hoover's personal instructions. Jimmy Hoffa did get one of the Kennedy – Monroe tapes, but only because it was leaked to him by one of the operatives. He wanted to make a buck and Hoffa's people paid $100,000 – a lot of money back then. But that surveillance was commissioned by the FBI, and almost all the tapes went to the FBI. J. Edgar Hoover had access to every goddamned thing that happened at the beach house, including what happened when the Kennedys were there, for nearly a year. Draw your own conclusions.' ")

(http://www.youtube.com/watch?v=ogYy0IJ4d-Q&NR=1: *Marilyn Monroe: A Case for Murder* documentary, 1988, part 4 of 5 – John Danoff said JFK "was tired of her and he gave her to Bobby...")

(*Say Goodbye to the President* documentary, 1985: John Danoff relayed, "Music. People talking...")

(http://www.youtube.com/watch?v=ogYy0IJ4d-Q&NR=1: *Marilyn Monroe: A Case for Murder* documentary, 1988, part 4 of 5 – Fred Otash countered, "I'm not the only man...")

(*Say Goodbye to the President* documentary, 1985: Account of Fred Otash.)

(SPADA 1991, p. 235: "Had he chosen to use it, Nixon had more than enough information on the Kennedys – information obtained through wiretaps that Fred Otash had installed in the Lawford home in 1959." Otash related, "Not regarding women, that came later. Just some inside information about what they were doing generally, their strategy for the 1960 campaign, that sort of thing.")

(HEYMANN 1998, p. 315: Ted Schwarz, who knew Otash, said, "Fred Otash… had been hired to bug Lawford's house…")

43. (SPOTO 1993, pp. 487-488: Spoto claimed that JFK and MM only met four times.)

(BADMAN 2010, p. 91: After the stay at Bing Crosby's Palm Springs home on March 24 – 25, "Marilyn and JFK would never share a bed or a sexually charged session again, and Marilyn never pursued it.")

(November 28th, 2006 article: www.freewebs.com/sugar22cane/marilynnews.htm: "Marilyn Monroe only had a one night stand with U.S. President John F. Kennedy and not an affair, according to a new biography of the screen beauty. In his book… writer Keith Badman claims the pair could not have conducted a significant relationship because their schedules rarely overlapped. However, Badman believes Monroe and Kennedy did spend the night together at Bing Crosby's home in Palm Springs, California.")

(SUMMERS 2000, p. 290: "Peter Lawford… knew Marilyn as early as 1950, when she was twenty-four. They met first at the William Morris Agency.")

(SUMMERS 2000, p. 289: "Two witnesses suggest that [Jack] Kennedy met Marilyn through him [Charles Feldman] as early as 1951. Feldman's longtime secretary, Grace Dobish, believes there was such a meeting. Alain Bernheim, who worked with Feldman and knew Marilyn well, thinks she was present at a dinner Feldman gave for Kennedy. Bernheim drove Kennedy home, however, and recalls that he left with another girl that night.")

(SUMMERS 2000, p. 290: Arthur James said, "Although Jack Kennedy was a Senator…")

(SUMMERS 2000, p. 289: "In the fall of 1954 John Kennedy... had undergone major [back] surgery in a New York hospital... A reporter who visited Kennedy, Priscilla McMillan... noticed... on the wall – a poster of Marilyn Monroe. The picture showed Marilyn in blue shorts standing with her legs spread apart. It had been fixed upside down so that her feet stuck up in the air.")

(SUMMERS 1994, p. 342)

(*History's Mysteries: The Death of Marilyn Monroe* documentary, 2000: James Bacon said, "Marilyn told me about her affair with JFK... It began when he was campaigning for president...")

(HERSH 1998, p. 106: Arthur P. Jacobs' employee Michael Selsman said he was informed of JFK's affair with MM in early January 1961 before the inauguration.)

(BARRIS, GEORGE. INTERVIEW WITH JAY MARGOLIS. 7 JANUARY 2011: "The Kennedys I think were very much aware of the fact that having relationships with movie stars could be detrimental to their career...")

(HEYMANN 1998, p. 240: Tom Jacobson (son of Max "Dr. Feelgood" Jacobson) relayed the effect his father's injections had on JFK.)

(http://www.youtube.com/watch?v=mzZ0VZORVmY: *JFK's Women: The Scandals* documentary, 2006, part 1 of 6: Anthony Summers talks about JFK's Addison's Disease and how cortisone treatments resulted in JFK's rising sexual libido.)

(THOMAS 2007, p. 60: "Always sickly, [Jack] Kennedy had been diagnosed in 1947 with Addison's disease, a failure of the adrenal glands... In 1950, cortisone was found to be an effective treatment... But the cortisone was not a cure-all, and it had some disturbing side effects, including inducing a state of euphoria. Addison's disease was not Kennedy's only health problem. His unstable back, damaged by war and football, also caused him excruciating pain.")

(HEYMANN 1989, pp. 147-148: George Smathers said, "My feeling was that Rose, like Eleanor Roosevelt, hated sex...")

(KELLEY 1979, pp. 132, 134-138: George Smathers relayed, "There's no question about the fact that Jack had the most active libido...")

(HEYMANN 1998, p. 243: Kennedy family friend Lem Billings corroborated Smathers' account, "He [Jack Kennedy] disappeared with Hjordis Niven, the wife of David Niven, below decks of the presidential yacht for ten minutes or so during his forty-fourth birthday party.")

(HEYMANN 1998, p. 235: "The pair were well known to the President's brother Bobby, who referred to them as Fiddle and Faddle. Formerly college roommates, Priscila Weir (Fiddle) and Jill Cowan (Faddle) joined on JFK's campaign drive as pollsters, then went to work at the White House, the former as an aide to Evelyn Lincoln, the latter assisting Pierre Salinger.")

(HERSH 1998, p. 103: On MM, George Smathers relayed, "She was a beautiful actress...")

(http://www.youtube.com/watch?v=MzQ27ElP9ik: *Marilyn Monroe: A Case for Murder* documentary, 1988, part 3 of 5 – James Bacon related, "Marilyn used to tell me about Jack. She had a big affair with him. It was kind of a slam-bang affair because she'd be ushered in...")

(KESSLER 2010, p. 12: "According to Secret Service agents, Kennedy had sex with Marilyn Monroe at New York hotels and in a loft above the Justice Department office of then-Attorney General Robert F. Kennedy.")

(HEYMANN 1998, pp. 227-229, 231: Secret Service agent Marty Venker's account.)

(JACOBS 2004, p. 161: "Marilyn would tell me breathlessly about Jack, though she never mentioned Bobby...")

44. (BADMAN 2010, pp. 78-79: "Some historians have also suggested that Monroe was having a fleeting affair with Kennedy in 1960 at the time he was campaigning in the Los Angeles area...")

(TARABORRELLI 2009, p. 329: "Marilyn wasn't sure she could make it...")

(SUMMERS 2000, pp. 292, 294, 298, 498-499: Account of Peter Summers.)

(*Say Goodbye to the President* documentary, 1985: Account of Peter Summers.)

(WOLFE 1998, p. 346: "When Jack, Bobby, and Teddy Kennedy arrived in Los Angeles, they checked into the Biltmore Hotel. The Kennedy suite, which was down the hall from Chief Bill Parker's private apartment…")

(HEYMANN 1989, p. 236: "Marilyn was part of the crowd of 100,000 that jammed the Los Angeles Coliseum…")

(HEYMANN 1998, p. 162: Peter said, "Of all his 'other' women…")

(HEYMANN 1989, pp. 235-236)

(http://latimesblogs.latimes.com/files/1960_1111_mirror_cover.jpg: Wilson, Earl. "Marilyn Monroe Will Divorce Arthur Miller." Los Angeles Mirror. 11 November 1960.)

(BADMAN 2010, p. 79: Buchwald, Art. "Let's Be Firm on Monroe Doctrine." Washington Post. 19 November 1960.)

(SUMMERS 2000, p. 352: "[John] Danoff had been involved in many surveillance operations for Otash, and claims Marilyn was the target of several… In 1961, according to Danoff, the Otash team succeeded in wiring the rooms and telephone lines at both Marilyn's apartment and the Lawford beach house. They were also 'hooked into' Marilyn's answering service… Danoff's main part in the operation, he says, was to sit in a vehicle monitoring receiver equipment. The bug at the Lawford house, he claims, transmitted desultory conversation between the President and Marilyn, and the unmistakable sounds of lovemaking. Danoff's recollection is that this occurred 'around Thanksgiving' in 1961. As we have seen, the President was in Los Angeles that November, and did meet Marilyn. Danoff is described as 'an honest informant' by a Treasury Department intelligence agent who used him in the sixties.")

(SUMMERS 2006, pp. 491-492: "…visit by the President [JFK] to Los Angeles on the weekend of November 18 – 19, 1961. He and Monroe were at the Lawford beach house on the 19th.")

(SPOTO 1993, p. 445: "From October 24 to November 4, the final interior scenes and process photography for the film [*The Misfits*] were completed at the Paramount Studios, Hollywood.")

(WEATHERBY 1976, pp. 202-203, 205-206: MM hints at an affair with one of the Kennedy brothers and also would not say a bad word about JFK.)

45. (BLAINE 2010, pp. 400-401: "To my knowledge, the only other time Marilyn Monroe was in the President's company had been in Santa Monica, at the home of Peter and Pat Lawford, during one of the President's visits to the Los Angeles area in 1961. The President stayed long enough to enjoy a brief swim and greeted the public on the beach area before we departed. These were the only two times that I or any of the agents I have discussed this with remember Marilyn Monroe being in proximity to the President. There will always be speculation on the private life of America's first families, but the reality is that it is the responsibility of the Secret Service to ensure that the first family has the ability to have privacy... What happens when the family retires is private, and the Secret Service has an obligation and duty to protect that privacy.")

(SUMMERS 2000, p. 375: "The *New York Times*, in its normal coverage, said the President returned to his hotel, the Carlyle, at 2:00 A.M....")

(BANNER 2011, pp. 196-197: Photograph at Arthur Krim's home showing MM and Isadore Miller near each other while JFK is on the other side of the room.)

(Schreiber, Flora Rheta. "Remembrance of Marilyn." <u>Good Housekeeping</u>. January 1963, p. 135: Isadore Miller said MM made sure to personally take him home.)

(HASPIEL 1993, pp. 194, 196: MM's young friend denied rumors of a tryst at the Carlyle as not possible because she had to take Isadore Miller home and Haspiel said he was there with her before 4:00 A.M.)

(SUMMERS 2000, p. 376: "Marilyn needed company and attention after she got home. Ralph Roberts, the masseur, remembers her calling him to request a massage. He shook himself awake, and hurried to her apartment to oblige.")

(BADMAN 2010, p. 155: MM's poem to JFK for his birthday began, "Let lovers breathe their sighs…")

(BROWN AND BARHAM 1993, pp. 80-81: Ralph Roberts mentioned the call MM made to him while she was staying with JFK at Bing Crosby's Palm Springs home from March 24 – 26, 1962.)

(SUMMERS 2000, pp. 348-350)

(SPOTO 1993, p. 487)

(TARABORRELLI 2009, pp. 409-411)

(BADMAN 2010, pp. 86-89)

(Hyams, Joe. "Marilyn's Chauffeur Is Upset." <u>Daily Times-News</u>. [Burlington, NC] 25 September 1962: Ralph Roberts tells of massaging MM and recalled advice he used to give her.)

(KELLEY 1986, pp. 301-302)

(HEYMANN 1998, pp. 306-307)

(HEYMANN 1989, pp. 365-366)

46. (BROWN AND BARHAM 1993, pp. 77, 80, 477: "In a pair of interviews, Ralph Roberts provided the glimpses of Monroe on Air Force One in disguise.")

(SUMMERS 1994, p. 342: "The most famous blonde in the world was smuggled… even on board Air Force One, disguised in a black wig and sunglasses.")

(LAWFORD 1988, p. 157: "Peter told me how he used to dress Marilyn in a brown wig, dowdy clothing, and glasses, then hand her a legal pad and pen. She would be sneaked into the Carlyle Hotel as Peter's personal secretary, Peter ordering her to take notes… The secretary trick was most effective when Peter took Marilyn on Air Force One or some other plane.")

(SCHWARZ 2009, p. 604: "Peter would take his 'assistant' onto Air Force One and the photographers would take only his picture. Not that the secret was 100 percent secure. There were many journalists who recognized Marilyn and understood what was happening. But as Jim Bacon discussed, this was not something they would publicize.")

(LEAMING 1998, pp. 403, 411-412: George Smathers said, "Well, it wasn't a big thing as far as he was concerned...")

(HERSH 1998, p. 104: George Smathers relayed, "What happened was that she... would like to be close to the President...")

(TARABORRELLI 2009, p. 418: Rupert Allan related, "If Kennedy had handled Marilyn differently...")

47. (Pace, Eric. "Judith Exner Is Dead at 65; Claimed Affair With Kennedy." New York Times. 27 September 1999: Dave Powers 1991 quote on Campbell.)

(EBBINS, MILTON. INTERVIEW WITH DONALD SPOTO. 6 AUGUST 1992: "Hell hath no fury like a hooker that becomes an author...")

(HERSH 1998, p. 311: Judy Campbell was not a prostitute nor could the FBI prove such was true.)

(Smith, Liz. "The Exner Files." Vanity Fair. January 1997, p. 30: Walter Winchell's May 9, 1962 column read, "Judy Campbell of Palm Springs and Bevhills is Topic No. 1 in Romantic Political Circles.")

(SELSMAN, MICHAEL. INTERVIEW WITH JAY MARGOLIS. 28 MARCH 2011)

(EXNER 1978, p. 86: Jack and Judy meet for the first time on February 7, 1960.)

(HERSH 1998, p. 299: Judy didn't know who JFK was when she met him.)

(EXNER 1978, pp. 100-104: Judy says she first made love to JFK on March 7, 1960.)

(EXNER 1978, pp. 111, 128: Judy wrote in her book, "Evelyn Lincoln and I became old telephone friends, or at least co-conspirators. She never failed to give Jack my messages and Jack never failed to return my calls... Since Evelyn Lincoln has now chosen to deny any knowledge of our relationship, I have decided to list some of the addresses and telephone numbers given to me by her and Jack during the time we saw each other. When I first knew Jack, Evelyn lived at 3132 Sixteenth Street, Northwest, apartment 507, telephone AD 4-5745. Other numbers were MA 4-1011, MA 4-9335, HO 2-5632. Her number at the Old Senate Office building, room 362, was CA 4-3121, extension 3341. The private number was RE 7-0064. After the election, Evelyn moved to 1440 Rock Creek Ford Road, Northwest, apartment 402, and the number was TA 9-5552. Jack's Georgetown home number was FE 8-2325; in New York it was PL 5-7600 and EL 5-4878, and his apartment was at 277 Park Avenue. The White House was NA 8-1414. At Hyannis, I could reach Evelyn at the Yachtman Hotel, Spring 5-4600. In Palm Beach, numbers for Jack were TE 2-7117 and TE 3-4622; Evelyn's, at the Palm Beach Towers, was TE 3-5761." The listing of these phone numbers would cease to be relevant had biographer Arthur Schlesinger, Jr. chosen not to deny that the Campbell/Kennedy relationship existed beyond seventy phone calls. Considering Schlesinger was a close Kennedy confidant of many years who worked alongside Jack Kennedy, his position on this matter was entirely predictable.)

(SPADA 1991, p. 287: "Giancana, Rosselli, and their fellow mobsters understandably expected that with their various assistances to the Kennedy administration, the FBI would turn a blind eye to their illegalities...")

(SCHLESINGER 2002, pp. 494-495: "White House logs show that Campbell telephoned some seventy times after January 1961 in pursuit of her friendship with John Kennedy. One cannot conclude whether she was doing it out of a weakness for presidents or whether she was put up to it by Giancana so that the underworld might get something on Kennedy.")

(EXNER 1978, p. 148: JFK as a celebrity gossip hound.)

(JACOBS 2004, pp. 138-139)

(HERSH 1998, p. 300: Judy told Hersh, "I now think he may have been interested in some of the women he asked about.")

(HERSH 1998, pp. 303, 306-312: Judy acted as courier to Sam Giancana on behalf of JFK. Shocked at first upon discovering the three-way connection, the FBI, especially J. Edgar Hoover, became wary of the JFK/Campbell/Giancana triangle.)

(SUMMERS 2000, p. 507: Giancana helped steal votes in Illinois for JFK.)

(SCHLESINGER 2002, p. 495: Giancana told Hoffa's attorney Edward Bennett Williams he's "working for the government.")

(*Say Goodbye to the President* documentary, 1985: Jimmy Hoffa's account from a 1973 clip.)

(THOMAS 2007, p. 85: "It is true that Kennedy's scattershot method produced many more headlines than indictments. The evidence adduced at the hearings was rarely strong enough to prompt the cautious Eisenhower Justice Department to bring a criminal case.")

(HERSH 1998, pp. 313-314: March 22, 1962 lunch between J. Edgar Hoover and JFK over his connection with Campbell/Giancana/Rosselli.)

(HERSH 1998, pp. 322-323: Judy told JFK about her pregnancy. Judy eventually resolved to have Giancana set up a doctor who could perform the abortion.)

(Smith, Liz. "The Exner Files." Vanity Fair. January 1997, pp. 38, 43: During late December 1962, Judy became pregnant with JFK's child and the following month, she had an abortion with the help of her friend Sam Giancana. She entered Chicago's Grant Hospital from January 26 – 28, 1963.)

(HERSH 1998, p. 322: Judy felt the Kennedys made their own rules.)

48. (THOMAS 2007, p. 40: Jack Kennedy "disappeared into a romantic world of historical fiction and derring-do... Jack Kennedy called *Pilgrim's Way* his favorite book.")

(HEYMANN 1998, p. 227: Secret Service agent Marty Venker explained that JFK was "intrigued by the whole mystique of the Secret Service.")

49. (EBBINS, MILTON. INTERVIEW WITH DONALD SPOTO. 6 AUGUST 1992: "If there was one, it was very well-hidden.")

(EBBINS, MILTON. INTERVIEW WITH DONALD SPOTO. 22 SEPTEMBER 1992: "I think that Bobby had an affair with her…")

(SELSMAN, MICHAEL. INTERVIEW WITH JAY MARGOLIS. 28 MARCH 2011: "The way I understand it is that Jack and Bobby had a routine ever since they were much younger…")

(http://www.youtube.com/watch?v=SFzm5cE35BA&feature=related: *The Death of Marilyn Monroe* documentary, part 2 of 5: Arthur Jacobs' employee Michael Selsman said, "The Kennedy brothers had a modus operandi when it came to women. Whereas Jack would begin in a relationship with a particular woman and then pass her on to Bobby.")

(SUMMERS 2000, p. 385: "Michael Selsman, now a Hollywood producer, in 1962 worked for Arthur Jacobs, a close friend of Marilyn's who ran her press relations. He was thus a colleague of Pat Newcomb, who personally handled Marilyn. Selsman says he had heard Newcomb and his employer, Jacobs, discussing Marilyn's affair with the President, and subsequently with Robert. They were concerned, he says, that exposure of the relationships would damage the Kennedys politically.")

(SUMMERS 2000, p. 503: Smathers said JFK told him he thought RFK's tryst with MM was getting out of hand.)

(*Say Goodbye to the President* documentary, 1985: Regarding his tryst with MM, Smathers said JFK wanted RFK to end it.)

(NAAR, JOSEPH. INTERVIEW WITH DONALD SPOTO. 22 JULY 1992: With women, RFK was "pushy, aggressive. 'I'm Bobby Kennedy, the Attorney General.' That was the attitude…")

(OPPENHEIMER 1995, pp. 312-313: George Terrien remembers RFK bragging about sleeping with MM after JFK was done with her.)

(*Say Goodbye to the President* documentary, 1985: Peter Dye said, "I know she was nuts about him because she told me…")

(*Say Goodbye to the President* documentary, 1985: Deborah Gould relayed, "From what Peter said then Bobby got very infatuated…")

(HEYMANN 1989, pp. 366-367: Peter said, "It wasn't Bobby's intention, but that evening they became lovers and spent the night in our guest bedroom. Almost immediately the affair got very heavy, and they began seeing a lot of each other...")

(HEYMANN 1998, p. 540: Regarding MM working on her last film, Peter said, "She looked good part of the time but for the most part appeared to be incoherent.")

(SUMMERS 2000, p. 336: Peter's third wife Debbie "Gould's understanding, quoting Lawford, is that Robert's involvement started when he went to Marilyn, as his brother's 'messenger boy,' to say that the relationship with the President could not continue...")

(SUMMERS 2000, p. 336: Debbie Gould relayed, "Marilyn took it quite bad and Bobby went away with a feeling of wanting to get to know her better. At the beginning it was just to help and console, but then it led into an affair between Marilyn and Bobby. From what Peter told me, he fell head over heels.")

(SUMMERS 2000, pp. 381-382: Peter said, "I'm a light sleeper and one night I woke up for some reason. It was dawn, and I looked out of the window and saw a figure standing on the balcony. It was Marilyn with a robe on, and it seemed like she was drunk and I went out and said, 'Are you okay?' There were tears streaming down her face. Pat by then had woken too, and we brought her in and talked to her.")

50. (SCHLESINGER 2002, pp. 590-591: At Arthur Krim's party after JFK's birthday gala, Adlai Stevenson said, "My encounters, however, were only after breaking through the strong defenses established by Robert Kennedy, who was dodging around her like a moth around the flame." Referring to the same event, Arthur Schlesinger, Jr. wrote in his diary for August 6, 1962: "I do not think I have seen anyone so beautiful; I was enchanted by her manner and her wit, at once so masked, so ingenious and so penetrating. But one felt a terrible unreality about her – as if talking to someone under water. Bobby and I engaged in mock competition for her; she was most agreeable to him and pleasant to me – but then she receded into her own glittering mist." Next, Schlesinger wrote in his book, "There was something at

once magical and desperate about her. Robert Kennedy, with his curiosity, his sympathy, his absolute directness of response to distress, in some way got through the glittering mist as few did.")

(SUMMERS 2000, p. 339: Lynn Sherman said, "There were many, many rendezvous there. The official car used to drive up, and you knew Robert Kennedy was in town...")

(SUMMERS 2000, p. 339: After MM's death, Lynn Sherman relayed that Pat "was complaining about Peter." Sherman said Pat had remarked, "But we all go through it – look what Ethel's been going through.")

(BROWN AND BARHAM 1993, p. 277)

(Miner, John. "Marilyn Uncensored." Playboy. December 2005, p. 200: MM says she wants to break up with RFK.)

(O'Neill, Anne W. "Ex-Prosecutor Says Monroe Dumped Robert Kennedy." Los Angeles Times. 14 December 1997)

(MOORE, TERRY. INTERVIEW WITH JAY MARGOLIS. 23 NOVEMBER 2010: Kay Spreckles Gable later told Terry Moore that shortly before her death, MM said she was deeply in love with RFK.)

(BROWN AND BARHAM 1993, p. 425: Terry Moore related regarding MM, "She told Kay that Bobby had just promised to make her First Lady when he became president. And this was only weeks before her death.")

(SPADA 1991, pp. 307-308: Account of Chuck Pick.)

(HEYMANN 1998, p. 314)

(SUMMERS 1994, p. 346: "Simon reported that Bobby was borrowing his Cadillac convertible for the purpose of going to see Marilyn Monroe.")

51. (Zolotow, Maurice. "MM's Psychiatrist a Troubled Man." San Antonio Light. [San Antonio, TX] 13 October 1973: 9-A)

("Psychiatrist Breaks Silence In Defense of Marilyn Monroe." Yuma Daily Sun. [Yuma, AZ] 23 October 1973)

(MAILER 1975, pp. 329-331: Even though Mailer doesn't point the finger at RFK as conspiring to kill MM, murder by the CIA or FBI is suggested: "This won't prove the Easterner's

[RFK's] most shining hour. He will next appear in San Francisco with his family after a Marine helicopter puts down at the pad next to Lawford's house on Sunday morning… What we can expect from all the stories is that if efforts were being made to protect Bobby Kennedy, none of the versions can afford to be accurate… If she could be murdered in such a way as to appear a suicide in despair at the turn of her love, what a point of pressure could be maintained afterward against the Kennedys.")

("Two Myths Converge: NM Discovers MM" Time. 16 July 1973, p. 70: Greenson publicly stated that Mailer's last chapter is "all wrong, filled with fallacious statements…")

(CONFIDENTIAL SOURCE: GREENSON, JOAN. UNTITLED 90-PAGE MARILYN MONROE MANUSCRIPT, p. 78: "I knew there had been a new man in her life, and I was asking her about her new boyfriend…" The complete work is located in Greenson Papers, Special Collections, UCLA, sealed from the public until January 1, 2039.)

(SUMMERS 2000, p. 336)

(GREENSON, HILDI. INTERVIEW WITH CATHY GRIFFIN. 4 JUNE 1991: "I think she mentioned it in a very veiled way to my daughter…")

(HEYMANN 1998, p. 311: General "is a common form of address for the attorney general.")

(SUMMERS 2000, p. 337: Dr. Robert Litman's notes from the Suicide Prevention Team's investigation into MM's death back in 1962: "Around this time, Marilyn started to date some 'very important men.' Greenson had very considerable concern that she was being used in these relationships…")

(BROWN AND BARHAM 1993, p. 275: Dr. Robert Litman relayed, "There was evidence of her intimate relationship with Robert Kennedy…")

(BROWN AND BARHAM 1993, p. 279: Litman said, "She was always able to attract the highest level of men…")

52. (SUMMERS 2000, p. 285: JFK to Clare Boothe Luce, "Dad told all the boys…")

(SUMMERS 2000, p. 285: Arthur Schlesinger, Jr. on RFK.)

(HEYMANN 2009, pp. 152-153: George Smathers on RFK/Mary Jo Kopechne affair.)

(HEYMANN 1998, p. 230: Peter on JFK/Mansfield affair.)

(STRAIT 1992, pp. 156, 178-179: "I had personal reason to believe Jayne's recollections of John F. Kennedy; once when the President was vacationing in Palm Springs, and another time when he was house guesting at Peter Lawford's Santa Monica beach home… [When Jayne and JFK met in Palm Springs] she was pregnant with her second daughter, Mariska, who she would always refer to as Maria because her father, Nelson Sardelli, was of Italian heritage… She regaled in telling the story. 'I was pregnant and Kennedy was wearing some kind of corset. He'd been hurt in the war, he said. We were a funny couple making love – a cripple and a balloon!' She quickly added that JFK 'was very considerate of my condition.' ")

(STRAIT 1992, pp. 153-160, 177-190: Mansfield's affairs with JFK and RFK.)

(HEYMANN 1998, p. 231: Strait on RFK/Mansfield affair.)

(STRAIT, RAYMOND. INTERVIEW WITH JAY MARGOLIS. 13 DECEMBER 2010: RFK/Mansfield tryst during early July 1963 at the Casino Royale in Washington, D.C.)

(STRAIT, RAYMOND. INTERVIEW WITH JAY MARGOLIS. 18 NOVEMBER 2010: Mansfield told JFK in late 1963, "Listen to me, buster…")

(HEYMANN 2009, p. 141: Art Buchwald on Jackie Kennedy.)

(http://www.highbeam.com/doc/1P3-1849455391.html: Carrington, Brenlee. "Bobby and Jackie Up In a Tree, K-i-s-s-i-n-g After JFK's Death?" <u>Winnipeg Free Press</u>. 30 August 2009: Heymann said to Carrington, a Winnipeg attorney, "As a biographer, it has always been my conviction that sexual or personal behavior is integral to a fuller understanding of a person's life, particularly in the case of public personalities.")

(HEYMANN 2009, p. 86: Aristotle Onassis' aide Johnny Meyer said, "Ari could be very pushy, but he also had a great deal of charm. If he couldn't get his way by being nice, he'd resort to bullying, a tactic also utilized by RFK. Both men were controlling figures. And both men hated each other. Onassis couldn't be critical enough of RFK. He was so positive Bobby had killed Marilyn Monroe that he hired a private investigator to document the murder. The P.I.'s findings were inconclusive.")

(HEYMANN 2009, p. 141: Onassis said, "The only thing JFK and RFK have in common…")

(HEYMANN 1998, p. 232: Peter Jay Sharp knows RFK would at times participate in JFK's notorious swimming pool orgies at the White House.)

(HEYMANN 2009, pp. 31-32: Peter Lawford described RFK and his affair with Carol Bjorkman.)

(HEYMANN 1998, p. 233)

53. (HEYMANN 2009, pp. 32-33: RFK and his affair with actress Lee Remick.)

(HEYMANN 1998, pp. 233-234)

(HEYMANN 2009, pp. 73-74: RFK and his affair with socialite Natalie Fell Cushing.)

(SPADA 1991, pp. 301-303: Milt Ebbins helping a nude MM into a very tight dress.)

(BROWN AND BARHAM 1993, pp. 75-77: The date of that same event with Milt Ebbins was April 14, 1962.)

(HEYMANN 1998, p. 67: Mort Downey, Jr. said, "Bobby didn't need sex as a daily fix the way Jack did…")

(HEYMANN 2009, pp. 88-89: Mort Downey, Jr. on RFK and his affair with actress Kim Novak.)

(HEYMANN 1998, p. 199: MM's friend reporter George Carpozi, Jr. and the RFK/Novak affair.)

(BRADEN 1989, pp. 152, 154-155: "I got back to the motel through the crowd and very shortly after there was a knock on the door. It was Bobby. He looked at me, saying nothing, and pulled his tie off. Then he spoke. 'It could have been me.' He put his arms around me and pulled me down on the bed alongside him.")

(Trueheart, Charles. "Joan Braden's Book Proposal: Kiss & Sell?; Memories of Rocky, RFK & Friends." Washington Post. 8 September 1987.)

(http://www.nytimes.com/1987/09/10/books/washington-book-proposal-withdrawn.html: Yarrow, Andrew L. "Washington Book Proposal Withdrawn." New York Times. 10 September 1987.)

(Anson, Robert Sam. "Secrets and Lies." Vanity Fair. November 1997, p. 114: Pierre Salinger told Seymour Hersh that in 1967, he found RFK in bed with his wife.)

(http://www.nydailynews.com/gossip/bwiddicombe/2007/08/02/2007-08-02_new_marilyn_death_docu_is_in_the_offing.html: Widdicombe, Ben. "New Marilyn death docu is in the offing." New York Daily News. 2 August 2007, p. 20: Keya Morgan on RFK's call girl at the Beverly Hills Hotel.)

(HEYMANN 1998, pp. 67, 79-80: RFK's affairs with Elizabeth Okrun and Amy Brandon, respectively.)

(HEYMANN 1998, pp. 159-162: RFK's affair with former showgirl Barbara Marx, wife of Zeppo Marx of the Marx Brothers, who eventually became Frank Sinatra's last wife until his death.)

(HEYMANN 1998, pp. 246-247: In the hardcover edition, see pictures between the pages for women RFK was interested in including actresses Mia Farrow, Claudine Longet, and Candice Bergen.)

54. (Scott, Walter. Personality Parade. 4 July 1971)

(TARABORRELLI 1997, p. 271: An anonymous Sinatra friend reflected, "Frank... said that he wanted Marilyn at Cal-Neva so he could keep an eye on her, because he'd heard that she had had an abortion in the last couple of weeks...")

(SUMMERS 2000, p. 385: "Natalie Jacobs heard about Marilyn's supposed pregnancy shortly before she died. 'Marilyn said she had had a miscarriage. Arthur did not know whether to believe her, or whether she had fantasized it...' Selsman says he too heard that Marilyn had an abortion in her last months.")

(SUMMERS 2000, pp. 384-385: Arthur James relayed, "It was obvious the poor girl was in trouble even by her standards…")

(JACOBS 2004, p. 169: "There was another strong medical tie: Marilyn's gynecologist was Red Krohn…")

(GUILES 1991, pp. 432-433: "One of the Jacobs Office publicists said that on July 20, Marilyn was admitted to Cedars of Lebanon Hospital under an alias…")

(MOORE 1977, p. 282: "On July 20, 1962, Marilyn told her friends that she was going to Lake Tahoe for a long week-end. But, according to a variety of unofficial sources, she was in the Cedars of Lebanon Hospital during the 'week-end,' for what was rumored to be another miscarriage.")

(NEWCOMB, PATRICIA. INTERVIEW WITH DONALD SPOTO. 3 AUGUST 1992: "I took her to the hospital once, a D & C… Here, at Cedars.")

(SELSMAN, MICHAEL. INTERVIEW WITH JAY MARGOLIS. 28 MARCH 2011)

(SPOTO 1993, p. 542: "The notes of her regular surgeon, Leon Krohn, M.D. (chief of the gynecological service at Cedars), leave no doubt that the later rumors of an abortion are sheer fiction.")

(BADMAN 2010, p. 215: "One Marilyn book even claimed that she went into Cedars for a 'D & C' (Dilatation and Curettage)…")

(CARPOZI, GEORGE, JR. INTERVIEW WITH DEBORAH CHIEL. 6 NOVEMBER 1992: "It was Bobby's baby.")

(BROWN AND BARHAM 1993, pp. 305-307: MM confidants attest to hearing about either a miscarriage or an abortion.)

(BROWN AND BARHAM 1993, p. 307: Rupert Allan recalled, "Nineteen sixty-two was a long time ago. If word that Marilyn had aborted a child by one of the Kennedys reached the press…")

(HEYMANN 1989, pp. 367-368: Peter said, "During July, Pat and I took her along on two junkets to Cal-Neva Lodge at Lake Tahoe…")

55. (HEYMANN 1989, pp. 367-368: Peter related, "During July, Pat and I…")

(http://www.youtube.com/watch?v=eF-ZnbysSCk&feature=related: *Marilyn: The Last Word* documentary, 1993, part 3 of 6: Former FBI agent Bill Roemer related, "I learned this from a microphone that I helped place in the headquarters of Giancana in a western suburb in Chicago and just before Marilyn died, the weekend before she died, Giancana indicated that he and Sinatra had taken her to the Cal-Neva Lodge at Lake Tahoe where Giancana had sex with her repeatedly during the weekend much to the dismay apparently of Marilyn. I think she was kind of in a fog at that particular time. She was very humiliated and depressed.")

(SUMMERS 2006, p. 495: "Rosselli may have been referring not to Monroe but to Campbell…")

(ROMANOFF, GLORIA. INTERVIEW WITH JAY MARGOLIS. 2 SEPTEMBER 2010: "Giancana, whatever you may think of him…")

(STRAIT, RAYMOND. INTERVIEW WITH JAY MARGOLIS. 13 DECEMBER 2010: "Frank was sleeping with her and I don't think he wanted Giancana to sleep with her.")

(TARABORRELLI 1997, pp. 271-273: Giancana's friend Tommy DiBella said, "No way. And I'll tell you why: because he knew how Sinatra felt about her, and Sam never screwed with another man's girl.")

(BROWN AND BARHAM 1993, p. 307: "Since Monroe had become an intimate with Patricia Kennedy Lawford, Bobby apparently prevailed on Pat Lawford to get Monroe out of town during his visit to Los Angeles the weekend of July 27 to 29. The Attorney General was flying in for a public appearance and several conferences on the progress of *The Enemy Within*.")

56. (CARPOZI, GEORGE, JR. INTERVIEW WITH DEBORAH CHIEL. 6 NOVEMBER 1992: "Peter Lawford picks her up and he says to her…")

(SUMMERS 2000, p. 512: "There was talk of Robert Kennedy having failed to meet Marilyn at Lake Tahoe.")

(SUMMERS 2006, p. 290: "Billy Woodfield recalled how, sometime afterward, Frank asked him to process and print a roll of photographs he had taken at the Cal-Neva. 'I developed the film and some of the pictures, about nine frames, showed Marilyn, on all fours...' ")

(CRAMER 2001, p. 409: "Then, before he left town, Joe would meet with Otash, who'd give him his reports: Marilyn in meetings with the Kennedys at the Lawfords' beach house... Bing Crosby's house with JFK... a weekend with Sinatra's friends at Frankie's new casino resort, the Cal-Neva Lodge, on the border at Lake Tahoe...")

(SUMMERS 2000, p. 397: "Langford's brother, Joe, says DiMaggio wanted to get in touch, but did not actually enter the Cal-Neva 'because there was a feud between him and Sinatra at the time.' Another witness... was told an eerie story by an employee. He recalled looking down from the casino, near dawn, to see Marilyn 'at the edge of the pool, barefoot, swaying back and forth. She was staring up the hill...' He followed her gaze, and there was DiMaggio standing in the driveway, 'staring back.' ")

(SUMMERS 2000, p. 397: Ralph Roberts relayed, "She told me it was a nightmare, a dreadful weekend. She said she didn't want to go particularly...")

(JACOBS 2004, p. 176: George Jacobs related an "S&M Mafia orgy" involving MM and Johnny Rosselli: Since Rosselli knew MM intimately before, Jacobs said, "She was *their* girl, not those Micks'.")

(BADMAN 2010, pp. 227-228)

(ISRAEL 1979, p. 339: Kilgallen wrote in her column on August 3, "Marilyn Monroe's health must be improving...")

(BADMAN 2010, p. 227: Kilgallen wrote in her column on August 3, "Marilyn's dress looks as if it was plastered to her skin and the skirt is hitched higher above the knees than any Paris designer...")

(STRAIT, RAYMOND. INTERVIEW WITH JAY MARGOLIS. 13 DECEMBER 2010: "She was kind of sprawled out like she passed out. She had her clothes on but her dress was up. It was white…")

(VAN METER 2003, p. 265: After seventeen years, Joe DiMaggio forgave Skinny D'Amato for what happened to MM at the Cal-Neva the second to last weekend of her life.)

57. (ROMANOFF, GLORIA. INTERVIEW WITH JAY MARGOLIS. 2 SEPTEMBER 2010: "Typically, Marilyn started taking pills at about eight o'clock. She'd time it. Eight o'clock. Nine o'clock. Ten o'clock…")

(SUMMERS 2000, p. 383: Gloria Romanoff relayed, "Marilyn drank champagne, and some vodka, and would take sleeping pills. The Lawfords walked her about, after midnight, trying to keep her awake, and I think they called Frank in, too. I remember Marilyn telling me one of her problems was that she'd taken pills so long, they didn't work for her the way they did for other people. So she'd begin about nine in the evening, and build up that lethal combination of booze and pills.")

(SUMMERS 2000, p. 382: "The staff, from the housekeeper to the bell boys, remember a sad, withdrawn figure. Mae Shoopman, then a cashier at the Lodge, recalls, 'She wasn't well. She kept herself disguised pretty much, kept herself covered with a black scarf, and stayed in her room a good deal of the time. In fact, everyone became alarmed about it, because she would go to sleep with the telephone at her ear open to the switchboard. I think she was frightened, and it was a way of not being alone.' It was thanks to the telephone operator, perhaps, that Marilyn did not die that weekend. Sitting up in the casino office, as the music blared and the late-shift croupiers hovered over the tables, the operator heard strange sounds and stertorous breathing on the line from Chalet 52. She called the manager, who raised the alarm, and Marilyn made it through another overdose.")

(WILSON 1974, p. 89: MM "had been found naked on the floor at the Cal-Neva Lodge at Lake Tahoe with the phone off the hook.")

(TARABORRELLI 1997, p. 272: Ted Stephens said, "All I know is this: We got this call from Peter Lawford…")

(TARABORRELLI 1997, p. 271: A close confidant said Frank Sinatra "had deep feelings for her, which is why she was there…")

(BROWN AND BARHAM 1993, p. 444: "Patricia Kennedy Lawford was with her constantly, except for a 'nap Marilyn took from 3:00 to 5:00 P.M.'… Utterly despondent, Monroe apparently began gulping sleeping pills immediately after dinner. She was asked politely – probably by Sinatra – to remain in her room… [Gary Weatherly related,] 'Sinatra was frightened that Monroe would die there and create a disastrous scandal…' [Around midnight] Back in her room, Monroe apparently gulped down more pills and was found comatose by Mrs. Lawford… Nurses who rushed to the stricken film star told Frank Sinatra later that she was only fifteen to twenty minutes away from death when Frank and Lawford burst into her room.")

(TARABORRELLI 2009, p. 467: George Jacobs related, "For her to maybe *die* at Cal-Neva while [Sinatra] was there? That would have been terrible. So, after he'd seen enough, he said, 'Get her out of here and get her out of here now.' And that was it.")

(BROWN AND BARHAM 1993, pp. 309-310: Peter told the district attorney years after MM's death, "She tried to kill herself the night of July twenty-eighth, and she finally succeeded on August fourth.")

(HEYMANN 1998 p. 320: Peter informed RFK at a pay phone that MM threatened a press conference with recorded telephone conversations as blackmail.)

(SUMMERS 2000, p. 396: Per Barbara Lieto, the pilot's widow, "When the plane finally landed at Los Angeles, after midnight, Marilyn was 'out of it, a mess…' The crew gave Lawford a ride to Santa Monica in their car. The pilot became further angered when Lawford insisted on stopping a few blocks from his home to make a half-hour telephone call from a public booth. Why, they wondered, could he not wait a mere five minutes, till he got to the beach house? With hindsight, one must wonder whether Lawford, too was now worried about security.")

(BROWN AND BARHAM 1993, p. 271: Hazel Washington said RFK's calls to MM were like "making love over the phone. And I do mean making love.")

(SUMMERS 2000, p. 340: "Marilyn's studio maid, Hazel Washington, remembers calls from Robert Kennedy.")

58. (TARABORRELLI 2009, p. 492: Keya Morgan and the MM sex tape.)

(http://www.mahalo.com/keya-morgan: "Marilyn Monroe Sex Tape": "On April 14, 2008, Morgan brokered the sale of a Marilyn Monroe Sex Tape for $1.5 million to an unidentified businessman in New York. Morgan arranged the sale of the black and white film, which allegedly shows Marilyn Monroe performing oral sex on an unidentified man. Morgan says that the film was discovered while he was researching an upcoming documentary film, *Marilyn Monroe: Murder on Fifth Helena Drive*. He claims that he interviewed police and FBI agents, and one mentioned that a copy of the sex tape was in the custody of the son of a deceased FBI informant. Morgan arranged the sale between the FBI informant's son and the businessman from New York.")

(http://www.cbsnews.com/stories/2008/04/15/earlyshow/ leisure/celebspot/main4015822.shtml?source=mostpop_story: "Former FBI Director J. Edgar Hoover, now known to have been an arch-rival of the Kennedy family, thought the man in the tape might be John or Robert Kennedy – and tried hard to prove that it was one of them, Morgan says. John is long rumored to have had an affair with Monroe.")

(Producer Keya Morgan on MSNBC with Dan Abrams: http://www.youtube.com/watch?v=T4XqkcwGdcQ)

59. (HEYMANN 2009, pp. 101-103: Clark Clifford saw movie of MM and related how Hoover was certain that RFK was the man in the video.)

(SUMMERS 2000, p. 523: "At dawn on December 15, 1966 – four years after Marilyn's death – a posse of police and District Attorney's investigators, armed with a search warrant, descended on Spindel's home in New York State...")

(Cohen, Joseph J. "Spindel Sues to Get Back Seized RFK Tape on Hoffa." World Journal Tribune. 18 December 1966: Bernie Spindel said, "My confidential file containing tapes and evidence concerning circumstances surrounding and the causes of the death of Marilyn Monroe...")

(Tomasson, Robert E. "SUIT ASKS RETURN OF BUGGING ITEMS: Tapes on Marilyn Monroe and Others Are Listed." New York Times. 21 December 1966.)

(STRAIT, RAYMOND. INTERVIEW WITH JAY MARGOLIS. 18 NOVEMBER 2010)

(STRAIT, RAYMOND. INTERVIEW WITH JAY MARGOLIS. 13 DECEMBER 2010)

60. (GREENSON 1967, p. 171: "Transference is the experiencing of feelings, drives, attitudes, fantasies, and defenses toward a person in the present," often the analyst, "which do not befit that person but are a repetition of reactions originating in regard to significant persons of early childhood, unconsciously displaced onto figures in the present.")

(GREENSON 1967, p. 155: "All people have transference reactions; the analytic situation only facilitates their development and utilizes them for interpretation and reconstruction... The two outstanding characteristics are: it is a repetition and it is inappropriate.")

(GREENSON 1967, pp. 52, 172: "Most psychoanalysts, however, are of the opinion that narcissistically fixated patients [as Greenson termed MM] require deviations from the standard psychoanalytic procedure.")

(GREENSON 1967, pp. 173-174, 184: "People who are essentially narcissistic will not be able to maintain a consistently analyzable transference relationship. Their relationship to the therapist will abound with fusions of self and object images, primitive forerunners of identification.")

(GREENSON 1967, p. 343: "borderline cases" and "their propensity for intractable transference reactions.")

(SUGARMAN 2000, pp. 279-282: In a paper entitled, "Countertransference," Greenson wrote, "Countertransference... is an inappropriate reaction of the therapist to his patient...")

(CONFIDENTIAL SOURCE: Greenson wrote to Dr. Kris on August 20, 1962, "If I behaved in a way which hurt her she reacted as though it was the end of the world..." The complete letter is located in Greenson Papers, Special Collections, UCLA, sealed from the public until January 1, 2039.)

(GUILES 1970, p. 372: "Clearly Dr. Greenson was concerned by her reliance upon the judgment of her hirelings.")

(CONFIDENTIAL SOURCE: Greenson wrote to Dr. Kris on August 20, 1962, "I have some misgivings about how correct was I in my form of treatment..." The complete letter is located in Greenson Papers, Special Collections, UCLA, sealed from the public until January 1, 2039.)

(ROMANOFF, GLORIA. INTERVIEW WITH JAY MARGOLIS. 2 SEPTEMBER 2010: "He's a real prize...")

(KIRSNER 2007, pp. 479, 483: "Unfortunately, Hazen was miserable much of the time and was scarcely a clear case of being helped by psychotherapy. But she was tied to Greenson by transferences and he (and Anna Freud) to her through money. Greenson stayed involved with her in one form or another in a helping role and also as family friend into the mid-1970s. But it was probably not a coincidence that he said he had enough of her when she stopped providing cash to Anna Freud and the Foundation. The treatment was clearly contaminated throughout by money.")

(YOUNG-BRUEHL 1988, pp. 412-413: "No millionaires materialized...")

61. (LITMAN, ROBERT, M.D. INTERVIEW WITH DONALD SPOTO. 23 APRIL 1992: "There was a real washing out of the usual doctor boundaries... I would never suggest that there was anything wrong in the relationship. He virtually adopted a person. There was a danger when someone gets that involved.")

(Miner, John. "Marilyn Uncensored." Playboy. December 2005, p. 197: MM spoke into her recorder, "Ever since you let me in your home and I met your family...")

(ROMANOFF, GLORIA. INTERVIEW WITH JAY MARGOLIS. 27 OCTOBER 2010: A friend of MM's for 14 years, I read Mrs. Romanoff selected passages from MM's free-association tapes as recollected by John Miner including, "Ever since you let me in your home and I met your family..." and she told me that while the words are not exact since they are framed by John Miner, Romanoff confirmed that many of the sentiments are very much MM's.)

(SPOTO 1993, pp. 599-611: Capell, Mailer, Slatzer "started" the murder rumors.)

(Oakland Tribune. [Oakland, CA] 5 January 1964: Greenson himself confirmed that the murder rumors began right after MM's death as he was receiving innumerable threats to his own life.)

(CONFIDENTIAL SOURCE: Greenson wrote to Dr. Kris on August 20, 1962, "And on top of it all, the notoriety, the press all over the world writing about it and constantly linking my name..." The complete letter is located in Greenson Papers, Special Collections, UCLA, sealed from the public until January 1, 2039.)

(KIRSNER 2009, p. 153: "Greenson told his colleagues that he decided to offer his family as a substitute for the family Monroe never had...")

(SUMMERS 2000, p. 400: At MM's insistence, her poet friend Norman Rosten became acquainted with Greenson during the spring of 1962. Greenson later wrote to Rosten on August 15, 1962, "I should have played it safe and put her in a sanitarium...")

(http://www.telegraph.co.uk/culture/film/7843140/Marilyn-Monroe-on-the-couch.html: Turner, Christopher. "Marilyn Monroe on the Couch: To Dr. Ralph Greenson, Marilyn Monroe was more than just a patient. Now, for the first time, his family recall their favourite 'big sister.'" Telegraph. 23 June 2010: Danny Greenson said, "He felt that therapy as he knew it wasn't working...")

(EBBINS, MILTON. INTERVIEW WITH DONALD SPOTO. 6 AUGUST 1992: "He made a statement that Marilyn was doomed and eventually...")

(RUDIN, MILTON. INTERVIEW WITH DONALD SPOTO. 31 OCTOBER 1992: "I think it helped kill him...")

(SELSMAN, MICHAEL. INTERVIEW WITH JAY MARGOLIS. 28 MARCH 2011: "Well, to the extent that every actor or actress is paranoid because their careers are absolutely perched on the knife's edge. She looks around at age 36...")

(ROMANOFF, GLORIA. INTERVIEW WITH JAY MARGOLIS. 2 SEPTEMBER 2010: "She never had any real money. The house she died in was the first home she ever owned and it meant everything to her...")

(CONFIDENTIAL SOURCE: Referring to July 1961, Greenson wrote to Dr. Kris on August 20, 1962, "I saw her at that time seven days a week, mainly because she was lonely..." The complete letter is located in Greenson Papers, Special Collections, UCLA, sealed from the public until January 1, 2039.)

(TARABORRELLI 1997, p. 272: Rudin related, "She could have a crisis over what she was having for lunch...")

(TARABORRELLI 2009, p. 369: Diane Stevens relayed, "Once, during a late night at the office, we sent out for Chinese food...")

(TARABORRELLI 2009, p. 374: Actress Maureen Stapleton related that MM "thought the waiter was reading her mind...")

(CONFIDENTIAL SOURCE: GREENSON, JOAN. UNTITLED 90-PAGE MARILYN MONROE MANUSCRIPT, p. 50: "She had visions of all kinds of crazy people climbing over her fence..." The complete work is located in Greenson Papers, Special Collections, UCLA, sealed from the public until January 1, 2039.)

(NEWCOMB, PATRICIA. INTERVIEW WITH DONALD SPOTO. 3 AUGUST 1992: "She was paranoid...")

Jay Margolis

(FARBER AND GREEN 1993, p. 103: Henry Weinstein said, "He might have been able to keep her propped up...")

(JACOBS 2004, p. 1: George Jacobs said, "Mr. S's lawyer Mickey Rudin... was a combination bag man, hit man, and Hollywood hustler.")

(STRAIT, RAYMOND. INTERVIEW WITH JAY MARGOLIS. 13 DECEMBER 2010: "He was a scumbag and everybody knew it. He was Sinatra's man...")

(KELLEY 1986, pp. 410-411: Greenson's sister Elizabeth Greenschpoon relayed, "I've known Frank a long time. He was a patient of my brother, who was a psychiatrist – Dr. Ralph Greenson...")

62. (RUDIN, MILTON. INTERVIEW WITH DONALD SPOTO. 31 OCTOBER 1992: "His wife was Swiss...")

(GREENSON 1978, pp. 493-495: "I told an emotionally immature young woman patient, who had developed a very dependent transference to me, that I was going to attend an International Congress in Europe some three months hence...")

(MURRAY 1975, p. 103: MM's housekeeper Mrs. Eunice Murray related, "Marilyn took a handsome chess piece from the set she had bought in Mexico – one knight to wrap in her handkerchief while she sang...")

(MORGAN 2007, p. 275: Michelle Morgan referred to a "pawn" that MM lost in New York after the birthday gala but as shown above, it was a white knight.)

(CONFIDENTIAL SOURCE: GREENSON, JOAN. UNTITLED 90-PAGE MARILYN MONROE MANUSCRIPT, p. 52: "Father was to give a lecture in Israel..." The complete work is located in Greenson Papers, Special Collections, UCLA, sealed from the public until January 1, 2039.)

(GREENSON, HILDI. INTERVIEW WITH CATHY GRIFFIN. 4 JUNE 1991: "That vacation we had, it was constant telephone calls...")

(HEYMANN 1998, p. 319)

(CONFIDENTIAL SOURCE: Greenson wrote to Dr. Kris on August 20, 1962, "I left Marilyn in the hands of a colleague whom she knew..." The complete letter is located in Greenson Papers, Special Collections, UCLA, sealed from the public until January 1, 2039.)

(CONFIDENTIAL SOURCE: GREENSON, JOAN. UNTITLED 90-PAGE MARILYN MONROE MANUSCRIPT, pp. 72-74: "Danny and I did get a call after her birthday..." The complete work is located in Greenson Papers, Special Collections, UCLA, sealed from the public until January 1, 2039.)

(FARBER AND GREEN 1993, p. 99: Hildi Greenson relayed, "She was bright and lovely and interesting...")

(MURRAY 1975, p. 107: "Marilyn didn't want to interrupt the psychiatrist's trip with her problems...")

(MURRAY 1975, p. 107: "A Dr. Wexler was on call for Dr. Greenson's patients...")

(CONFIDENTIAL SOURCE: GREENSON, JOAN. UNTITLED 90-PAGE MARILYN MONROE MANUSCRIPT, pp. 74-75: "It was clear that there was really no way Marilyn was going to make it through that picture without my father here..." The complete work is located in Greenson Papers, Special Collections, UCLA, sealed from the public until January 1, 2039.)

63. (SPOTO 1993, pp. 528-529: Greenson's angry letter postmarked June 22, 1962 to friend Lucille Ostrow.)

(FARBER AND GREEN 1993, pp. 98, 106: "Janice Rule, who was in analysis with Greenson at the time Marilyn died, remembers how 'crucified' he felt by the press.")

(MEYERS 2010, p. 269: On June 22, 1962, Greenson wrote a letter to Anna Freud about MM, a letter located in the Library of Congress.)

(MEYERS 2010, p. 269: On July 2, 1962, Anna Freud wrote back to Greenson about MM, a letter located in the Library of Congress.)

Jay Margolis

(BERTHELSEN 1987, pp. 152-153: Anna Freud spent one week with MM in 1956 during the shooting of *The Prince and the Showgirl* in London.)

(SPOTO 1993, p. 375: MM's psychiatrist "Hohenberg had a suggestion for Marilyn, and forthwith whisked her off to meet her old friend Anna Freud, an analyst with a thriving London practice. Marilyn had several therapy sessions with Sigmund Freud's daughter.")

(GREENSON, HILDI. INTERVIEW WITH CATHY GRIFFIN. 4 JUNE 1991: "That felt very good, winning my suit...")

64. (FARBER AND GREEN 1993, p. 99: Hildi Greenson remarked, "You always treaded on eggshells with Marilyn...")

(http://www.telegraph.co.uk/culture/film/7843140/Marilyn-Monroe-on-the-couch.html: Turner, Christopher. "Marilyn Monroe on the Couch: To Dr. Ralph Greenson, Marilyn Monroe was more than just a patient. Now, for the first time, his family recall their favourite 'big sister.'" Telegraph. 23 June 2010: Danny Greenson said, "Until she came along he [my father] was assiduous in not saying anything about who his patients were...")

(CONFIDENTIAL SOURCE: GREENSON, JOAN. UNTITLED 90-PAGE MARILYN MONROE MANUSCRIPT, p. 1: "I glanced at my watch. It was almost time..." The complete work is located in Greenson Papers, Special Collections, UCLA, sealed from the public until January 1, 2039.)

(CONFIDENTIAL SOURCE: GREENSON, JOAN. UNTITLED 90-PAGE MARILYN MONROE MANUSCRIPT, p. 5: "Out of the car emerged a petite girl..." The complete work is located in Greenson Papers, Special Collections, UCLA, sealed from the public until January 1, 2039.)

(FARBER AND GREEN 1993, p. 98: Leo Rosten said, "Romi was furious with me because I didn't want to come down and meet her...")

(NEWCOMB, PATRICIA. INTERVIEW WITH DONALD SPOTO. 3 AUGUST 1992: "He was always on her side against everybody else...")

(GUILAROFF 1996, pp. 164-165: "She crossed the lawn with some difficulty, leaning on a dour middle-aged man...")

(ROMANOFF, GLORIA. INTERVIEW WITH JAY MARGOLIS. 2 SEPTEMBER 2010: "She wasn't deceptive with people. She was almost childlike in that respect...")

(Zolotow, Maurice. "MM's Psychiatrist a Troubled Man." San Antonio Light. [San Antonio, TX] 13 October 1973, p. 9-A: Greenson on MM: "She was afraid of people...")

(CONFIDENTIAL SOURCE: Greenson wrote to Dr. Kris on August 20, 1962, "I suggested to her that she look for a little house which she could buy so that she could have a place of her own..." The complete letter is located in Greenson Papers, Special Collections, UCLA, sealed from the public until January 1, 2039.)

(GREENSON, HILDI. INTERVIEW WITH CATHY GRIFFIN. 4 JUNE 1991: "He thought she was a waif who needed a home...")

(HEYMANN 1998, pp. 310-311)

(CONFIDENTIAL SOURCE: GREENSON, JOAN. UNTITLED 90-PAGE MARILYN MONROE MANUSCRIPT, pp. 20-21: "After the dishes were done, Marilyn usually went home..." The complete work is located in Greenson Papers, Special Collections, UCLA, sealed from the public until January 1, 2039.)

(http://www.telegraph.co.uk/culture/film/7843140/Marilyn-Monroe-on-the-couch.html: Turner, Christopher. "Marilyn Monroe on the Couch: To Dr. Ralph Greenson, Marilyn Monroe was more than just a patient. Now, for the first time, his family recall their favourite 'big sister.' " Telegraph. 23 June 2010: Chris Turner wrote, "Marilyn couldn't drive, Joan says, because fans would deliberately crash into her so they could meet her, so Joan would ferry her around in a battered Hellman convertible instead.")

(http://www.telegraph.co.uk/culture/film/7843140/Marilyn-Monroe-on-the-couch.html: Turner, Christopher. "Marilyn Monroe on the Couch: To Dr. Ralph Greenson, Marilyn Monroe was more than just a patient. Now, for the first time, his family recall their favourite 'big sister.' " Telegraph. 23 June 2010: Joan Greenson said, "It was a two-way street...")

(CONFIDENTIAL SOURCE: GREENSON, JOAN. UNTITLED 90-PAGE MARILYN MONROE MANUSCRIPT, p. 17: "Whenever Marilyn had feelings about a subject, it was always with a great deal of intensity..." The complete work is located in Greenson Papers, Special Collections, UCLA, sealed from the public until January 1, 2039.)

(GREENSON, HILDI. INTERVIEW WITH CATHY GRIFFIN. 4 JUNE 1991: "I was awfully sorry for her in many, many ways. She had an intensity in every direction...")

(SUMMERS 2006, pp. 175-176: Greenson treated Sinatra in psychoanalysis.)

(WEXLER 2002, p. 240: "Greenson himself was a dramatic individual and undoubtedly would have made a splendid actor...")

(KIRSNER 2009, p. 153: "The approach Greenson recommended in his 1967 textbook could not have been further removed from his treatment of Marilyn Monroe between 1960 and her death in 1962.")

(http://www.telegraph.co.uk/culture/film/7843140/Marilyn-Monroe-on-the-couch.html: Turner, Christopher. "Marilyn Monroe on the Couch: To Dr. Ralph Greenson, Marilyn Monroe was more than just a patient. Now, for the first time, his family recall their favourite 'big sister.' " Telegraph. 23 June 2010: Joan Greenson said, "It may have been foolhardy...")

65. (CONFIDENTIAL SOURCE: Greenson wrote to Dr. Kris on August 20, 1962, "First of all she was a patient and I felt responsible for her..." The complete letter is located in Greenson Papers, Special Collections, UCLA, sealed from the public until January 1, 2039.)

(SPOTO 1993, p. 502: One of Greenson's colleagues said, "At the time, everyone was experimenting with ways to treat schizophrenics, and [Milton] Wexler had his own method. Greenson used Wexler as his supervisor, and thus gave his unorthodox treatment of Monroe an apparent legitimacy. One of the techniques was to invite the patient into the home – not only to provide what may have been lacking earlier, but to have a constant connection so the patient would never have undue anxiety on weekends, or [suffer] any separation trauma.")

(TARABORRELLI 2009, p. 375: "Wexler… felt strongly that Marilyn Monroe suffered at least from borderline paranoid schizophrenia after sitting in on three sessions with her in Dr. Greenson's home…")

(TARABORRELLI 2009, p. 375: Wexler relayed, "One misconception about her treatment is that it was Dr. Greenson's idea that she move in with his family. She never moved in with the Greensons. Instead, it was my suggestion…")

(http://www.telegraph.co.uk/culture/film/7843140/Marilyn-Monroe-on-the-couch.html: Turner, Christopher. "Marilyn Monroe on the Couch: To Dr. Ralph Greenson, Marilyn Monroe was more than just a patient. Now, for the first time, his family recall their favourite 'big sister.'" Telegraph. 23 June 2010: Danny Greenson said, "My father's heart was in the right place…")

(SPOTO 1993, p. 501: Greenson told Weinstein, "Henry, don't you pay any attention to these fantasies of hers. She has a lot of them…" Spoto wrote, "By this time, Greenson himself was so deeply overwhelmed by his projection and countertransference that he may well have seen himself as the father figure to whom she was sexually attracted… 'I think,' Weinstein said years later with compassion for them both, 'that Ralph was dependent on her.'")

(TARABORRELLI 2009, p. 171: Dr. Liden said Gifford told him in 1965, "My daughter was Marilyn Monroe…")

(FARBER AND GREEN 1993, p. 85: Author Leo Rosten, Greenson's friend since 1938, discussed how Greenson loved to talk about his patients.)

66. (CONFIDENTIAL SOURCE: On August 20, 1962, Greenson wrote to Dr. Marianne Kris, "I had become a prisoner now of a form of treatment which I thought was correct for her but almost impossible for me..." The complete letter is located in Greenson Papers, Special Collections, UCLA, sealed from the public until January 1, 2039.)

(HEYMANN 1998, p. 322: Peter said, "Greenson had thus been set up by Bobby to 'take care' of Marilyn.")

(SUMMERS 2000, p. 422: Coming home after MM died, Greenson "kept repeating that he was sure it had been an accident.")

(SPADA 1991, p. 326: Danny Greenson said, "Marilyn was dead when my father arrived at her house...")

(NOGUCHI 1984, pp. 80-81: "From my forensic experience with suicide victims, I believe that the sheer number of pills Monroe ingested was too many to swallow 'accidentally.' ")

(SUMMERS 2000, p. 415: "Dr. Greenson would later say he had brought in Dr. Engelberg to try to wean Marilyn away from sleeping pills...")

(CONFIDENTIAL SOURCE: District Attorney's Report dated September 27, 1982. Investigator Alan B. Tomich interviewed MM's physician Dr. Hyman Engelberg who relayed, "I don't know of anything Dr. Greenson gave her. Maybe he did. I cannot answer for him... Only one had been prescribed by me. I had prescribed Nembutal to help her sleep... I knew nothing about any chloral hydrate. I never used chloral hydrate.")

(HEYMANN 1998, p. 312)

67. (BUCHTHAL AND COMMENT 2010, p. 213: While at Payne Whitney in New York, MM wrote to Greenson on February 2, 1961, "PS: Someone when I mentioned his name you used to frown with your moustache and look up at the ceiling. Guess who? He has been (secretly) a very tender friend. I know you won't believe this but you must trust me with my instincts. It was sort of a fling on the wing. I had never done that before but now

I have – but he is very unselfish in bed. From Yves I have heard nothing – but I don't mind since I have such a strong, tender, wonderful memory. I am almost weeping...")

(GREENSON, HILDI. INTERVIEW WITH CATHY GRIFFIN. 4 JUNE 1991: "It's just ludicrous...")

(HEYMANN 1998, p. 322)

(HEYMANN 1998, p. 322: Peter related, "The most surprising revelation of Marilyn's 'free-association' tapes was that in addition to her affairs with the Kennedys, she was also involved with Dr. Greenson, who appeared to be deeply in love with her...")

(GRIFFIN, CATHY. INTERVIEW WITH JEANNE AND C. DAVID HEYMANN. 11 MARCH 1991: John Miner asked Cathy Griffin an intriguing question on Greenson and MM's alleged sexual affair. In addition, Griffin concluded MM may have had sex with Greenson.)

(GILMORE 2007, p. 198: "Like a jealous lover, Greenson manipulated Marilyn's thinking and her choices...")

(GILMORE 2007, p. 198: Ralph Roberts relayed, "He was having her get rid of the people who loved her and were devoted to her...")

(STRAIT, RAYMOND. INTERVIEW WITH JAY MARGOLIS. 18 NOVEMBER 2010: "Women like that who are very lonesome and feel like they've been abandoned...")

(JACOBS 2004, p. 136: George Jacobs relayed, "She was the ultimate Girl Who Can't Say No. In view of a deeply unloved childhood, if a man showed interest...")

(LEAMING 1998, p. 391: Greenson's weakness for "damsels in distress.")

(SUMMERS 2000, p. 394: Joan Greenson's birthday is on July 19, 1940.)

(CONFIDENTIAL SOURCE: GREENSON, JOAN. UNTITLED 90-PAGE MARILYN MONROE MANUSCRIPT, pp. 79-80: "I must admit, I don't really remember what everyone gave me, except for Marilyn..."

The complete work is located in Greenson Papers, Special Collections, UCLA, sealed from the public until January 1, 2039.)

(CONFIDENTIAL SOURCE: GREENSON, JOAN. UNTITLED 90-PAGE MARILYN MONROE MANUSCRIPT, pp. 23-25, 29-30, 32: "Why was it that no matter what she did she was striking?..." The complete work is located in Greenson Papers, Special Collections, UCLA, sealed from the public until January 1, 2039.)

(JAFFE 2004, p. 171: Greenson said to a candidate in training, "In addition to the problem of motivation in the beginning when you assess the patient, there is the problem of a change in motivation that happens when, for example, the patient develops an acute sexual transference...")

(FARBER AND GREEN 1993, p. 109: Accounts of Drs. Leo Rangell and Melvin Mandel.)

(WAHL 1974, pp. 71-72, 75)

(FREEMAN 1993, p. 155: "Only a person who feels loved feels beautiful...")

68. (Miner, John. "Marilyn Uncensored." Playboy. December 2005, p. 197: MM thanks her psychiatrist Greenson for solving her orgasm problem.)

(SUMMERS 2000, p. 255: "Marilyn, he [Greenson] observed, felt that she was frigid. She 'found it difficult to sustain a series of orgasms with the same individual.'")

69. (SPOTO 1993, p. 658: "The only five-week summer vacation [Greenson] took from 1959 to his death in 1979 was in 1962. With no other woman patient was he so involved, and the language of this passage is virtually a copy of his descriptions of MM in his August 20 letter to Marianne Kris.")

(GREENSON 1964, pp. 202-203. The complete work is located in Greenson Papers, Special Collections, UCLA.)

(SUMMERS 2000, p. 254: "Dr Greenson listened to Marilyn's 'venomous resentment' toward Arthur Miller. She claimed her husband was 'cold and unresponsive' to her problems, attracted to other women, and dominated by his mother. She accused

Miller of neglecting his father and not being 'nice' to his children. She said Miller would tell Greenson a different story, but not to believe him.")

(SUMMERS 2000, p. 328: "As for his patient's attitude toward men, Dr. Greenson was to note Marilyn's increasing trend toward random promiscuity. In her last months she was to tell him she was having sex with one of the workmen remodeling her house. Once she invited in a taxi driver who brought her home late at night.")

70. (GREENSON 1964, pp. 203-206. The complete work is located in Greenson Papers, Special Collections, UCLA.)

(SUMMERS 2000, p. 255: "Much later, after Marilyn's death, Greenson told colleagues that he thought the Miller marriage had collapsed 'to a considerable degree' on sexual grounds.")

(JACOBS 2004, pp. 158-159: "Marilyn... was masochistic. She would get fat just to see if men would still like her...")

(GREENSON, HILDI. INTERVIEW WITH CATHY GRIFFIN. 4 JUNE 1991: "She would have no plans whatsoever for an evening... I think at one point she asked the taxi driver to come in and have dinner with her...")

(FARBER AND GREEN 1993, pp. 95-98: Hildi said her husband found out about MM's random promiscuity and "realized this wasn't healthy..." so he often allowed MM to stay for supper like a family member and often attended Greenson's chamber music recitals.)

(FARBER AND GREEN 1993, p. 97: With dark glasses and a black wig, MM joined Danny while he looked for an apartment. She would often use this disguise to attend many of Greenson's lectures.)

(CONFIDENTIAL SOURCE: GREENSON, JOAN. UNTITLED 90-PAGE MARILYN MONROE MANUSCRIPT, pp. 55-56: "Father liked to give lectures, and he was an excellent public speaker..." The complete work is located in Greenson Papers, Special Collections, UCLA, sealed from the public until January 1, 2039.)

(ROSTEN 1973, pp. 99-100: "Finally, after coffee and cake and idle Sunday chatter, the other musicians showed up...")

(FREEMAN 1993, p. 27: A friend of Greenson's Paul Moor said, "Romi may have been the world's worst violinist...")

(CONFIDENTIAL SOURCE: GREENSON, JOAN. UNTITLED 90-PAGE MARILYN MONROE MANUSCRIPT, pp. 59-60: "She would sit in the living room in the big wing-backed chair..." The complete work is located in Greenson Papers, Special Collections, UCLA, sealed from the public until January 1, 2039.)

71. (WEXLER 2002, pp. 241-242)

(SUGARMAN 2000, p. 282: Greenson wrote, "One of the most frequent signals of countertransference reaction is... reacting sexually... to the transference manifestations...")

72. (http://www.jamesgrady.net/hollywood/ghostinthemachine.htm: Author/Screenwriter James Grady's article in the summer of 1992 entitled, "The Ghost in the American Machine.")

(ARNOLD 1987, p. 42: Photographer Eve Arnold took a picture of MM holding the James Joyce book *Ulysses*.)

(Schickel, Richard. "Jottings from an earnest soul." Los Angeles Times. 1 November 2010, pp. D1, D4: MM read books on James Joyce, Heinrich Heine's poetry, and a book on Goya.)

(TARABORRELLI 2009, p. 261: MM and Dostoyevsky's play *The Brothers Karamazov*.)

(http://www.youtube.com/watch?v=ogYy0IJ4d-Q&NR=1: *Marilyn Monroe: A Case for Murder* documentary, 1988, part 4 of 5 – Interview with *Goddess* author Anthony Summers: "morality of atomic testing.")

(STRASBERG 1992, p. 250: Ralph Roberts told Susan Strasberg that MM went to see RFK at the Lawfords' on July 4, 1962 instead of visiting Susie's parents Lee and Paula.)

(SUMMERS 2000, p. 539: "As reported in the FBI briefing, the [meeting] had been... either in the first two weeks of that month, or – at the earliest – in late June... The record, though, makes it more likely that the [meeting] was with Attorney General Robert Kennedy.")

(DePaulo, Lisa. "The Strange, Still Mysterious Death of Marilyn Monroe." Playboy. December 2005, p. 196: DiMaggio's best friends Engelberg and Positano say MM's diary did exist. In fact, Morris Engelberg said DiMaggio told MM to write everything down that RFK was telling her.)

(ENGELBERG 2004, p. 282: Joe, Jr. "was willing to disclose what Marilyn had told him about Bobby Kennedy. She said she spoke with RFK three or four times a week...")

(SUMMERS 2000, p. 467: "Joe DiMaggio's friend, Harry Hall, who accompanied him to the house later on Sunday, says DiMaggio 'looked for what he referred to as a book, and it was gone. All her personal notes were gone.'")

(CRAMER 2001, p. 416)

(BROWN AND BARHAM 1993, p. 379: Tom Reddin said, "If you've been intimate with the President and the Attorney General...")

(http://www.youtube.com/watch?v=KxfQUUCw8p4&feature= related: "In Search of..." *The Death of Marilyn Monroe*, History Channel documentary, 1980, part 3 of 3: Deputy Coroner's Aide Lionel Grandison.)

(WOLFE 1998, p. 36: Former OCID detective Mike Rothmiller told Wolfe how he saw a copy of MM's diary, not the original.)

(ROTHMILLER, MIKE. INTERVIEW WITH JAY MARGOLIS. 26 SEPTEMBER 2010: Donald Wolfe accurately quoted Rothmiller and his recollection of the contents in MM's red diary.)

(SUMMERS 2000, p. 399: Skinny D'Amato and how the exposure of RFK's affair with MM and the exposure of sensitive political information would have been the "big fall" for RFK and his family name.)

(STRAIT, RAYMOND. INTERVIEW WITH JAY MARGOLIS. 13 DECEMBER 2010: At Cal-Neva, MM also told Johnny Rosselli, in addition to Skinny D'Amato, about her plans to get back at the Kennedy brothers.)

(VAN METER 2003, p. 192: Skinny D'Amato on MM's troubles with RFK.)

(STRAIT, RAYMOND. INTERVIEW WITH JAY MARGOLIS. 18 NOVEMBER 2010: JFK indeed had his sights set on Ms. Dickinson.)

73. (http://www.youtube.com/watch?v=Iy56XWtUb8s&feature=related: *Marilyn Monroe: A Case for Murder* documentary, 1988, part 5 of 5 – Interview with former FBI agent Bill Roemer: "Certainly the mob wouldn't have wanted to murder her at that particular point because they would've wanted something to go on and on so they could've used that to blackmail the Kennedys. So, I don't see that they would have the motivation.")

(GIANCANA 2010, p. 411: "With Marilyn Monroe, Mooney would show them [the Kennedy brothers] just how truly vulnerable they were.")

(SUMMERS 2000, p. 507: "Giancana knew too much about the Kennedys. By organizing massive vote-stealing in Illinois, he had helped Kennedy win the presidency in the first place.")

(GIANCANA 2010, pp. 387, 392: "For the task of tailing the Attorney General and the President, Mooney selected his CIA coconspirator Bob Maheu…")

(RAPPLEYE AND BECKER 1991, pp. 181, 184: "Maheu did, in fact, have connections to the mob. One was through Jimmy Hoffa, who hired Maheu to do electronics work in 1957. Another was through his close friend Edward Bennett Williams, the powerhouse Washington attorney who represented Hoffa before the McClellan Committee and, before that, Frank Costello. But his closest contact to the mob, his friendship with a true Mafioso, was John Rosselli.")

(http://www.guardian.co.uk/world/2008/aug/20/usa?INTCMP=SRCH: Carlson, Michael. "FBI agent and CIA fixer who became Howard Hughes's bagman." *Guardian*. 20 August 2008: "When Maheu was hired to serve a subpoena on an elusive Las Vegas casino…")

(FBI 2009, document dated July 13, 1961: "Rosselli admitted that he has known Robert Maheu…")

(RAPPLEYE AND BECKER 1991, p. 158: On his close friend John Rosselli, Maheu reflected, "All my children fell in love with him…")

(HANCOCK 2003, p. 106: "The FBI continued to monitor Rosselli during 1964 and 1965...")

(COCKBURN AND ST. CLAIR 2001, p. 104: "It was in late 1961 that Sam Giancana approached his CIA contact, a D.C.-based private detective named Robert Maheu, with a personal problem – he suspected his girlfriend, Phyllis McGuire, one of the McGuire Sisters singing group, of having an affair in Las Vegas with comedian Dan Rowan, of Rowan and Martin. In return for his assistance in the Castro assassination plots, Giancana wanted the Agency to bug Rowan's Vegas hotel room.")

(http://www.guardian.co.uk/world/2008/aug/20/usa?INTCMP=SRCH: Carlson, Michael. "FBI agent and CIA fixer who became Howard Hughes's bagman." Guardian. 20 August 2008: "When Maheu's operatives were caught in the act...")

(HERSH 1998, pp. 289-290: "The case was turned over to the FBI, whose agents were told in late April 1961 that the CIA was working with Sam Giancana and the mob...")

(FBI 2009, document dated March 6, 1967: "I was informed of the following on a highly confidential basis by former Attorney General Kennedy during a conference in my office on May 9, 1962: He indicated that a few days prior thereto he had been advised by CIA that Robert A. Maheu had been hired by CIA to approach Sam Giancana with a proposition of paying $150,000 to hire some gunmen to go into Cuba and kill Castro. He further stated CIA admitted having assisted Maheu in making the 'bugging' installation in Las Vegas [of Dan Rowan] which uncovered this clandestine operation and for this reason CIA could not afford to have any action taken against Giancana or Maheu. Mr. Kennedy stated that upon learning CIA had not cleared its action in hiring Maheu and Giancana with the Department of Justice he issued orders that CIA should never again take such steps without first checking with the Department of Justice. Mr. Kennedy further advised that because of this matter it would be very difficult to initiate any prosecution against Giancana, as Giancana could immediately bring out the fact the United States Government had approached him to arrange for the assassination of Castro. He stated the same was true concerning any action we might take against Maheu for any violation in which he might become involved.")

(RAPPLEYE AND BECKER 1991, pp. 213, 217: "On May 22, 1961, Hoover dispatched a memo to Robert Kennedy... The memo carried a significance beyond the political machinations of the FBI director. It established on the record that the President's brother was aware that the CIA had engaged a top Mafioso, one of the very gangsters Kennedy had targeted for aggressive prosecution, in their 'dirty business.' ")

(GIANCANA 2010, p. 386: Sam Giancana related, "So they offered me one hundred fifty thousand bucks for the hit.")

(HEYMANN 1998, p. 264)

(*JFK: A Presidency Revealed* History Channel documentary, 2003: Robert Maheu was allegedly a close confidant of the Kennedys.)

(http://www.youtube.com/watch?v=ogYy0IJ4d-Q&NR=1: *Marilyn Monroe: A Case for Murder* documentary, 1988, part 4 of 5 – Fred Otash on how the CIA "wanted a derogatory profile on the Kennedys.")

(BROWN AND BARHAM 1993, p. 450: Otash wanted his epitaph to read in effect: "The only detective who worked for and against the Mafia; for and against the CIA; for and against the FBI; for and against Marilyn Monroe.")

(BROWN AND BARHAM 1993, p. 452: Fred Otash said, "It was a game. In fact, I put in one system and, at a crucial point, sent tape copies to three sources...")

(SCHLESINGER 2002, pp. 482-483: "Maheu brought in John Rosselli, a minor crook-about-town he had known in Las Vegas. Rosselli, who had no illusions about his middling rank in the underworld, brought in the Chicago big shot Sam Giancana, who was a don and could make the right connections.")

(*Say Goodbye to the President* documentary, 1985: "The idea that emerged later was for the American Mafia to assassinate Castro on behalf of the CIA...")

(STRAIT, RAYMOND. INTERVIEW WITH JAY MARGOLIS. 13 DECEMBER 2010: "He knew that Giancana's people did it. He knew that. He knew who paid the money...")

(STRAIT, RAYMOND. INTERVIEW WITH JAY MARGOLIS. 13 DECEMBER 2010: "I don't think the FBI was on the site at the time all this stuff happened. I think they stayed as far away from that as they could get.")

(WOLFE 1998, pp. 92-93: Suppressed 20/20 Sylvia Chase interview with Fred Otash.)

(BROWN AND BARHAM 1993, pp. 456-458: Via a transcript edited by Otash, Schwarz read the sanitized version of the tapes versus Strait's first-hand listening of the actual tapes that indicated murder and multiple persons in the room, hushing and whispering.)

(STRAIT, RAYMOND. INTERVIEW WITH JAY MARGOLIS. 18 NOVEMBER 2010: "I had all those tapes in my garage in a sealed-up box for ten years... I never opened them...")

(STRAIT, RAYMOND. INTERVIEW WITH JAY MARGOLIS. 13 DECEMBER 2010: The voices on tape could not be understood over wiretaps: "Not at all. No. They didn't have too much to say. They had a job to do and they went in there and did it.")

(STRAIT, RAYMOND. INTERVIEW WITH JAY MARGOLIS. 18 NOVEMBER 2010: "Giancana in Chicago is the one who ordered the direct hit on her. Two of his people were there in the bedroom with her...")

(STRAIT, RAYMOND. INTERVIEW WITH JAY MARGOLIS. 18 NOVEMBER 2010: "That Newcomb, she hid in the closet...")

(WOLFE 1998, pp. 3, 463: Neighbors say Newcomb screamed, "Murderers! You murderers! Are you satisfied now that she's dead?")

(STRAIT, RAYMOND. INTERVIEW WITH JAY MARGOLIS. 18 NOVEMBER 2010: "The last words he ever said to her were...")

(EBBINS, MILTON. INTERVIEW WITH DONALD SPOTO. 22 SEPTEMBER 1992: "Number one, he never would've killed Marilyn because Frank was in love with Marilyn!")

(ROMANOFF, GLORIA. INTERVIEW WITH JAY MARGOLIS. 2 SEPTEMBER 2010: "Giancana, whatever you may think of him, would never have violated his friendship with Frank, not for one moment.")

(MOORE, TERRY. INTERVIEW WITH JAY MARGOLIS. 23 NOVEMBER 2010: "Giancana was very nice to her. I think the Kennedys didn't want him to be friends with her any longer.")

(GIANCANA 2010, pp. 412-414: The authors argued that MM was murdered in the presence of four men with *one* Nembutal/chloral hydrate suppository. They assume she died in her main bedroom.)

(STRAIT, RAYMOND. INTERVIEW WITH JAY MARGOLIS. 13 DECEMBER 2010: "There were two of them in the house. The others were Freddy Otash and Peter Lawford...")

(STRAIT, RAYMOND. INTERVIEW WITH JAY MARGOLIS. 18 NOVEMBER 2010: "Peter was drunk and hysterical. Fred slapped the shit out of him...")

(STRAIT, RAYMOND. INTERVIEW WITH JAY MARGOLIS. 18 MARCH 2011: On Lawford and Newcomb's presence in MM's home before she died, "I know that they were both there. I do not know that they arrived together.")

(STRAIT, RAYMOND. INTERVIEW WITH JAY MARGOLIS. 18 NOVEMBER 2010: "Fred was there in the house as she was dying...")

(STRAIT, RAYMOND. INTERVIEW WITH JAY MARGOLIS. 13 DECEMBER 2010: "Peter got scared and hysterical so he called Fred.")

(STRAIT, RAYMOND. INTERVIEW WITH JAY MARGOLIS. 18 NOVEMBER 2010: "Fred says, 'You meet me at Marilyn's house.' And Fred showed up with his sound man...")

(http://www.youtube.com/watch?v=OK5WFA5qOOc&feature
=related: *Marilyn: The Last Word* documentary, 1993, part 4 of
6: With the release of Sam and Chuck Giancana's book *Double
Cross*, Anthony Summers suggested that it's possible that Sam
Giancana, acting on orders from the CIA, ordered to have
MM killed in an attempt to embroil RFK in a scandal.)

(STRAIT, RAYMOND. INTERVIEW WITH JAY
MARGOLIS. 13 DECEMBER 2010: Strait is certain MM
died in her main bedroom. He also maintains that there
were two men sent out to kill her not four as Sam and Chuck
Giancana mention.)

(SPOTO 1993, p. 585: A suppository was not used on MM.)

(SLATZER 1992, p. 276: Sam Giancana's daughter Antoinette
vehemently denied that the Mafia had a hand in MM's death.)

(STRAIT, RAYMOND. INTERVIEW WITH JAY
MARGOLIS. 13 DECEMBER 2010: Strait is adamant that
the CIA had nothing to do with MM's death.)

74. (SUMMERS 2000, p. 433: Peter Lawford's ex-wife Debbie
Gould said Peter told her, "Marilyn took her last big enema.")

(SUMMERS 2000, p. 433: "Amy Greene, Marilyn's friend in
New York, says Marilyn took frequent enemas, as early as the
mid-fifties.")

(TARABORRELLI 2009, p. 494: "It's been maintained by
many people that Eunice Murray customarily gave Marilyn
Monroe enemas.")

(SLATZER 1975, p. 315: Noguchi's autopsy report read: "The
colon shows marked congestion and purplish discoloration.")

(http://www.youtube.com/watch?v=IS0nLApY4Tg&feature
=related: *The Death of Marilyn Monroe* documentary, part 5
of 5: John Miner's account of how a crime scene was never
established as shown by newsreel footage.)

(BROWN AND BARHAM 1993, pp. 438-439)

Jay Margolis

75. (ABRAMS, ARNOLD, M.D. INTERVIEW WITH DONALD SPOTO. 2 NOVEMBER 1992: "The odds that she took pills and died from them are astronomically unlikely... I have never seen anything like this in an autopsy. There was something crazy going on in this woman's colon...")

(Rebello, Stephen. "Somebody Killer Her." Playboy. December 2005, p. 188: Miner maintains MM couldn't have given herself the enema that killed her.)

(WOLFE 1998, pp. 7, 453: Clemmons "then asked if Monroe was in the practice of using a hypodermic needle or syringe. Engelberg said she was not, and that the medications prescribed were all oral; however, the doctor stated he had been treating her for diarrhea and had recently administered some injections... This comment by Dr. Engelberg to Sergeant Clemmons has gone unreported for over thirty years. It was discovered in the transcript of a talk given by Jack Clemmons on March 22, 1991, to the Los Angeles organization 'Marilyn Remembered.' He has recently reconfirmed the statement. It has a significance relating to the autopsy. Regarding the digestive tract, Dr. Noguchi states, 'The colon shows marked congestion and discoloration.' This heretofore unexplained notation has given substance to erroneous speculation that the mode of death was via a suppository or enema infusion of barbiturates. But according to Monroe's New York internist, Dr. Richard Cottrell, she had episodes of colitis brought about by emotional stress, and in 1961 she was diagnosed as having an ulcerated colon...")

(MINER, JOHN. INTERVIEW WITH DONALD SPOTO. 11 JUNE 1992: "Dr. Curphey in one of his more exuberant moments said, 'Oh, she gobbled 40 pills all at one time.' That's not possible...")

(BROWN AND BARHAM 1993, pp. 427-428: John Miner said, "If you're trying to kill the lady and need to make no mistakes, then this is the way to do it. Foolproof.")

(HEYMANN 1998, p. 324: John Miner related, " 'The thought of her having been killed deliberately [via enema] by someone – namely, murder – did not cross my mind at the time [but] if you wanted to kill somebody,' that method would 'leave no residue in the stomach.' ")

76. (WOLFE 1998, p. 459: "At Murray's request, Norman Jefferies stayed on into the evening. Jefferies recalled that his mother-in-law was unnerved by the day's events, and he watched television with her, while Marilyn remained in her room.")

(SUMMERS 2000, p. 537: "Bolaños… said that – in a telephone call on the night she died – Marilyn told him 'something that will one day shock the whole world.' At the time of the interview – in 1983 – I did not take him too seriously. Today, having glimpsed FBI's Security file on Marilyn, one wonders.")

(SUMMERS 2000, p. 416: "José Bolaños says he telephoned Marilyn from the Ships Restaurant, not far from her home, between nine-thirty and ten o'clock… He does say Marilyn ended the conversation by simply laying down the phone – she did not hang up while he was on the line.")

(WOLFE 1998, p. 461: "There was a commotion at the door, and Marilyn went to see what it was." José Bolaños said MM put the phone down and never came back on the line. She had left the room to investigate a noise.)

(WOLFE 1998, p. 36: "Norman Jefferies also verified the existence of the diary. He recalled that Marilyn kept her red diary either in her bedroom or locked in the file cabinet located in the guest cottage. Jefferies said that on the night she died, her filing cabinet was broken into and many of the contents were removed.")

(Miner, John. "Marilyn Uncensored." Playboy. December 2005, p. 199: MM discussed why she used enemas.)

(SPOTO 1993, pp. 585, 587: "…an enema – something on which Marilyn often relied for other purposes.")

(VITACCO-ROBLES 1999, p. 106: The guest cottage had a bath directly adjacent to it so water was indeed easily accessible for an enema.)

(VICTOR 1999, p. 137: "It is Haspiel's opinion that Marilyn was murdered as part of a conspiracy reaching up to the highest echelons of government, an opinion based upon tapes reputedly recorded by wiretapper Bernie Spindel.")

(HASPIEL 1993, pp. 199-200: "Suddenly without thinking further, the politician [RFK] grabbed for a pillow across the bed...")

(http://www.nydailynews.com/gossip/ bwiddicombe/2007/08/02/2007-08-02_new_marilyn_death_ docu_is_in_the_offing.html: Widdicombe, Ben. "New Marilyn death docu is in the offing." New York Daily News. 2 August 2007, p. 20: An FBI agent witnesses RFK enter MM's home. Keya Morgan said, "He saw Bobby Kennedy and other men go inside the house. He heard them screaming and yelling in the guest cottage. They were in the guest cottage, not in her bedroom where her body was found.")

(WOLFE 1998, p. 461: "Norman Jefferies recalled that between 9:30 and 10:00 P.M., Robert Kennedy, accompanied by two men, appeared at the door. They ordered Jefferies and Murray from the house.")

(WOLFE 1998, p. 463: Wolfe noted that the men with RFK were later identified as "two detectives assigned to Kennedy as security officers.")

(SUMMERS 2000, p. 416: "At about ten o'clock, Ralph Roberts learned next day, a woman with a 'slurred voice' called his answering service. Told Roberts was out, the caller hung up.")

(AMADOR, ELIAS, M.D. INTERVIEW WITH JAY MARGOLIS. 11 JANUARY 2011)

(SUMMERS 2000, p. 516: Detective Sergeant Byron said, "Engelberg told me he'd had a call from the housekeeper who said Marilyn was either dead or unconscious...")

(SMITH 2005, pp. 74-75: "Tom Reddin, Parker's assistant, now retired, told me that, in fact, a great deal of secret investigation into Marilyn's death took place, as was evidenced by a bulky file which he knew to exist. We now know that the inquiry was carried out by John Dickie at the behest of Chief Deputy District Attorney Manley J. Bowler. The file included details of an interview with Robert Kennedy, but none of this was ever released. The file disappeared, a slim 'public' file taking its place, Tom Reddin said... It would seem [Chief Parker] was totally satisfied that Robert Kennedy was not in any way involved with Marilyn's demise, and his defense for his high-handed – indeed unlawful – actions would likely be that justice, as he saw it, demanded that Robert Kennedy and the President be protected from such an infamous conspiracy. Tom Reddin, who knew his boss as few others would, speaks extremely highly of him. It would appear, therefore, that if he had not been convinced of the innocence of the Kennedys he would in no way have involved himself in such an enormous deception.")

(SUMMERS 2000, p. 425: Helen Parker recalled her husband telling her regarding MM's death, "This thing has to be straightened out in more ways than one.")

(*The Marilyn Files* documentary, 1991: Jack Clemmons and Sam Yorty's comments about Police Chief William Parker.)

(WOLFE 1998, p. 49: Former mayor Sam Yorty said, "Hamilton's Intelligence Division was Parker's version of the FBI. Parker believed that he was the man who would one day succeed J. Edgar Hoover, and Bobby and Jack Kennedy led Parker to believe he was their choice.")

(STRAIT, RAYMOND. INTERVIEW WITH JAY MARGOLIS. 13 DECEMBER 2010: When MM was being smothered by a pillow, the voices of the men in the room were indistinguishable.)

(STRAIT, RAYMOND. INTERVIEW WITH JAY MARGOLIS. 18 NOVEMBER 2010: Strait agreed that an enema was given to MM.)

(SUMMERS 2000, p. 469: "Two fragmentary reports, one from a police source, one from a former member of the Twentieth Century-Fox staff, Frank Neill, suggest Kennedy arrived in the city by helicopter, putting down near the studio's Stage 18, in an open space then used by helicopters serving the area near the Beverly Hilton.")

(BROWN AND BARHAM 1993, p. 328: "The chopper had been approved to land at just after 11:00 A.M., as duly noted in the studio's security log... Neill later noted that Kennedy was preoccupied, gazing from side to side before sliding into the backseat. Through the open door, Neill caught a glimpse of the carefully tanned face of Peter Lawford.")

(SLATZER 1975, p. 232: Mrs. Murray related, "I saw that the telephone was under her. She was lying on it.")

(WOLFE 1998, pp. 461-462: Norman Jefferies said that when he and Mrs. Murray returned, they discovered MM in the guest cottage. Jefferies also noted that the phone was under her.)

(http://www.youtube.com/watch?v=ORac4GJKbqA&feature=related: "In Search of..." *The Death of Marilyn Monroe*, History Channel documentary, 1980, part 2 of 3: Mrs. Murray said, "I believe that Marilyn did *not* commit suicide purposefully...")

(SUMMERS 2000, p. 425: Helen Parker on her husband drawing a question mark in the air regarding the MM case.)

(DOUGHERTY 2001, p. 179: "Did someone know she was in trouble?...")

(BROWN AND BARHAM 1993, p. 455: Ted Schwarz, author of *Candy Barr*, reported how Otash told him that he heard over surveillance that RFK and Peter Lawford knew MM was in trouble but let her die instead. However, Raymond Strait made it clear to me that Otash was also at the house as MM was dying.)

77. (WOLFE 1998, p. 14: Undertaker Guy Hockett said rigor mortis places the death sometime before midnight between 9:30 and 11:30 P.M.)

(SLATZER 1992, p. 259: "Dr. J. DeWitt Fox shares Jack Clemmons' view that Marilyn was killed by a combination of two different drugs, but believes they were administered in a different way.")

(SLATZER 1975, p. 315: Noguchi's autopsy report read: "The stomach is almost completely empty...")

(http://www.youtube.com/watch?v=MzQ27ElP9ik&feature=related: *Marilyn Monroe: A Case for Murder* documentary, 1988, part 3 of 5 – Interview with medical expert Dr. Sidney Weinberg: "Let me tell you about the doubts that were raised in my mind...")

(SUMMERS 2000, pp. 541-542: Noguchi's consideration of murder: "She had a bruise, on her back or near the hip, that has never been fully explained...")

(EBBINS, MILTON. INTERVIEW WITH DONALD SPOTO. 6 AUGUST 1992: "When there's an overdose of drugs, the first thing the doctor would give her was a shot of adrenaline.")

(Carroll, Ronald H., and Alan B. Tomich. "The Death of Marilyn Monroe – Report to the District Attorney." December 1982, p. 13: "In the November 23, 1982 edition of the Globe, a weekly tabloid published in West Palm Beach, Florida, the headline article states that a former ambulance driver by the name of James Hall alleges that he saw Marilyn Monroe murdered.")

(Blackburn, John, Chuck Orman, and Dan McDonald. "I Saw Marilyn Murdered." Globe. 23 November 1982, Volume 29, Number 47, p. 4: Hall said he arrived at MM's "between three and four in the morning.")

(CONFIDENTIAL SOURCE: In a recorded phone call sometime after August 11, 1982, Carroll told Hall, "One of the things I'm concerned about. You mentioned the man in the business suit used a needle in the heart...")

(WOLFE 1998, p. 77: "The time discrepancy is perhaps explained by Hall's disclosure that he worked a twenty-four-hour shift...")

(SUMMERS 2000, pp. 514-515, 604: Including Joe Tarnowski and Tom Fears, "No less than seven former employees of Schaefer's, one now a company vice president [Carl Bellonzi] recall hearing about the call in 1962.")

(CONFIDENTIAL SOURCE: In a recorded call sometime after August 11, 1982, Hall told investigator Alan Tomich, "You go in and you turn to the left and the bed was facing longways as you're looking at it...")

(http://www.youtube.com/watch?v=TyCkSTsaO_M: *Marilyn Monroe: A Case for Murder* documentary, 1988, part 2 of 5: James Hall's account: "We did what we could to save her...")

(*The Marilyn Files* documentary, 1991: James Hall said, "She was naked. She had no sheet, no blanket... There was no water glass. No alcohol.")

(SPADA 1991, p. 325: "According to Hall, when he arrived with his partner, Marilyn was in the guest bedroom...")

(NEWCOMB, PATRICIA. INTERVIEW WITH DONALD SPOTO. 3 AUGUST 1992: "Whoever the writer was who said I leaned over the body screaming, 'She's dead! She's dead!' I never saw the body. So what is he talking about, this ambulance driver?...")

(SUMMERS 2000, p. 514: Hall "says Marilyn's assistant, Pat Newcomb, was distraught, and already there when he arrived, and that Marilyn was not yet dead.")

(GUILES 1970, p. 384: "Pat was awakened by a phone call at 4 A.M. It was lawyer Mickey Rudin...")

(Carroll, Ronald H., and Alan B. Tomich. "The Death of Marilyn Monroe – Report to the District Attorney." December 1982, p. 13: "Mr. Hall first contacted the Los Angeles District Attorney's Office on 8/11/82. Thereafter, under a code name 'Rick Stone,' he telephonically contacted this office several times.")

(Blackburn, John, Chuck Orman, and Dan McDonald. "I Saw Marilyn Murdered." Globe. 23 November 1982, Volume 29, Number 47, p. 4: Hall said, "My driver and I had just dropped a patient off at a hospital...")

(MURRAY 1975, pp. 125-126: "Sometime during the earlier part of the day, the bedside table was delivered and Marilyn wrote a check for it.")

(SLATZER 1975, p. 312: In the original autopsy report, Noguchi noted only two bruises, "A slight ecchymotic area is noted in the left hip and left side of lower back.")

(BROWN AND BARHAM 1993, pp. 382-383: Noguchi mentioned for the first time there were bruises on MM's arms, not included in the original autopsy report!)

(SLATZER 1992, p. 207: Hall took credit for bruises on MM's arms that Noguchi mentioned to Brown and Barham.)

(Blackburn, John, Chuck Orman, and Dan McDonald. "I Saw Marilyn Murdered." Globe. 23 November 1982, Volume 29, Number 47, pp. 4-5: Hall continued, "So, my partner and I rolled her off the bed and dragged her across the carpet into the hall...")

78. (Blackburn, John, Chuck Orman, and Dan McDonald. "I Saw Marilyn Murdered." Globe. 23 November 1982, Volume 29, Number 47, p. 5: "Incredibly, when Hall was shown a photograph of Eunice Murray as she looked at the time, he shook his head and declared: 'This is not the woman who was screaming hysterically outside the house and hovered over us the entire time we were working on Marilyn...'")

(SPADA 1991, pp. 325-326: James Hall relayed, "Just as Marilyn started coming around, this doctor arrived. I believe it was Dr. Greenson. He had a bag with him...")

(SLATZER 1992, p. 210: Hall said, "I absolutely believe that Dr. Ralph Greenson murdered Marilyn Monroe...")

(*The Marilyn Files* documentary, 1991)

(GRIFFIN, CATHY. INTERVIEW WITH JEANNE AND C. DAVID HEYMANN. 11 MARCH 1991: Jeanne and C. David Heymann wrote in their notes, "One of the possible scenarios offered by Griffin was that Dr. Greenson murdered Marilyn Monroe by injecting her in the heart with some substance, brown...")

(AMADOR, ELIAS, M.D. INTERVIEW WITH JAY MARGOLIS. 11 JANUARY 2011: "If that's true, that's murder. That is point-blank murder. That's never done for any reason except to kill.")

(*The Marilyn Files* documentary, 1991: "In 1982, Hall claimed that he and his partner Murray Liebowitz drove one of the ambulances to Marilyn's house that night.")

(WOLFE 1998, p. 77: "Hall later identified the hysterical woman as Pat Newcomb, the man in the jumpsuit as Peter Lawford, the doctor as Ralph Greenson, and the police officer as Sergeant Marvin Iannone. Hall's revelation was a fascinating but improbable account of events surrounding the circumstances of Marilyn Monroe's death. If his story was to be believed, it would explain the neighbor's sighting of the ambulance and police car late Saturday night.")

(*The Marilyn Files* documentary, 1991: James Hall said, "They moved her and they put her into the master bedroom. When Jack Clemmons, the first officer at the scene got there, he said she looked exactly like what she was: a dead body that had been laid in that position on the bed in the master bedroom, facedown covered with a sheet...")

79. (Blackburn, John, Chuck Orman, and Dan McDonald. "I Saw Marilyn Murdered." Globe. 23 November 1982, Volume 29, Number 47, p. 5: "Private investigator John Harrison, who had been conducting polygraph examinations for 40 years, reports: 'When I was first brought into this, I thought the whole thing was a fairy tale...' ")

(Blackburn, John, Chuck Orman, and Dan McDonald. "I Saw Marilyn Murdered." Globe. 23 November 1982, Volume 29, Number 47, p. 5: "Hall was interviewed while under hypnosis by Henry Koder, a professional forensic hypnotist with more than 20 years of law-enforcement experience and veteran of hundreds of major crime investigations...")

(WOLFE 1998, pp. 80-81: In 1992, polygraph examiner Donald E. Fraser relayed to Wolfe that he tested Hall ten years after the release of the article from Globe, "There's no question that James Hall is telling the truth...")

(http://www.youtube.com/watch?v=i-v5j497lO4: *The Marilyn Files* Live TV Special, 1992, part 3 of 6: Fraser gave Hall polygraphs on August 10, 1992.)

(SPADA 1991, p. 326: Danny Greenson said, "I hate all this speculation, and especially that guy who says he saw my father plunge a needle into Marilyn's heart. That's ridiculous...")

(GREENSON, HILDI. INTERVIEW WITH CATHY GRIFFIN. 4 JUNE 1991: "I sometimes have a feeling that this ambulance driver went on a call that night somewhere else...")

(CONFIDENTIAL SOURCE: District Attorney's Report dated September 27, 1982. Investigator Al Tomich interviewed MM's physician Dr. Hyman Engelberg who said he didn't see any needle marks from an injection to MM's chest, "I would have noticed any gross things. I didn't notice any such thing.")

(WOLFE 1998, p. 81: In a telephonic interview, Murray Liebowitz validated that Hall was his partner, not Ken Hunter, and that MM did indeed die in the guest cottage, not in her main bedroom.)

(SUMMERS 2000, p. 514: "Hall's story receives some corroboration from his family. His father, Dr. George Hall, a retired police surgeon, says his son told him of the incident at the time. Hall's former wife and sister say the same.")

(WOLFE 1998, p. 80: "Interviews with Hall's father, his former wife, his sister, and his longtime friend Mike Carlson confirm that Hall told them his story shortly after Marilyn's death.")

(WOLFE 1998, p. 75: "Her body exhibited signs of cyanosis – the classic indication of rapid death. In cyanosis the body takes on a bluish cast due to the rapid depletion of oxygen and reduced levels of hemoglobin...")

(http://www.youtube.com/watch?v=0nMEfgElwPE&feature=related: Leigh Wiener said in a late 1980s documentary, "They'll look like a frozen cube of ice...")

(WOLFE 1998, p. 10: James Bacon said, "I stayed there long enough to get a good view of the body...")

(http://www.youtube.com/watch?v=MzQ27ElP9ik&feature=related, *Marilyn Monroe: A Case for Murder* documentary, 1988, part 3 of 5: John Miner's account: "Her body was examined minutely by both of us under magnification to see if we could find any needle mark...")

(SLATZER 1992, pp. 134-136: John Miner related, "We both examined the body very carefully with a magnifying glass for needle marks. It would have taken a substantial dosage of barbiturates to kill her, and that would have produced a noticeable bruise. If drugs had been administered by way of injection, there would have been evidence of it. Any needle produces at least a small ecchymosis, a bruise... There were no needle marks on the body. There was no indication that the drugs had been administered by way of hypodermic needle. If there had been needle marks, they would have been apparent on such a very careful examination of the body... The duodenum was felt all the way down to the ileum, which is at the end of the small intestine but there was nothing obstructive.")

(NOGUCHI 1984, p. 67: "I found no needle marks, and so indicated on the body diagram in the autopsy report. But, interestingly I did find evidence which might have indicated violence – and I also marked that evidence on the diagram. On Monroe's lower left back was an area of slight ecchymosis, a dark reddish-blue bruise that results from bleeding into the tissues through injury. And the color of the bruise indicated that it was fresh rather than old," which supported James Hall's account of dropping her.)

(NOGUCHI 1984, p. 221: In the John Belushi case, Noguchi wrote, "The very fact that the fresh punctures had been so difficult to discover worried me...")

(WOLFE 1998, p. 28)

(SLATZER 1992, p. 258: Dr. J. DeWitt Fox explains how blue post-mortem lividity could have hidden a needle injection on MM's chest. Sergeant Clemmons agreed with Fox and James Hall. Hall told Melvin B. Bergman for *The Marilyn Files* that since he and Liebowitz had discovered MM in the guest cottage, she later must have been moved from the guest cottage to the bedroom where Sergeant Clemmons officially discovered her. MM's body was then placed facedown on the bed to hide the needle mark from Greenson's injection of pentobarbital.)

(Carroll, Ronald H., and Alan B. Tomich. "The Death of Marilyn Monroe – Report to the District Attorney." December 1982, p. 15: "Lividity, as described to our investigators, is a process by which blood drains...")

(SLATZER 1975, p. 311: Under the heading EXTERNAL EXAMINATION, Noguchi noted in his autopsy report, "Lavidity [sic] of face and chest...")

(BROWN AND BARHAM 1993, p. 373: John Miner's admission that since the kidneys appeared to be clean of the barbiturates then an injection would have bypassed the stomach.)

(Carroll, Ronald H., and Alan B. Tomich. "The Death of Marilyn Monroe – Report to the District Attorney." December 1982, pp. 13, 15-16: "According to Hall, the doctor ultimately plunged a giant syringe filled with a brownish fluid into her heart, after which she quickly died while on her back on the floor...")

(WOLFE 1998, p. 29: "The faint lividity noted on her posterior must have occurred immediately after death, when Monroe's body was on its back for a period of time before being placed facedown...")

(AMADOR, ELIAS, M.D. INTERVIEW WITH JAY MARGOLIS. 11 JANUARY 2011: MM was given an enema containing thirteen to nineteen 100-mg Nembutals and seventeen 500-mg chloral hydrates. Dr. Amador originally estimated between 15 – 20 Nembutals; however, 13 – 19 was the amount of Nembutal left in MM's bottle at the time the enema was given to her. The autopsy report noted that 10 chloral hydrates were remaining from a bottle of 50.)

(BROWN AND BARHAM 1993, p. 340: Clemmons related that Greenson was "cocky, almost challenging me to accuse him of something.")

(HEYMANN 1998, p. 322: Peter Lawford said, "Greenson had thus been set up by Bobby to 'take care' of Marilyn.")

(Blackburn, John, Chuck Orman, and Dan McDonald. "I Saw Marilyn Murdered." Globe. 23 November 1982, Volume 29, Number 47, pp. 5, 7: Dr. Sidney Weinberg stated, "Knowing the results of the toxicology examination and the negative findings in the stomach...")

(WOLFE 1998, p. 463: Wolfe incorrectly surmised, "In the presence of Bobby Kennedy, she was injected with enough barbiturate to kill fifteen people.")

(SLATZER 1992, pp. 257-258: John Miner said, "The amount of drugs found in Marilyn's body was so large that had it been administered by injection [containing high dosages of Nembutal and chloral hydrate], the star would have died almost immediately...")

80. (Carroll, Ronald H., and Alan B. Tomich. "The Death of Marilyn Monroe – Report to the District Attorney." December 1982, p. 16: "Since Mr. Hall's statements have surfaced another person, a Mr. Ken Hunter, has been located who claims to have been

an ambulance driver who responded to the Monroe residence in the early morning hours of August 5, 1962. He reports that he arrived at the scene in the morning hours with his partner, whom he believes with reasonable certainty to have been a Mr. Murray Liebowitz, and entered the Monroe residence within one or two minutes of their arrival... He reports that after he and his partner made the cursory observations of the body, they both left the scene.")

(SUMMERS 2000, pp. 462-463: "The D.A.'s staff talked to a former ambulance driver called Ken Hunter...")

(http://www.cbsnews.com/stories/2006/04/22/48hours/main1534542.shtml: Tape-recorded interview with Schaefer Ambulance driver Ken Hunter conducted by investigator Al Tomich on December 14, 1982.)

(CONFIDENTIAL SOURCE: Complete December 14, 1982 tape-recording of Al Tomich interviewing Ken Hunter.)

(*The Marilyn Files* documentary, 1991:

LANDAU: We came home quite late. It must have been close to 1 o'clock. There was quite a few cars and an ambulance here. We didn't know what happened until we found out she was dead.

NARRATOR: We asked him if he noticed any police cars.

LANDAU: Yes, there was a police car.

NARRATOR: When was that?

LANDAU: That was the same night.

NARRATOR: At the same time?

LANDAU: It was here with the ambulance.)

(http://www.youtube.com/watch?v=ymremwgTl-Q: *Marilyn: The Last Word* documentary, 1993, part 1 of 6: Abe Landau says, "We were out to a dinner party and we arrived home. It must have been close to 1 o'clock. And we spoke to someone who said Marilyn Monroe had died.")

(WOLFE 1998, p. 79: "There was a bigger problem with Hunter's story: Ken Hunter didn't work for Schaefer in 1962. Carl Bellonzi, Vice President of the Schaefer Ambulance Service, who has worked for the company for over forty years, stated in 1993 that Ken Hunter wasn't employed by Schaefer until the mid-1970s, and that Hunter never worked the West Los Angeles area. He was an employee in the 1970s and 1980s in the Orange County office.")

(BELLONZI, CARL ANGELO. INTERVIEW WITH DONALD WOLFE. 11 SEPTEMBER 1993)

(*The Marilyn Files* documentary, 1991: James E. Hall's social security number and employment records prove that he did indeed work for Schaefer Ambulance in August 1962.)

(WOLFE 1998, p. 80: "Hall's social security records and Schaefer's payroll deductions indicate that Schaefer wrongfully denied that Hall was his employee. Dated October 4, 1962, a photo in the *Santa Monica Evening Outlook* shows James Hall transporting a crime victim for Schaefer Ambulance Service.")

81. (http://www.youtube.com/watch?v=TyCkSTsaO_M: *Marilyn Monroe: A Case for Murder* documentary, 1988, part 2 of 5: Female reporter said Walt Schaefer "is now dead but in a 1985 interview, he said an ambulance did go to the scene that night but it was *not* driven by James Hall.")

(SLATZER 1992, p. 185: Walt Schaefer "did admit that Hunter had worked for him. He also admitted that Liebowitz had been Hunter's partner.")

(LEIB, SYLVIA. INTERVIEW WITH JAY MARGOLIS. 3 FEBRUARY 2011: James Hall *was* Murray Liebowitz's partner and they both went to MM's house that night.)

(SLATZER 1992, pp. 185, 187: Walt Schaefer first reported that MM died at Santa Monica Hospital then later told Slatzer he lied due to political pressure from the Kennedys that could ruin his business.)

(SUMMERS 2000, p. 463: In 1985, contradicting his wife's statement to me, Murray Leib related to Summers, "I wasn't on duty that night...")

82. (SLATZER 1992, p. 183: Abe Landau said, "My wife and I were out to a party. We came home quite late. It must have been close to 1:00 A.M. There was the ambulance. There was a police car and quite a few other cars.")

(http://www.youtube.com/watch?v=TyCkSTsaO_M: *Marilyn Monroe: A Case for Murder* documentary, 1988, part 2 of 5: Abe Landau's "Grand Central Station" account and the female narrator mentioned a "mysterious midnight traffic jam in front of Marilyn's house the night she died.")

(FRANKLIN 2002, pp. 111-112: Officer Lynn Franklin, through correspondence with Fred Otash and James Hall, placed Sergeant Marvin Iannone and Peter Lawford on the scene at 11:45 P.M. and Fred Otash agreed that at this time an ambulance was present.)

(BROWN AND BARHAM 1993, pp. 447-448: No later than ten minutes after midnight on August 5, Officer Lynn Franklin pulls over Peter Lawford for speeding with RFK and Greenson in tow.)

(*The Marilyn Files* documentary, 1991: Minutes after Greenson injected MM in the heart, James Hall observed, "At about this time, two men came in. The one man was wearing a Los Angeles police officer's uniform. The other was in civilian clothes. The guy in the civilian clothes went up to Patricia Newcomb...")

(WOLFE 1998, p. 77: "Hall noticed that a police officer arrived and briefly spoke to the man in the jumpsuit. The officer then went into the main house before returning to sign Hall's EPA call slip. Hall later identified the hysterical woman as Pat Newcomb, the man in the jumpsuit as Peter Lawford, the doctor as Ralph Greenson, and the police officer as Sergeant Marvin Iannone.")

(WOLFE 1998, p. 64: "Before departing, Captain James Hamilton promoted Marvin Iannone to lieutenant and transferred him to the down-town office of the Intelligence Division.")

(WOLFE 1998, p. 61: "Iannone was known to work for Hamilton in Intelligence, and whenever the President or the Attorney General visited the Lawfords'...")

83. (KIRSNER 2007, p. 478: On August 20, 1962, Greenson wrote to Anna Freud regarding MM's death, "This has been a terrible blow in many ways...")

(SUMMERS 2000, p. 337: "Dr. Litman says today that Greenson spoke to him of a 'close relationship with extremely important men in government,' that the relationship was 'sexual,' and that the men concerned were 'at the highest level.' ")

(CONFIDENTIAL SOURCE: Greenson wrote to Dr. Kris on August 20, 1962, "I am amazed how deeply people seemed to be affected by this death..." The complete letter is located in Greenson Papers, Special Collections, UCLA, sealed from the public until January 1, 2039.)

(NEMIROFF 1992, pp. 52, 83: Greenson and his exclusive definition of immortality implied that MM was not included since he believed narcissistic people could not love other people.)

(MECACCI 2009, pp. 31-32: On January 20, 1963, Anna Freud wrote to Greenson, "I am terribly sorry about Marilyn Monroe...")

(MECACCI 2009, p. 30: Sandler, Ken. "Marilyn Monroe's Psychiatrist Speaks Out In Her Defense." Medical Tribune. 24 October 1973: Greenson relayed, "It is controversial, I know that...")

(CONFIDENTIAL SOURCE: Sandler, Ken. "Marilyn Monroe's Psychiatrist Speaks Out In Her Defense." Medical Tribune. 24 October 1973: Greenson said, "I think it is wrong to connect her death with any sort of political intrigue. It is fantastic and not true.")

84. (BROWN AND BARHAM 1993, p. 426: Greenson said, "We made some mistakes at the end. And, if you really want to know what happened to Marilyn, why don't you ask Robert Kennedy.")

(Zolotow, Maurice. "MM's Psychiatrist a Troubled Man." San Antonio Light. [San Antonio, TX] 13 October 1973: 9-A)

(SUMMERS 2000, p. 337: Greenson told the Suicide Prevention Team of a "close relationship with extremely important men in government.")

85. (*Say Goodbye to the President* documentary, 1985: In 1964, while on the phone with Greenson, William Woodfield recorded Greenson's "Talk to Bobby Kennedy" statement.)

(ROMANOFF, GLORIA. INTERVIEW WITH JAY MARGOLIS. 2 SEPTEMBER 2010: "It is unbelievable to see that kind of behavior in a professional man.")

(http://www.telegraph.co.uk/culture/film/7843140/Marilyn-Monroe-on-the-couch.html: Turner, Christopher. "Marilyn Monroe on the Couch: To Dr. Ralph Greenson, Marilyn Monroe was more than just a patient. Now, for the first time, his family recall their favourite 'big sister.' " Telegraph. 23 June 2010: Danny Greenson related, "I don't know why he said that...")

86. (FARBER AND GREEN 1993, p. 106: Greenson told his patient actress Janice Rule, "There is no way in my lifetime I will ever be able to answer any of this...")

(FARBER AND GREEN 1993, p. 107: Greenson related, "Some of them saw no reaction in me...")

(BROWN AND BARHAM 1993, pp. 392-393: Freeman said Greenson would blame himself for MM's death.)

(GREENSON, HILDI. INTERVIEW WITH CATHY GRIFFIN. 4 JUNE 1991: "My husband at one time talked to the APA, where he was asked how come he took Marilyn into therapy and he said, 'Well, I think she deserved a psychiatrist who had experience. Where should she go? To a beginner?' ")

(FARBER AND GREEN 1993, pp. 107-108)

(FARBER AND GREEN 1993, p. 108: Greenson relayed, "You can't sit there like a computer...")

(SUMMERS 2000, p. 422: Greenson said, "She was a poor creature, whom I tried to help and ending up hurting.")

(MARSHALL 2005, p. 434: A colleague of Greenson's remarked, "The fire went out in Greenson...")

(FARBER AND GREEN 1993, p. 110: Greenson replied to Blaustein, "I wanted to be somebody else.")

87. ("Marilyn." Independent Press-Telegram. [Long Beach, CA] 5 August 1973: Greenson and his alleged dinner engagement until around midnight. Greenson claimed that Mrs. Murray called him three hours later: "At 3 A.M. his phone rang...")

(CONFIDENTIAL SOURCE: On August 4, 1962, Greenson attended a dinner party at the home of actor Eddie Albert and his wife Margo.)

(*Say Goodbye to the President* documentary, 1985: Mrs. Murray said MM was discovered "around midnight." Sergeant Clemmons agreed Mrs. Murray said midnight and Clemmons also stated that Greenson and Engelberg did not disagree with Mrs. Murray.)

(CONFIDENTIAL SOURCE: District Attorney's Report dated September 27, 1982. Investigator Al Tomich interviewed MM's physician Dr. Hyman Engelberg regarding rumors that he arrived at midnight. Engelberg responded, "Nonsense. Absolute, utter nonsense.")

(SLATZER 1975, pp. 172-173: Picture 60 is a photograph of a man pointing at the broken window Greenson claimed he shattered to enter MM's bedroom. One wonders how Greenson stuck his full hand into the window without cutting himself.)

(SMITH 2005, pp. 30-33: Police report #62-509 463 and follow-up police report show serious time discrepancies.)

(GREENSON, HILDI. INTERVIEW WITH CATHY GRIFFIN. 4 JUNE 1991: Eunice Murray "wished she had awakened at midnight and called but she didn't. She fell asleep again and she only called at around two.")

(HEYMANN 1998, p. 323)

(CONFIDENTIAL SOURCE: District Attorney's Report dated September 27, 1982. Investigator Al Tomich interviewed MM's physician Dr. Hyman Engelberg who relayed, "I recall this. I don't know if Greenson or Mrs. Murray told me but the door was locked to the bedroom. Mrs. Murray first looked in through the window and saw her and the way they got in was I guess through the window...")

(CONFIDENTIAL SOURCE: District Attorney's Report dated September 27, 1982. Investigator Al Tomich interviewed MM's physician Dr. Hyman Engelberg who relayed, "I was parked in the basement of the parking area of a small apartment house and somebody parked in back of me...")

88. (SUMMERS 2000, pp. 416-417: "At about 3:30 A.M., at the Greenson home in Santa Monica, the psychiatrist's daughter, Joan, heard the telephone ring in her parents' bedroom...")

(CONFIDENTIAL SOURCE: GREENSON, JOAN. UNTITLED 90-PAGE MARILYN MONROE MANUSCRIPT, p. 82: "My parents were going to a dinner party, and were not having dinner at home..." The complete work is located in Greenson Papers, Special Collections, UCLA, sealed from the public until January 1, 2039.)

(GREENSON, HILDI. INTERVIEW WITH CATHY GRIFFIN. 4 JUNE 1991: "I was very worried, and my daughter was here and we immediately stayed up. We just went downstairs and sat around...")

(CONFIDENTIAL SOURCE: GREENSON, JOAN. UNTITLED 90-PAGE MARILYN MONROE MANUSCRIPT, p. 83: "I finished my snack, and went back to my parents' bedroom and told my mother I was going back to bed..." The complete work is located in Greenson Papers, Special Collections, UCLA, sealed from the public until January 1, 2039.)

89. (GREENSON, HILDI. INTERVIEW WITH CATHY GRIFFIN. 4 JUNE 1991: "Her room was locked and with a bolt lock. It wasn't a lock that you could go through with a credit card and open it or undo it...")

(SPOTO 1993, p. 486: "Cherie [Redmond] wished to secure Marilyn's financial papers, checks and related private materials in a closet or in one of the small bedrooms – 'but there isn't one door in the place that locks,' as she wrote to her New York counterpart, Hedda Rosten (who was taking care of mail and minor secretarial duties at Fifty-seventh Street). As the next owners after Marilyn discovered, none of the inoperative interior locks were repaired while she was in residence. (Cherie finally had one installed for her small file cabinet, on March 15).")

(MARSHALL 2005, p. 282: "Linda Nuñez, who moved into the 5th Helena home after Marilyn's death, explained... that no one in her family ever had a key to any of the locks on any of the interior doors of the home...")

(BROWN AND BARHAM 1993, p. 441: "We found out... that Monroe's housekeeper, Eunice Murray, had a skeleton key to Monroe's bedroom. It was attached to her own key ring. Greenson had insisted on it because Murray was often on suicide watch. Therefore, there should have been no need to break in the movie star's bedroom window.")

(http://southernwingsaircraft.com/howmarilyndied.html: "Eunice Murray stated more than once years later that the door actually was not locked. She even put this in writing in a questionnaire [to Roy Turner] saying the door was not locked. Plus it is easy to believe Mrs. Murray and Dr. Greenson would have a skeleton key to Marilyn's door as it was a simple deadbolt lock that used a universal key. So if you take away the lack of decoration and take away the locked door, add in the fact that everyone interviewed on her last day said she was in good spirits that evening then there is no evidence she wanted to kill herself.")

(SMITH 2005, pp. 102-103: "In fact, Marilyn's masseur and close friend Ralph Roberts, said the door was never locked. He was in a position to know this, also, for he often gave Marilyn massages late in the evening when she was settling down for sleep. Cherie Redmond, who was Marilyn's business secretary when she died, commented to Hedda Rosten, who was doing secretarial work for Marilyn in New York, that she couldn't find a working lock in the house.")

(SPOTO 1993, pp. 575-576: "Between March 15 and June 30, according to their invoice # 7451, the A-1 Lock & Safe Company of 3114 Wilshire Boulevard, Santa Monica, installed only two locks in the house: a cabinet lock for Cherie Redmond's files, and a replacement lock for the front door of the house. Additional locks were not installed until August 15 and 21, after Marilyn's death (A-1 invoice # 7452)...

On February 9, 1987, archivist and genealogist Roy Turner wrote to Eunice (whom he had befriended), asking 'Was Marilyn's door locked when you found her?' She replied in one handwritten word following his question: 'No.' ")

(SUMMERS 2000, p. 515: "Four years ago, however, Mrs. Murray appeared entirely lucid. In 1982, in a conversation with researcher Justin Clayton, she said she had 'found Marilyn's door ajar' at about midnight. As Clayton vividly recalls, Mrs. Murray then stopped dead, suddenly raising her hand to her mouth, and said, 'I mean, I found the door locked.' ")

(TARABORRELLI 2009, p. 474: "More intriguingly, Eunice would later say that there was no lock on Marilyn's door. If that's the case, then the entire story of how she was found seems to fall apart.")

(SLATZER 1975, pp. 289-290: see for the A-1 Lock & Safe Company Creditor's Claim and Invoices)

90. ("Marilyn." <u>Independent Press-Telegram</u>. [Long Beach, CA] 5 August 1973)

(SPOTO 1993, p. 570: Determining the exact time of Joe DiMaggio, Jr.'s call to be 7:00 P.M.)

(WOLFE 1998, p. 460: According to DiMaggio, Sr., Joe Jr.'s call with MM lasted 15 minutes.)

(CONFIDENTIAL SOURCE: Greenson wrote to Dr. Kris on August 20, 1962, "When I left at 7:15…" The complete letter is located in Greenson Papers, Special Collections, UCLA, sealed from the public until January 1, 2039.)

(MURRAY 1975, p. 135: "I knew that the new white wool carpet filled the space under the door…")

(GREENSON, HILDI. INTERVIEW WITH CATHY GRIFFIN. 4 JUNE 1991: "People say that there were four hours before it was reported…")

(CONFIDENTIAL SOURCE: GREENSON, JOAN. UNTITLED 90-PAGE MARILYN MONROE MANUSCRIPT, p. 84: "He had gone over to Marilyn's house after he had gotten the call from Mrs. Murray. Her bedroom

Marilyn Monroe: A Case for Murder

door was locked..." The complete work is located in Greenson Papers, Special Collections, UCLA, sealed from the public until January 1, 2039.)

(CONFIDENTIAL SOURCE: District Attorney's Report dated September 27, 1982. Investigator Al Tomich interviewed MM's physician Dr. Hyman Engelberg who relayed, "I thought that at the time she took the pills, it was a suicide attempt. That was my opinion...")

(SUMMERS 2000, p. 458: "Eunice Murray agrees that Rudin called, but insists the lawyer said nothing about the troubling call Marilyn had supposedly had with Lawford. She assumed it was merely a casual inquiry and, without checking on Marilyn, said all was well.")

(RUDIN, MILTON. INTERVIEW WITH DONALD SPOTO. 31 OCTOBER 1992: Rudin said he got a call from Greenson telling him MM was dead and this was before midnight.)

91. (MURRAY 1975, p. 134: "The last time Eunice had left her room was when attorney Rudin phoned... But she had not gone through the hall to answer the phone, but through the bathroom... at the back of the house. Had there been one telephone or two in the room when Rudin phoned? Eunice hadn't noticed. One, however, must have been missing at that time if Rudin was checking because of a call Marilyn had made.")

(*Say Goodbye to the President* documentary, 1985: Mrs. Murray admits to being in the living room at the time Greenson arrived and she conceded MM was not yet dead.)

(SUMMERS 2000, p. 515: "Mrs. Murray, the housekeeper, caused a sensation in 1985. While being interviewed by me for the BBC, she delivered herself of the version usually offered for public consumption. Then, as the camera crew were starting to clear up, she said suddenly, 'Why, at my age, do I still have to cover this thing?' Mrs. Murray then astonished us by saying Robert Kennedy had indeed visited Marilyn on the day she died, and that a doctor and an ambulance had come while she was still alive. She said much the same to the ABC Team.")

(SMITH 2005, p. 46)

(WOLFE 1998, p. 462: Norman Jefferies corroborated Mrs. Murray's statement that she was in the living room shortly before MM died.)

(SMITH 2005, pp. 30-33: Police report # 62-509 463)

(SUMMERS 1994, p. 347: "Dr. Greenson confirmed privately, years later, that Robert Kennedy was present that night and that an ambulance was called.")

(GREENSON, HILDI. INTERVIEW WITH CATHY GRIFFIN. 4 JUNE 1991: "We had been out at a dinner party and that was another if. Apparently Lawford called Mickey Rudin...")

(HEYMANN 1998, p. 323: "The Greensons returned from their dinner party and went to bed, only to be awakened at 2 A.M. by the telephone.")

(SPOTO 1993, p. 575: On the morning of August 5, Mrs. Murray claimed she went outside MM's house and used a fireplace poker to "part the draperies" of the only unbarred window.)

(NEWCOMB, PATRICIA. INTERVIEW WITH DONALD SPOTO. 3 AUGUST 1992: Newcomb recalled there was no "middle-divider" to the draperies Eunice Murray claimed she parted.)

92. (WOLFE 1998, pp. 5-8: "When the sergeant turned to talk to the housekeeper, he found that Murray had left the room. Searching through the sparsely furnished house, which seemed rather small and inelegant for the home of a film star, he found Murray in the service porch off the kitchen, where both the washer and the dryer were running. She appeared agitated as she folded a stack of laundry on the counter. Clemmons thought it odd that the housekeeper was doing laundry in the middle of the night while her employer lay dead in the bedroom. While she continued folding, he asked, 'When did you discover that something was wrong with Miss Monroe?' 'Just after midnight,' Murray replied. 'Then I called Dr. Greenson, and he arrived at about twelve-thirty...' Returning to the bedroom, Clemmons asked the doctors why they'd waited four hours before calling the police. Greenson caustically replied, 'We had to get permission from the studio publicity department before we could call anyone.'

'The publicity department?' Clemmons wondered aloud. 'Yes, the 20th Century-Fox publicity department. Miss Monroe is making a film there.' 'What did you do during those hours?' he asked. The doctors became more evasive, but Clemmons pressed the point. 'We were just talking,' Engelberg mumbled. 'About what?' Clemmons queried. 'What were you talking about for four hours?' The doctors shrugged their shoulders and stared at him blankly.")

(*Say Goodbye to the President* documentary, 1985: Mrs. Murray said she discovered MM around "midnight.")

(SPOTO 1993, pp. 578-579: Greenson said he "had to get permission from the publicity department at the studio before we could notify anyone.")

(SMITH 2005, p. 15)

(BROWN AND BARHAM 1993, pp. 340-341: "Actually he [Greenson] might have put it another way. Not only had he called the studio publicity department, he had waited until the department's work was done before calling the police.")

(SUMMERS 2000, p. 541: Ronald Carroll said, "We would have looked further if we had known, back then...")

(*Say Goodbye to the President* documentary, 1985: Natalie Trundy Jacobs recalled how MM was either dead or dying around 10:30 – 10:40 P.M.)

93. (NEWCOMB, PATRICIA. INTERVIEW WITH DONALD SPOTO. 3 AUGUST 1992: Newcomb and the alleged 4:00 A.M. call from Rudin. Oddly, Spoto reported this call one hour later at 5:00 A.M. in his book on page 574.)

(GUILES 1970, p. 384: "Pat was awakened by a phone call at 4 A.M. It was lawyer Mickey Rudin...")

(WOLFE 1998, p. 15: "Though Newcomb said she had driven to the Monroe residence after Rudin's call, her car wasn't there. Photos and newsreel footage show...")

(RUDIN, MILTON. INTERVIEW WITH DONALD SPOTO. 31 OCTOBER 1992: "I didn't have her phone number.")

(EBBINS, MILTON. INTERVIEW WITH DONALD SPOTO. 6 AUGUST 1992: "It's strange that Mickey called Pat Newcomb. That's the first time I heard of that.")

94. (JACOBS, NATALIE TRUNDY. INTERVIEW WITH DONALD SPOTO. 28 FEBRUARY 1992)

(SUMMERS 2000, p. 461: Natalie said Arthur Jacobs had to "fudge the press.")

(SPADA 1991, p. 323: Natalie is certain that "Pat Newcomb was the first one at the house.")

(SMITH 2005, pp. 28-29)

(SPOTO 1993, pp. 573-574)

(SELSMAN, MICHAEL. INTERVIEW WITH JAY MARGOLIS. 28 MARCH 2011)

(GREENSON, HILDI. INTERVIEW WITH CATHY GRIFFIN. 4 JUNE 1991: "One thing that puzzles me very much – I've forgotten now who the people were who went to a concert in the Hollywood Bowl...")

95. (WOLFE 1998, pp. 86-87: "The 1962 Beverly Hills phone directory reveals that Pat Newcomb and Natalie Trundy, the future Mrs. Jacobs, were next-door neighbors. Newcomb lived at 150 South Canon Drive, and Natalie Trundy resided at 152 South Canon Drive. When recently asked if she had discussed Marilyn's death with her neighbor when she returned home from the Bowl, Natalie stated, 'Pat Newcomb wasn't home Saturday night, and didn't return to her apartment until late Sunday.' ")

(MARSHALL 2005, p. 409: Pat Newcomb and Natalie Trundy were neighbors.)

(EBBINS, MILTON. INTERVIEW WITH DONALD SPOTO. 6 AUGUST 1992: On Arthur Jacobs, "Pat Newcomb knew where he was every minute...")

(EBBINS, MILTON. INTERVIEW WITH DONALD SPOTO. 6 AUGUST 1992: "The maid was his mistress!" Peter's maid Erma Lee Riley had attested over the years that Peter never left his home that night but since she's his mistress, her account is suspect.)

(WOLFE 1998, p. 88: "On Sunday morning, as Pat Newcomb drove away from Marilyn's house yelling, 'Keep shooting, vultures!' she was seated in the passenger seat of Mrs. Murray's Dodge because she had driven there with Lawford and her car was still at his beach house.")

(SLATZER 1975, pp. 244-245: Slatzer's interviews with Mrs. Murray and Pat Newcomb. Newcomb claimed she brought her own car to MM's house, which is not true. Arriving at Peter's at 9:30 P.M. per "Bullets" Durgom, she was wearing what appeared to be her pajamas, covered by a dark coat. Newcomb never left MM's house once she arrived.)

(MURRAY 1975, p. 141: "The police practically had to forcibly evict her. But first she was allowed to telephone her psychiatrist...")

(NAAR, DOLORES. INTERVIEW WITH JAY MARGOLIS. 4 NOVEMBER 2010: "All I remember is 'Bullets' Durgom. George Durgom. There were other people there but I don't remember.")

(SUMMERS 2000, p. 513: Durgom said, "The one thing I remember clearly is Pat Newcomb coming in, at maybe 9:30. She stood on the step and said, 'Peter, Marilyn's not coming. She's not feeling well.' ")

(SUMMERS 2000, p. 513: "Durgom says that 'at about 10 or 11 o'clock' Lawford tried to call Marilyn and could not get through. As a result, after a call to Marilyn's lawyer, Milton Rudin, 'the lawyer and somebody else went over to the house.' ")

(RUDIN, MILTON. INTERVIEW WITH DONALD SPOTO. 31 OCTOBER 1992: Rudin said he got a call from Greenson telling him MM's dead and this was before midnight.)

(STRAIT, RAYMOND. INTERVIEW WITH JAY MARGOLIS. 18 MARCH 2011: As for Pat Newcomb and Peter Lawford's attendance at MM's house that last night on August 4, "I know that they were both there. I do not know that they arrived together.")

(SUMMERS 2000, p. 514: Per employee Juliet Roswell, Arthur Jacobs arrived at MM's house by 11:00 P.M.)

(SMITH 2005, p. 28: Natalie Jacobs related, "That was about 10:30 P.M., and at that time of night it would not take him above thirty minutes to reach Marilyn's house. I never saw him the next two days.")

(SPADA 1991, p. 323: No worry over MM during Peter's dinner party.)

(SUMMERS 2000, p. 459: "Both Mr. and Mrs. Naar are adamant that, during the supper party… there was no talk of concern for Marilyn, not a word about 'good-bye' phone calls.")

96. (*Say Goodbye to the President* documentary, 1985: Former Mayor Sam Yorty recalled, "Chief Parker told me confidentially that Bobby Kennedy was supposed to be north of Los Angeles…")

(WOLFE 1998, pp. 51-52: "In the process of his investigation, however, [Chief of Detectives] Thad Brown discovered something startling – the Attorney General *had* been in Los Angeles on Saturday, August 4. Thad's brother, detective Finis Brown, related [to Anthony Summers], 'I talked to contacts who had seen Kennedy and Lawford at the Beverly Hilton Hotel the day she took the overdose.'")

(FRANKLIN 2002, pp. 108-113: Officer Franklin pulled over Peter Lawford, RFK, and Dr. Ralph Greenson all in the same car at 12:10 A.M. on August 5, 1962.)

(BROWN AND BARHAM 1993, pp. 445-448)

(http://www.youtube.com/watch?v=IS0nLApY4Tg&feature=related: *The Death of Marilyn Monroe* documentary, part 5 of 5. Beverly Hills police officer Lynn Franklin said, "Just as I approached Olympic Boulevard, a Lincoln Continental went through the intersection eastbound heading for Downtown Los Angeles at roughly 80 miles per hour. So I threw on the red light and went in pursuit. When I pulled the car over, the only one who I recognized immediately was Peter Lawford. And in the backseat, once I shined the light back there, I recognized Robert Kennedy, the Attorney General.")

(WOLFE 1998, p. 463: Wolfe incorrectly stated that the car Lawford was driving was a black Mercedes. As Officer Franklin has always stated, it was a Lincoln Continental.)

(ROTHMILLER, MIKE. INTERVIEW WITH JAY MARGOLIS. 26 SEPTEMBER 2010)

(NAAR, JOSEPH. INTERVIEW WITH DONALD SPOTO. 22 JULY 1992)

(NAAR, JOSEPH. INTERVIEW WITH JAY MARGOLIS. 2 SEPTEMBER 2010: "People like Warren Beatty think I know exactly what happened. That I'm covering it up because I'm a friend of the [Kennedy] family and that what really happened is that Bobby came down and killed her. It's such bullshit. Warren heard all sorts of things. In those days, everybody was talking about how Bobby killed her. 'Bobby had her killed.' ")

(SLATZER 1975, pp. 238-239: Sergeant Jack Clemmons relayed, "I heard that Marilyn and Bobby Kennedy were having an affair. But a friend of mine, who had been in the movie industry and who still knew a lot of people in the business, asked me if I was the first officer on the death scene. I told him I was, and he said, 'Do you know what they are saying?' I asked him who he meant by 'they,' and he said, 'the people in the entertainment field…' and he said it was going around that Bobby Kennedy had Marilyn done away with, and he said, 'I'll tell you one thing, everybody in the business believes it.' ")

(FRANKLIN 2002, p. 127: "At a Beverly Wilshire Hotel Chamber of Commerce Breakfast, Chief B.L. Cork presents Det. Lynn Franklin the CHA Award. The highest Honor ever bestowed upon a Beverly Hills Cop.")

(BROWN AND BARHAM 1993, p. 446: Officer Franklin related that Peter "appeared drunk, terrified, and coming apart at the seams.")

(SCHWARZ 2009, p. 624: Otash recalled that Peter "looked like hell, trembling in the manner of a junkie going through cold turkey withdrawal.")

(SPADA 1991, p. 328: Milt Ebbins' account of a drunk Lawford.)

(EBBINS, MILTON. INTERVIEW WITH DONALD SPOTO. 6 AUGUST 1992)

97. (BROWN AND BARHAM 1993, pp. 343, 503: Lady Lawford is adamant that neighbors saw RFK in and out of Peter's beach house that last Saturday.)

(BROWN AND BARHAM 1993, p. 330: Ward Wood said, "It was Bobby all right...")

(*Say Goodbye to the President* documentary, 1985: Ward Wood's account.)

(STRAIT, RAYMOND. INTERVIEW WITH JAY MARGOLIS. 18 NOVEMBER 2010: "Bobby skipped out of town and said he was never there but everybody knew he was there. You cover your tail as best you can...")

(WOLFE 1998, p. 58: "Meanwhile, in Los Angeles, reporter Joe Hyams learned that Lawford's neighbors were upset that a helicopter had touched down on the Santa Monica shore behind the Lawford residence in the early hours of Sunday morning, August 5, blowing sand into their swimming pools. Ward Wood, another neighbor, had told a police department contact that he saw Bobby Kennedy arrive in a Mercedes at the Lawford mansion 'late Saturday afternoon or in the early evening.' ")

(SUMMERS 2000, p. 471: Helicopters "were permitted to land on the beach...")

(SUMMERS 2000, p. 471: "As she [Deborah Gould] understood it from Lawford, 'He [RFK] left by helicopter to the airport.' Former Herald Tribune Bureau Chief, Joe Hyams, and photographer William Woodfield, teamed up for several days after Marilyn's death to dig deeper into the events of the fatal night. They hired a former policeman, who has been interviewed for this book, to help with the research. Hyams and the former policeman both say they learned that a helicopter touched down on the beach, close to the Lawford house, late that night. They discovered this in separate interviews with Lawford's neighbors.")

(SUMMERS 2000, pp. 472-473: "Photographer William Woodfield... had recently used a helicopter for air-to-ground shooting, while preparing an article on Frank Sinatra's luxurious private plane. The helicopter in question was one regularly chartered by Sinatra and Lawford. Within three days of Marilyn's death, Woodfield says, he revisited the pilot, who had flown him before, at Clover Field, Santa Monica. That is the nearest airfield to the Lawford beach house. Woodfield says he went… to the pilot on the pretext of preparing a follow-up article on the use of helicopters by celebrities, an idea he had discussed when they previously met. It promised welcome publicity for the pilot and his company, and he proved agreeable. He raised no objection when Woodfield asked to leaf through the helicopter's logbook, supposedly in search of famous customers who had recently used the service. Seated quietly with the log, Woodfield turned back a few days to the page covering the night of August 4, 1962. He found what he had hardly dared to hope for. An entry for the night of Marilyn's death showed that a helicopter had been rented to pick up a passenger at the Lawford beach house and to deposit him at the main Los Angeles airport. 'The time in the log,' Woodfield recalls, 'was sometime after midnight – I think between midnight and two in the morning. It showed clearly that a helicopter had picked up Robert Kennedy at the Santa Monica Beach.' ")

(SUMMERS 2000, p. 517: James Zonlick remembered, "Hal had picked Robert Kennedy up at the beach house and left him at Los Angeles International Airport…")

(SUMMERS 2000, p. 517: Patricia Conners recalled, "Next morning, I remember saying, 'Did you hear that Marilyn Monroe died?' ")

(SUMMERS 2000, p. 468: "Certainly the parish priest confirms, Kennedy was in Gilroy by 9:30 A.M. on Sunday, attending Mass at the church of St. Mary.")

(LAWFORD 1969, p. 36: Carmine S. Bellino and RFK's strict dedication to Mass.)

98. (WOLFE 1998, p. 36: Contents of MM's red diary.)

(SUMMERS 2000, p. 541: "Marilyn Monroe, weeks before her death, was a security risk – and the fault was the Kennedys.")

99. (WOLFE 1998, pp. 13-14: Norman Jefferies and Eunice Murray noticed that Pat Newcomb didn't want to leave the premises. Jefferies saw Newcomb looking through MM's drawers searching for something, presumably the little red diary RFK couldn't find the night before.)

(MURRAY 1975, p. 141: "This time no verbal suggestion could cause her [Pat Newcomb] to leave. The police practically had to forcibly evict her. But first she was allowed to telephone her psychiatrist and arrange to have him pick her up at the corner of Sunset and Carmelina, a few blocks away. Eunice offered to drive her there.")

(BROWN AND BARHAM 1993, p. 52: Dr. Litman related, "Marilyn never knew that Murray was a psychiatric assistant planted in the Brentwood house to watch for warning signs.")

(SPOTO 1993, p. 481: Eunice Murray's son-in-law Philip LaClair stated that Mrs. Murray "had no formal training as a nurse – not even a high school education – but she was a kind woman and became a valuable asset to Greenson. She always followed his orders very closely.")

(MURRAY 1975, p. 12: Mrs. Murray says, "I am not formally trained in the field of psychology. Although I have read widely and have worked with psychiatrists in aiding their patients, I make no claim of possessing great knowledge of motivations.")

(WOLFE 1998, pp. 381, 387: "Friends of Marilyn's regarded Mrs. Murray as peculiar. Whitey Snyder described her as 'a very strange lady. She was put into Marilyn's life by Greenson, and she was always whispering – whispering and listening. She was this constant presence, reporting everything back to Greenson…' It wasn't until the last weeks of Marilyn's life that she began to realize that a web of deception had been woven around her. In July 1962, she confided to Ralph Roberts that she had found something disturbing about Dr. Greenson's enveloping influence. Roberts wrote to Susan Strasberg, 'She was radically turning on Dr. Greenson and Mrs. Murray, the woman he'd put with her, she felt to spy on her.' ")

(BROWN AND BARHAM 1993, p. 391: "Just before her death, Monroe had learned that Murray was a psychiatric nurse and that Ralph Greenson had placed her in the actress's home as a combination spy and caretaker. 'Marilyn caught on just before she died and felt very betrayed,' recalled Ralph Roberts. 'Plans to fire [Mrs. Murray] were already in the works.' ")

(STRASBERG 1992, p. 230: "Marilyn said it felt like she had a keeper.")

(SPOTO 1993, p. 482)

(TARABORRELLI 2009, p. 388)

(SMITH 2005, p. 105)

(WOLFE 1998, p. 36: "On Monday, August 6, Jefferies returned to the Monroe residence with Eunice Murray to open the house for Inez Melson, Marilyn's former business manager and executrix of the estate. The driver for the Coroner's Office arrived while they were waiting for Melson. Jefferies recalled that Murray had the red diary in her possession and gave it to the driver along with one of Marilyn's address books. Jefferies couldn't explain when or how Murray had obtained the diary.")

(*The Marilyn Files* documentary, 1991: Lionel Grandison said, "I sent the drivers to her house to pick up any property or any information that would lead us to the next of kin. They came back with a book. The infamous little red book…")

(WOLFE 1998, p. 36: Lionel Grandison explained how the next day the red diary was gone and that only three people at the Coroner's Office knew the combination to the safe.)

100. (SUMMERS 2000, p. 516: Account of Detective Sergeant Robert E. Byron.)

(BYRON, DOROTHEA. INTERVIEW WITH JAY MARGOLIS. 13 SEPTEMBER 2010)

(BUNTIN 2009, p. 280: Chief Parker and his reservations about the Kennedys' relationship with Frank Sinatra.)

(SUMMERS 2000, pp. 424-425: Helen Parker related how Chief Parker protected RFK in the MM case.)

(BROWN AND BARHAM 1993, p. 440: "With the stroke of a pen, Chief Parker…")

(BROWN AND BARHAM 1993, p. 467: Rothmiller said, "Since nobody really ever investigated this death – they only covered up – all the trails were allowed to turn cold.")

(BROWN AND BARHAM 1993, p. 430: Rothmiller relayed, "This is precisely what they did with the Monroe investigation... they protected the name of the Kennedy dynasty..." "Intelligence chiefs" did this in 1962, 1975, and 1982.)

(STEWART, DANIEL K. INTERVIEW WITH JAY MARGOLIS. 14 JANUARY 2011)

(BROWN AND BARHAM 1993, pp. 437-438: Assumption of suicide tainted the Monroe investigation.)

(CARPOZI, GEORGE, JR. INTERVIEW WITH JOANNE GREEN-LEVINE. 21 JANUARY 1992: "They never conducted a criminal investigation...")

(DAMBACHER, ROBERT. INTERVIEW WITH JAY MARGOLIS. 9 MARCH 2011: "I was a Deputy Coroner at the time. My partner's name was Cletus Pace. So Cleet and I were dispatched at eight in the morning to go out to Westwood Village Mortuary to pick up her remains...")

(http://www.youtube.com/watch?v=IVaVYw7zJrI&feature=watch_response_rev: *The Death of Marilyn Monroe* documentary, part 1 and 5. *New York Herald Tribune* reporter Joe Hyams said, "I had a source at the telephone company and my source came back and said the Secret Service has already been here and taken our records. Kind of weird.")

(http://www.youtube.com/watch?v=IS0nLApY4Tg&feature=related: *The Death of Marilyn Monroe* documentary, part 5 and 5. *New York Herald Tribune* reporter Joe Hyams said, "The fact that the Secret Service had impounded all those telephone tapes was really weird because that's very uncommon. That's the first time in my memory as a reporter that they ever, ever stepped in that fast to start a hush.")

(SUMMERS 2000, p. 448: Joe Hyams contacted the telephone company "the morning after her death.")

(WOLFE 1998, p. 50: Florabel Muir wrote on August 8, 1962, "Strange 'pressures' are being put on Los Angeles police...")

(SUMMERS 2000, p. 451: Jack Tobin said, "Hamilton told me he had the telephone history of the last day or two of Marilyn Monroe's life...")

(http://www.youtube.com/watch?v=IS0nLApY4Tg&feature=related: *The Death of Marilyn Monroe* documentary, part 5 of 5. Arthur Jacobs' employee Michael Selsman relayed, "I believe that the Kennedys were concerned that Pat, being a close friend of Marilyn's, would become very emotional and might at some point mention something to somebody about the extent of the relationship between the Kennedys and Marilyn.")

(http://www.youtube.com/watch?v=IS0nLApY4Tg&feature=related: *The Death of Marilyn Monroe* documentary, part 5 of 5. *New York Herald Tribune* reporter Joe Hyams said, "Eunice Murray, who was Marilyn's housekeeper and who had found the body, disappeared. And Pat Newcomb disappeared but she reappeared very hastily working for the Kennedys in Washington. It just began to look like a vast cover-up.")

(BARRIS, GEORGE. INTERVIEW WITH JAY MARGOLIS. 7 JANUARY 2011: "I'll tell you about Pat Newcomb...")

101. (SUMMERS 1994, p. 350: Anthony Calomaris relayed, "He said she was murdered, that it wasn't a suicide, that the Kennedys were involved.")

(SUMMERS 1994, pp. 344, 349: When MM and RFK saw each other at the Lawford mansion on February 1, 1962, Hoover was listening in over wiretaps.)

(THOMAS 2007, p. 117: Ethel Kennedy and the anonymous recommendation of Police Chief William Parker to the head of the FBI.)

(THOMAS 2007, pp. 194, 429: Seattle Intelligencer. 7 August 1962)

(SUMMERS 2000, pp. 484-485: "Three years after Marilyn's death, in 1965, Joe DiMaggio stood in a ceremonial lineup for baseball hero Mickey Mantle at New York's Yankee Stadium. Robert Kennedy came along the line, smiling and shaking hands. Rather than shake Kennedy's hand, DiMaggio quickly backed away.")

(HEYMANN 2009, p. 77: "DiMaggio refused to shake Bobby's hand that day, giving rise to a New York Daily News sports page headline: 'Joltin' Joe – No Fan of RFK's!' ")

(SUMMERS 2000, p. 421: Harry Hall said DiMaggio "held Bobby Kennedy responsible for her death. He said that right there in the Miramar.")

(HAYS 2005, p. 8: "In 1966, Chief Parker died of a heart attack during an engagement as a guest speaker at a military banquet.")

102. (BROWN AND BARHAM 1993, p. 345: "To Allan, the master publicist, Lawford's story sounded as though it had been written for him by a public relations expert...")

(EBBINS, MILTON. INTERVIEW WITH DONALD SPOTO. 6 AUGUST 1992)

(EBBINS, MILTON. INTERVIEW WITH DONALD SPOTO. 22 SEPTEMBER 1992)

(ASHER, WILLIAM. INTERVIEW WITH DONALD SPOTO. 25 SEPTEMBER 1992)

(*Say Goodbye to the President* documentary, 1985: Interview with producer George "Bullets" Durgom.)

(EBBINS, MILTON. INTERVIEW WITH DONALD SPOTO. 6 AUGUST 1992: "There were two numbers. Peter didn't have the other number.")

(RUDIN, MILTON. INTERVIEW WITH DONALD SPOTO. 31 OCTOBER 1992: Rudin claimed he didn't call Greenson but rang the housekeeper.)

("Peter Lawford Phoned MM on Her Last Night." San Antonio Express. [San Antonio, Texas] 9 August 1962)

103. (LAWFORD 1992, pp. 77-80: Lady May Lawford, Peter's mother, suspects her son of foul play on August 4, 1962.)

104. (Scott, Vernon. "Debunking MM murder rumors latest Hollywood industry." European Stars and Stripes. [Darmstadt, Germany] 7 October 1985: Milt Ebbins related, "But when Pat

and Peter divorced, Peter became persona non grata with the Kennedys... If Peter had bailed Bobby out of a jam, don't you think they would have been friends for life?")

(http://www.people.com/people/archive/article/0,,20089693,00.html: Boyes, Malcolm. "The Passing of Peter Lawford Rekindles Memories of the Joys and Sadness of a Camelot Lost." People. 14 January 1985, Vol. 23, No. 2)

(ROMANOFF, GLORIA. INTERVIEW WITH JAY MARGOLIS. 2 SEPTEMBER 2010: "I don't think there was a lot of affection between Bobby Kennedy and Peter Lawford...")

(FRANKLIN 2002, p. 109: On RFK snapping at Peter, "Lawford didn't react; apparently he was used to verbal whippings.")

105. (ASHER, WILLIAM. INTERVIEW WITH DONALD SPOTO. 25 SEPTEMBER 1992)

106. (NAAR, DOLORES. INTERVIEW WITH JAY MARGOLIS. 4 NOVEMBER 2010: "We were to pick her up...")

(SPADA 1991, p. 321)

(NAAR, JOSEPH. INTERVIEW WITH DONALD SPOTO. 22 JULY 1992)

(NAAR, JOSEPH. INTERVIEW WITH JAY MARGOLIS. 2 SEPTEMBER 2010)

(SPADA 1991, p. 323: During Peter's party, Dolores Naar recalled, "I picked up on nothing. Except that during the evening there was a call and Peter said, 'Oh, it's Marilyn again' – like she does this all the time. His attitude didn't change. It was very light, up evening." Erma Lee Riley, Peter's maid, agreed: "There wasn't a word of worry about Marilyn.")

(NAAR, DOLORES. INTERVIEW WITH JAY MARGOLIS. 3 NOVEMBER 2010: "I was in the room.")

(NAAR, DOLORES. INTERVIEW WITH JAY MARGOLIS. 4 NOVEMBER 2010: "So you don't need to go.")

(SMITH 2005, p. 180: "Peter Lawford telephoned to say that Marilyn had taken too many pills, and he sounded anxious about her. Joe Naar offered to go and find out what was happening. He dressed in readiness, but Lawford called again before he set off. He said it was unnecessary to go, that it had been a false alarm. Dolores Naar recalls Lawford telling them that Marilyn's doctor had given her a sedative and she was resting.")

(SUMMERS 2000, p. 514)

(WILSON 1973, pp. 320-321)

(WILSON 1974, p. 89)

(RUDIN, MILTON. INTERVIEW WITH DONALD SPOTO. 31 OCTOBER 1992)

107. (LEAMER 1996, p. 569: Best friend Joe Naar believed Peter's descent into alcohol was because of guilt over MM's death.)

(MARTIN, JEANNE. INTERVIEW WITH JAY MARGOLIS. 11 NOVEMBER 2010: "Let the woman alone. Just let the whole story alone...")

(ROLLYSON 1993, p. 211: MM to Richard Meryman, "I never quite understood it – this sex symbol – I always thought symbols were...")

(http://www.youtube.com/watch?v=Iy56XWtUb8s&feature=related: *Marilyn Monroe: A Case for Murder* documentary, 1988, part 5 of 5 – Interview with former FBI agent Bill Roemer.)

(MECACCI 2009, p. 29: "Marilyn's death was in the end a relief for everyone: for the Kennedys, who had been freed from the nightmare of a scandal; for the CIA and the FBI...")

(SUMMERS 2000, p. 528: On July 8, 1964, Hoover wrote to Bobby, "His book will make reference to your alleged friendship with the late Miss Marilyn Monroe. Mr. Capell stated that he will indicate...")

108. (SLATZER 1975, p. 122: "We breezed toward San Diego, far ahead of the Saturday morning traffic buildup.")

(SPOTO 1993, p. 227: "On the afternoon of Saturday, October 4, Marilyn (who never liked to shop alone) asked Natasha to accompany her on a shopping expedition to Jax, a store on Wilshire Boulevard. There she selected several pairs of lounging trousers, shirts, blouses and accessories and wrote a check against her account at the Bank of America for $313.13.")

(SCHREINER, GREG. INTERVIEW WITH JAY MARGOLIS. 3 JANUARY 2011: Slatzer was nowhere in MM's address books.)

(CHENOWETH, DORAL. INTERVIEW WITH JAY MARGOLIS. 6 DECEMBER 2010: "The famous picture with Bob and Marilyn was used many times in books about Slatzer and Monroe. That was taken by a guy named Fred Pfening, Jr...")

(Wallace, Tom. "He Sure Made Time On That Couch With Marilyn Monroe!" Confidential. May 1957, pp. 20-23: "Maybe it's a little late in this story to point this out: A glamour puss like Monroe will make it legal with a sports celebrity like DiMaggio, or a famous man of letters like Arthur Miller. But on the other hand, if a guy is lucky enough to catch up with her between hubbies, it's good to know that there's always a spot for an ordinary little guy to move in – like Slatzer, or you, or you.")

(GILMORE 2007, pp. 144, 202-208: "The sad truth about Slatzer, who is so often quoted by so-called Marilyn historians, was that he was an alcoholic, compulsive pathological liar who had turned his sickness to profit...")

(FOWLER 1991, p. 288: "Robert Slatzer was never married to Marilyn Monroe. He met the star only once. That was in Niagara Falls, New York, where he had his only pictures taken with her while she was making the movie, *Niagara*, with Joseph Cotton in 1951 – 1952. Slatzer never met Marilyn before or since that time. Also, Slatzer never even met Walter Winchell or Joe DiMaggio in his life.")

(CARPOZI, GEORGE, JR. INTERVIEW WITH DEBORAH CHIEL. 7 NOVEMBER 1992: "Back in 1974, I had a call from Andy Ettinger...")

(DOUGHERTY 2001, p. 168: "The individual who claims to have been married to her after our marriage...")

(MARSHALL 2005, pp. 235-236: Italian TV director Claudio Masenza wrote, "A few days later I met Allan Snyder and, after the interview, I asked him how well he knew Slatzer when Marilyn was alive...")

(*Say Goodbye to the President* documentary, 1985: As for the entries in MM's red diary, "Slatzer could have got his story years later from published sources.")

(Davis, Lisa. "The Right Photographer." Los Angeles Times. 27 June 1993)

(SCHREINER, GREG. INTERVIEW WITH JAY MARGOLIS. 3 JANUARY 2011: MM's stand-in Evelyn Moriarty told Slatzer, "Bob, you were never on that set...")

(*Runnin' Wild: All About Marilyn*, January 1992, Number 5: Milton Greene's son Anthony snapped at Slatzer, "C'mon Bob. You've got to stop somewhere. You've got to get back to reality.")

109. (JAMES 2007, p. 367: Jeanne Carmen claimed she met MM "during the early 1950's... at a bar near the Actors Studio in New York City.")

(JACOBS 2004, pp. 76-78, 154-155, 261)

(SCHREINER, GREG. INTERVIEW WITH JAY MARGOLIS. 3 JANUARY 2011: Jeanne Carmen was nowhere in MM's address books.)

(CARPOZI, GEORGE, JR. INTERVIEW WITH DEBORAH CHIEL. 7 NOVEMBER 1992: "Have you heard of the name Jeanne Carmen?... She doesn't exist as Marilyn's friend...")

(JAMES 2007, p. 485: Jeanne Carmen claimed that sometime after 5:30 A.M., "early in the morning on August 4th," MM called Carmen complaining about harassing phone calls all night long. Since she didn't get any sleep, she said MM wanted her to come over with pills and Carmen declined.)

(JAMES 2007, p. 486: MM's alleged call to Jeanne Carmen at 8:00 P.M. and Carmen's version of the stuffed tiger story.)

(SUMMERS 2000, p. 411: Don Feld and the stuffed tiger story.)

(JAMES 2007, p. 488: On MM supposedly telling Carmen that Greenson came over and gave her an injection.)

(Blackburn, John, Chuck Orman, and Dan McDonald. "I Saw Marilyn Murdered." Globe. 23 November 1982, Volume 29, Number 47, p. 5: On Greenson, James Hall related, "Strange, but when he was trying to find her heart, he had to count down her ribs – like he was still in premed school and had really never done this before.")

(JAMES 2007, p. 487: Carmen said MM relayed RFK's angry response to her, "You know damn well what I'm looking for. The fucking bug you used to record me with.")

(SUMMERS 2000, p. 521: "Apparently he was still looking for the recording device...")

(JAMES 2007, p. 488: Jeanne Carmen said, "I reminded her that my birthday was on the following day and I thanked her for the card she'd sent me...")

(JAMES 2007, p. 489: Jeanne Carmen claimed, "Marilyn called me again one last time at around 10 P.M.... The phone rang again about a half hour later but I didn't answer it.")

(SUMMERS 2000, p. 416: Carmen claims MM called her at 10:00 P.M. and even later than that.)

(JAMES 2007, p. 535: Jeanne Carmen said in her book that Anthony Summers wrote the best biography on MM.)

(ROMANOFF, GLORIA. INTERVIEW WITH JAY MARGOLIS. 2 SEPTEMBER 2010: "I have to tell you, she came very late to the scene. They shared the same address on Doheny Drive for a period...")

(SUMMERS 2006, p. 466: "Carmen... occupied neighboring apartments at 882 Doheny Drive in West Hollywood. An old telegram sent to Carmen at that address confirms that she lived there... Western Union message dated Jul. 31, 1961, in collection of Jeanne Carmen.")

110. (CLARK 2000, pp. 117-118: " 'I'll set the alarm for seven o'clock'...")

111. (CLARK 1995, p. 134: "I came back and told Tony there was no truth in the rumour about the pregnancy...")

(CLARK 1995, p. 140: "Sure enough, at 10 A.M. we had an official message from Parkside to say MM was not well, and a doctor had been called...")

112. (CLARK 1995, pp. 142-143: "Plod called me over to Parkside for a chat. He could say nothing directly, but he hinted that MM had been pregnant but had now miscarried...")

113. (CLARK 2000, pp. 130-131: "Less than an hour later, she was awake again...")

114. (CLARK 2000, p. 132: " 'Are you OK, Marilyn?'...")

(CLARK 2000, p. 136: A doctor asked Colin Clark, "And what are you doing here, Mr. Clark, if I may ask...")

115. (SPOTO 1993, pp. 375-376: "While she was performing some of her best scenes in late August, Marilyn learned she was expecting a baby...")

116. (LEAMING 1998, pp. 270-271: "Marilyn didn't show up at the studio again on Thursday [August 30]. Instead she saw Arthur [Miller] off at the airport. The next day [August 31], Milton Greene telephoned Irving Stein in New York to report that Marilyn was pregnant...")

117. (CLARK 1995, p. 140: As for the diary entry dated Thursday, 6 September, "AM [Arthur Miller] had found the name of a London physician from a friend and had recommended him over the phone.")

(CLARK 2000, pp. 139-140: "Milton tells me that Arthur is returning from New York this afternoon. I'm sure that will help. Marilyn told me she's going to work especially hard...")

118. (http://www.wowowow.com/culture/liz-smith-forget-vampires-hollywoods-greatest-undead-marilyn-monroe-473422: Smith, Liz. "Forget Vampires… Hollywood's Greatest Undead Is – Marilyn Monroe!" 18 May 2010)

119. (http://www.independent.co.uk/news/obituaries/colin-clark-611377.html: Trewin, Ion. "Colin Clark, Writer and film producer in the shadow of his father and brother." Independent. 18 December 2002)

(SUMMERS 2000, p. 224: "In 1980, in his autobiography, entertainer Sammy Davis, Jr. wrote of Marilyn: 'While she was making *The Prince and the Showgirl* with Laurence Olivier, she was going through one of the most difficult periods of her life. She was having an affair with a close friend of mine. He was a photographer... They met clandestinely, often at my house. She was always being followed there, and we had to get up all sorts of intrigues to keep the affair secret. I used to pretend we were having a party, and Marilyn would arrive and leave at different times from my pal.' Milton Greene was, of course, a photographer, and he did count Sammy Davis among his friends. It was Greene, indeed, who introduced Davis to Marilyn. In 1984, asked about Davis' story, Greene laughed hugely and asked, 'Did he really say that? You may be right, but I'm not saying anything. I think the best way to keep it, is that we were close friends and associates and we loved each other. Period.' ")

120. (OATES 2001, p. 680: MM opened an envelope and was shocked by what was inside, "It was a square of white toilet paper upon which someone had carefully block-printed, in what appeared to be actual excrement, WHORE.")

(OATES 2001, p. 737: The Sharpshooter injects MM with a needle to the heart.)

(MARSHALL 2005, p. 237: "Jordan lessens his credibility further when he goes on to misidentify a picture of Arline Hunter in his book as Marilyn.")

121. (SPOTO 1993, p. 408: In 1958, "Carl Sandburg... met Marilyn briefly during the filming of *Some Like It Hot*.")

(MEYERS 2010, p. 176: Sandburg met MM again in 1960 during the time she was making *Let's Make Love*.)

(Scheer, Julian. "Carl Sandburg Talks About Marilyn Monroe." Cavalier. January 1963, pp. 12-15: In 1960, Sandburg was working on a screenplay called *The Greatest Story*

Ever Told. The photos Sandburg glances at in the pictures that accompany the article are the same photos that were taken in which MM's hair was prepared by a hairdresser right before her arrival and these pictures are credited to photographer Len Steckler.)

(http://lensteckler.com/PhotographyCollectionsFolder/VisitSeries.aspx: One afternoon during December 1961, in his own New York apartment, photographer Len Steckler took the first photographs of MM with Carl Sandburg.)

(http://www.dailymail.co.uk/tvshowbiz/article-1248938/Never-seen-photos-Marilyn-Monroe-pictured-months-death-sale.html: "Never-before seen photos of Marilyn Monroe pictured months before death go up for sale." Daily Mail Reporter. 5 February 2010: Len Steckler related, "Hours later I went to open the door and there I was face to face with Marilyn Monroe...")

("Tribute to Marilyn, from a friend... Carl Sandburg." Look. 11 September 1962, pp. 90-94: The second photographs of Carl Sandburg and MM together displayed in this article are credited to photographer Arnold Newman: January 20, 1962 at the Los Angeles home of Henry and Irena Weinstein.)

(CONFIDENTIAL SOURCE: GREENSON, JOAN. UNTITLED 90-PAGE MARILYN MONROE MANUSCRIPT, pp. 62-64: "One of Marilyn's friends that we did get an opportunity to meet was Carl Sandburg..." The complete work is located in Greenson Papers, Special Collections, UCLA, sealed from the public until January 1, 2039.)

(TARABORRELLI 2009, pp. 432-433: Between these pages are Arnold Newman's photographs of MM and Carl Sandburg.)
(http://www.gettyimages.com/detail/53466917/Arnold-Newman-Collection)

Index

Abernathy, Raymond, 4, 11, 18, 246–247
Abrams, Dr. Arnold, 138, 152
Abrams, Dan, 105–106
Ahearn, Det. James, 63, 78
Albert, Eddie and Margo:
    Greenson's alleged August 4 attendance at dinner party of, 169–170, 172
Allan, Rupert:
    JFK's callous treatment of MM, 84
    Lawford's "alibi" for night MM died, 195
    MM's death, 33
    MM's June 13 telegram to RFK, 69
    MM's last abortion, 100
    MM's miscarriage during *The Prince and the Showgirl*, 218
    MM's press conference threat, 60
    Press agent for John Springer, 55
Amador, Dr. Elias W.:
    Acknowledgements, v
    Greenson's undiluted pentobarbital injection to MM in the heart, 152, 156
    Impossibility of accidental suicide in MM's case, 26, 57, 152
    MM's empty stomach, 14
    MM's last call to the answering service of Ralph Roberts, 141
    MM receiving an enema in the evening, 56–57
    MM receiving an intramuscular pentobarbital injection in the afternoon, 57
Armstrong, Grover, 188, 251, 254
Asher, Bill:
    Disbelief in MM's tryst with RFK, 88
    Lawford's alleged panic phone calls, 196, 200
    MM and her alleged Saturday afternoon walk on the beach, 32
    MM's death, 200–201
Autopsy report, 241–247

Bacon, James, 75, 77, 154
Badman, Keith, 19, 35, 50, 51, 60, 75, 78, 82, 83, 99, 103
Barham, Patte B., 19, 23, 25, 26, 33, 36, 37, 51, 60, 62, 67, 69, 83, 92, 99, 105, 130, 132, 134, 138, 139, 143, 149, 155, 165, 167, 171, 181, 184, 185, 189–190, 195
Barr, Candy, 35
Barris, George:
    Acknowledgements, vi

Author of *Marilyn: Her Life In Her Own Words*, 8
Conviction that MM was murdered, 9
Cosmopolitan story on MM, 7–8
Debunking suicide in MM's case, 8
Discussing the Kennedy brothers, 76
Final August 3 phone call from MM, 7–8
Foreword, viii
Meeting MM for first time on set of *The Seven Year Itch*, 8
Meeting MM for her birthday on set of *Something's Got to Give*, 8
MM's determination as a model, 9
MM's good spirits shortly before her death, 8
MM's loneliness and shyness, 9
MM's unidentified neighbor to the east at Gloria Steinem's book signing, 36–37
Pat Newcomb, 31, 192–193
Bates, John, 27
Beatty, Warren, 184
Beck, Dave, 63
Bellonzi, Carl Angelo, 160
Bergman, Melvin B., 152
Bjorkman, Carol, 95–96
Blackburn, John, 148, 153
Blaine, Gerald, 81, 82
Blane, Paul, 94
Blaustein, Julian, 169
Blonde (Oates), 220
Blonde (film), 220
Blu-ray disc, 221
Bobby and Jackie: A Love Story (Heymann), 48, 94
Bolaños, José, 140, 213
Bowler, Manley J., 24–25
Braden, Joan, 97
Brown, Peter H., 19, 23, 25, 26, 33, 36, 37, 51, 60, 62, 67, 69, 83, 92, 99, 105, 130, 132, 134, 138, 139, 143, 149, 155, 165, 167, 171, 181, 184, 185, 189–190, 195
Brown, Thad, 62, 181
Buchwald, Art, 79–80, 94
Buntin, John, 63, 189
Burke, Richard E., 46
Byron, Dorothea, 188–189
Byron, Det. Sgt. Robert E., 4, 17, 142, 170, 171, 188, 190

Cal-Neva Lodge, 66, 73, 98, 100, 101–102, 104, 105, 131
Calomaris, Anthony, 61, 193
Campbell, Judith "Judy," 46, 84, 85–86, 87, 101
Campbell, William, 85
Capell, Frank, 59, 110, 111, 205
Captain Newman, M.D. (book), 121
Captain Newman, M.D. (film), 121, 169–170
Carlson, Michael, 132, 133
Carlyle Hotel, 42, 81, 82, 83, 95
Carmen, Jeanne, 211, 212, 213–214
Carpozi, George, Jr.:
 Intramuscular pentobarbital injection to MM in afternoon, 57
 Jeanne Carmen as fraud, 212
 Lawford/RFK/Greenson conspiracy to murder MM, 33
 MM aborts RFK's child, 99
 RFK's fallen promise to meet MM at Cal-Neva, 102
 Robert Slatzer as fraud, 208–209
 Suicide Prevention Team misused to cover up MM's murder, 191
Carroll, Ronald "Mike," 144–146, 176
Carter, William R., 86–87
Case, Det. Archie, 63, 78
Castro, Fidel, 85–86, 87, 131, 132–133, 186
Chaplin, Charlie, 224

Chaplin, Charlie, Jr., 72
Chase, Sylvia, 73–74, 133–134
Chenoweth, Doral, 207–208
Chiel, Deborah, 208, 212
Chloral hydrate, 4, 5–6, 10, 11, 12, 13–14, 23, 25, 26, 56, 57, 64, 135, 136, 138, 139, 140, 141, 152, 156, 157, 213
Clark, Alan, 219
Clark, Barbara, 83
Clark, Colin, 215–220
Clemmons, Sgt. Jack, 10, 18–19, 142, 143, 153, 155, 156, 163, 170, 173, 176, 187, 191
Cleopatra, 8–9
Clifford, Clark, 106–107, 108
Confidential magazine, 208
Conners, Hal, 185–186
Coroner to the Stars (Noguchi and DiMona), 25, 26, 65
Cramer, Richard Ben, 15, 73, 130
Crosby, Bing, 43, 49, 51, 73, 75
Curphey, Theodore J., 1, 11, 14, 17, 18, 24–25, 26, 64, 139, 188
Cushing, Natalie Fell, 96

D'Amato, Paul "Skinny," 103–104, 131
Dambacher, Robert, 191
Danoff, John, 74, 80, 132
Davis, Sammy, Jr., 220
DD Group (Death Discussion Group), 41, 69, 209
Del Raso, Joe, 131
DePaulo, Lisa, 53, 54
DeSapio, Carmine, 72
DiBella, Tommy, 101–102
Dickinson, Angie, 84, 97, 131, 133
DiMaggio, Joe, Jr., 16, 28, 130, 172–173, 199
DiMaggio, Joe, Sr., 9, 15–16, 17, 28, 39, 66, 70–71, 73, 75, 100, 101, 102, 103, 104, 106, 107, 112, 130, 173, 194

Donaldson, Martha, 51–52
Double Cross (Giancana and Giancana), 132, 134–136, 137, 200
Dougherty, Jim, 19, 143, 209
Douglas, William O., 17
Dunne, Dominick, 43
Durgom, George "Bullets," 40, 180, 184, 196–197, 198, 204
Dye, Peter, 89, 90

Ebbins, Milt, 2, 28, 31–32, 35, 49, 65, 84, 88, 96, 111, 135, 144, 174, 177, 179, 184–185, 195–196, 197–199, 200
Edwards, Sheffield, 133
Eicher, Kay, 209
The Enemy Within (book), 62–63
The Enemy Within (film), 102
Engelberg, Dr. Hyman, 3–4, 5, 6–7, 19, 20–21, 22, 56, 58, 122, 139, 142, 153, 154, 170–171, 174, 175, 176, 179, 188, 196, 198, 212
Engelberg, Morris, 15–16, 130
Ettinger, Andy, 208–209

Farberow, Dr. Norman, 11, 14, 61
Fears, Tom, 146
Feld, Don, 212
Fell, Fifi, 96
Flanagan, Agnes, 100, 212
Fox, Dr. J. DeWitt, 26, 57, 58, 143, 154, 155
Franklin, Det. Lynn, 164–165, 176, 181–184, 185, 199
Fraser, Donald E., 153–154
Freeman, Lucy, 125, 169
Freud, Anna, 109–110, 116, 117, 166, 167, 169
Freud, Sigmund, 169
The Fruitful Bough (Kennedy), 36, 44

431

Gates, Daryl F., 34, 62, 63, 78
Gentry, Curt, 51
Giancana, Chuck, 132, 135, 136–137
Giancana, Sam "Mooney," 47, 48–49, 85–86, 87, 101–102, 103, 130, 132–133, 134, 135, 136–137, 186, 200
Giancana, Sam (Mooney's nephew), 132, 135
Gianola, Leonard "Needles," 135, 137
Gifford, Charles Stanley, 120–121
Gilmore, John, 59–60, 122
Globe newspaper, 10, 148–151, 152, 153, 156, 157
Goddess: The Secret Lives of Marilyn Monroe (Summers), 6, 37–38, 51, 212, 214
Goldman, Ivan G., 62
Gould, Deborah, 61, 65, 89, 138
Gould, Milton, 67–68, 69
Grandison, Lionel, 11, 131, 187–188, 210
Greene, Amy, 218
Greene, Anthony, 211
Greene, Josh, 216
Greene, Milton H., 211, 216, 218, 220
Greenson, Danny:
    Discounting James Hall, 154
    Greenson's discretion to family about patients before MM, 117
    Greenson's recorded "Talk to Bobby Kennedy" remark, 168
    June 2 visit to MM's home, 114–115
    MM and dressing incognito, 127
    MM and Payne Whitney Psychiatric Clinic, 111
    Statement that MM intentionally committed suicide, 20, 120
    Statement that MM was dead when Greenson arrived, 121
Greenson, Hildi:
    Alibi for night of MM's death, 171, 176
    Defensively discounting James Hall, 154
    Discounting phone call to Hollywood Bowl, 179
    Greenson's alleged plan to wean MM from barbiturates, 5
    Greenson's alleged unawareness of August 3 prescription, 6
    Greenson bringing MM into his home, 126, 127
    Interviewed by private investigator Cathy Griffin, v, 4, 5, 6, 20, 92, 114, 117, 118, 119, 122, 127, 154, 171, 173, 176, 179
    MM and doctor shopping, 4
    MM and dressing incognito, 92
    MM and free-association tapes, 41
    MM and incessant phone calls to Greenson in Europe, 114
    MM and RFK, 92
    MM and state of mind, 115, 117, 118, 119
    Response to rumors of MM and Greenson affair, 122
    Statement that MM committed suicide accidentally, 20
    Statement that MM's door was locked and bolted night of death, 171
    Statement that Mrs. Murray awakened at midnight then fell asleep again, 173
    Winning law suit against Swiss newspaper *Blick*, 117
Greenson, Joan:
    Alibi for night of MM's death, 171
    Driving MM home, 118–119
    Foreword, vii
    Greenson's alleged handling of MM's medication, 4–5
    Greenson's alleged plan to wean MM from barbiturates, 20
    Greenson's alleged unawareness of August 3 prescription, 6

Greenson's European vacation, 114
Greenson's European vacation cancelled, 115
Greenson's unorthodox psychiatric methods, 120
Information about MM's unidentified neighbor to the east, 36
Intensity of MM and her emotions, 119
June 2 visit to MM's home, 114–115
Meeting MM for the first time, 117
MM and attendance at family chamber music recitals, 127
MM and Carl Sandburg, 224
MM and dressing incognito, 127
MM and free-association tapes, 122
MM and her natural sexiness, 123–124
MM and paranoia, 112
MM and RFK, 91–92
MM and unjust firing from *Something's Got to Give*, 69
Statement that MM was dead when Greenson arrived, 173–174
Greenson, Dr. Ralph:
Alibi for night of MM's death, 169–176
Alleged plan to wean MM from barbiturates, 3, 5
Alleged sexual affair with MM, 122–129
Alleged unawareness of August 3 prescription, 3–4, 6–7
August 20, 1962 correspondence to Dr. Marianne Kris, 5, 6, 21, 30, 31, 45, 58, 109, 110–111, 114, 118, 120, 121, 166, 173, 174
Calls police to report "suicide," 18–19
Countertransference, 108–109, 121, 124, 129
Cryptic remarks,166–169

Discounting MM's affairs with JFK and RFK, 23
Discounting MM murder rumors, 23, 91
Experiencing countertransference feelings while treating MM, 108–117
Improbability of administering intramuscular injections, 37, 212–213
Interviewed by Zolotow, 4, 21–22, 29–30, 31, 91, 118, 167
MM and free-association tapes, 39, 41, 42–43, 64–67, 69–70, 71, 110
MM and her alleged lack of sleep night before death, 29–30, 31, 32
Murder suspect, 33–34, 42–43, 148–157, 165, 175–176, 182–183, 204–206
Obsession with MM, 117–122
Presence at death scene, 14, 33, 165–166
Spoto's allegations against Greenson, 138
Strange remarks to Suicide Team on MM's death, 14, 18
Tells family MM accidentally committed suicide, 19–20
Tells Suicide Team MM had affairs with both Kennedy brothers, 23, 91–92
Greenschpoon, Elizabeth, 113
Griffin, Cathy, v, 4, 20, 92, 117, 119, 122, 152, 154, 171, 176, 179
Griffiths, Susan, 221
Guilaroff, Sydney, 39–40, 118
Guiles, Fred Lawrence, 5, 53, 54, 98, 148, 177
Guthman, Edwin, 66

Hackett, David L., 61
Hall, Harry, 15, 130

433

Hall, James Edwin, 64, 136, 143–157, 159, 160, 161–163, 164–165, 174, 180, 204, 212–213
Hamel, Veronica, 72
Hamilton, James, 61, 62–64, 78, 142, 165–166, 192
Harrison, John, 153
Haspiel, Jimmy, 82, 141
Hazen, Lita, 109–110
Hersh, Seymour M., 75–77, 83, 84, 85–87, 97, 133
Heymann, C. David, v, 17, 21, 28–29, 33–34, 35, 36, 41–42, 43, 44, 45–46, 47, 48–49, 51, 59, 66–67, 69, 72, 74, 76, 77, 78, 79, 89–90, 91, 92, 93, 94–96, 100, 101, 106–107, 122, 125, 128–129, 152, 156, 182, 204, 206
Hockett, Don, 4
Hockett, Guy, 4, 143
Hoffa, Jimmy, 27, 47, 63, 72, 73, 86, 107, 186
Hoover, J. Edgar, 51–52, 61, 62, 63, 72, 74, 87, 88, 91, 105, 106, 107, 142, 193–194, 205
Houston, Lawrence, 133
Hryniszak, Roman, 210
Hughes, Howard, 9, 74, 208
Hunter, Arline, 221
Hunter, Ken, 157–161, 164
Huston, John, 58
Hyams, Joe, 53, 63, 83, 185, 186, 191, 192

Iannone, Sgt. Marvin D., 78, 152, 153, 165–166, 190
In the President's Secret Service (Kessler), 77
Irvin, Monte, 104

Jacobs, Arthur P., 31, 33, 34, 39, 54, 55, 56, 60, 98, 99, 176–179, 180

Jacobs, George, 34, 46, 48, 49, 51, 77–78, 98, 102–103, 113, 123, 126, 211–212
Jacobs, Natalie, 33, 98, 176–179, 180
Jacobson, Dr. Max, 76
Jacobson, Tom, 76
James, Arthur, 72, 75, 98
James, Brandon, 211, 214
Jeanne Carmen: My Wild, Wild Life (James), 211, 214
Jefferies, Norman:
  Ambulance on scene ahead of Greenson, 175
  Destroys evidence with Mrs. Murray, 138
  Escorts Mrs. Murray into living room before MM died, 142, 151
  Finds unconscious MM leaning on phone, 141–142
  Lawford and Newcomb arrive together before MM died, 142, 176, 180
  MM died in guest cottage, 136, 175
  Mrs. Murray gives MM's red diary to driver for Coroner's Office, 187
  Negating Greenson's official version to police, 176
  Observes frightened MM after RFK's afternoon visit, 39
  Ordered out of house by RFK and two men, 139–140
  Pat Newcomb arrives before MM died, 142, 148
  Pat Newcomb frantically searches MM's drawers, 186–187
Jordan, Ted "Eddie," 221
Joyce, James, 71, 129
Judd, Ashley, 221
Justice, Michelle:
  Acknowledgements, vi
  Whitey Snyder debunking Slatzer's claims to know MM, 210

Kelley, Kitty, 49, 76, 113
Kennedy, Edward "Teddy," 36, 46, 93, 95
Kennedy, Ethel, 39, 51, 69, 89, 90, 93, 94, 95, 96, 97, 99, 186, 194
Kennedy, John "Jack":
  Affair with MM, 39–40, 45–46, 49–50, 75–76, 77–81
  Famous libido, 76–77, 88
  Frank Sinatra, 46–51
  Judy Campbell, 46, 84–88
  Maine cruise four days after MM's funeral, 17
  MM plays secretary, 83–84
  No May 20 tryst with MM at Carlyle Hotel, 81–83
  Sam Giancana, 47–48, 49, 85–87, 132
Kennedy, Jacqueline "Jackie," 28, 41–42, 45, 47, 48, 49, 50, 69, 76, 77–78, 93, 94, 95, 96, 107
Kennedy, Joseph, Sr., 36, 44, 46–47, 48, 76, 77, 200
Kennedy, Robert "Bobby":
  Affair with MM, 39–40, 42, 66, 88–92
  Alibi for night of MM's death, 27
  August 4 visit to MM, 27–30, 59
  Extra-marital affairs, 42, 93–97
  Frank Sinatra, 47–49, 51
  Greenson's recorded "Talk to Bobby Kennedy" remark, 167–168
  J. Edgar Hoover, 193–194
  MM's abortion, 98–100
  MM sex tape, 105–107
  MM's taped phone conversations, 66, 105
  Murder suspect, 9–10, 15–16, 33–34, 139–143, 208
  Photoplay article, 51–52
  Plane to San Francisco, 185–186
  Police connections, 61–64, 188–192
  Presence at death scene, 139–143, 156, 157, 165, 166
  Red diary, 37–38, 129–131, 141, 186–188
  Sam Giancana, 85–86, 133
  Trip to Oregon, 17
Kessler, Ronald, 77, 82
Kilgallen, Dorothy, 27, 103
King, Martin Luther, Jr., 51, 97
Kirsner, Douglas, 111, 120
Koder, Henry, 153
Kopechne, Mary Jo, 93
Krim, Arthur, 81
Kris, Dr. Marianne, 5, 6, 15, 21, 30, 58, 108, 110, 116, 127
Krohn, Dr. Leon "Red," 98, 99–100

Landau, Abe C., 23, 159, 164
Langford, Ray, 102
Lawford, Lady May, 185, 197
Lawford, Pat Kennedy, 16–17, 28, 43, 68, 75, 78, 85, 90, 97, 98, 100, 101, 102, 105, 129–130, 197, 199
Lawford, Patricia Seaton. *See* Stewart, Patricia
Lawford, Peter:
  Alibi for night of MM's death, 195–203
  Alleged final 7:30 P.M. phone call to MM, 15, 195–196
  August 4 afternoon visit to MM, 27–30
  Interviewed by Heymann, 21, 28–29, 33–34, 35, 41–45, 47–49, 50–51, 59, 66–67, 69, 72, 79, 89–90, 92, 93, 96, 100, 101, 125, 128–129, 156, 182, 204, 206
  Maine cruise four days after MM's funeral, 17
  MM's last weekend at Cal-Neva, 100, 101, 102, 104–105
  Murder suspect, 15, 17, 33–35, 204–206

Presence at death scene, 136, 142, 152–153, 165
Pulled over by Officer Lynn Franklin, 165, 181–182
Relationship with Frank Sinatra, 43, 46–47, 48–49, 72, 100, 101, 104–105
Wiretaps in home, 72–74
Leaming, Barbara, 123, 218
Leib, Murray. *See* Liebowitz, Murray
Leib, Sylvia, 161–164
Leigh, Wendy, 9–10
Levathes, Peter, 67
Liden, Donald, 120–121
Liebowitz, Murray, 152, 156, 157, 159, 160, 161–162, 163, 204
The Life and Curious Death of Marilyn Monroe (Slatzer), 207, 209
Life magazine, 21, 154, 205
Litman, Dr. Robert, 7, 11, 14, 17, 18, 25, 56, 58, 61, 91, 92, 110
Look magazine, 223, 224
Lovell, Gloria, 211
Lytess, Natasha, 1, 207

Maheu, Robert Aime, 132–133
Mailer, Norman, 22, 59, 91, 167
The Manchurian Candidate, 51
Mandel, Melvin, 124
Mann, May, 190
Mansfield, Jayne, vi, 25, 43, 93–94, 112, 123
Marcello, Carlos, 47, 72
The Marilyn Files, 25, 26, 142, 148, 152, 160, 187
The Marilyn Files (TV Special), 64, 164
Marilyn: The Last Months (Murray and Shade), 53
Marilyn: The Last Word, 38, 72
Marilyn Monroe: A Case for Murder, 143, 148, 154, 161, 164
Marilyn Monroe: The Final Days, 20–21
Marilyn Monroe: Murder on Fifth Helena Drive, 105

Marshall, David, 41, 59–60, 69, 171, 209
Martin, Dean, 2, 35, 69, 204
Martin, Jeanne, 2, 31, 35, 62, 204–205
Martin, Ralph G., 36, 81
Masenza, Claudio, 209
McCullough, Jimmie, 104
McDonald, Dan, 148
McGuire, Phyllis, 133
McKesson, William, 17
Mecacci, Luciano, 205
Melson, Inez, 187
Meryman, Richard, 21, 205
Meyer, Johnny, 95
Miller, Arthur, 70, 71, 79–80, 123, 126, 215, 216, 217, 218–219
Miller, Isadore, 53, 81–82
Miner, Dr. John Willis, v, 17–18, 19, 23, 24–25, 39, 41, 42–43, 57, 58, 64–65, 66, 68–69, 70, 71, 110, 122, 125, 129, 138–139, 140, 154, 155, 156, 163
The Misfits, 58, 78, 80, 221
Mitchell, James, 210
Monroe, Marilyn:
1956 miscarriage, 215–219
Atomic testing, 129–130
Autopsy report, 241–244
Cal-Neva Lodge, 66, 100–105
Concentration of drugs at time of death, 56–58
Coroner Curphey's press conference statement, 11–13
Drug enema, 23, 26, 56–57, 135–136, 138–139, 213
Final abortion, 98–100
Finances, 45, 112–113
Firing, 7, 69
Free-association tapes, 64–67, 70–71, 110, 125, 140
Greenson's fatal heart injection, 150, 152, 155, 156
Heavy pill use, 104
Insomnia, 112, 224
Lack of pill residue in stomach,

10–11, 14, 25–26, 57–58, 143–144, 244
Last morning alive, 53–56
Manic-depressive, 20–21
MCA dispute, 67
Paranoia, 111–112
Prescription "mix-up," 3–7
Press conference threat, 59–60, 105
Previous suicide attempts, 1, 15
Red diary, 38, 66, 129–131, 140, 141, 186–188, 210, 213
Sex tape with RFK, 105–107
State of mind before death, 1–2
Taped phone conversations with RFK, 66, 105
Wiretaps in house, 72–74, 107–108, 128–129
Montand, Yves, 122
Moore, Terry, vi, 1, 9, 90, 135
Morgan, Keya, 97, 105–106, 140, 141
Moriarty, Evelyn, 210
Muir, Florabel, 27, 135, 191–192
Murray, Eunice, 4, 5, 14, 19, 22, 23, 25, 28, 29–31, 32, 39, 53–54, 56, 64, 114, 115, 118, 119, 136, 138, 139–140, 141, 142, 148, 149, 151, 170, 171–172, 173, 174, 175, 176, 177, 180, 186, 187, 188, 190, 191, 192, 195, 198, 199, 203, 204
My Story (Campbell), 85
My Week with Marilyn (Clark), 215, 218, 219–220
My Week with Marilyn (film), 220

Naar, Dolores, 180, 201–203, 204
Naar, Joseph T., 2, 32, 35, 88, 89, 183–184, 185, 196, 198, 200, 201, 202, 203, 204
Neill, Frank, 142
Nelson, Valerie J., 61
Nembutal, 3–4, 6–7, 10, 11, 12–14, 19, 22, 23, 25, 26, 29, 36, 37, 56–57, 58, 135, 136, 138–139, 141, 152, 155–156, 157, 172, 186, 202, 213
Newcomb, Margot Patricia "Pat":
  Admission to bringing MM to Cedars of Lebanon for a D & C, 98–99
  Alleged phone call from Mickey Rudin, 148, 177
  Arrival at Peter's August 4 evening party, 180, 204
  Avoids Suicide Prevention Team, 14
  Defensive discounting of James Hall, 148
  Discounting MM's tape recordings, 66
  Discounting Mrs. Murray's account, 176
  Discounting RFK as murder suspect in MM's death, 34
  Dismissed by Greenson day of MM's death, 29
  Driven by Peter Lawford to MM's house before death, 142, 176, 180, 204
  Friendship with George Barris, 31, 192–193
  Hired by Kennedys after MM's death, 192–193, 197, 206
  Hysterical after MM's death, 142, 192
  Interested in same men as MM, 31
  Interviewed by Margolis, 2–3
  Interviewed by Slatzer, 27, 179–180
  Larry Schiller, 54, 55, 56
  Maine cruise with Kennedys four days after MM's funeral, 17
  Mentioned by Greenson as one of last persons to see MM alive, 22
  Michael Selsman, 55, 56, 192
  MM and Engelberg, 6
  MM and Greenson, 6, 117–118
  MM and her alleged lack of sleep night before death, 29–30, 31

MM and her alleged last walk at Santa Monica beach, 29, 32
MM and paranoia, 112
MM and Payne Whitney Psychiatric Clinic, 15
MM didn't lock doors, 172
Natalie Trundy, 177–179
Phones Arthur Jacobs at the Hollywood Bowl, 176–179
Presence in MM's home before death, 135, 136, 142, 148, 151, 152–153, 159, 175, 176, 180, 204
Publicity campaign after MM's death to deceive public, 33
Searching for MM's red diary, 186–187
Seen by James Hall before MM died, 148, 151, 152–153, 159
Seen by Norman Jefferies before MM died, 142, 175, 176
Trip to Hyannis Port and Paris after MM's death, 135, 192–193, 206
Newman, Arnold, 224
Niagara, 207, 208, 210, 211, 221
Nicoletti, Chuck, 135
Nixon, Richard, 74
Noguchi, Dr. Thomas, v, 17, 18, 22, 23, 25, 26, 36, 56, 57, 58, 59, 65, 121, 138, 143, 144, 149, 154, 155, 163, 197
Norma Jean & Marilyn, 221
Norma Jean: My Secret Life with Marilyn Monroe (Jordan), 221
Novak, Kim, 48, 96–97

Oates, Joyce Carol, 220
O'Donnell, Kenneth, 79, 84, 96
Onassis, Aristotle, 95
Onassis, Jackie Kennedy, *See* Kennedy, Jacqueline

O'Neill, Anne W., 64
Oppenheimer, Jerry, 51, 89
Orman, Chuck, 148
Ostrow, Lucille, 115
Otash, Fred, 27, 37–38, 39, 40, 59, 65, 66, 70, 72, 73–74, 80, 101, 102, 103, 108, 130, 132, 133–134, 136, 142, 143, 164–165, 184, 204, 205
Oui magazine, 14, 25–26

Pace, Cletus, 191
Parker, Helen, 142, 143, 189
Parker, William H., 61, 62, 63–64, 142, 143, 181, 188, 189–190, 191, 194
People magazine, 199
Peters, Jean, 208
Pfening, Fred D., Jr., 208, 211
Photoplay magazine, 51–52
Pick, Chuck, 91
Playboy magazine, 54, 55
Plecher, Marjorie, 1
Pollard, Betty, 37
Pollard, Elizabeth, 36, 37
Positano, Rock, 16, 130
Powers, Dave, 84
The Prince and the Showgirl, 116, 215, 219, 221
Pulp Fiction, 221

Rangell, Leo, 124
Rathman, Richard, 188
Reddin, Tom, 61, 62, 130, 142
Redmond, Cherie, 171
Refractile crystals, 14, 25, 143
Reis, May, 56
Remick, Lee, 48, 96
Reynolds, Debbie, 10
RFK: A Candid Biography of Bobby Kennedy (Heymann), 41, 42, 50–51, 91
Robello, Stephen, 65

Roberts, Ralph, 13, 23–24, 53, 56, 57–58, 60, 67, 82, 83, 88, 102, 122, 129–130, 141, 172, 213
Robin, Betty, 3
Robinson, Edward, Jr., 72
Roemer, Bill, 101, 205
Romanoff, Gloria, vi, viii, 1, 2, 6, 10, 15, 16, 20, 28, 70, 71, 101, 104, 109, 112–113, 118, 168, 199, 214
Rosenman, Judge Samuel, 68
Rosselli, Johnny, 47, 85, 86, 87, 101, 102, 103–104, 131, 132–133
Rosten, Hedda, 127, 171, 216, 218
Rosten, Leo, 115, 117, 121
Rosten, Norman, 111, 127
Rothmiller, Mike, 36, 62, 131, 183, 190
Rowan, Dan, 133
Rudin, Milton "Mickey," 3, 20, 111, 112, 113, 119, 148, 173, 174–175, 176, 177, 179, 180, 188, 195–196, 197, 198, 199, 202, 203
Rule, Janice, 116, 119, 127, 168–169
Runnin' Wild: All About Marilyn, vi, 32, 67, 153–154, 160, 163, 210
Russell, Jane:
   Acknowledgements, vi
   Foreword, vii
   MM's emotional sensitivity, vii, 220
   Suspicions of RFK's involvement in MM's death, 9–10

Sahl, Mort, 195, 198
Salinger, Nicole Gillman, 97
Salinger, Pierre, 97
Sandburg, Carl, 3, 223–225
Sandler, Ken, 167
Santa Monica Hospital, 161–164
Say Goodbye to the President, 30–31, 65, 74, 88, 133, 168, 175, 176, 181, 196–197, 210
Schaefer Ambulance, 64, 136, 143–157, 160–164, 165, 204, 212–213
Schaefer, Walt, 146, 157, 160, 161, 163
Schenck, Joe, 1
Schiller, Larry, 53–54, 55–56
Schlesinger, Arthur, Jr., 93
Schreiber, Flora Rheta, 53, 82
Schreiner, Greg:
   Acknowledgements, v–vi
   Carmen as fraud, 212
   Evelyn Moriarty sets Slatzer straight, 210
   Slatzer as fraud, 207
Schwartzberg, Phil, 188
Schwarz, Ted, 72, 74, 134, 143
Scott, Walter, 98
The Secret Happiness of Marilyn Monroe (Dougherty), 209
Selsman, Michael, vi, 34–35, 39, 54–55, 56, 60, 75–76, 84, 88, 99, 112, 178–179, 192
The Seven Year Itch, 8, 221
Shade, Rose, 29, 54, 180
Sharp, Peter Jay, 95
Sherman, Lynn, 90, 185
Shimon, Joe, 132
Shneidman, Dr. Edwin S., 61
Siegel, Dr. Lee, 7, 9
Simms, Judy E., 60
Sinatra, Frank, 2, 15, 34, 43, 46–48, 49, 51, 70, 71, 72, 73, 77, 80, 85, 86, 98, 100, 101–102, 103, 104–105, 111, 113, 119, 122, 126, 130, 131, 185, 186, 189, 211, 214
Sinatra, Tina, 47
Slatzer, Robert:
   Investigation into MM's death (truthful), 23, 27, 28, 30, 37, 38, 54, 56, 59, 60, 110, 136–137, 142, 149, 151–152, 155, 156, 161, 163, 164, 179–180

Alleged relationship with MM (liar), 207–211, 221
Slusher, Juanita Dale, *See* Barr, Candy
Smathers, George, 49–50, 76, 83, 88, 93
Smith, Jean Kennedy, 81, 96
Smith, Liz, 84, 87, 219
Smith, Matthew, 142, 177, 180
Smith, Stephen "Steve," 43, 46, 96
Snyder, Allan "Whitey," vi, 1, 209–210
Something's Got to Give, 2, 4, 7, 8, 53, 96, 111, 152, 210, 221, 224
Spada, James, 32, 51, 91, 148, 151, 154, 177, 178, 180, 201, 202
Speriglio, Milo, 19
Spindel, Bernie, 38, 72, 73, 107–108, 141
Spoto, Donald, v, 5, 6, 7, 14, 15, 17, 28, 29, 31, 32, 34, 53, 56, 57, 59, 61, 64, 65, 66, 75, 83, 84, 88, 89, 98–99, 110, 111, 112, 113, 117–118, 135, 136, 138, 139, 140, 144, 148, 172–173, 174–175, 176, 177–178, 179, 187, 195–196, 197, 200–201, 203, 207, 218
Spotts, Neil, 190–191
Spreckles, Kay, 90
Springer, John, 55, 111
Stapleton, Maureen, 112
Star magazine, 41
Steckler, Len, 223
Stein, Irving, 218
Stephens, Ted, 104
Stevens, Diane, 111–112
Stevens, Inger, 20, 119
Stewart, Daniel K., 44, 190
Stewart, Patricia, 41, 44–45
Strait, Raymond, vi, viii, 25, 43, 59, 65, 70, 74, 93, 94, 101, 103, 108, 113, 123, 131, 133, 134–135, 136, 137, 141, 142–143, 180, 185
Strasberg, Lee, 205
Strasberg, Paula, 130

Strasberg, Susan, 67, 88, 129
Suicide Prevention Team, 1, 5, 7, 11, 14–15, 17, 23, 25, 56, 61, 91, 110, 122, 166, 168
Summers, Anthony "Tony," v, 3, 6, 14, 18, 30–31, 33, 35, 37–38, 40, 51, 55–56, 58, 61, 62, 63, 64, 65, 72, 75, 76, 78, 80, 81, 83, 85, 88, 90, 91, 92, 94, 98, 101, 102, 122, 129, 130, 131, 137, 138, 140, 142, 143, 146, 154, 157, 163, 171, 175–176, 177, 178, 180, 181, 185–186, 188, 189, 191–192, 193, 207, 211, 212, 213, 214
Summers, Peter, 78, 79, 80

Tabachnick, Dr. Norman, 11, 14
Taraborrelli, J. Randy, 51, 78, 83, 104, 120, 138
Tarantino, Quentin, 220, 221
Tarnowski, Joe, 146
Taylor, Elizabeth, 8–9, 69, 114
Terrien, George, 89
That Shining Hour (Lawford), 97
The Thinking Body (Todd), 83
Thomas, Evan, 42–43, 44, 63, 87
Timeline, 227–239
Time magazine, 22, 23, 59
Tobin, Jack, 192
Todd, Mabel Ellsworth, 83
Tomich, Alan B., 146–148, 154, 157–160, 170
Tortorella, James "Mugsy," 135, 137
Travilla, William, 67
Trewin, Ion, 219
Trundy, Natalie. *See* Jacobs, Natalie
Tuckerman, Nancy, 41–42
Turner, Christopher, 20, 119, 168
Turner, Roy, 172

Van Meter, Jonathan, 104
Venker, Marty, 77, 82, 88

Wahl, Charles William, 124
Wald, Jerry, 102
Washington, Hazel, 100, 105
Wasserman, Lew, 67
Watts, Naomi, 220
Weatherby, William J., 80–81
Weinberg, Dr. Sidney B., 10–11, 25–26, 57, 143–144, 152, 156
Weinstein, Henry, 112, 120, 224
Wexler, Dr. Milton, 114, 115, 120, 128
Wiener, Leigh, 154
Williams, Edward Bennett, 86, 132
Williams, Michelle, 220
Wilson, Earl, 79, 203
Winchell, Walter, 27, 84
Wolfe, Donald H., v, 39, 40, 63, 73, 78, 131, 133, 139, 140, 142, 146, 153–154, 156, 160, 162, 165, 177, 179, 183, 186–187
A Woman Named Jackie (Heymann), 41, 50–51
Wood, Ward, 185
Woodfield, William Read, 4, 54, 63, 101, 102, 168, 185, 186

Yorty, Sam, 63, 142, 181
Young-Bruehl, Elisabeth, 110

Zanuck, Darryl F., 69, 207
Zolotow, Maurice, 4, 21–22, 29, 31, 59, 91, 118, 167
Zonlick, James, 185–186

Made in the USA
Lexington, KY
10 January 2013